Lyndon LaRouche and the New American Fascism

# DENNIS KING

# Lyndon LaRouche and the New American Fascism

DOUBLEDAY

*New York • London • Toronto • Sydney • Auckland*

Published by Doubleday, a division of Bantam Doubleday Dell Publishing Group, Inc. 666 Fifth Avenue, New York, New York 10103

**Doubleday** and the portrayal of an anchor with a dolphin are trademarks of Doubleday, a division of Bantam Doubleday Dell Publishing Group, Inc.

To those journalists with whom I have worked most closely on the LaRouche story: Russ Bellant, Chip Berlet, Bryan Chitwood, Ed Kayatt, and Patricia Lynch. Without their input, this book could never have been written.

Photo of LaRouche in early 1970s courtesy of *The Militant* (by Ed Weaver).
Photo of Operation Mop Up courtesy of *People's Daily World.*
Photo of airport literature table courtesy of Chip Berlet.
Photos of Carol White, NCLC demonstration, and LaRouche antidrug speech courtesy of Linda Ray.
Photos of Roy Frankhouser, Paul Goldstein, LaRouche's estate, and 1986 Leesburg raid courtesy of *Loudoun Times-Mirror* (by Douglas Graham).
Photo of Mitchell WerBell III courtesy of Steve Deal.
Photo of Richard Dupont copyright © by Andy Freeberg.
Photos of Janice Hart and Mark Fairchild and 1988 photo of LaRouche courtesy of AP/Wide World Photos.

Library of Congress Cataloging-in-Publication Data

King, Dennis.
    Lyndon LaRouche and the new American fascism / Dennis King.—1st ed.

        p.   cm.
    Includes index.
    1. LaRouche, Lyndon H.—Political and social views.
2. Politicians—United States—Biography.   3. Fascism—United
States.   4. United States—Politics and government—1981–
I. Title.
E840.8.L33K55   1989
324.2′092′4—dc19   88-13868
[B]
ISBN 0-385-23880-0
Copyright © 1989 by Dennis King
All Rights Reserved
Printed in the United States of America
April 1989
First Edition
BG

# Contents

It is not necessary to wear brown shirts to be a fascist . . . It is not necessary to wear a swastika to be a fascist . . . It is not necessary to call oneself a fascist to be a fascist. It is simply necessary to be one!

—LYNDON H. LaROUCHE, JR.,
*"Solving the Machiavellian Problem Today"*

# Introduction

In the mid-1970s a former Trotskyist named Lyndon LaRouche emerged from the wreckage of the New Left with a few hundred young followers in tow. Claiming to have "subsumed" Marxism, he announced that henceforth he and his associates would champion the industrial capitalists rather than the proletariat. Organizers for his National Caucus of Labor Committees (NCLC) began contacting everyone they and their fellow radicals of the anti-Vietnam War movement had reviled—the CIA and FBI, the Pentagon, local police red squads, wealthy conservatives, GOP strategists, and even the Ku Klux Klan. Their announced objective was to build a grand coalition to rid American politics of the Enemy Within—the evil leftists, liberals, environmentalists, and Zionists.

Over the next decade the LaRouchians made extraordinary inroads into American politics, surpassing the achievements of any other extremist movement in recent American history. Their success was all the more impressive in being achieved during a period of economic prosperity and political stability.

They built a nationwide election machine that fielded thousands of candidates in Democratic primaries in the mid-1980s, frequently picking up 20 percent or more of the vote and winning dozens of nominations for public office. In 1986 LaRouchians won the Democratic nominations for lieutenant governor and secretary of state in Illinois. Although this triggered attacks from the media and Democratic Party regulars, so-called LaRouche Democrats continued to win nominations and garner high vote percentages through 1988. In addition, their movement raised over $200 million in loans and donations from the American public during the 1980s, a sum far in excess of what any other extremist group had ever collected in this country. LaRouche, who was a perennial presidential candidate, used much of this money to purchase frequent half-hour network television spots. In effect, he became the televangelist of secular extremism, with each TV appearance helping him raise money to pay for the next one.

LaRouche also set up an international political intelligence "news service," a kind of parallel CIA, which gained him the ear not just of CIA officials but also of top National Security Council aides. He and his followers became valued although unofficial consultants to the Reagan administration during its first term. With NSC and Pentagon approval —and a little boost from the Department of State—they helped to promote the Strategic Defense Initiative ("Star Wars") throughout the United States and overseas. They also served the interests of the administration and the GOP through various forms of snooping, smear campaigns, dirty tricks, and propaganda. This included things the Republicans could not directly carry out, such as the rumor campaign in 1988 about Michael Dukakis's mental health. Over the years the beneficiaries of LaRouche's snooping and trickery (whether solicited or not) included Ronald Reagan during his 1980 New Hampshire primary race, Labor Secretary Ray Donovan, U.S. Senator Jesse Helms, Panamanian dictator Manuel Noriega, New Orleans crime lord Carlos Marcello, auto magnate John DeLorean, and the South African Bureau of State Security. The LaRouchians also helped out the late Teamsters boss Jackie Presser. Indeed, they made themselves useful in the late 1970s and early 1980s to officials on every level of the nation's most powerful union, providing "truth squads" that helped hoodlum elements maintain control of restive locals.

The media consistently avoided dealing with the fact that LaRouche had become a significant player in American politics. He was often described (by people who had not bothered to read his writings) as an eccentric whose ideas were too bizarre to worry about. The truth was that LaRouche was a man with a coherent program, subtle tactics, and —what is usually lacking in American politics—a long-range plan of how to get from here to there. Both in word and in deed, he was a serious ideologue in the classic European fascist mold. His pendulum swing from left to right in the 1970s had followed the pattern of Benito Mussolini, who was a socialist newspaper editor before founding Italy's Fascist Party. Likewise, LaRouche's occasional reversion to left-wing rhetoric when useful fit the pattern of the early Nazi brownshirts, who, after all, fancied themselves as "National Socialists."

LaRouche's classic fascist tactics included making demogogic appeals to mutually opposed constituencies (for instance, white supremacists and black nationalists) to unite them around a supposedly higher program. His synthetic ideology combined anti-Semitism with extreme militarism and the need for an authoritarian regime to rescue the industrial capitalist system from what he believed was an impending crisis. In the late 1970s, his followers began cultivating conservative businessmen with the message that LaRouche was the man to save the nation. Meanwhile, they set in motion their plan for a populist mass movement of farmers, small businessmen, and blue-collar workers, whose anger over drugs, unemployment, and high interest rates was to be channeled against the "Zionists." The political theory at work evidently was that simultaneous pressure from above and below, as in Germany in 1933, would put LaRouche into power at the propitious moment.

The American public had encountered few authentic homegrown fascists since the days of the German-American Bund and the Silver Shirts in the 1930s. Fascism had become, in the eyes of most, a relic of Europe's past with little relevance to politics today, and especially not to American politics. Before LaRouche, the closest approximations to a fascist movement in postwar America were the so-called hate groups—cross-burning Klansmen in bed sheets and goose-stepping neo-Nazi misfits in homemade uniforms. LaRouche for his part, being an educated man seriously committed to gaining power, avoided the simple-minded tactics and self-isolating symbols of these groups. When he wanted to signal his ultimate goals, he did so with finesse. For instance, during a 1988 presidential campaign ad on network television he urged in a low-key genial manner the rebuilding of Germany's Reichstag and the uniting of Europe from the Atlantic to the Urals. This was to be accomplished through an alliance of Germany and America to save the West, as LaRouche had repeatedly urged. Clearly, any display of a swastika banner would have been redundant.

LaRouche's relative urbanity made him more dangerous than the traditional hate-group leaders. Although the economic crisis and 1930s-style mass movement that he dreamed of did not arrive in the 1980s, he developed ties with many influential Americans in odd places, from Oklahoma oilmen through Detroit racketeers through conservative think-tankers in Washington. He tapped into their willingness to listen, although as yet only half-seriously, to the seemingly unthinkable. He made the fascist option a subject of legitimate debate by calling it something else (such as "humanism") or simply leaving it unnamed.

The sophistication that LaRouche brought to the American ultraright included his use of recruitment and control tactics borrowed from religious cults. Some observers, after encountering an especially cultish LaRouche follower, would define the group as being more like the Hari Krishnas than a political organization (and hence as less of a problem than the traditional hate groups). But the LaRouche organization's brainwashing methods deepened the commitment of its members to an extraordinary degree. The few hundred LaRouche cadres often performed organizational and fund-raising feats that an ordinary sect or a mainstream political organization would require many thousands of volunteers to carry out. Yet the NCLC ultimately was a political vanguard organization more than a cult, although it used cult methods in an intensive manner. (In this it was far from unique: Hitler's SS merged cultism and politics, as did Mao's Communist Party. Cult-style brainwashing was employed in the 1980s not just by the NCLC but by PLO terrorists, Peruvian guerrillas, Central American death squads, and Christian fundamentalist political cadres in the Republican Party— to cite but a few examples. None of these groups were dismissed simply as a "cult" by the media.)

LaRouche avoided serious opposition for many years not just because of the cult label, but also because the media chose to portray him as a kook. Curiously, he delighted in encouraging this viewpoint by confirming to all and sundry that indeed he *did* believe the Queen of England pushes drugs. Yet underneath this useful pose of eccentricity (which cost him little yet sidetracked so much potential trouble for him) LaRouche strove to tap into something quite serious: the undercurrents of collective irrationalism in American politics. As he well knew, a significant portion of the American public had proven susceptible in the past, under conditions of economic distress or rapid social change, to ideas not unlike what he was espousing. During the Great Depression, this paranoid style in American politics had developed briefly into a large-scale pro-fascist movement, with millions of citizens listening to the radio priest Father Coughlin and joining the America First Committee. Even in the prosperous conditions after World War II, periodic eruptions continued: McCarthyism, the John Birch Society, the 1968 George Wallace campaign, the anti-busing movement of the 1970s.

To be sure, none of these postwar movements were really fascist. They lacked a truly fascist ideology, as well as a vanguard to provide the *will* to fascism. But what they lacked LaRouche attempted in the 1980s to provide. He created in his voluminous writings an ideology that embodied the essence of fascism in an updated, Americanized form. He recruited a vanguard to organize around his program, while pioneering in slick new tactics to inject his ideas into strata of our society that traditionally had shown themselves susceptible to paranoid populism. Many of his counterparts in the Ku Klux Klan and other traditional white supremacist circles had so little self-confidence that they rarely tried to organize outside their own rural or blue-collar strata. But LaRouche reached out boldly to people of wealth and power, as well as to the forgotten and disinherited, striving to develop both a public and a private dialogue on any terms, no matter how opportunistic.

The NCLC chairman also built an organizational structure of extraordinary complexity to support his multileveled political organizing. In its mid-1980s form, it was dominated by the NCLC National Executive Committee, a dozen stalwarts operating under LaRouche's daily instructions. The NCLC had regional or local units in over twenty cities, each with its own steering committee. It also had a national office staff in Leesburg, Virginia, divided into "sectors"—legal, finance, operations, intelligence, and security. This central bureaucracy ran the "entities"—a network of political action committees, publishing ventures, educational and fund-raising arms, and business fronts.

The public directly encountered only the entities, not the shadowy NCLC. The National Democratic Policy Committee (NDPC) was the chief vehicle for LaRouchian electoral activity. The Fusion Energy Foundation (FEF) was its scientific think tank and an important lobbying tool. The NCLC also sponsored the Schiller Institute, an international propaganda arm headed by LaRouche's German wife, Helga Zepp-LaRouche.

Much of the NCLC's financial resources were poured into a propaganda machine that disseminated anti-Semitic literature nationwide in artfully disguised forms. The most important publication was the NCLC's twice-weekly newspaper, *New Solidarity* (called *The New Federalist* after 1986). *The Campaigner*, a monthly, was the theoretical journal. Persons who stopped at LaRouchian airport literature tables were most likely to see the weekly newsmagazine *Executive Intelligence Review* (*EIR*), as well as paperback books published by the New Benjamin Franklin Publishing House. The titles were catchy: *Dope, Inc., The Hitler Book,* and *What Every Conservative Should Know about Communism.*

Although the ultimate goals of the LaRouche network were political, the fund raising was an obsessive daily routine. Hundreds of LaRouche followers fanned out each morning to airports around the country or to the NCLC's telephone "boiler rooms" at shifting locations. While selling literature and cadging donations, their chief aim was to solicit loans (often from senior citizens), which were rarely repaid. Potential lenders were told they would be helping a patriotic or humanitarian cause (such as SDI or research to cure AIDS) while supposedly earning a high interest rate. The weekly *EIR*, high-priced special reports, videocassettes, the frequent television ads in which LaRouche addressed the nation in a "presidential" manner—all were used to gain the confidence of potential lenders. The income from loans and donations was shuttled from entity to entity in a never-ending shell game to avoid creditors and the IRS, and to guarantee that the maximum would always be available for LaRouche's pursuit of political influence and power.

The NCLC National Executive Committee thus served not just as a general staff, but as a board of directors, with LaRouche as chairman of the board. His presidential campaigns provided a cover of constitutionally protected activity for what became an increasingly predatory financial empire. When faced with criminal and civil proceedings, he claimed "political persecution" and often sued the investigating agency or creditor for violation of his civil rights. His intelligence-gathering and propaganda networks also helped protect the financial operation by investigating the investigators and launching smear campaigns against creditors. The system was not foolproof: After 1986, dozens of LaRouche's followers were indicted for credit-card and loan fraud and other offenses. In October 1988, LaRouche himself was indicted on charges of defrauding lenders of over $30 million. But his fund raisers still continued to rake in large amounts each week. (LaRouche and six top aides were convicted on fraud and conspiracy charges in December 1988.)

LaRouche's political and financial network did not end at the borders of the United States. He had created an international web that included political parties in eight countries inspired by his ideology and financed in part by his fund-raising schemes. Together with the NCLC, they comprised the International Caucus of Labor Committees (ICLC). The largest branch was in West Germany, with vigorous organizations also in France, Italy, Sweden, Canada, Mexico, Colombia, and Peru and support networks in at least a dozen other countries. Each ICLC member party had its own array of front groups. Their combined membership apart from the NCLC was no more than one thousand, but their influence in several countries was far greater than the numbers alone would suggest. Their high level of motivation, financial support from the U.S. organization, and open and covert support from military officers, government officials, or trade union leaders in countries with strong right-wing tendencies all played a role. The result was the world's best-organized, wealthiest, and ideologically most sophisticated neofascist operation of the 1980s—ruled not from the jungles of Paraguay, as in a B-grade movie, but from a country estate thirty minutes from Washington, D.C.

In 1981, the creator of this political network ruminated—in his only published work of overt fiction, a short story—about the possible circumstances under which an individual who threatens the social order can act out his dreams. There is a "fabric of social controls," LaRouche wrote, which usually restrains such individuals. These controls supposedly are based on the ability to identify and keep track of potential troublemakers "in the equivalent of some computer filing system." But what if the system "misses a problem-case with special capabilities"? Does not the "very habit of reliance on the system" become the system's main vulnerability? In LaRouche's story, a "paranoid technologist" is believed to have invented an "infernal machine" to blow up downtown Chicago. The detective-hero of the story (not surprisingly, LaRouche himself) struggles to deduce what is going on after the authorities clamp a security screen around the incident.

In the chapters that follow, we shall invert this process. We shall pierce the screen that has concealed the real story of political "technologist" Lyndon LaRouche and his potentially explosive ideology and movement. Why did society's containment system miss this "problem-case"? How did LaRouche break out of quarantine? Did powerful people know all along who and what he was, deciding simply to use him for their own purposes? Why did he remain invulnerable to prosecution for so many years? How did he inspire so much fear in those who should have led an early fight to drive him back into quarantine? This book will examine these questions as well as investigate the motives of the remarkable range of allies that LaRouche gathered along the way—hoodlums, spooks, Klansmen, mercenaries, defense scientists, political wheeler-dealers, diplomats, retired generals, New Right ideologues, foreign dictators, and White House aides. What was LaRouche's secret appeal that attracted people from both the heights and the depths of our society, and still attracts them today?

# Part One

# The Vanguard

Cry for the duck?
You silly chickens!
This is a hawk.
See now how he moves.

—Lyndon H. LaRouche, Jr.
  "Morning Is a Wonderful Day"

# One

# Makings
# of an Ideologue

In the mid-1960s Lyndon LaRouche saw protest movements burgeoning throughout America and sensed for the first time the real
possibility of political power. What he needed to start with, he decided,
was a cadre of several hundred full-time organizers, tightly organized
and armed with the correct strategy and tactics. He understood that
such a vanguard could only seize power in a social crisis far greater than
that triggered by the Vietnam War or the civil rights struggle. But he
believed such a crisis was inevitable. If the organization and program
were developed years in advance, the masses could be swiftly mobilized
at the right moment.

This appeared to be standard Marxist doctrine, but LaRouche added
his own unique twist: The members of the revolutionary party must be
intellectually of a superior breed—a philosophical elite as well as a
political vanguard. In the following years this innovation became more
and more important in his thinking, and he broke completely with
Marxism. He began to portray his philosophical elite as the forerunners
of a biological master race, which he called the "golden souls" after

Plato's aristocratic usage. They would rise to power, he taught, by championing the interests of industrial capitalism.

LaRouche's swing from far left to far right was not without precedent: Mussolini was also a socialist before throwing in his lot with the upper classes and launching Italian fascism. But in LaRouche's case there was an additional twist. He had adopted Marxism as a young man to escape the ultraconservatism and religious fundamentalism of his parents. His shift to the right in the 1970s would be partly a return to this mental universe of his childhood.

Lyndon Hermyle LaRouche, Jr., was born in Rochester, New Hampshire, on September 8, 1922, the oldest of three children. His father, the son of a French-Canadian immigrant, was a United Shoe Machinery Corporation roadman earning a comfortable salary. His mother, the former Jesse Weir, came from an evangelical Protestant background. Both parents regarded themselves as orthodox Quakers, Lyndon Sr. having converted from Roman Catholicism in his teens.

Lyndon Jr.'s first ten years were spent in Rochester, where his two sisters were born and where he attended the School Street elementary school. The rest of his childhood and youth were spent in Lynn, Massachusetts, to which the family moved after Lyndon Sr. resigned from United Shoe to launch his own business.

LaRouche has described his childhood as that of "an egregious child, I wouldn't say an ugly duckling but a nasty duckling." He felt socially isolated. This was partly because of his precociousness. He learned to read at five and was soon dipping into adult books in the family library. Kids at school called him "Big Head." A greater problem was his parents' strictures. When he was about to begin first grade he was summoned to the family dining room and told that under no circumstances could he fight with other children, even in self-defense. This resulted, according to LaRouche, in "years of hell" from bullies at school.

Despite their belief in nonviolence, LaRouche's parents did not fit the popular stereotype of gentle and tolerant Quakers. The couple were ferocious sectarians who accused their co-religionists of closet Bolshevism and embezzlement of religious funds. They wanted their son to share these beliefs. LaRouche recalls being herded with other children into a basement when he was eight years old to listen to a woman evangelist fulminate against the evils of communism. She denounced him to his parents when he accidentally crumpled his song sheet.

LaRouche writes that his mother spent most of her time on "church work" and that his father's chief interest, apart from his career, was in assisting this work. How this affected LaRouche is suggested by his vehement opposition as an adult to matriarchal elements in religion (e.g., the goddess Isis and the Virgin Mary), as well as his numerous psychological tracts about an archetypal "witch mother" who renders her children and husband "impotent."

Visits to his grandparents provided young LaRouche some relief from the rigid home atmosphere. He was especially fond of his maternal grandfather Weir, a United Brethren minister in Ohio, who stimulated his interest in biblical history. Forty years later this interest would resurface in LaRouche's conspiracy theories about the ancient Near East.

LaRouche continued to feel like a social leper in high school. He withdrew into his books, took long walks in the woods, and accumulated an enormous resentment against his peers. He found solace in the great philosophers, especially Descartes, Leibnitz, and Kant, whose works helped him rationalize his social isolation. He was the victim, he mused, of an educational system based on the evil ideas of John Dewey and British empiricism. This belief persisted into adulthood. In his 1979 autobiography, *The Power of Reason,* he describes his high school tormenters as "unwitting followers of David Hume" (the eighteenth-century philosopher).

Kant's ideas in particular prompted LaRouche to question his parents' beliefs and their plans for him to become a minister. He stopped carrying the King James Bible to school every day. But when his sisters rebelled more openly, LaRouche disapproved. He regarded them as shallow creatures, concerned only with winning the approval of their peers.

In spite of his growing doubts about religion, LaRouche supported his parents' war against their Quaker brethren. The immediate issue was a trust fund for religious education left by a wealthy uncle of LaRouche's mother. The LaRouches objected to the money being given to the liberal-minded American Friends Service Committee (AFSC).

The bitterness of this dispute is reflected in a 1937 tract LaRouche Sr. published under the pseudonym Hezekiah Micajah Jones. Its rambling and abusive style and obsession with conspiracies foreshadow LaRouche Jr.'s writings forty years later. The elder LaRouche denounced the Friends' handling of religious trust funds as a "swindle." Quaker ministers, he said, were preaching the "principles of Communism," and he could count on his fingers the number who were not part of the plot. He singled out Quaker reform leader Rufus Jones for urging "love for everyone including, without doubt, Satan." "The Orthodox Quaker," LaRouche Sr. vowed, "will not join hands with the ungodly, nor will he go down into Babylon and join forces." Only Orthodox Quakers, he said, have a "right to the name Christian."

Turning to world affairs, the pamphlet berated certain Quakers who had criticized "one of the governments opposed to Communism" (apparently either Mussolini's Italy or Hitler's Germany) at a world peace conference in Philadelphia. The pamphlet also chided participants at a regional Friends conference in Providence, Rhode Island, for not responding favorably to an anti-Jewish speech by a Palestinian Arab. According to LaRouche Sr., the speaker presented his views "well and authoritatively . . . his attitude should be given more consideration."

In October 1941, the Lynn Meeting disowned LaRouche Sr. for his disruptive behavior. His wife and nineteen-year-old son resigned in protest. The LaRouches later established a schismatic Quaker group in Boston, and the bitterness persisted for decades. In a 1978 article, LaRouche Jr. charged that the American Friends Service Committee had used "intelligence-mode 'dirty tricks' operations" to isolate his parents.

Before Pearl Harbor, LaRouche attended Northeastern University in Boston. By his own account he received poor grades and incurred his father's wrath. In late 1942 he entered a Civilian Public Service (CPS) camp for conscientious objectors, as did many other young Quakers. The camp, in West Campton, New Hampshire, was administered by the AFSC. LaRouche promptly joined a small faction at odds with the administrators.

After a little over a year LaRouche became fed up with CPS life, which he later compared to "a 'soft' model of the Nazi concentration camps." The experience had taught him, he said, the "unbridgeable dividing line" between "bestiality" (i.e., the AFSC) and "humanity." He contacted the Selective Service to enlist in the Army as a noncombatant.

LaRouche has given two versions of this decision. In a 1974 autobiographical piece, he said that after engaging in political discussions with socialists and ex-Communists in the camp and being introduced to the first volume of Marx's *Das Kapital,* he decided to join the Army. In a second version, written after his swing to the right, he does not mention any Marxist influences, and claims he intended to join the Army all along. According to this version, he entered the CPS camp for a few months as a temporary concession to his parents, to soften the blow of his inevitable enlistment.

The late Boston publisher Porter Sargent, who was LaRouche's close friend in the CPS camp, confirmed the first version to the *Boston Phoenix.* He said LaRouche had been a "serious deep pacifist," well versed in "all the ways of active nonviolence."

LaRouche was inducted into the Army in early 1944 and served as a private in medical and ordnance units in the China-Burma-India theater. While stationed near Calcutta he attempted, without much success, to organize GIs to work with the local Communist Party. In his 1974 reminiscences, he told of meeting P. C. Joshi, a Calcutta Communist leader. Joshi supposedly rejected the twenty-three-year-old LaRouche's suggestion that the Indian Communists should stage an immediate uprising in Bengal against the British colonial government. LaRouche said he walked out of Joshi's headquarters thoroughly disillusioned with Stalinism: "By the time [I] reached the bottom of the stairs, [I] was a sort of hardened Trotskyist."

This story also underwent heavy revision. A 1983 LaRouche campaign biography, prepared under his close supervision, says that his contacts with Indians, including lowly street sweepers, left him deeply "gratified and touched" by their admiration for U.S. capitalism. He returned to America, according to this version, determined to provide India with a "flow of capital-goods exports."

LaRouche was mustered out of the Army in May 1946. Later that year he gave Northeastern University a second try. He intended to major in physics, but soon quit in protest over what he regarded as an all-pervasive academic "philistinism." His autobiographical writings do not mention any subsequent attempt to gain a university degree.

In December 1948, LaRouche applied for membership in the Socialist Workers Party (SWP), an affiliate of the Trotskyist Fourth International. This was no trivial decision. The Cold War and the resulting Red Scare were already underway. Dozens of Communist Party members had been indicted on conspiracy charges. The trade union movement was in the throes of a political purge that would soon extend to the academic world and the arts. The SWP, which had been targeted under the Smith Act during the war, remained on the Attorney General's list of subversive organizations and was under close FBI surveillance. As Senator Joseph McCarthy began his demagogic rise, both the SWP and the Communist Party feared that fascism was taking hold in America. Many leftists tore up their party cards, hoping to avoid the worst to come.

LaRouche was admitted to full party membership in early 1949 and adopted a party pseudonym to avoid trouble with employers and the FBI. Journalists have speculated that his choice, "Lyn Marcus," was intended to suggest a personal affinity with Lenin and Marx, although LaRouche says it was based on the nickname "Marco Polo" given to him during the war.

LaRouche went to work at the GE River Works in Lynn, under the SWP policy of industrial colonizing—the sending of intellectuals to work in factories in the hope of recruiting worker cadres. Within months he was put under party discipline for advocating a "tactical alliance" with the Stalinists. He soon tired of the proletarian life, and was glad to escape into a part-time job with his father. Although the SWP's sectarian dogmatism was beginning to remind him of his parents' religiosity, he thought the party could be changed from within. He spent much time with the late Larry Trainor, a middle-aged printer who headed the Boston SWP, seeking approval for his maverick views. Former Boston comrades recall him as an earnest young man whose life seemed to revolve around the Trotskyist movement's endless ideological debates.

In 1954, LaRouche moved to New York City and married fellow SWP member Janice Neuberger. The party's national center was in New York, and he hoped to gain recognition as one of its rising ideological stars. He became friendly with Janice's close friends Myra Tanner Weiss and the late Murray Weiss, who led a small SWP faction. Myra Weiss recalls that "Lyndy" was a "quite dedicated" party member. He faithfully attended branch meetings, distributed party literature, and participated in election campaigns. He also wrote long erudite documents which he circulated to party leaders. Several shorter pieces appeared under his name in SWP publications, and he occasionally gave party-sponsored lectures on economics. But according to Murray Weiss, he remained on the party's outskirts, never able to win the leadership's trust.

Through the years LaRouche has given various versions of his relationship to the SWP. In a 1970 essay he described his SWP membership from 1949 until his expulsion in 1966 as "my seventeen-year passage." The essay provided exhaustive details of his long struggle for a pristine revolutionism untainted by ideological compromise. However, his 1983 biography, written to win conservative support, omits any reference to the SWP. It depicts his involvement in unspecified "left politics" as lasting only for a brief period in the late 1940s. According to this account, LaRouche wrote to Dwight D. Eisenhower, urging him to run for President in 1948. When Eisenhower failed to enter the race, LaRouche reluctantly joined the left as the best alternative for struggling against "Trumanism."

LaRouche has also repeatedly suggested that he served as a government informant within the SWP. In an October 1986 interview on ABC Radio's Bob Grant show he said he went back into the SWP after the early 1950s "because the FBI approached me to go back." He explained: "I promised [the FBI] if I found anything that was wrong, as a citizen I would tell them." But Janice LaRouche does not believe her ex-husband worked for the FBI. She believes he was sincere in his

Marxist beliefs, and only discarded them years later. Other former SWP members who knew LaRouche agree with Janice.

The LaRouches' only child, Daniel, was born in 1956. At this point, LaRouche began to channel more and more of his energy into building a management consulting career. For several years he was associated with the George S. May Company, and often made a thousand dollars a week or more helping corporations reduce labor costs. He outlined his approach to troubleshooting in a 1962 essay: If management tells you to keep your nose out of an area, that is precisely where you should snoop first.

LaRouche became interested in computer technology after reading Norbert Wiener's book *Cybernetics*. Recognizing that computers were the wave of the future, he pioneered in computer-complex installations and software design. He also tried his hand at computer theory, speculating on the possibility of a total-systems technology to manage the entire U.S. economy.

Janice recalls that he could work "for forty hours at a stretch without sleeping or eating." During one of these round-the-clock binges, ruminating on Marvin Minsky's artificial intelligence theories, he experienced a quasi-mystical inspiration that deeply altered his view of reality. "During the night I sat and paced, alternately, sleepless, going through the matter repeatedly," he wrote in *The Power of Reason*. "In that moment, I saw clearly, for the first time, the nature of the solution to the 'particle-field paradox'—not as something I understood . . . but as a solution I could 'see.'" LaRouche has never revealed the precise nature of this solution, yet he wrote that his experience was "on a relative scale of things . . . one of greatness. I know what the realized pinnacles of human personal development are in our time and, to large measure, in earlier times. I have, essentially, matched them."

He began to fancy himself an expert on psychoanalysis as well as physics. According to *The Power of Reason*, he held free counseling sessions with a troubled young man named Griswold, who supposedly was driven away by a tactless remark of Janice's. LaRouche heard several months later that Griswold had committed suicide. The news of this tragedy, LaRouche writes, was the "last straw" in his accumulated resentments against Janice. They separated in 1963, and he moved into an apartment on Morton Street in Greenwich Village with Carol Schnitzer, an SWP comrade who became his main collaborator in the founding of the National Caucus of Labor Committees. Soon "Lyn Marcus" and "Carol LaRouche" (they never married) were deeply immersed in factionalism in and around the SWP. They organized support work for a Trotskyist-influenced strike of New York City welfare workers in 1965, and held conspiratorial meetings with expelled SWP members.

LaRouche lost interest in his consulting business and spent most of his time studying and writing, seeking to develop a new version of Marxism that could bring him a personal following. His experience with the SWP's ineptness had convinced him that "no revolutionary movement was going to be brought into being in the USA unless I brought it into being."

# Two

# Do You Believe in Marxist Magic?

LaRouche's pretensions to the mantle of Lenin and Trotsky were by no means odd in the America of the mid-1960s. As the movement against the Vietnam War began to stir, new activist organizations sprouted like mushrooms. Antiwar students battled the police in New York in 1964 and gathered by the tens of thousands in Washington the following year. Many burned their draft cards at public rallies. "Free universities" were founded as an alternative to an official academia believed to be corrupted by defense contracts and CIA recruiters. Anticommunism rapidly fell out of fashion. When the House Un-American Activities Committee tried to probe Communist influence in the fledgling antiwar movement, students who were subpoenaed treated the committee with contempt, turning the hearings into forums to denounce the war. Meanwhile, the Harlem riots of 1964 became the prototype for ghetto rebellions across the country. Malcolm X and then the Black Panthers gave a political voice to this rage. For the first time in decades, the Establishment appeared to be on the defensive. Young radicals pored over the writings of Che Guevara and Mao Zedong, embibing the belief that sheer revolutionary will can move mountains.

It was within this heady New Left atmosphere that LaRouche, a product of the Old Left but attuned to the new possibilities, made his first bid for leadership beyond the orbit of the SWP. He initially focused on the American Committee for the Fourth International (ACFI), a Trotskyist splinter group with about twenty members.

He vowed to transform it into a proper "cadre organization," then expand into the larger world beyond Trotskyism. Tim Wohlforth, former leader of the ACFI, recalls that for six months during 1965–66 he and LaRouche met almost every day to plot factional intrigues.

The ACFI was under the influence of Britain's Socialist Labour League (SLL), a bitter rival of the SWP. In October 1965, Wohlforth, LaRouche, and other schismatics traveled to Montreal to meet with Gerald Healy, the SLL chairman, to discuss a plan for a new revolutionary party in the United States. The first stage would be to merge the ACFI with a somewhat larger SWP spin-off, the Spartacist League. The second stage would be to reach out to radical students. A tentative unity plan was agreed on, which LaRouche later called the "Montreal Concordat," as if the persons involved had been Great Power diplomats. He hoped to become the chairman of the fused organizations. However, Healy repudiated the scheme and forced LaRouche to resign from the ACFI. The "franchise" for Healyism in America went to the more pliable Wolhforth.

It is ironic that LaRouche should have chosen a satellite of Healy's SLL for his first foray outside the SWP. The SLL later became famous under a new name, the Workers Revolutionary Party, as the vehicle for actress Vanessa Redgrave's anti-Zionism. As early as the mid-1960s it displayed some of the features of a political cult. Over the next two decades Chairman Healy developed, as did LaRouche, a full-blown political megalomania. The WRP split in 1985, and the anti-Healy faction went public with charges about subsidies from the Libyans and Healy's affairs with young women comrades. The British tabloid press had a field day with this "Reds in the Bed" scandal.

LaRouche learned important lessons from Healy. He later wrote about the SLL leader's use of goon squads and psychological intimidation to control his followers. While LaRouche had naïvely tried to win support through ideological persuasion, Healy had gone for the jugular. The basic method, LaRouche wrote, was an old one: First, you "isolate and publicly degrade dangerous individuals." Once they are psychologically "broken," you "assimilate" them into your machine as "useful party hacks." LaRouche stated that "any experienced leader in the socialist movement knows exactly how [such] 'brainwashing' is accomplished." But he boasted that he had personally resisted the process: "Healy was dealing with a person who knew all about that game; it didn't work out as he planned."

LaRouche concluded that he could easily have won "hegemony" over the ACFI but for Healy's interference. "My commitments, temperament and creative abilities," he said, "seem to generate a certain amount of 'charisma.' " But he would need an organization of his own, with no rival gurus allowed. As for Trotskyism, it was basically dead. A viable revolutionary movement could only be launched "from scratch." LaRouche observed, "Once you have struggled free of the sewer, you do not jump back into it."

He began to offer Marxist classes under the sponsorship of the Free School of New York. Its summer 1967 catalogue described his course on dialectical materialism as supposedly fulfilling "training requirements of revolutionary leadership cadres." LaRouche did not bother with the trendy theories of Herbert Marcuse or the simplistic essays of Chairman Mao. His students read the three volumes of Marx's *Das Kapital.* In preparation they studied Hegel, Kant, and Leibnitz. This was to winnow out all those lacking in a "passion for more profound scientific accomplishments." The ones who persisted were invited to daylong LaRouche seminars and were encouraged to do political organizing under his direction—"laboratory work," he called it. One of the first projects was a campaign against real estate speculators featuring the slogan "Tax Landlords, Not People." LaRouche meanwhile wrote *The Third Stage of Imperialism,* a pamphlet that warned about "cancerous speculative growth" in the U.S. economy.

LaRouche targeted the Students for a Democratic Society (SDS), which had become *the* activist organization on campuses from coast to coast. A lesser tactician would have charged in with his tiny band of disciples and challenged the existing tendencies head-on. Instead, LaRouche concentrated on enticing to his banner key members of SDS's most ideological element—the campus cadre of the Progressive Labor Party.

The PLP was a Maoist group led by former members of the Communist Party USA. Its campus members and supporters had joined SDS in 1965 with the aim of taking control. Most SDS members were political novices, but those in the PLP had a coherent ideology, clarity of program, and the guidance of adults who understood how to manipulate loosely organized mass movements. By 1967 a few hundred PLP student enthusiasts across the country exerted much influence, in spite of the hostility of the SDS national office.

The PLP had an Achilles' heel, however. This was its doctrine of the student-worker alliance—that campus radicals should take the antiwar movement and PLP ideology to the blue-collar working class. Although the strategy made sense from a Marxist point of view, it resulted in pressure on students to do things they didn't really want to do: get jobs in campus cafeterias, work in garment factories during the summer, and sell *Challenge* (the PLP newspaper) at factory gates. LaRouche offered a face-saving way out. Linking up with the working class is fine, he said, but it should be delayed until student cadres have mastered *Das Kapital* and Hegel's *Science of Logic*. In the meantime the student movement can best serve the masses by leafleting against landlords in neighborhoods around the campus.

Initial contact with the PLP was established through a LaRouche disciple at Columbia who had several chums in the PLP—he had attended Great Neck South High School on Long Island with them. He persuaded them to attend one of LaRouche's classes. LaRouche was careful not to frighten them away with any frontal assaults on the PLP's doctrines. Instead he urged a united front around shared goals. Steve Fraser, who was one of the Great Neck PLPers, recalls how LaRouche's cerebral form of charisma gradually won them over. He said that LaRouche would lecture for hours, extemporaneously and almost nonstop. "He ranged over the widest imaginable intellectual landscape," Fraser said. "He would show how the toolmaking capacity of monkeys was supposedly connected to the falling rate of profit. It was mindboggling and thrilling. It also demanded a higher intellectual effort than I had ever faced, and a certain moral rigor . . . LaRouche challenged you existentially."

In November 1967, LaRouche's disciples and several New York PLP members launched the "SDS Transit Project." The initial aim was to protest subway fare increases, but the group soon took on other issues. As the months passed, more PLP supporters were brought to LaRouche's classes and strategy sessions. When they began to raise his ideas at PLP meetings, they angered some of the more dogmatic members. But the PLP leadership hesitated to expel them.

In the spring of 1968, demonstrations erupted at Columbia against the university's role in Pentagon research and its plan to build a gymnasium in Harlem's Morningside Park. Activists occupied several buildings, presented "nonnegotiable demands," and shut the university down. The event electrified students across the nation as they watched the spectacle of chanting protesters on TV against a colorful backdrop of red banners. It seemed to give symbolic form to their rage and romanticism. Thousands of students who knew nothing about Marxism began calling themselves SDS members and Marxists. SDS was transformed not only into a household name but also, briefly, into a formidable political force.

Members of the PLP and the SDS Transit Committee were in the forefront of the Columbia strike. Tony Papert, chairman of Columbia PLP but heavily influenced by LaRouche, led the occupation of Low Library in support of black students barricaded in Hamilton Hall. When the police arrived he held out with a handful of associates, gradually attracting more and more students. Other buildings were seized, and the campus was effectively shut down. A strike steering committee was established, on which Papert and his friends wielded great influence. It seemed to the PLP's national leaders that the strike would become a PLP triumph, strengthening its hand within SDS nationally. But when the PLP leadership tried to give further instructions to their Columbia club, they discovered that LaRouche had most of the leverage.

LaRouche himself kept a relatively low profile on campus as the strike approached its inevitable denouement, the famous charge by the NYPD's Tactical Police Force that routed the forces of Revolution. That summer, with the campus still sizzling, he taught Marxism at a fraternity house turned "liberation school." Gaunt, bushy-bearded, and attired in rumpled old clothes, he seemed the quintessential off-campus guru basking in the admiration of student rebels.

Meanwhile, the PLP, having expelled Papert for "revisionism," found itself isolated within Columbia SDS. Control passed almost entirely into the hands of SDS chapter chairman Mark Rudd, who was close to the SDS national leadership. Rudd had cooperated at first with the Papert group, but had little sympathy for them. He built his own influence through flamboyant speeches and press interviews. A strong PLP organization could have handled him by emphasizing tactics and program, and did in fact prevent honcho-type leadership from emerging during several later campus rebellions. But the Papert group, which began calling itself the SDS Labor Committee, was unable to outmaneuver Rudd on its own. It thus began to operate independently of the Columbia SDS chapter, under LaRouche's direct command.

The real significance of LaRouche's recruitment of Papert and his handful of friends only became apparent during the following year. The student movement had entered its most volatile period during which—as the Columbia strike had shown—aggressive organizers could ignite campus-wide protests attracting thousands of previously moderate students. Often two or three such organizers on a campus could rapidly set up a strong new SDS chapter or gain dominance within an already existing one. Meanwhile, SDS's membership had grown to more than 50,000 nationwide while influencing hundreds of thousands of students indirectly. Yet it remained an amorphous organization in many ways. The conditions were thus favorable for the scattered but centrally directed organizers of the PLP to realize their goal of capturing SDS and becoming a pivotal force in the antiwar movement as a whole.

During the 1968–69 school year, the PLP and the SDS national office waged a nationwide power struggle, preparing for the 1969 convention. The PLP's influence grew more rapidly than the national office's but not quite rapidly enough. LaRouche's raid had prevented the PLP from gaining national prestige from the Columbia strike and also had deprived it of several of its best campus organizers. For instance, Steve Fraser, whom the PLP sent to Philadelphia to take command of SDS, ended up joining LaRouche. When a major strike erupted at the University of Pennsylvania in early 1969, it was the Labor Committee, not the PLP, that ran the show.

The result was that the PLP went into the 1969 Chicago convention without a solid majority. The mutual hostilities passed the point of no return and the PLP was forced to take over prematurely. It could not prevent the deposed leadership and a large minority from setting up a parallel organization—the "real" SDS. Although the latter soon fell apart, the PLP majority faction was unable to recover momentum. Isolated from the off-campus peace movement, SDS dwindled in size over the next two years.

The main cause of the split was the sectarianism and ideological extremism of the two major factions, not the actions of LaRouche's followers, who were reviled as elitists by both camps. But LaRouche's 1967–68 raid on the PLP had definitely helped to tip the balance. It was his first lesson in how a small but adroitly led group, through the right tactics at the right time and place, can help to produce a "manifold shift" in the larger political arena. The lesson would hold him in good stead in his later forays into mainstream politics.

LaRouche could never have influenced SDS without encouraging bold tactics, especially during the Columbia and University of Pennsylvania strikes. But when he and his followers were wooing the New Right in the early 1980s, they apparently felt an acute need to rewrite the history of their SDS involvement. A 1983 LaRouchian pamphlet claimed that they had "agreed to penetrate" SDS in 1967–68 in order to "discredit and neutralize the leftism emerging at that time." The pamphlet did not say who the other party to this agreement was, but strongly implied it was some government agency.

The LaRouche organization did begin to cooperate with local police and the FBI in the mid-1970s. But former leading Labor Committee members say the idea of a "penetration operation," circa 1968, is preposterous. LaRouche's disciples entered SDS filled with revolutionary fervor. Their political strategy to develop "class-wide organizing" and "mass strikes" was second to none in its radical implications. While advocating militancy, they scrupulously avoided the provocateurish rhetoric and deeds that were the hallmark of police infiltrators.

In fact, the LaRouchians were themselves the target of government surveillance and harassment. The FBI's COINTELPRO operatives produced a leaflet, *The Mouse Crap Revolution,* aimed at discrediting Tony Papert among Columbia students and driving a wedge between the Labor Committee and other factions. In Philadelphia the FBI and the local police Red Squad engaged in a classic frame-up of Steve Fraser. Explosives were planted in his refrigerator, and he was charged with plotting to blow up the Liberty Bell. (The indictment, which drew heavy fire from civil libertarians, was eventually dismissed.)

The most telling refutation of the penetration-agent myth comes in a complaint the LaRouchians themselves filed in 1982 in a federal court lawsuit against the FBI. It describes "constant and intrusive" visits by federal agents to NCLC members' employers and landlords, hundreds of arrests on petty matters such as street-corner soliciting, the use of police informers to infiltrate the organization, and the compiling of over 25,000 pages of surveillance files. All of this was supposed to have taken place between 1968 and 1976. If LaRouche was a government agent, he was being provided with as much cover as the Howard Hughes–CIA Glomar expedition!

In the wake of the SDS split, LaRouche picked up recruits sick of faction fights and mindless slogans. Already his followers were organizing independently of SDS under a new name, the National Caucus of Labor Committees (NCLC). By 1973 the NCLC had over six hundred hard-core members in twenty-five cities and the most literate paper on the far left, *New Solidarity.* LaRouche also had attracted a small following in Europe, chiefly in West Berlin and Stockholm.

He centralized the organization and began purging those of independent mind. First to get the ax, in 1971, were the "Bavarians," a dissident circle whose chief spokesman was Steve Fraser. LaRouche then surrounded himself with individuals willing to carry out his every whim. Most important were Konstandinos (Gus) Kalimtgis ("Gus Axios" or "Costas Axios") and Nick Syvriotis ("Criton Zoakos"), former members of a left-wing Greek exile sect. Together with a third crony, Andy Typaldos ("Andreas Reniotis"), they became known as LaRouche's "Greek mafia" and served as his key lieutenants for almost a decade.

NCLC members developed their own cultish jargon—e.g., "creative mentation," "class-for-itself," "left hegemony," "Promethean hubris." Many dropped out of school or quit their jobs to organize full-time. Often they cut themselves off from family and friends, reordering their lives totally around the NCLC. They came to believe that the Revolution was just around the corner: The NCLC would seize control of most major American trade unions within six months, overthrow the government within the decade, and rule the world by the year 2000. To hasten the process they began disrupting meetings of other groups, seizing the microphone to give vehement speeches to the effect that everyone except themselves was working for the CIA.

Other SDS offshoots were behaving even more strangely as the exhilarating days of campus rebellion receded. The Weathermen worked themselves into a frenzy via ultrafanatical indoctrination sessions, then dove underground to make bombs. The Revolutionary Union built a personality cult around Chairman Bob Avakian, who later fled to Paris claiming the ruling class was about to kill him. The PLP marched through Boston's streets with sticks and Communist T-shirts to combat the supposedly imminent threat of fascism.

Most of the ultraleft sects of the early 1970s adhered to standard variations of Marxist-Leninist doctrine. But LaRouche injected into the NCLC a conspiracy theory of politics quite different from anything in the Marxist tradition. In its early stages, before he latched on to hardcore anti-Semitism, this theory held that the Rockefeller family, through its alleged control of the CIA and a vast network of agents on every level of society, was responsible for most of the world's ills. The Rockefellers, LaRouche taught, were plotting a nuclear holocaust. Time was running out. The world's fate rested on the shoulders of the tiny NCLC. Anyone who couldn't see this was part of the plot. Soon the NCLC enemies list, like that of Richard Nixon, was burgeoning. It included not only most of the Establishment but also NCLC defectors, leaders of rival sects, and distinguished scholars whose only apparent sin was their refusal to recognize LaRouche's genius.

Such fanaticism, however, was sharply at variance with the flashes of Machiavellian cynicism that began to appear in LaRouche's own writings. In a 1970 essay on the dog-eat-dog world of left-wing factionalism, he observed that ideology is mostly "designed for the purpose of deceiving—usually to deceive the authors above all others." He added that most leftist honchos operate on the hope that their "credulous followers and opponents" can be suckered into accepting a given factional position at face value. In reality, LaRouche argued, the typical leftist leader "says in print and public debate that with which he wishes to conceal his actual practice."

LaRouche put this theory of deception and manipulation to the test. In the spring of 1973, he launched his followers on the most extraordinary odyssey in the history of American extremism: a journey to the farthest limits of the left and from thence, by circuitous paths, to the outermost reaches of the right.

# Three

# Operation Mop Up

LaRouche's writings in the late 1960s displayed an intense curiosity about the history and methods of European fascism. His research, so his followers thought, was aimed at learning how to *prevent* fascism. But his analysis differed in subtle ways from that of other leftists. One of the first observers to spot something amiss was his old rival Tim Wohlforth. In a 1968 article, Wohlforth noted LaRouche's "preposterous theory" that the Nazi murder of six million Jews had been motivated solely by economics. "It seems," wrote Wohlforth, "that when [the Nazis] worked the Jews to a point where there was no labor power left in them, they simply sent them to the gas chambers to save the cost of upkeep for unproductive slaves." Wohlforth saw LaRouche's theory as just a one-sided analysis of Nazi motives. He didn't suspect that LaRouche one day would develop his own brand of fascism.

In 1971, LaRouche published a major article on the prospects for fascist base building in America. Only with a mass base, he observed, could a "storm trooper" organization have "saleable qualities" that might attract support from "leading governmental and financial inter-ests." He predicted that such a movement would emerge soon on the basis of a "populist" ideology and diverse appeals to rival ethnic groups. This movement would begin to furnish the capitalists with gangs to "break strikes and break up socialist and union meetings." Although at first it might include fascist-minded Jews, it would sooner or later turn on the Jewish community. The Jews, LaRouche observed, were "a most visible and thus 'ripe' " candidate for the role of scapegoat.

LaRouche also predicted that a new type of left-wing group, defined as "left-protofascist," would take part in the street violence on the side of overtly right-wing ethnic fascists. In subsequent articles he examined how the alleged controllers of fascism, the American capitalist class, might use advanced brainwashing techniques to transform leftist college students into precisely this type of left-fascist "zombie." He meanwhile began to teach his own leftist followers to regard themselves as "Prometheans," an elite far above the rest of humanity.

LaRouche's implication was clear: The NCLC must learn from fascism and adopt some of fascism's tactics. But his followers still regarded themselves as good Marxists (in spite of their elitist pretensions) and retained a visceral hatred of fascism. If LaRouche wanted to steer them to the right, he would have to turn the NCLC into a controlled environment for ideological reeducation—a political cult.

The NCLC's transformation occurred in three overlapping stages during 1973–74. First, LaRouche ordered his followers into the streets for a campaign of savage attacks on rival leftist groups called Operation Mop Up. This forced them to either deepen their commitment or get out. It also isolated them irrevocably from the rest of the left.

Second, LaRouche staged "ego-stripping" sessions at NCLC meetings, instilling in his followers a sense of shame over any ideological wavering or lack of courage they might have displayed during Mop Up.

Finally, he whipped up an atmosphere of hysteria inside the NCLC based on allegations of an assassination plot against himself. The acceptance of these bizarre allegations severed most of the remaining links between NCLC members and everyday reality.

Operation Mop Up was preceded by months of squabbling between the NCLC and the Communist Party USA. NCLC members had frequently disrupted CP meetings with long harangues from the floor. The CP began tossing them out and published articles alleging that they were government agents. Matters escalated in early 1973 when the NCLC announced a conference in Philadelphia to build a national organization for welfare recipients and the unemployed. CP members and other local activists started a campaign to discredit the conference, calling its NCLC organizers racists as well as agents. The NCLC leadership was furious. A *New Solidarity* front-page editorial, entitled "Deadly

Crisis for CPUSA," warned the CP that if it didn't back off it would face an all-out counterattack. The CP failed to take the threat seriously.

On the conference's opening day the anti-NCLC coalition sent a sound truck through the black community and staged a picket line with signs comparing the NCLC to the Ku Klux Klan. This failed to stop the event, which was attended by several hundred white middle-class activists and a handful of welfare mothers. The harassment did, however, give LaRouche the pretext he needed. He called an emergency meeting of the East Coast NCLC. "From here on in," he declared, "the CP *cannot hold a meeting* on the East Coast . . . We'll mop them up in two months." The NCLC, he promised, would seize "hegemony" on the left—i.e., replace the CP as the dominant organization.

Many NCLC members were shocked and frightened by LaRouche's announcement, but he anticipated their reluctance: "I know you better than you know yourselves, and for the most part you're *full of crap,*" he said. "This isn't a debating society anymore."

A front-page *New Solidarity* editorial, "Operation Mop Up: The Class Struggle Is for Keeps," echoed LaRouche's call. "We must dispose of this stinking corpse [the CP]," the editorial said, "to ensure that it cannot act as a host for maggots and other parasites preparing future scabby Nixonite attacks on the working class. . . . If we were to vacillate . . . we would be guilty of betraying the human race. Our job is to pulverize the Communist Party."

Meanwhile, the NCLC leadership prepared an extraordinary psycho-theological document, "The CP Within Us," to bolster morale. The key to winning Mop Up, it argued, was to expunge the inner voice of cowardice and hesitation (i.e., the CP) within each NCLC member.

Months prior to Mop Up, LaRouche had ordered the most physically agile NCLC members to undergo training for street fighting. This training was now stepped up. Members were organized into flying squads armed with metal pipes, clubs, and *numchukas* (Korean martial arts devices consisting of two sticks attached by a chain). The idea was to go into action as mini-phalanxes with the *numchuka* wielders in the center.

Mop Up began in New York, then spread to Philadelphia, Buffalo, Detroit, and other cities. Attackers were sometimes brought from out of town so their faces wouldn't be recognized. In several cities they broke up public meetings and invaded leftist bookstores, beating anyone who tried to bar their way. In New York they ambushed individual CP leaders on the street. In Detroit they administered a savage beating to a partially paralyzed left-wing activist on crutches. In Philadelphia, twenty-five to thirty NCLC members raided a meeting of the Public Workers Action Caucus. "The steps were a mass of blood," said a

PWAC activist. "As soon as I walked out I was hit by a pole." Although no one was critically injured in any of the attacks, several were hospitalized with broken bones and many required medical treatment for cuts and bruises.

The NCLC rhetoric kept pace with the attacks. "The red Communist Party has turned into a den of yellow cowards," announced a LaRouche spokesman in Philadelphia. "CP Recruiting Pallbearers for Its Own Funeral," blared a headline in the April 30 *New Solidarity*.

When members of the Socialist Workers Party and other Trotskyist groups came forward to defend the CP despite past differences, the NCLC responded with an announcement that henceforth the Trotskyists would be fair game. Undeterred, dozens of SWP supporters showed up to guard the CP's New York mayoral candidate, Rasheed Storey, after the NCLC announced it would break up a speech he was scheduled to give at Columbia. Doug Jenness, a member of the defense squad, recalls that about forty LaRouchians "filtered into the hall, some wearing leather jackets. They had staves concealed under blankets. When Storey started speaking, they stood up and moved forward, putting on brass knuckles and displaying *numchukas.*" Storey and other speakers were whisked out the back. The battle then began in earnest. Although the NCLC was finally driven from the hall, six members of the defense squad required treatment.

An unsigned front-page *New Solidarity* article, "Their Morals and Ours" (named after an anti-Stalinist treatise by Trotsky), expressed anger at the attitude of LaRouche's former Trotskyist comrades. The SWP, the article complained, "has been saying, 'Smash the Communist Party' for almost forty years, yet when some left organization proceeds to actually smash the CP, the SWP leaders and members roll their glazed eyes heavenward, expecting the entire galaxy to fall upon them."

"Their Morals and Ours" revealed the tactical thinking behind Mop Up. It boasted that fifty NCLC members could "rout" three hundred CP members and that the CP would have to mobilize at least six times as many fighters to even become a "serious obstacle."

This bravado strongly resembled the passage in *Mein Kampf* in which Hitler, describing an altercation between Nazis and leftists in a Munich meeting hall in 1921, crowed that "our enemies, who must have numbered seven and eight hundred men, [were] beaten out of the hall and chased down the stairs by my men numbering not even fifty."

"Their Morals and Ours" also said that destroying the CP meant showing that it was "a 'paper tiger,' rightfully an object of pitying contempt in the eyes of the working person." This idea was further developed in another *New Solidarity* article: "All those mighty 'Communists' can do is hide behind the nightsticks of the local police, while publishing tear-jerking accounts of their own casualties."

Again, there is a similar formulation in *Mein Kampf:* "Any meeting which is protected exclusively by the police discredits its organizers in the eyes of the broad masses. . . . [A] heroic movement will sooner win the heart of a people than a cowardly one which is kept alive only by police protection."

Such parallels did not go entirely unnoticed within the NCLC. Christine Berl, one of LaRouche's top disciples (who quit the following year), recalls that she was assigned to prepare a report for a 1973 NCLC conference on how Hitler built up the Nazi Party. "It scared me," she says. "I began to see it was the very tactics Lyn was using." Berl says that she presented her doubts in the form of a puzzle: How do we distinguish ourselves from the Nazis? The audience was unable to give a clear answer.

New York in 1973 was hardly comparable to Munich in 1921. There were no Freikorps veterans and ruined shopkeepers to flock to LaRouche's banner. And his street fighters were middle-class intellectuals, not desperate lumpen proletarians. Indeed the majority of them were not fighters at all. Most Mop Up attacks were carried out by just a few dozen persons. Even the most enthusiastic of these became nervous as the CP and SWP fought back, their defense squads often outnumbering the attackers. "I pissed blood for a month," recalls a female NCLC member who was injured while charging a Detroit SWP rally. The Chicago regional NCLC sent a memo to New York stating that it wasn't strong enough to "deal directly" with the CP. Would the leadership send "defense reinforcements"? Until such reinforcements arrived, the Chicago organization would keep most of its activities "low-key or underground," the memo said. By May, the NCLC leadership was finding it difficult to whip up enthusiasm for fresh attacks even in New York.

It is widely believed among leftists that the police in some cities encouraged Mop Up. This suspicion is understandable in light of well-documented police harassment of left-wing groups in the late 1960s and early 1970s. But former LaRouchians who participated in Mop Up say they don't recall any police encouragement. At the time, the NCLC regarded the police as the enemy, acting in cahoots with the CP and the SWP to repress the true forces of Revolution. This view was vehemently expressed in the pages of *New Solidarity* as the police cracked down on Mop Up in city after city. Several NCLC members were arrested in Philadelphia, including a top LaRouche aide. More were arrested in Boston. In Buffalo felony indictments brought the local Mop Up to a grinding halt. In New York City two NCLC members were charged with second-degree assault and possession of a deadly instrument after they attacked black CP leader Ron Tyson. One of Tyson's attackers was rearrested a week later for assaulting an SWP member.

The only evidence of a law enforcement role in Mop Up points not to local police but to the FBI. The findings of a federal judge in an SWP lawsuit against the FBI suggest that once Mop Up was under way, the bureau's New York office attempted to aggravate it as part of a campaign of anonymous mailings and other malicious pranks to keep leftist sects at each other's throats. Federal Judge Charles D. Breitel of the Southern District of New York reviewed classified FBI files in 1979 as a court-appointed Special Master acting for plaintiff SWP. His report noted that a letter had been sent to the NCLC during Mop Up listing the names, home telephone numbers, and addresses of SWP members. "Unless the Government is prepared to allow disclosure of all information" in the deleted part of the file, Breitel ruled, "it should be conclusively presumed that the letter was sent by the FBI . . ."

LaRouche knew just how far he could push Mop Up. Before the stalemate with the CP could turn into a rout for his followers, he declared victory and called everything off. In fact, Mop Up did no real political harm to the CP. A few meetings were canceled in the first weeks, but thereafter the CP continued its normal activities behind a screen of defense squads. However, Mop Up was a great success for LaRouche. It induced his followers to believe that those they had attacked, and who had fought back, were permanently the enemy. No longer were non-NCLC leftists seen as rivals within a common Marxist tradition. They had become unredeemable devils, traitors to the working class, subhuman police agents, *fascists.* Mop Up thus marked a bizarre new stage in the NCLC's political evolution—the stage of antifascist fascism.

# Four

## The Great Manchurian Candidate Scare

In the summer of 1973, LaRouche began sessions of what he called "ego-stripping." He suggested this would cure his followers of the cowardice and bourgeois moral qualms they had displayed during Mop Up. The big problem with most NCLC members, he said, was their psychosexual fears. LaRouche proposed to use fear to fight fear:

"I am going to make you organizers—by taking your bedrooms away from you . . . ," he announced. "What I shall do is to expose to you the cruel fact of your sexual impotence . . . I will take away from you all hope that you can flee the terrors of politics to the safety of 'personal life.' I shall do this by showing to you that your frightened personal sexual life contains for you such terrors as the outside world could never offer you. I will thus destroy your rabbit-holes, mental as well as physical. I shall destroy your sense of safety in the place to which you ordinarily imagine you can flee. I shall not pull you back from fleeing, but rather destroy the place to which you would attempt to flee."

The ego-stripping sessions were similar to the confrontational therapy practiced by psychological cults. LaRouche would pick an NCLC member at random, or perhaps one who had failed at some political assignment. The group would heap nonstop attacks on every aspect of the victim's behavior. Supposedly it was a sign of psychic liberation if he or she broke down and started sobbing hysterically. LaRouche said this was the way in which the individual "abruptly 'breaks free' as if from a drugged state; a sudden personality change occurs, in which the group sees the real person come forth, assume control of himself, or herself, and bring the ego-state under control." Thus ego-stripping was "an act of social love."

Christine Berl, who participated in these sessions, gives a different view. The so-called social love, she writes, was "pure psychological terror" and resulted in an extreme form of "depersonalization." The T-group members were "transformed into sniveling informers vying with each other for [LaRouche's] approval. Even couples were encouraged to 'inform' on each other's 'progress,' particularly by singling out any behavior that could be construed as apolitical, or that was suspected of being 'resistant' to the aims of the sessions."

LaRouche took to calling himself Der Abscheulicher (the Abominable One). Along with the ego-stripping, he began to instill in his followers an outlook of all-pervasive paranoia. In the unconscious mind, he warned, there lurked dark forces producing impotence, homosexuality, zombie states, madness. These "pit creatures" would destroy anyone who let his or her guard down. Meanwhile, in the outside world, Rockefeller, the CIA, and a vast network of secret agents and assassins were poised to attack at any moment. Safety could be attained only by following LaRouche's every command, replicating his thoughts and remaking oneself in his image.

Some NCLC members were unconvinced of this, despite their deep admiration for LaRouche's intellectual abilities. Matters came to a head in January 1974, when LaRouche seized upon a fantasy that united the demons of the unconscious mind and the assassins of the outside world into a single horrifying vision. This was the Great Manchurian Candidate Scare, which wiped the slate clean of skepticism among the members and completed their transformation into a totalitarian political cult.

The prologue to this momentous event took place in the summer of 1973, when LaRouche traveled to West Germany to meet with members of the European Labor Committees, a newly formed NCLC affiliate. In early August, LaRouchians in the United States began to read in *New Solidarity* how Konstantin George, a member of the German organization, had been drugged and brainwashed by the East German secret police while visiting a girlfriend in East Berlin. George had then been sent back over the wall, so the story went, to spy on the European Labor Committees and finger LaRouche for assassination by a KGB-

CIA hit team. The plot was foiled when LaRouche recognized the symptoms of brainwashing in George's behavior, and deprogrammed him using techniques "absolutely unprecedented in 'psychological science.'" The details of these techniques were not revealed, but NCLC members were warned to be on the lookout for other brainwashing victims.

The George affair did not unduly alarm the NCLC membership. Not only was the story extremely confused, but it was rumored that George had denied it. Real fear seized the organization only after LaRouche announced the uncovering of a second zombie—a Manchurian Candidate in every respect—Christopher White, a twenty-six-year-old NCLC member and British national who had earned the personal resentment of LaRouche. In 1972, Carol Schnitzer had left LaRouche and married White, who was ten years her junior. The Whites had withdrawn to London, promising to organize a British NCLC branch.

In December 1973, LaRouche ordered them to return to New York for an NCLC year-end conference. White had good reason to feel nervous about this. He had done a poor job of organizing the British branch, and was a prime candidate for ego-stripping even apart from the love triangle. During the flight over the Atlantic, he viewed the film *Trinity.* According to his recollection of the plot (in an article he wrote two months later), the hero has a girlfriend "at least ten years older than himself." She is murdered, and the hero then arranges the execution of a "rather paternal figure." White became increasingly agitated. When the plane landed, he began to shout that the CIA was planning to kill both his wife and LaRouche.

Instead of calling a doctor, Carol called LaRouche. Chris was rushed into a deprogramming session at LaRouche's apartment. LaRouche's security aides and Dr. Gene Inch, a physician and NCLC member, rushed to the scene. Meanwhile, members from across the country had gathered in New York for the conference. The suspense began to mount as alarming rumors emanated from LaRouche's apartment. It was said that White had been tortured and brainwashed in a London basement by the CIA and British intelligence, who had programmed him first to kill his wife upon the utterance of a trigger word and then to finger LaRouche for assassination by Cuban exile frogmen.

LaRouche mobilized the entire NCLC. They passed out fliers on a massive scale in New York and other cities, describing White's alleged tortures in lurid detail. The national office issued over forty press releases in a two-week period. LaRouche and the Whites filed a complaint with the United Nations Commission on Human Rights and launched a lawsuit against the CIA. NCLC members frantically solicited their parents and friends to serve on an Emergency Commission of Inquiry.

LaRouche's proof for the story was his tapes of the deprogramming. But *New York Times* reporter Paul Montgomery listened to them and gathered only that White was emotionally distraught. "There are sounds of weeping and vomiting," Montgomery wrote. "Mr. White complains of being deprived of sleep, food and cigarettes. . . . There is also what appears to be an attempt to hypnotize Mr. White." Montgomery wrote that at one point, after White failed to contradict one of LaRouche's suggestions, LaRouche exclaimed, "Now do you see Carol? Do you believe?" At another point, White complained of a pain in his arm. When LaRouche said the pain was merely part of the "program," White suddenly shouted: "The pain is real . . . I have to tell you what's real and stop this crazy fantasy world. Because it's not my fantasy."

The NCLC brought in three psychiatrists. None would substantiate the Manchurian Candidate story. Dr. Israel Samuelly suggested that White was suffering from "schizophrenic catatonia with paranoiac features." Most of the persons listed on the Emergency Commission either quit or said they had never agreed to serve in the first place.

Within the NCLC, the atmosphere of hysteria was so intense that facts didn't matter. LaRouche drilled his followers on what each could expect if kidnapped by the CIA: "When they really start the heavy programming," he said, "first of all they give you heavy electric shock. *Heavy* electric shock. . . .

"But then, you know what they do to you? It's not the pain that brainwashes people.

"What kills you is when you eat excrement as a way of inducing your torturer to lay off the pain. In permitting a bottle to be inserted in your anus and sitting on it on a chair for hours while interrogation continues, as a way of avoiding greater pain. Lying on the floor and whining like a puppy, as a way of getting your torturers to lay off. Or permitting yourself to be subjected to homosexual rape, oral and anal. . . . They say your father was nothing, your father was a queer, your father was a woman. . . ."

As for the skeptics in his audience, LaRouche cried, "Any of you who say this is a hoax—you're *cruds!* You're *subhuman!* You're not serious. *The human race is at stake.* Either we win or there is no humanity."

*New Solidarity* followed up with an editorial entitled "Will You Eat Shit for Rockefeller's CIA?" It warned that the enemy would use "every form of degradation known to man." During the next few weeks, each NCLC member was terrified that he or she had been brainwashed. (LaRouche emphasized that the victims would have total amnesia about the experience—until the moment of utterance of the fatal trigger word.) The leadership was flooded with requests for deprogramming from those who found themselves harboring vaguely murderous thoughts about LaRouche. One member went berserk, screaming, "Cancel me! Cancel me!" and had to be hospitalized. According to LaRouche, this individual's "code barrier" had gone out of control.

The hysteria prompted the issuance of an "intake procedure" manual by Carol White. "The brainwashed comrade's version of events should be taken down," Mrs. White wrote, "and particular attention should be paid to his fantasies—reference to witches, devils, sensitivity to hissing sounds . . ."

Predictably, any member who expressed skepticism became immediately suspect. Christine Berl called the story hogwash and withdrew from any active role in the leadership. LaRouche said that the CIA, acting through her boyfriend, had taken over her mind. A friend warned her that a plot was afoot to kidnap and deprogram her—to liberate her from her brainwashed condition. They waited outside her door, but she didn't come out. Less fortunate was Alice Weitzman, also a skeptic, who was held captive in her apartment and forced to listen to Beethoven at high volume—a deprogramming technique suggested by LaRouche. Weitzman managed to throw a note out the window. A passerby picked it up and alerted the police. When officers went to the apartment, they heard screams, forced their way in, and freed her. Later that day, they arrested six NCLC members on kidnapping charges. (The case was ultimately dismissed after Weitzman refused to press charges.)

NCLC security chief José Torres was another skeptic. "The spook stuff [went] on for weeks," he recalls, "and for that time I was the functioning head of the LC because nobody would do shit." Torres decided he'd had enough. "I [took] Chris White aside and said, 'Do you know who I am?' And he said, 'Yes, I know you.' I said, 'Look, I'm going to bust you up right now if you give me any bullshit about being brainwashed because you weren't brainwashed so why the fuck did you put us on like this?' And he said, 'It's too late to turn back now.' He couldn't back out now, it was all crap, all of it."

Torres says he told LaRouche about this, but LaRouche dismissed it as part of White's brainwashing. Torres later concluded that White had known "exactly what he was doing" and had been motivated by a desire to avoid a psychological dressing-down. Says Torres: "White knew how Konstantin George had been deemed a victim of brainwashing and forgiven. So why not be brainwashed? He did it, and . . . Lyn . . . believed him and that was all it took. . . . He just kept feeding Lyn, and Lyn constructs the whole big thing out of it."

At the time, an NCLC leaflet described the deprogramming of White as "opening up a whole new area of psychology—the solution to psychosis." But LaRouche apparently decided in later years that the incident was best forgotten. His 1979 and 1987 autobiographies, although boastful about his alleged discoveries in many fields of knowledge, are silent about his cure for psychosis.

Most NCLC defectors agree with José Torres that LaRouche appeared genuinely spooked during the Chris White affair. They point out that on several later occasions LaRouche's belief in being a target of assassination seemed to fill an inner need. Yet the frequent security alerts to protect LaRouche also serve an extremely practical goal: They keep the NCLC membership in a state of mindless hysteria, scrambling frantically to raise money for LaRouche's coffers.

Various articles and speeches at the time by LaRouche and top aides suggested a high degree of calculated behavior.* Key passages dealt with the psychological weaknesses of the NCLC membership, their vulnerability to brainwashing, and the various manipulative techniques that might be used on them (for instance, playing on fears of homosexuality and triggering an infectious group paranoia). Although these methods were described—as in LaRouche's January 3, 1974, speech— as something the CIA was planning, they bore an uncanny resemblance to what LaRouche himself was doing to the NCLC membership.

To brainwash someone (so the LaRouchian theory went), it is first necessary to "terrorize" him into regarding "the entire world as a police-controlled environment." This was done during the Chris White affair, when many members believed themselves in imminent danger of being picked up by the CIA and/or the New York City police for tortures worse than death. The victim must believe that the entire world is falling apart and there is only himself to blame. This was also done: NCLC members were told that if they didn't stop the CIA conspiracy, the entire human race would die—and *they* would be responsible. Finally, the victim must be placed in a controlled environment, an artificial family. This, too, corresponds to life in the NCLC.

* That LaRouche knew exactly what he was doing was charged by Dr. Fred Newman, a Stanford University-trained logician-turned-Marxist-activist who worked with the NCLC during the Manchurian Candidate Scare. Newman was the author of *Explanation by Description* (1968), a study of how we believe what we believe. After splitting with the NCLC in mid-1974, he wrote a pamphlet analyzing how LaRouchians believe what LaRouchians believe. He charged that LaRouche had a "systematic plan" to transform his followers' ordinary middle-class values into an explicitly fascist consciousness, chiefly through the generating of an artificial paranoia at every level of the organization. (Newman went on to build his own political cult, the New Alliance Party, which through the years has mimicked LaRouche's tactics to an uncanny degree.)

LaRouche also described brainwashing as a system of doublethink, or metalogic, by which a person comes to believe that it is not he but the rest of the world that is brainwashed. "The victim's sense of reality is turned inside out," he explained. Christine Berl and Alice Weitzman accused him of brainwashing the membership, he said, because the CIA had brainwashed them to say this.

The doublethink during the Chris White affair went far beyond anything during Mop Up. Thus leading NCLC members who had readily supported Mop Up, such as Berl and Torres, challenged LaRouche's credibility during the spring of 1974. They had believed in Mop Up because it possessed at least a veneer of rational justification: CP members indeed had assaulted NCLC members and spread exaggerated accusations about them on several prior occasions. Berl and Torres thus could convince themselves that the CP was a counterinsurgency force standing in the way of Revolution. But the Chris White story had no empirical basis at all. It required a leap of faith, not just contorted logic. NCLC members with a strong sense of reality found it intolerable. One by one during 1974 they defected.

Those who remained were capable of believing in anything La-Rouche might suggest, even neo-Nazism.

# Five

# The Beethoven Gang

One would think that the many black, Hispanic, and Jewish members in the NCLC would have become an embarrassment to LaRouche as he swung to the ultraright. But he developed his own unique viewpoint on the relationship between ethnic minorities and fascism.

In a 1971 essay, still writing from an ostensibly Marxist perspective, LaRouche tried to imagine how fascism might come to America. He looked at Rabbi Meir Kahane's Jewish Defense League, Joe Colombo's Italian-American Civil Rights League, George Wallace's American Party, and various black nationalist groups. These, LaRouche argued, were the germs of a uniquely American fascism. America is an "ethnic-cultural polyglot," and a powerful fascist base can't be built on one ethnic community alone. A successful U.S. fascism must include multiethnic alliances different from anything in Hitler's lexicon.

LaRouche predicted that the "mutually segregated" ethnic fascist groups would join with youth from the drug/rock counterculture in a "common front" around a "populist" cover ideology. This coalition would launch the "direct street-battle between socialism and fascism," growing into "the sort of large organization which U.S. fascism must become to be taken seriously."

He was aware that a fascist movement embracing white Christian ethnics, Jews, blacks, and Hispanics, even in segregated units, would seem to be a strange combination. But was it not fascism's nature to unite apparent opposites? (The NCLC acted on this principle in later years when it attempted, unsuccessfully, to unite elements of the KKK, Black Muslims, Jewish Defense League, and mob-linked labor racketeers under its leadership.)

The first application of "ethnic fascism" came in 1973, when the NCLC set out to organize street-fighting units, fascist in all but name, among black and Hispanic ghetto youth. LaRouche first alluded to this idea in his April 1973 speech announcing Operation Mop Up. "You think this CP stuff [Mop Up] is scary?" he asked. "Well, I'll tell you something that's really gonna scare you. In a few months we're gonna have 10,000 enraged ghetto youth, we're gonna organize street gangs. . . ."

At an NCLC convention in late May he launched the Revolutionary Youth Movement (RYM), which he said would be a "paramilitary organization" reaching out to the type of ghetto youth who believe they can "make it as Superfly." It would "cut through" their "hustle" mentality and organize them on the basis of "what they really feel underneath," their feelings of despair and of "increasingly pure rage." RYM would teach them that rage is not just "robbing the corner candy store." Rage is the determination to "take it all"—to seize control of America in alliance with other enraged groups.

LaRouche predicted that his message would "spread like wildfire" in the ghetto. Thousands would join RYM, where they would learn military discipline and revolutionary theory. "These youth will be able to debate philosophers," he boasted.

During that summer and fall, NCLC's small cohort of college-educated blacks, wearing Black Panther-style leather jackets and sunglasses, fanned out to Manhattan's Lower East Side, Brooklyn's Bedford-Stuyvesant, Newark's Central Ward, and other poor neighborhoods. The message was that gang members could become "Prometheans"—like Zeke Boyd, a former Panther and the token black on the NCLC security staff.

LaRouche's organizers developed ties with the Outlaws, the largest gang in Bedford-Stuyvesant. *New Solidarity* said the Outlaws were a peaceful bunch attending RYM classes to learn to appreciate classical music. According to Christine Berl, this was not entirely accurate. "I gave the Beethoven class," she recalls. "They had guns in the room."

The NCLC tried to persuade RYM members to reject the subculture of the streets. A black NCLC member told *The Village Voice* that ghetto youth "spend their time practicing the jungle boogie. . . . They look like they're masturbating in public. I tell these kids I don't want to talk to them until they're human." Tolerance was never the NCLC's strong point. But like Marine recruits, the RYM members accepted this drill-instructor message without taking offense. The leader of the Outlaws, twenty-one-year-old Tea, said that if RYM was "ever ready to fight the government and pick up guns, the Outlaws will be right behind them."

A former LaRouchian, Dan Jacobs, writes that the RYM project was doomed to failure because the NCLC was never willing to accept the ghetto youth as anything more than exotic auxiliaries to stand around and look tough at rallies.

But the New York Police Department was not about to tolerate "red gangs," as LaRouche called them. It came down hard on RYM, arresting Tea, Tango, Sly, Ace, and others on charges including attempted murder, robbery, and illegal weapons possession. RYM members also were arrested in Newark and Philadelphia. *New Solidarity* complained in article after article that the arrests were politically motivated, but the NCLC was politically too isolated to mount an effective defense. RYM members became disillusioned and dropped away.

At the same time NCLC members were learning to talk out of both sides of the mouth. While RYM organizers urged ghetto youth to "take it all," *New Solidarity* editorials sent a very different message to ethnic whites: "Soon, you will lose your job—probably to a 'welfare loafer,' a methadone-crazed dope-fiend . . . some gang member brought in from a ghetto neighborhood." The NCLC also physically attacked black activists and disseminated blatantly racist propaganda. This began during Mop Up, when blacks were priority targets. A black CP leader was assaulted on the street near party headquarters in Manhattan. A CP meeting in Harlem was terrorized by a contingent wearing hockey helmets. A meeting of the Martin Luther King Coalition in Buffalo was attacked by an all-white Mop Up squad which beat up several people. *New Solidarity* meanwhile carried headlines such as "CP Turns Rebels into Niggers" and bestowed demeaning nicknames on black CP members—e.g., "Ron 'Race Riot' Tyson."

In Newark the NCLC targeted poet turned activist Amiri Baraka, who had attracted national attention by his crusade for black community empowerment. NCLC members convinced themselves that Baraka was a CIA agent and hence fair game. They circulated a pamphlet called *Papa Doc Baraka: Fascism in Newark.* This and various *New Solidarity* articles called him a "gutter dweller," an "animal," a "mad dog," "Aunt Jemima," and "Superfly." A cartoon on the pamphlet's cover portrayed him as a hyena with Negroid lips drooling over a baby's corpse. Baraka became the NCLC's Symbolic Black, just as Henry Kissinger would become its Symbolic Jew.

Baraka's and LaRouche's followers began to fight it out in the streets, much to the delight of right-wing elements in Newark's white ethnic community led by law-and-order advocate Anthony Imperiale. Followers of Imperiale began to echo some of the NCLC's charges against Baraka, and met with Newark NCLC members to explore the possibility of joint action. Individuals claiming to be affiliated with the Ku Klux Klan also approached NCLC members to express support. In September 1973 the NCLC staged an anti-Baraka demonstration which turned into a slugfest inside the Newark City Council chambers. Ten NCLC members were arrested, including Gus Kalimtgis, co-author of the Baraka pamphlet.

The NCLC developed a plan to take its anti-Baraka campaign nationwide. "The country will be saturated with our newspapers, leaflets, with the Baraka pamphlet, with meetings, forums, press conferences, rallies," boasted *New Solidarity*. It called on "every working class organizer" and "all trade unionists" in the country to join the fight. That fall violent clashes between the NCLC and black nationalists occurred on several campuses. At Harvard the NCLC security staff set a trap. They called a meeting, armed themselves, and waited for members of the Boston-based Mau Mau to filter into the room. "A signal was given," said a former NCLC member. "Suddenly a sea of *numchukas* rose in the air and came down." One of the Mau Mau tried to pull a gun; NCLC members wrestled him to the floor. "They beat the shit out of him with sticks, then one of our guys stood over him with a shotgun while he lay there bleeding. The rest of the Mau Mau beat a retreat."

In the summer of 1974 the NCLC tried to whip up public fear of a new black nationalist threat: Zebra killers. In the San Francisco Bay Area, members of a tiny prison-based cult had killed several whites for ritualistic reasons. The NCLC, with no evidence whatsoever, claimed that similar killers were about to erupt into the streets of New York City from a Bronx drug addiction treatment program run by leftist doctors. "You could be white. You could be black . . ." said an NCLC leaflet circulated in Manhattan. "This summer you will be walking down the street with your family and a cruising car will pull up beside you. A group of young black men will jump out of the car and surround you. As they close in on you, you may notice that their eyes show no emotion, their pupils are pinpoints. Your throat will be slashed, your wife will be stabbed, your children's heads will be smashed against the pavement. The attackers will be grinning or laughing."

It is hard to imagine how black NCLC members went along with this. Sheer hysteria undoubtedly played a role, but more important was

LaRouche's ideological "reframing" of the NCLC membership's view of racism. He began, as he often does, with what seemed to be a valid point: Poverty in black ghettos is perpetuated by destructive lifestyles and a self-defeating psychology. Unless these problems are addressed, the cycle of poverty cannot be ended. The point is a commonplace today, but in the early 1970s it was not something most sociologists or civil rights activists were ready to confront. LaRouche did confront it, in striking rhetoric, when he lashed out at "the illusion that the ghetto can survive by parasitizing on itself." Black NCLC members thus could fancy he was the one white radical leader who would never try to patronize them. White members could pride themselves on belonging to the single radical party hard-nosed enough to reject the politics of liberal guilt. But LaRouche developed no constructive program from his insights. He simply used them to bolster the NCLC's synthetic paranoia: Ghetto street culture was invented by the CIA to control blacks, jazz is a form of brainwashing, Black Power advocates are part of the CIA-Rockefeller plot to set up black America for enslavement and genocide in concentration camps. LaRouche thus turned his followers' views on racism and black liberation inside out. Black and white NCLC members rushed into the streets to battle Baraka with a clear conscience, believing they were saving the black community from the CIA. They also used epithets like "nigger" and "animal" without any qualms, telling themselves the terms merely referred to the targeted individual's enslavement to false values invented by the CIA.

This topsy-turvy logic helped NCLC leaders justify alliances and political positions they never would have dreamed of in previous years. In 1974, at the height of the antibusing agitation in Boston, they traded intelligence with a leader of the stridently antibusing ROAR, based in white ethnic South Boston. They also sponsored their own antibusing congressional candidate in that troubled community. This was justified on the logic that busing was a CIA plot to divide the working class.

In Michigan, NCLC members began meeting with followers of KKK grand dragon Robert Miles, who had been convicted of bombing school buses in Pontiac, Michigan, to protest local busing. They even nominated the great knight hawk (sergeant at arms) of Miles's Klan, Vernon Higgins, as their 1974 candidate for the Michigan House of Representatives from Pontiac. Although Higgins turned out to be an FBI informer, the NCLC was not deterred from further dealings with Klansmen. In 1975, members began what would be an eleven-year alliance with Roy Frankhouser, the Pennsylvania grand dragon and Miles's close friend. When Frankhouser went on trial that year in Philadelphia on charges of transporting stolen explosives to Michigan for associates of Miles, the LaRouchians sponsored a press conference to support him.

Curiously, the closer the ties the NCLC developed with Klansmen, the more it downplayed antiblack rhetoric. Instead, LaRouche moved into an anti-Jewish mode, attempting to promote anti-Semitism in black as well as white communities. The NCLC was not alone in this tactic. Klan and neo-Nazi leaders had long recognized the wisdom of tactical alliances with secondary enemies to concentrate maximum force against the primary enemy. In the mid-1960s the neo-Nazi leader George Lincoln Rockwell had suggested an alliance with the Black Muslims. Such thinking became more common in the 1970s as anti-Semitism and anti-Zionism took strong hold in black communities. When Louis Farrakhan emerged as America's premier black anti-Semite in the 1980s, he won the sympathy of many Klansmen and neo-Nazis, including Frankhouser. But LaRouche, unlike the Klan, did more than pay lip service to the idea of a black-white anti-Jewish front. In 1978 his National Anti-Drug Coalition began massive propaganda in black communities charging that Jews control the narcotics traffic. Issuing a warning to black Americans on the "Zionist evil," LaRouche said: "We [blacks and the NCLC] are poised to destroy this enemy politically, if we collaborate."

His overtly antiblack campaign of 1973–74 may have been short-lived, but it was of great importance in the NCLC's development. It was LaRouche's first really complicated experiment in ideological reframing—the tactic of changing a person's emotional response to an idea by changing the context in which it is communicated. The antiblack campaign was essentially a dry run for what he next did to his Jewish followers, leading them step by step to believe that true liberation for Jews lay in the rejection of everything Jewish. The NCLC's left-wing Jews had the typical viewpoint of young leftists of the period: that racism against blacks is more evil and more worthy of protest than anti-Semitism. Once they violated the ultimate leftist taboo by attacking blacks, it was relatively easy to get them to attack their fellow Jews.

# Six

# The Jewish Question

When the LaRouchians began reaching out to the Ku Klux Klan and other white supremacist groups, they justified it as a tactical move. The main enemy, a 1975 NCLC internal memorandum argued, was "Rocky's [Nelson Rockefeller's] fascism with a democratic face" backed by liberals and "social fascists" (non-NCLC leftists). The NCLC should "cooperate with the Right to defeat this common enemy."

There was semantic trickery here. Not only did the memos lump together neo-Nazis with conservatives in an amorphous right (thus sanitizing the former), but groups traditionally opposed to fascism were tarred with the fascist label. It was the same logic used by Stalin in the early 1930s when he told the German Communists to cooperate with Hitler on the ground that the Social Democrats were the main enemy. (The term "social fascist" was first coined by the Stalinists to express this idea.)

The 1975 memo also argued that organizing on the right would bring the NCLC large financial contributions, allies with real influence, and new recruits. After the Revolution it would be "comparatively easy" to crush those who refused to be recruited.

The memorandum divided the "right wing" into "pro-Rocky" and "anti-Rocky" factions (i.e., pro- and anti-big business). The "pro-Rocky" side included William F. Buckley and other alleged big business penetration agents. The "anti-Rocky" side appeared to include the various Klansmen and neo-Nazis who had expressed interest in the NCLC. The implication was that these anti-Rocky rightists could be a positive force for social progress.

Some LaRouchians sincerely believed this, but the NCLC leadership was preparing itself for an ideological shift rather than merely a tactical one. The previous year the NCLC had developed an important friend in neo-Nazi circles—Ken Duggan, editor of *The Illuminator*. Duggan met regularly with NCLC security staffers, especially Scott Thompson, and urged them to move further to the right.

Duggan was soon arrested for stabbing a political rival, and was convicted of attempted murder. While awaiting sentencing at Rikers Island, the New York City detention center, he used a bedsheet to hang himself from a light fixture. But during his brief relationship with the LaRouchians he introduced them to a number of contacts and potential allies, the most important being Willis Carto.

Carto, founder of the Liberty Lobby, was by far the most successful and influential American anti-Semite of the 1970s. He was an intellectual disciple of the late Francis Parker Yockey, who roamed Europe and North America in the 1950s futilely attempting to build an underground movement. Carto met Yockey only once—in San Francisco in 1960, when Yockey was in jail awaiting trial for possession of false passports. Several days after their meeting, Yockey committed suicide in his cell by taking cyanide. Carto, already an ultrarightist, dedicated himself to carrying out Yockey's mission to save Western civilization.

This mission was set forth in Yockey's *Imperium*, a 600-page synthesis of Nazi racialism and Oswald Spengler's philosophy of history. The book was dedicated to the "Hero of the Second World War" (Hitler). But Carto, although devoted to Yockey's ideas, had no illusions about Yockey's tactics. Instead of engaging in inept conspiracies, he concentrated on building a political movement and developed a populist cover ideology. Although he discreetly sold *Mein Kampf* and *The Protocols of the Elders of Zion* by mail, he publicly denied being either a Nazi or an anti-Semite—he was merely "anti-Zionist."

Carto defended Hitler's heritage, not by saying the Holocaust had been a good thing, but by denying that it ever took place. He founded the Institute for Historical Review to prove that the alleged murder of six million Jews was a hoax invented by Zionists to make people feel sorry for them. Carto went so far as to publicize a theory that the gas ovens at Auschwitz were really just an industrial facility for converting coal into oil, operated by happy well-fed Jewish prisoners.

Carto's Liberty Lobby, based in Washington, D.C., and nominally headed by Colonel Curtis B. Dall (a former son-in-law of President Franklin D. Roosevelt), enjoyed friendly ties with conservative congressmen. It published a weekly tabloid, *The Spotlight,* which by 1979 enjoyed a paid circulation of almost 200,000. Its articles championed income-tax rebels, protested the plight of family farmers, and promoted quack cancer cures such as laetrile. Its favorite political targets included the Rockefellers, the Rothschilds, Henry Kissinger, the Council on Foreign Relations, and the "Zionist entity" in Palestine.

As early as 1975, Carto chatted frequently with Scott Thompson, and LaRouche himself visited Liberty Lobby headquarters to meet with Colonel Dall. A multileveled collaboration soon developed between the two organizations. They shared intelligence on various targets, including William F. Buckley and Resorts International. *The Spotlight* published articles by Thompson and other NCLC members writing under pen names. It also sold LaRouchian tracts through its mail-order service.

An initial point of agreement was on the need to expose the Rockefellers. However, Carto believed the NCLC hadn't cast its conspiracy nets wide enough. A 1976 *Spotlight* review of an NCLC report on terrorism complained that the NCLC still failed to recognize the role of the Jewish bankers. LaRouche received the message loud and clear. A wave of articles in *New Solidarity* blamed the Rothschilds and other Jewish bankers for a wide range of crimes, including the assassination of Abraham Lincoln. A 1977 piece by LaRouche admitted the Liberty Lobby had been ahead of the NCLC in identifying the main enemy. (LaRouche subsequently met with Carto in Wiesbaden. Questioned about this meeting during a 1984 deposition, LaRouche recalled that they had discussed "the Jewish question" as well as the "abomination" of America's postwar occupation of Germany.)

The NCLC also developed ties with persons on the fringes of the Liberty Lobby. Mitchell WerBell III, a friend of Carto, became LaRouche's security adviser. Colonel Tom McCrary, a Georgia rightist often praised in *The Spotlight,* accompanied Gus Kalimtgis on a national speaking tour. Edward von Rothkirch, a Lobby contact who ran a small press service in Washington and had once threatened to sue the LaRouchians for appropriating his firm's name, now became friendly. Several leaders of the American Agricultural Movement, a group championed by *The Spotlight,* began to work with the LaRouchians on farm issues. By the time LaRouche launched his 1980 presidential campaign, he felt free to call himself the candidate of *The Spotlight*'s readership, which he hailed as the quarter million strong " 'Gideon's Army' of American nationalism."

LaRouche's own "nationalism" had taken a quantum leap after he went to Wiesbaden in 1977 to straighten out the German organization and romance a young woman named Helga Zepp. While in Wiesbaden he became fearful of left-wing terrorists. He hunkered down in his villa and did some hard thinking.

When he returned to the United States late that year, with Helga as his bride, the war on Jews began in earnest. *New Solidarity* and other NCLC publications started to be full of attacks on wealthy Jewish families, B'nai B'rith, Zionism, the State of Israel, the American "Jewish Lobby" and the Jewish religion. *New Solidarity* published crude anti-Semitic jokes as well as articles suggesting that Zionists were a kind of subhuman species.

Actually LaRouche and some of his followers had ruminated along these lines even in their leftist days. In a 1973 article, "The Case of Ludwig Feuerbach," LaRouche argued that the Jewish religion is a fossilized reflection of the life in ancient and medieval times of the Jewish "merchant-usurer." The Jew of that epoch was a wretch who "had not yet evolved to the state of Papal enlightenment, a half-Christian, who had not developed a Christian conscience." Today's Jew is no better. His culture is "merely the residue left to the Jewish home after everything saleable has been marketed to the Goyim." Any religious feelings today's Jew may have are nothing but "infantile object elation." LaRouche also offered an anti-Semitic brand of psychoanalysis: "The brutally sadistic moral castration of the Jewish boy by the domineering 'Jewish mother' is the basis for one of the most horrifying models of male sexual impotence . . . the 'business Jew.' "

Following this article, *The Campaigner* published an anti-Israel tirade by Nancy Spannaus, one of LaRouche's top aides. The Israelis, she wrote, have a "psychotic" fear of anti-Semitism. In particular Jerusalem's Orthodox Jews are "crazed with the fear of death" and thus engage in "frightful orgies of sex and violence." Their religion is only the "thinnest disguise for exacerbated peasant paranoia."

LaRouche's 1974 tirade against the Jews was buried in a footnote. Many NCLC members passed over it. Others thought it was just LaRouche engaging in provocative remarks to help his Jewish followers confront their personal hang-ups. As for Spannaus's remarks, everyone knew she was a difficult personality. But the anti-Semitic agitation which began in 1977–78 was much more difficult to ignore or rationalize. It was not just a footnote or personal aberration; it was a systematic expression of hatred, revulsion, and scorn targeting every aspect of Jewish history, culture, religion, and home life.*

How could the Jewish members of the NCLC—at that time, a quarter of the membership—let this pass without expressing outrage? Defectors say that many members either didn't hear the message or simply tuned it out. They were working on the streets or in LaRouche business enterprises sixteen hours a day. Many of them were too exhausted to read *New Solidarity*. Those who did read it were in such a state of hysteria—mobilizing for the latest NCLC campaign to prevent imminent nuclear war—that the message didn't register.

Former NCLC member Linda Ray, in her 1986 article "Breaking the Silence," describes another factor—the NCLC habit of knee-jerk rationalization. Ray, who is Jewish, says that whenever anyone tried to tell her the NCLC was anti-Semitic, she instantly denied it, pointing to supposedly anti-Nazi statements in *New Solidarity*. She recalls reading in *New Solidarity* about LaRouche's concept of a subhuman oligarchical species. "Although I knew it did not make scientific sense, I presumed that it was a deep intellectual metaphor that was over my head." Years later a friend showed her a *New Solidarity* article in which the Star of David was used to symbolize the drug trade. "I quickly replied . . . 'It is just a graphic arts symbol'—which I had naïvely thought for years. But as soon as I said it out loud I realized that I sounded ridiculous. It was as if I was waking from a nightmare."

Ray's article explains the state of mind of many NCLC rank-and-filers. It does not explain the acquiescence of the NCLC national and regional leadership cadre, many of them Jewish, who helped develop the anti-Semitic line and implemented it with alacrity. Here, as during

---

* A sampling from NCLC publications, much of it written by LaRouche: Early Jewish settlers in America were prominent in the slave trade. Those who came over in the early twentieth century became the founders of organized crime, rising to power through rum-running, drug pushing, and pornography. Their corrupting influence was supplemented by that of Viennese refugees in the 1930s—an intellectual "cholera culture" and "intellectual pus" undermining American values. Their chief organization, the B'nai B'rith, resurrected the "tradition of the Jews who demanded the crucifixion of Jesus Christ, the Jews who pleaded with Nero to launch the 'holocaust' against the Christians." They manipulated the U.S. government, against its best interests, to support the "kosher nostra" government of Israel. Also they founded the Zionist Lobby, "the most visible of the internal enemies of the United States—and of the human race." The policies of the Zionist Lobby are "pure evil." Any American "professing Zionist loyalties" is, by definition, "a national security risk." As for Israel itself, it is a "zombie-nation" and follows policies "a hundred times worse than Hitler." Its denizens display a "nauseating Jewish hypocrisy over the murder of one of their children" while "bellow[ing] and belch[ing] in smug contentment every time hundreds of thousands of . . . Palestinians are butchered."

Mop Up and the Chris White affair, a few rebelled but most bowed to LaRouche's will.

Kevin Coogan, a member of the intelligence staff, did some background research on Carto and the Liberty Lobby. Shocked by what he discovered, he quit. Several other members of the national office staff also resigned. They prepared unsigned reports and met privately with journalists, stating that the NCLC had become an anti-Semitic organization and that LaRouche was espousing Nazi ideas. But none were willing to go public against LaRouche.

Security staffer Bob Cohen played a key role in stirring up the discontent. He met with several trusted comrades to point out the similarities between LaRouche's writings and *Mein Kampf.* But when his friends decided to quit, Cohen backed out. His reverence for LaRouche kept him in the organization until 1981.

Cohen's brother-in-law and fellow security staffer, Paul Goldstein, came back seething from a trip down South with LaRouche. The hulking former college athlete had been present, as LaRouche's bodyguard, when anti-Semitic jokes were traded among the good old boys. Goldstein, former friends say, was almost ready to quit. But the leadership put him through an ego-stripping session led by Helga LaRouche. The session focused on his alleged sexual fantasies, and he was told his wife would be ordered to leave him if he didn't shape up. Goldstein, reduced to tears, capitulated totally. Thereafter, he was one of La-Rouche's most loyal followers.

A few more NCLC members protested when LaRouche announced that only one and a half million Jews, not six million, were killed in the Holocaust. Contemptuously ignoring his followers' complaints, he issued a press release reaffirming the 1.5 million figure.

By 1980–81 the protest over LaRouche's anti-Semitism died down. Most NCLC members who subsequently quit did so for personal reasons, not over matters of principle. Unlike earlier defectors, most would do nothing to oppose LaRouche. Don and Alice Roth charged in a resignation letter that the membership had undergone a process of "moral anaesthetization." They cited a joke that they said had become popular in the national office: "How many Jews can you fit into a Volkswagen? One hundred. Four on the seats and ninety-six in the ashtray."

In psychological terms the anti-Semitism that seized the NCLC in the late 1970s was similar to the violent fantasies that gripped it during Operation Mop Up. Instead of assaulting Communists with *numchukas,* the NCLC now attacked Jews via brutally worded propaganda tracts. Once again LaRouche helped his followers overcome their moral qualms by reframing reality for them through semantic tricks and false syllogisms.

The resulting belief structure involved four layers: a redefinition of "Jew," a redefinition of "Nazi," a denial of the concepts of "left" and "right" in politics (to totally disorient the believer), and, for Jewish LaRouchians, a guilt trip and special fears.

To redefine the meaning of "Jew," LaRouche concocted a distinction between real and false Jews. He said his political attacks were not aimed at all Jews, just those who advocate evil policies like Zionism. Using Orwellian semantics, he called the latter "nominal Jews," the "Jews who are not Jews." Who then are the real Jews? LaRouche said they are the Jewish members of a "humanist" faction drawing its inspiration from Philo of Alexandria, a first-century Jewish Neoplatonist.

Here LaRouche was at his wiliest. For Philo has no following in modern Judaism. His only professed followers are LaRouche's own NCLC members, whose interpretation of Philo bears little relation to the latter's actual writings.

The bogus nature of the "real Jew" faction was further revealed in LaRouche's polemics against the "unremitting evil" of Zionism. To be a real Jew, he suggested, one must repudiate the State of Israel, Zionism, and the mainstream leadership of the Jewish community. But a sizable minority of Jews are already anti-Zionist and estranged from the mainstream Jewish leadership—e.g., some of the Hassidim and many secular Jewish leftists. Are they "real Jews"? Not at all. In LaRouchian propaganda the Hassidim are portrayed as evil cultists while leftist Jews appear as dope-pushing terrorists. In the final analysis the Jewish members of the LaRouche organization—a few score individuals—are the only real Jews in the world!

LaRouche redefined what a Nazi is in tracts such as "The Truth About 'German Collective Guilt'" and "Hitler: Runaway British Agent." He argued that Hitler was put into power by the Rothschilds and other wealthy Jews-who-are-not-really-Jews. These evil oligarchs invented Nazi racialism and brainwashed the Nazis to accept it. They then urged Hitler and his cronies to persecute the German Jews so the latter would flee to Palestine, where the Rothschilds had decided to set up a zombie state as a tool of their world domination. But as this scenario unfolded, the German people developed their own agenda: a "sound and intense . . . nationalist enthusiasm" to invade Britain (the Rothschild headquarters). Hitler at first acquiesced in this desire, but unfortunately he was ideologically weak—he backed off and returned to the puppet masters' game plan by attacking the Soviet Union. Thus did LaRouche place the ultimate blame for Hitler's crimes on the Jews-who-are-not-Jews-but-really-are-the-Jews-anyway.

LaRouche didn't deny that Hitler and the Nazis were partly responsible for many horrendous crimes as the Rothschilds' junior accomplices. But he instructed NCLC members to focus on a newer and deadlier plot. The Rothschilds and other "British" families—and the Israelis—were preparing to launch a Holocaust a *hundred* times worse than Hitler's. This new Holocaust was aimed at consolidating "British" power, and would involve the death of billions of human beings via nuclear war, plagues, famine, and a New Dark Age—horrors that would make the "Nazi thing" seem like a "slight mistake." The New Dark Age conspirators were "a hundred times worse" than Hitler, and anyone collaborating with them (like Jimmy Carter) was also a hundred times worse.

With his followers thus confused, LaRouche was able to switch labels on his concepts. The New Dark Age conspirators were not only far worse than the Nazis of the Hitler era, they *were* Nazis. The real Nazis were the hundred-times-worse Nazis. Menachem Begin was a Nazi, Ariel Sharon was a Nazi, the "Jewish Lobby" in America was "Nazi."

It followed from this relabeling that anyone who opposed Israel and the "Jewish Lobby" was, objectively, *anti*-Nazi. LaRouche's followers thus ended up with a topsy-turvy view in which the real Nazis were seen as anti-Nazis, and anti-Semitism was perceived as a moral necessity—to "save" the Jews from themselves. The LaRouchians accordingly worked seven days a week to build a fascist movement while imagining they were building an antifascist movement. LaRouche had used their fears of fascism to further fascist goals.

There was always the possibility that some NCLC members would wake up and begin to critically examine these Orwellian labels. Stage three guarded against such a possibility. In "The Secrets Known Only to the Inner Elites," LaRouche announced that the left and the right in politics don't really exist. They are a fiction concealing the struggles of two conspiratorial elites—the humanist elite (LaRouchians or proto-LaRouchians) and the oligarchical elite (the Jews-who-are-not-Jews, etc.). Hence, in judging a given party or faction one should not ask where it stands on the political spectrum, but which elite is manipulating it. Depending on the answer, there are good Communists and bad Communists, good conservatives and bad conservatives, good Klansmen and bad Klansmen. During World War II there were good Nazis (the Wehrmacht) and bad Nazis (the Rothschild agents-of-influence in the Nazi Party leadership).

With the traditional political spectrum abolished, LaRouche's followers no longer had to deal with the glaring contradictions between their old leftist and new fascist politics. For all intents and purposes, the NCLC's political past no longer existed. Fascism and communism no longer existed. All that mattered were LaRouchism and anti-LaRouchism, which were whatever LaRouche said they were.

When LaRouche first promulgated these views in the late 1970s, he played on his Jewish followers' guilt feelings, their anxiety over their possible tainted status in the NCLC, and their nightmares about the Holocaust. In a 1978 article on the "cult origins of Zionism," he warned the NCLC Jews: If you don't put aside your doubts and totally devote yourself to our political goals, you are "just as guilty" as Adolf Hitler. Indeed, you are *more* guilty, since the consequences of an NCLC failure to take power will be human death on a far greater scale than under Hitler. But I know you: Underneath your veneer of loyalty to the NCLC you still have a residual sense of loyalty to your fellow Jews—the false Jews. Insofar as you feel that residual loyalty, you are "on the pathway to becoming a Nazi"—a supporter of the evil oligarchy's plan to kill off two-thirds of the human race. Forget your narrow bestial ethnic loyalties! Instead ask yourself: "What is a Jew good for? What can a Jew contribute to humanity generally which obliges humanity to value the Jew?"

LaRouche used even sterner language to warn his Jewish followers of the possible consequences of disloyalty: "You have no right to hide behind the whimpering, morally degraded profession [of excuses]. . . . Either you take responsibility for the ultimate consequences of your conduct or you have no moral right to complain against whatever evil the world's developments bestow upon you."

To get the full flavor of this threat, one must understand that, in 1978, many NCLC members fervently believed that LaRouche would soon take power in America. Jewish members thus could easily have felt worried—at least on a subliminal level—for their own safety.

# Part Two

# What LaRouche
# Wants

The war in which I am presently
engaged against the forces of the
Whore of Babylon . . . is not a
war merely for some particular
policy, but a battle for that Great
Design under which sovereign
nations dedicated to general-
ized scientific and technological
progress form a powerful alliance to crush the remaining
power of the oligarchist faction,
to rid our planet of that faction.

—LYNDON H. LaROUCHE, JR.,
*The Power of Reason,* 1979

# Seven

# The Grand Design

In the early 1970s LaRouche bolstered his followers' morale with fantasies of an insurrection that would soon put them in power. Select NCLC members were sent to a secret boot camp near Argyle, New York, to study riflery, the use of explosives, and small-arms tactics. One of the former instructors, Gregory Rose, said they learned "how to take this hill, that hill." They also played Capture the Flag. Members not attending the camp participated in local NCLC "militias." Former NCLC member Linda Ray recalled: "We were each handed a pole. We were told we were preparing for class warfare. We practiced marching in circles." A top LaRouche aide produced a study of Tito's World War II partisans as the prototype for LaRouche's army. Relevant intelligence was collected, such as on the troop strength and readiness of California's National Guard.

As the NCLC moved to the right, the idea arose of winning over military officers to help LaRouche achieve power. U.S. Army intelligence reports reveal that in the mid-1970s NCLC members began calling and sending suggestive memos to high-ranking officers. For instance, Ron Kokinda called the XVIII Airborne Corps commander at

Fort Bragg in 1976 to warn him that a Carter victory in the presidential election would pose a threat to the Republic. Kokinda also sent a letter to General Frederick C. Weyand, the Army Chief of Staff, claiming that Carter and the Wall Street bankers were plotting to destroy the Constitution. The way to stop them, he advised, was to crush Wall Street's "command structure" and undertake a massive "economic reorganization."

NCLC security staffers sought out officers with strong political views, such as Major General John K. Singlaub, removed as commander of U.S. forces in Korea in 1977 after criticizing President Carter's defense policies. Singlaub recalls being approached when he was stationed at Fort McPherson in Georgia: "They said, 'You military people are going to be the savior of the country. . . . We want to work closely with you.' " Singlaub cut them off and denounced them in press interviews.*

According to former NCLC members, the national office staff was briefed in May 1979 on how a military coup would make LaRouche dictator. The NCLC's "right-wing allies" supposedly would bring this about sometime before the 1980 election. Meanwhile in a campaign speech LaRouche called for the abolition of democracy and alluded to a plan for a march on Washington. The context suggested something like Mussolini's 1922 march on Rome.

Whatever LaRouche might tell his followers to feed their sense of self-importance, he knew he could only establish his dictatorship if a "leading strata of capitalists and governmental agencies" were willing to sponsor it. For this, a major crisis would be necessary. As the signs of such a crisis multiplied, a faction of the capitalists would begin to call for new leadership. A coalition would emerge of midwestern industrialists, technocrats, the Teamsters union, military officers, and dissident CIA agents to win over the silent majority and isolate the nation's "liberal third." NCLC advisers would permeate the coalition and coordinate its efforts. But LaRouche cautioned his followers to let their prospective allies take the lead at first, while the NCLC built up its independent political base.

LaRouche thought he recognized the seeds of the impending crisis in the international monetary system. The Third World and Eastern Europe had run up hundreds of billions of dollars in debts to Western banks. Many debtor countries were hard-pressed to pay the interest, to say nothing of the principal, and the total debt was mounting steadily. What if just one major debtor nation decided to default? LaRouche predicted a "chain-reaction collapse" of the debt structure leading to

---

* In a 1983 letter to the author, he compared the LaRouchians to the Nazis and said they were one of the most dangerous extremist groups in America.

"a depression far worse than that of the 1931–33 period." The only way out would be for "someone in a leading position in the U.S.A." to override the greed of the bankers and bring the nation "back to its senses." LaRouche's grandiose tone suggested that this "someone" would be himself.

LaRouche urged the formation of a debtors' cartel and a don't-pay strategy. His followers toured Latin America, contacting hundreds of government officials, labor leaders, and military officers. They produced dozens of research studies and propaganda tracts, and La-Rouche himself wrote *Operation Juarez* (1982), a brilliant call to arms against the International Monetary Fund austerity programs. The small LaRouchian parties in Mexico, Peru, and Colombia gained access to high government officials. LaRouche became known in Latin America as a serious economist and political strategist. He met with Presidents José López Portillo of Mexico and Raúl Alfonsín of Argentina. Peru's President, Alán García, met with a LaRouchian delegation in Lima. Fighting the IMF meanwhile became a continent-wide demagogic rallying cry. Tens of thousands of students marched against the IMF in Buenos Aires. Fidel Castro seized on the issue and developed his own version of Operation Juarez. But no Latin American leader was willing to take the final step—actual default as opposed to rhetorical threats—that might cut off the credit keeping their economies afloat. LaRouche wasn't discouraged, however. He still believed the catastrophe was only a few years away and that he alone would know how to save civilization. He called his long-range plan, to be implemented once he took power, the Grand Design for Humanity.

The Grand Design was based, like his plan for triggering the debt bomb, on an anti-Semitic conspiracy theory. LaRouche claimed that the world is dominated by a Zionist oligarchy—a cabal of international usurers—with headquarters in London. In *The Power of Reason* he stated that he was fighting to restore sovereignty to the United States and other key nations so they could "rid our planet" of this oligarchy, so that mankind could create the social conditions for the next step in evolution: the super race of "golden souls." LaRouche said that creating this super race was the true objective of his life.

The Grand Design is the key to all of LaRouche's multileveled efforts, including his amassing of great wealth. In working out its details, he became the first systematic thinker in the history of international fascism to deal with the state, the economy, culture, race, military strategy, and a host of tactical questions within a consistent philosophical framework. This tour de force contains genuine insights on many questions and borrows from LaRouche's major achievement in economics—his model of a totally mobilized economy. The Grand Design is embodied in a score of articles and books, including *The Case of Walter Lippmann* (1977). As reworked for popular consumption in various propaganda tracts, it has exerted a subterranean influence on ultrarightists from Argentina through West Germany. Given the uniqueness of this body of ideas—the fact that they fill a void in international fascism—it is inevitable that LaRouche's ideological influence will continue for years, even if he should die tomorrow.

The Grand Design begins with a total rejection of "British liberal notions of 'democracy,' " notions which are "is like a farm without a farmer, in which the chickens, sheep, cows, horses and pigs form 'constituencies.' " His own humanist republic would have "nothing to do with elections, parliaments, or such differentia," but would ruthlessly suppress all "nonrepublican" (i.e., non-LaRouchian) influences. The American people wouldn't lose anything, because our democracy is merely a façade for an already existing dictatorship of the "monetarist faction"—i.e., the oligarchy. LaRouche would replace this bad dictatorship with a good one—a "class dictatorship-in-fact" of the industrial capitalists, with labor leaders like the Teamsters as junior partners to provide a "broader social base." Within this dictatorship the interests of capital and labor would be "understood to be identical," and strikes by labor unions would not be tolerated.

But this dictatorship would not actually be run by the capitalists. A special elite who have mastered the "humanist" (LaRouchian) philosophy would take command. These favored few would have exclusive power to shape the laws of the new order—laws aimed at curbing the selfish tendencies of society's "less moral strata"—and they would not tolerate any "direct violation of humanist outlook and methods" even from capitalists.

To make this palatable, LaRouche adopted Big Brother's "freedom is slavery" slogan, only phrased more arcanely. Freedom has nothing to do with tolerating "violations of universal law" (i.e., of LaRouche's will). Freedom is "exactly the opposite"; it is the "abhorrence of such error." In other words, freedom is the abhorrence of freedom.

LaRouche's "freedom" would involve total control over the individual's innermost thoughts. He distinguishes between thoughts "which lead to increasing human perfection—which we call good," and thoughts "which abort progress or worse—which we call evil." His Republic would "mobilize the good within the individual citizen to rule over the evil within himself." The individual citizen would have little choice to do otherwise. The state "does not 'concede' freedom to the individual, but *demands* that he or she partake of it in the general interest of the state . . ." Anyone who refuses to go along "has no consciously defensible premise on which to say to his fellows: 'I have a right to live as a free man.' "

LaRouche would revise the criminal justice system to reflect this. No longer would a criminal be someone who commits criminal acts; it would be anyone who thinks criminal thoughts. Such thoughts would include putting one's own interests and those of one's family above the interests of the Republic. "Every citizen who holds the view, 'I can't worry about society and the world; I must attend to my family responsibilities,' is exhibiting a degree of relative infantilism tending in the direction of the criminal mind," says one LaRouchian manifesto. Indeed, such a mentality not only tends toward criminality, it *is* criminal.

LaRouche's system of government would require immediate purges of any opposition. The police would be empowered to conduct "surgically precise preventive action." The first target would be the Jews and others who operate as agents of the London-based oligarchy. LaRouche describes the conspiracy as a four-tiered ziggurat of (from the top down) Jewish bankers on Wall Street, Jewish community leaders, Jews and pro-Jewish Gentiles in the government and media, and finally the gutter networks of Communists, environmentalists, and peaceniks. This conspiracy has kept the nation subservient to London, enabling "speculative capital" to bleed dry "industrial capital" through usury. The influence of the conspirators dates back to Benedict Arnold and is so deeply rooted that only a complete purge can restore the nation's sovereignty. As a *New Solidarity* editorial put it, "America must be cleansed for its righteous war by the immediate elimination of the Nazi Jewish Lobby . . . from the councils of government, industry and labor." (Note the Orwellian use of the word "Nazi.") A second editorial called for an FBI task force to "root out the cancer in the American body politic that is the so-called Zionist Lobby." The task force would include a "permanent Special Prosecutor's office." Jewish leaders would be investigated and their organizations "dismantled or registered as foreign agents." A special congressional committee would "clean out Senators and Congressmen who maintain their covert relationships with Zionist spies." Anyone who opposed this would be "branded as a traitor." The Zionist "octopus" would be "eliminated" at all costs.

Such appears to be LaRouche's program for a fascist state: dictatorship by the party elite, a purge of the "Zionists," suppression of all opposition, brainwashing-style pressure on those who refuse to internalize the party elite's ideology, denial of citizenship to subhumans, and revisions in the criminal code to make it all "legal." The Grand Design's next stage is the "total mobilization of the entire nation" in preparation for Total War.

The Nazis used the term "total mobilization" to discuss Germany's war economy, but LaRouche believes they never understood the idea. They simply looted until there was nothing left to loot, then went under. *Real* total mobilization means ever-expanding scientific discovery, technological innovation, and industrial investment. And these must expand *faster* than the needs of the war machine.

But LaRouche certainly agreed with the Nazis that total mobilization requires a centralized, disciplined economy. Scientific and technological progress cannot be left to "British" free enterprise. LaRouche envisioned an economy dominated by a cluster of giant "brute-force" projects with his humanist elite cracking the whip. He often cited the Apollo Project and the Manhattan Project, but his chief model seemed to be Hitler's Peenemünde rocket center, where the V-2 rockets were developed for manufacture by slave laborers at underground plants. The cost of such projects would be offset by the "spin-offs"—new civilian-sector products, cheap new sources of energy like fusion power, and miraculous gains in productivity. These in turn would produce more resources for the military economy.

The key to the ever-expanding military potential would be the "creative powers of the mind," mobilized via fanaticism to serve the Grand Design. To encourage such creative powers—especially the ability to invent and master advanced military technologies—the educational system would be completely transformed. Children would be taught NCLC "humanism" as well as "classical German" doctrines. They would also be taught the "hypothesis of the higher hypothesis," La-Rouche's own method of insight (one thinks about how one thinks while one thinks). As many children as possible would be transformed into Wernher von Braun-type geniuses. Thus the rate of innovation in science and technology would accelerate through the roof, and the speedy adoption of the most useful innovations would be guaranteed by the educational machine churning out millions of engineers and skilled technicians—the high-tech force to operate weapons systems of ever-increasing complexity. The young scientists, engineers, and technicians would be Spartan-type "soldier-citizens," led by "engineer-officers," thoroughly dedicated to the mobilization process. They would be the cutting edge of armed forces vastly expanded through Universal Military Training (not just the draft) into an invincible "pyramid of maximum in-depth war-fighting capabilities."

Of course, there is one thing missing from this Star Wars fascism. The soldier-citizens wouldn't be Germans. But they would memorize Schiller's poetry, listen to Beethoven night and day, and master classical German philosophy as well as emulating the V-2 scientists. Even today, NCLC publications suggest they revere their Teutonic heritage

and the alleged critical role played by Germany (not England) in founding the real America—and hence regard America as having special ties
with Germany transcending those with any other NATO ally.

The ultimate aim of LaRouche's total mobilization would be world
conquest. As LaRouche said in 1978, he would be the President who
would *win wars.* He would lead the nation in establishing the "permanent hegemony of the Neoplatonic-humanist [LaRouchian] forces over
the globe." The oligarchical "forces of evil" would be crushed everywhere, bringing the nations under "firm-handed (if loving)" rule. The
"progressive liquidation" of oligarchist regimes would not end until
"total victory"—the crushing of the world's "last bastion of oligarchical
policy."

Just as LaRouche took issue with Hitler's version of total mobilization, so he criticized his military strategy of waging a two-front war
against both the West and the Soviet Union. Hitler should have
mopped up the Rothschilds' headquarters, Britain, before marching
east. The London blitz was not carried out boldly enough. LaRouche
here makes explicit his Nazi sympathies. The war on Britain was an
expression of Germany's "republican-nationalist impulse," and the
enthusiasm to crush Britain was "sound." Britain was "then, as now,
the enemy of continental Europe, including the German nation."
Hitler was "London's most deadly enemy" (hence by implication he
was Europe's hero in spite of his mistakes).

LaRouche would do things right, one stage at a time. The United
States should plan first for a war against Britain, not the Soviet Union.
There must be a "total elimination of Britain's worldwide political,
economic, and military leverage." If it doesn't surrender it should face
the use of "force" against its outpost in the Middle East—Israel—and
London itself should receive the "treatment" meted out to Japan in
1945.

While crushing Britain, LaRouche would carry out the unification of
other Western nations by installing "humanist" regimes in each. Nuclear blackmail would be a helpful means to this end: "The might of the
United States . . . will moderate the heteronomic impulses of the err-
ing." Once the smaller nations recognized that American policy "has a
fist within it," changes of government would "spontaneously erupt
around the globe" (presumably like the fascist putsches that erupted in
Eastern Europe in the 1930s). LaRouche provided a rationale in terms
of international law. One must distinguish, he said, between the sovereignty of nations in the abstract and the sovereignty of particular incumbent governments. To extend the principle of sovereignty from the
former to the latter is "specious," he said.

With the entire West unified, purged, and totally mobilized, America would be ready to go after the "last bastion" of the enemy—the Soviet Union. This would not be a matter of a few bombs or a putsch. La-Rouche believed that war between the two superpowers "cannot be less than total war," and that to win such a war one would have to hit the enemy with an atomic, bacteriological, and chemical triple punch. LaRouche called this "ABC paving" because it supposedly " 'paves' the entire front of assault to the purpose of exterminating every possible means of opposition." The attack would occur in waves: maximum-strength ABC bombardment of "all adversary logistical and political [i.e., civilian] targets out of short-term reach" would be followed by ABC tactical bombardment of front-line targets and then by rapid advance of ground forces through the ruins with continuing ABC support. The war would become a "meatgrinder," with the West hopefully emerging from each phase with a marginal gain in relative strength. Whichever side possessed greater surviving "in-depth logistical and deployable reserve capabilities" (i.e., whichever side was better at total mobilization) would win.

LaRouche conceded that the initial nuclear exchange would "eliminate between 120 and 180 million lives in the United States," and that the Soviet Union would lose "up to 30 percent of its population." He even admitted as "credible" the claim by scientists that the radioactive cesium-137 levels would "eliminate all higher animal life on earth." Although he said that such considerations do not apply when great powers "threaten the total conquest of one another," he apparently later decided that so final a solution for himself as well as the enemy was not really desirable. Shortly after writing the above, he began his intensive propaganda push for Star Wars, which some on the right see as a miracle shield that might make a first strike marginally possible.

Assuming a victory short of mutual annihilation, what should happen next? LaRouche says that the "pacification process of military occupation" must begin with wiping out the "oligarchist component" in the Soviet Union. It also must include the "creation and defense" of new cities on the occupied territory as the "chief mediators of scientific and technological progress into urban and rural life." This "citybuilding" policy should be the chief objective of the occupying force, LaRouche says.

This is nothing new. SS chief Heinrich Himmler also had a citybuilding plan for a string of Aryan cities to be built under SS sponsorship from the Ukraine to the Caucasus as strategic foci for the ruthless pacification of that vast region. Himmler glorified the medieval German king Heinrich I, who earned the title of "citybuilder" by constructing fortresses on the eastern frontier to hold back the Magyars. Himmler even regarded himself as Heinrich I's reincarnation and built a shrine to him. A photo accompanying a LaRouche article on pacification suggests that his dream is similar to Himmler's. According to the caption, it shows U.S. Army soldiers working in a vast cavern "underneath the Greenland polar ice cap." This supposedly demonstrates that GIs have "the potential to serve as an army of citybuilders." Any former SS veteran in West Germany would get the point, for the main U.S. base in Greenland is at Thule, which happens to be the name the Nazis gave to the alleged Arctic homeland of the Aryans. The name also suggests the Thule Society, the Munich occult lodge believed by many neo-Nazis to have recruited Hitler for his historic mission. And in the popular mythology that has grown up around Nazism, a team of Nazi scientists is supposed to have escaped in submarines at the end of the war to a secret UFO base under the polar ice to prepare for the eventual rise of a Fourth Reich.

In imposing the "benefits of a Republican order" on occupied countries, LaRouche sometimes cites Alexander the Great as a model conqueror. Most historians would agree that Alexander's policies were relatively benign. But the LaRouchians also have another model: Timur the Great, also known as the "Prince of Destruction," a Mongol who conquered most of Central Asia in the fourteenth century. They depict him as a "humanist," although he was a genocidal monster who probably killed more civilians than any conqueror prior to Hitler. His soldiers decapitated the entire population of Baghdad, piling up the victims' heads in a pyramid to rot in the sun.

In 1983 an NCLC drama troupe staged for the faithful a version of *Tamburlaine,* Christopher Marlowe's lurid Elizabethan tragedy about Timur. *New Solidarity* explained that the play was selected because it provided a sympathetic portrait of a hero who, like LaRouche, "makes his own rules." Marlowe's Tamburlaine, the reviewer said, is a "citybuilder" who demonstrates his humanism by using conquered emperors as a footstool. As to his stern measures, the reviewer chided NCLC members for their lack of understanding: "Some get queasy when Tamburlaine skewers the Virgins of Damascus, and [some] pout heads-in-hands during speeches about piling millions of carcasses at the gates of hell. But, as long as their [sic] is a place in hell for the present-day [oligarchical] emperors; so, there must be a place in the minds of men for Marlowe's *Tamburlaine.*"

# Part Three

# LaRouche and Star Wars

We are shaping increasingly the course of important events. . . . We play the enemy forces as a hundred-pound fisherman successfully plays a powerful sailfish or oversized tarpon.

—LYNDON H. LaROUCHE, JR., "Resisting the Pressures of 'Littleness,'" 1981

# Eight

## The Greatest Invention Since Fire

In a historic speech delivered on March 23, 1983, President Reagan announced the Strategic Defense Initiative, a plan for a space-based missile defense system. To most of the Washington press corps, the so-called Star Wars speech came as a bolt out of the blue. But the LaRouchians were not at all surprised. For years they had advocated their own version of SDI and were in close contact with officials who helped develop Reagan's proposal.

LaRouche began speculating about a space-based particle- or laser-beam weapons system as early as 1975. His organization included scientists who grasped the basic principles and were able to explain them in layman's terms for him. During the late 1970s he became more and more intrigued. Beam weapons seemed to fit well with his dreams of world conquest. A miracle shield against ballistic missiles would make large-scale offensive wars thinkable for the first time since the beginning of the nuclear age.

The Fusion Energy Foundation, established in 1974 as a cover for the NCLC intelligence staff's science and technology division, became the chief LaRouchian propaganda vehicle for beam weapons. In the late

1970s it gained a measure of credibility in the scientific community and the aerospace and nuclear power industries by publishing the monthly *Fusion,* which championed high technology. It also sponsored seminars and conferences on scientific and political topics. Its officers included Dr. Morris Levitt and Dr. Steven Bardwell, both physicists, and John Gilbertson, a nuclear engineer.

The FEF tried to cultivate Major General George Keegan, Jr. (ret.), a former Air Force intelligence chief who believed the Soviets were gaining a dangerous edge in beam technologies. When Keegan called for stepped-up research in this field, FEF members offered their support. They published a pamphlet, *Sputnik of the Seventies* (1977), praising Keegan and calling particle-beam weapons "crucial to this nation's survival." But Keegan was suspicious of their intentions and soon cut them off.

The FEF continued to publicize the issue on their own, with frequent articles about the latest American and Soviet advances in relevant fields of theoretical and applied physics. They recognized that fusion energy research had potential applications in the beam weapons field, and that many of the scientists for any large-scale Pentagon effort would have to come from civilian fusion research. By discussing the two technologies together, *Sputnik of the Seventies* was right on target: Many fusion scientists whom the FEF cultivated in the late 1970s ended up in SDI research in the 1980s.

There is no mystery about how the FEF won the respect of fusion scientists. It launched a campaign to get them more government funding. FEF staff members testified before Congress, lobbied, held press conferences, and crisscrossed the nation on speaking tours. Meanwhile, LaRouche followers at airports displayed pro-fusion posters and literature. Hundreds of thousands of Americans first learned about fusion from their encounters with these seven-days-a-week salesmen.

The FEF undeniably met a real need, and not just for a handful of scientists. OPEC oil price hikes had made cheaper energy sources a national priority, and fusion energy was the most promising long-range solution. But fusion researchers had been inept at presenting their case to the public. Thus the Carter administration poured billions of dollars into synfuel, only a few million into fusion. To frustrated scientists the FEF was a heaven-sent ally.

Support for the FEF's work was especially strong among government fusion scientists. According to Department of Energy documents obtained under the Freedom of Information Act, the contacts began during the Ford administration. At first the FEF spokesmen made a comical impression. One DOE scientist circulated a memo describing how they had tried to convince him of the need for a new world monetary system based on the Soviet ruble. But during the Carter years the FEF proved its effectiveness in building a fusion constituency. Researchers and administrators in the DOE's Office of Fusion Energy (OFE) began to take it seriously, speaking at its conferences and praising its work. They were willing to overlook its sinister politics, including its scurrilous attacks on Energy Secretary James Schlesinger. The FEF might be nasty, but it was useful.

The relationship between the OFE and the LaRouchians had a peek-aboo quality. This was reflected in a September 1978 letter from OFE director Edward Kintner to Stephen Dean, head of the Magnetic Confinement Systems Division, who had previously spoken at FEF events. Kintner, apparently under pressure from superiors, ordered Dean "not to appear" at an FEF meeting later that month because it was a fund-raising event and because the FEF had expressed "policy disagreement" with top DOE officials. (The FEF had accused these officials of being part of a treasonous plot.) Yet Dr. Kintner's memo also displayed a remarkable solicitude for the LaRouchians: "This [directive] by no means precludes . . . staff participation in FEF events in general. . . . Please assist FEF in arranging for a substitute speaker if possible so as to minimize problems for the FEF."

The substitute who showed up was Kintner's deputy, Dr. John Clarke. He didn't just talk on fusion technology—he gave a strong endorsement of the FEF. "You are one of the few organized groups I know of," he said, "that has the courage to stand up and advocate high technology as a solution to some of the problems of the world, and for that I think that we owe you a debt of gratitude." This statement was used in *Fusion* advertisements to solicit subscribers and new FEF members. When Clarke received inquiries about it, he acknowledged on DOE stationery that the quote was accurate. In a letter to a Georgia Tech professor he said that although he didn't agree with the FEF's politics, he thought they performed a "valuable function in our society."

Shortly after Clarke's speech, a senior scientist from the DOE's Office of Energy Research addressed an FEF conference in Pittsburgh. Scientists from Lawrence Livermore National Laboratory and Princeton University's Tokamak fusion reactor project also participated. *Fusion* crowed that the event was attended by representatives of major corporations and that it "marked a quantum jump in FEF's stature as the political leadership of the scientific and engineering communities." While this was an exaggeration, it suggested the hidden agenda behind the FEF's touting of high technology.

In 1979 Stephen Dean left the government to set up Fusion Power Associates, a nonprofit firm backed by energy and defense corporations. This was a setback for the LaRouchians inasmuch as it co-opted their "leadership" role on fusion. But Dean and the LaRouchians continued to have a warm relationship. In August 1979 he appeared on the podium with LaRouche at a U.S. Labor Party rally in Lansing, Michigan. He also accompanied the FEF's Uwe Henke von Parpart on an FEF-arranged trip to India, where they met with fusion energy buff Indira Gandhi and other notables.

When Dean was questioned about the FEF at a 1980 U.S. Senate energy hearing, he testified that "fusion community people attempt to treat the variety of different people that come to us equally and respectfully, independently of whether we agree with their political views. . . . Some of the comments and positions taken by the FEF are in fact positions we support on the merits." He added in a 1984 phone interview: "I don't think they've done the country any harm. It makes life exciting to have them around."

OFE scientists were not the only ones impressed by the FEF. By 1980 it claimed thousands of dues-paying members and over 80,000 *Fusion* subscribers. FEF director Levitt spoke at West Point on the military applications of fusion power, and Uwe Parpart gave a presentation at Lawrence Livermore. Almost $2 million in donations poured in during fiscal 1980–81.

John Bosma, editor of *Military Space* magazine, explained the enthusiasm for the FEF as being partly due to the "top drawer" technical expertise of *Fusion* magazine. He had worked for Boeing Aerospace in Seattle in the late 1970s, and recalled senior managers and engineers "waving *[Fusion]* around and saying, 'This is great stuff.'"

Another key to the FEF's success was its championing of nuclear power at a time when antinuclear sentiment was sweeping the nation. The 1979 Three Mile Island near-disaster alarmed millions of Americans. Environmentalists staged large demonstrations at nuclear power construction sites such as Seabrook in New Hampshire. Jane Fonda's *The China Syndrome* portrayed nuclear engineers as liars and murderers.

The nuclear power industry was dismayed and angered. The FEF played on this by charging a giant plot to undermine American world leadership in science and technology. *Fusion* blamed the Three Mile Island incident on saboteurs. It offered slogans and bumper stickers for an industry counterattack: "More Nukes, Less Kooks" and "Feed Jane Fonda to the Whales." It also suggested that the United States should emulate the Soviet Union's hard line against "zero-growthniks." The February 1980 issue hailed a Soviet government scientist, A. P. Aleksandrov, who had attacked scientists opposed to building nuclear plants near cities. Said Aleksandrov, as quoted by *Fusion:* "Nuclear plants are very safe."

The FEF provided an opening wedge for other activities. LaRouche's intelligence staff prepared reports for power companies on antinuclear activists. His 1980 presidential campaign committee solicited donations from executives of nuclear power and aerospace corporations. Dozens of scientists and engineers (including a top man from Three Mile Island) signed a full-page *Fusion* advertisement backing LaRouche for President.

Although some FEF supporters were turned off by its strident attacks on Darwinism, rock music, and Isaac Newton, it continued to grow. One reason was its support for a 1980 congressional bill to establish fusion power as a major national energy goal. The bill's sponsor, Representative Mike McCormack (D.-Wash.), envisioned a development push modeled on the Apollo Project. He estimated it would cost about $20 billion. In a speech before the House he predicted that the development of fusion energy would be "the second most important energy-related event in human history—second only to the controlled use of fire."

McCormack didn't need the LaRouchians to tell him this. Many distinguished scientists had urged increased fusion funding. Nevertheless, the sweeping nature of the McCormack bill was not dissimilar to that of a 1976 fusion research and development draft bill prepared by the FEF. During the late 1970s, FEF staffers sent a steady stream of proposals to McCormack's office. They attempted to mobilize support for his 1980 bill through speaking tours and press interviews, encouraging a barrage of postcards and telegrams to Congress. Simultaneously they attacked the Senate version, accusing its sponsor, Senator Paul Tsongas (D.-Mass.), of attempting to sabotage fusion development.

The campaign for the McCormack bill proved to be a dry run for the LaRouchians' beam weapons campaign. FEF director Levitt warned that the United States was falling dangerously behind the Soviet Union in industry, education, and defense. The McCormack bill could create a "strategic focal point" to mobilize the nation for a historic comeback. "Fusion is strategic militarily," Levitt said.

In November 1980, President Carter signed the Magnetic Fusion Engineering Act, which set the goal of a successful magnetic fusion demonstration plant by the year 2000. Although the bill provided only token funding, the FEF hailed it as a historic step. After Ronald Reagan assumed office, the massive fusion funding McCormack had envisioned went into SDI instead, and many fusion scientists shifted into SDI research. The FEF and LaRouche uttered nary a word of protest. They recognized that SDI offered a far better opportunity to push their ideological agenda.

# Nine

# The "Higher" Peace Movement

In the spring of 1981, two years before President Reagan's Star Wars speech, *New Solidarity* reported that the President was "known to favor a space-based ABM system." The FEF promptly held a seminar in Washington on "anti-missile beam potentials"and other national-security implications of fusion energy. But the LaRouche campaign for beam weapons did not get into full swing until the following winter, when LaRouche supposedly received a message from a mysterious personage known only as "Mister Ed."

LaRouche had received dozens of messages of advice from Mister Ed since the mid-1970s, often in the form of "E to L" (Ed to LaRouche) memoranda. This time the message suggested that he launch a major push for beam weapons. LaRouche, believing that Mister Ed spoke for a faction of the Central Intelligence Agency, "accepted the assignment," according to a report LaRouche's attorneys filed in Boston federal court five years later.

In February 1982, LaRouche held a forum in Washington to propose a campaign for beam weapons. It would be a good counter to the nuclear freeze movement, he said. The following month he issued a research and development proposal which was followed in May by an FEF "white paper." In August the FEF circulated a report on Capitol Hill regarding a scheme for X-ray laser weapons favored by Dr. Edward Teller, the father of the H-bomb. The FEF held briefings for congressional aides to promote Teller's idea.

LaRouche's publications reported on the various high-level lobbying efforts for space weaponry—including the September 1982 White House meeting between Teller and President Reagan. *New Solidarity* printed the text of Teller's speech the following month at the National Press Club, and dubbed his proposal the "LaRouche-Teller initiative." The FEF's Dr. Bardwell embarked on a tour of college campuses to convince audiences to join "the higher peace movement."

LaRouche apparently was forewarned about Reagan's March 1983 speech. The previous month he had instructed his followers to intensify their campaign of petitions and lobbying and to make beam weapons "a household word in America . . . during the month of March." The day after Reagan's speech, LaRouche hailed it as probably the most important action "by any President in twenty years," adding that "true greatness . . . touched President Ronald Reagan last night . . . a moment of greatness never to be forgotten."

The media turned to the FEF to explain Reagan's proposal. The wire services, syndicated columnists, and *The Washington Post* all quoted FEF spokesmen. Meanwhile LaRouche began to assert that he was really SDI's "intellectual author." According to Dr. Ray Pollock, the National Security Council's director of defense programs at that time, LaRouche's followers "flooded Capitol Hill" with literature claiming this. Pollock said that although some White House officials were annoyed, no steps were taken to set the record straight.

The FEF was undeniably one of the best sources for up-to-date information on SDI in its early stages. An October 1983 FEF seminar in the U.S. Senate's Dirksen Office Building was packed with government officials and foreign diplomats to hear FEF scientists explain the latest developments. John Pike, associate director for space policy at the Federation of American Scientists, recalled that he first learned about Teller's Excalibur project from the LaRouchians. Pike said it was apparent that they had talked to "people with access to classified information." *Beam Defense,* a 1983 book by the FEF's staff, contained, Pike said, "one of the most comprehensive and detailed studies" publicly available on particle beams and X-ray lasers. It won a 1984 award from the Aviation/Space Writers Association.

The LaRouchians were reaping the rewards of their foresight and hard work. When they published their first article on beam weapons in 1975, warning about alleged Soviet breakthroughs, they attracted little notice. But they persisted, building their network of contacts among scientists.

One of their first targets was Teller. As late as 1976 they had described him as a Rockefeller agent and a plotter of genocide. But when Teller delivered a speech attacking the ecology movement and its zero-growth theories, the LaRouchians began praising him. LaRouche set his sights on a private meeting with Teller to explore the possibilities of an alliance. FEF staffers hoped that Dr. Stefan Possony, a Teller colleague at Stanford University's Hoover Institute, would arrange it. LaRouche dedicated his magnum opus, *The Case of Walter Lippmann*, to Possony and Teller as "the writer's former opponents who exhibited the integrity to modify their views on important questions." (They were not his only dedicatees; the list also included Fidel Castro, Helmut Schmidt, and the spirit of Benjamin Franklin.) But Possony, whose taste in rightist politics ran more along World Anti-Communist League lines, never delivered the goods, although he did address two FEF conferences before dropping away.

In a 1984 phone interview Teller called LaRouche "a poorly informed man with fantastic conceptions." Teller said he had chatted with FEF members on the phone from time to time, but had rejected all invitations to meet with LaRouche. He acknowledged he had made a mistake in not objecting when they began publishing articles suggesting he was working with them. "I was reluctant to criticize someone for agreeing with my ideas," he explained.

In 1983 the LaRouchians strongly urged Teller to reciprocate their support. He asked a close personal friend, Dr. Robert Budwine of Lawrence Livermore, to take the matter in hand. Budwine knew very little about the LaRouchians, but agreed to meet with them to take the pressure off Teller. He ended up traveling to Paris and Bangkok, at LaRouchian expense, to speak at beam weapons conferences sponsored by the LaRouche publication *Executive Intelligence Review*.

Budwine became deeply intrigued by the LaRouchians and was drawn for several months into the periphery of their cult life. Among other things, he attended the NCLC annual conference in January 1984 at LaRouche's Virginia mansion, where the baroque harpsichord background music struck him as "an attempt to re-create an eighteenth-century salon." He formed friendships with Uwe Parpart and other NCLC members, and spent several hours in private discussions with LaRouche on Indo-European root languages, Riemannian geometry, and other LaRouche hobbies.

Budwine's scientific training ultimately made him a poor subject for recruitment. "They kept talking about this great method they have, but I kept asking: 'What kind of method is it that consistently gives you the wrong answers?' " He began to read up on cults and brainwashing, and came to the conclusion that "LaRouche is not a serious man, he's even less than that . . . LaRouche is crazy."

The LaRouchians continued to go to great lengths to entice Star Wars scientists. Roy Woodruff, former head of arms development at Livermore, recalls at least twenty phone calls from Chuck Stevens, a *Fusion* reporter and former nuclear engineering student. Again and again, Woodruff refused to speak with him, but Stevens persisted. "He sat at the West Gate and waited for me," Woodruff said. "I went out another gate to avoid him."

*New Solidarity* articles often praised Dr. Lowell Wood, chief of Livermore's "O Group," a top SDI research team. Wood said in 1984 that FEF representatives called him from time to time and that he also ran into them at scientific conferences. Asked if they had influenced the development of SDI, he was hesitant to deny it. He said they had boasted to him about meetings with top presidential aides and Pentagon officials. Although he never attempted to confirm these claims, he said that many administration officials had mentioned to him the "quality, speed, and accuracy" of LaRouche's intelligence operation.

Dr. John Nuckolls, Livermore's associate director for physics and the man to whom the O Group reported, received calls from the LaRouchians throughout the late 1970s and early 1980s. Their attempts to "break the classification barrier," he said, made "interaction difficult." He couldn't decide if their promotional activities on behalf of fusion energy and SDI were "positive or negative." However, he thought it might "be useful to have someone at the grass roots—assuming they are at the grass roots." He said he didn't want to either attack or defend them. "We have a common interest," he said.

For Dr. Winston Bostick and Dr. Friedwardt Winterberg, physicists on the outer fringes of Star Wars, this common interest involved more than SDI. Bostick, former chairman of the Stevens Institute of Technology physics department, participated in beam weapons-related research at the Kirtland Air Force Base weapons laboratory from 1979 to 1983. He was also a leading figure in the FEF, speaking at its conferences, writing for *Fusion,* and serving on the editorial board of another FEF publication, the *International Journal of Fusion Energy.* In a 1984 telephone interview he said he supported LaRouche's attempts to promote "German military, scientific, cultural, and economic traditions."

Winterberg was a fusion specialist with the University of Nevada's Desert Research Institute. He volunteered ideas on beam weapons to the Air Force in the late 1970s, and later speculated on the subject for LaRouchian publications. In 1980 he described LaRouche as having the "most scientifically founded" program of any candidate for the U.S.

presidency. The FEF published his *Physical Principles of Thermonuclear Explosive Devices* (1981) and also sent him on overseas speaking tours.

One of the most important government scientists contacted by the LaRouchians was Dr. Richard DeLauer, Under Secretary of Defense for Research and Engineering from 1981 to 1984. DeLauer, who first became aware of their activities in the late 1970s when he was executive vice president of TRW Inc., granted an interview to an *Executive Intelligence Review (EIR)* reporter in his Pentagon office in 1981. He fulminated on the weaknesses of American science, which he blamed on the "greening of America" and "gurus" who "took advantage of food stamps." Asked about his assessment of Soviet progress on space-based ABM systems, he said his views came in large part from reading *EIR*—"you guys are supposed to know more about it than anybody else."

In mid-1984, after being attacked by the LaRouchians for alleged foot dragging on SDI, DeLauer claimed that his statement about *EIR*'s expertise had been mere sarcasm, an expression of his "exasperation" with the interviewer. "I have no use for that guy [LaRouche] and his opinions," he said. But he praised the FEF for its pronuclear stance: "In their support of nuclear power—in that sense—I support them." He had even donated money to the FEF as "the only active group that opposes Jane Fonda." Asked about a sexually demeaning anti-Fonda bumper sticker sold by the FEF, he chuckled and said: "I got another one [FEF slogan] for you: 'More people have been killed in the back seat of Ted Kennedy's car than in a nuclear accident.' "

A far more useful contact was the NSC's Dr. Pollock, one of the key policymakers behind Reagan's Star Wars speech. Pollock said he was first contacted by the LaRouchians while working at Los Alamos National Laboratory in the late 1970s. He began to chat on the phone with *Fusion* reporter Stevens to find out the latest gossip about the fusion research community.

When Pollock moved to Washington to work at the Department of Energy, he sometimes lunched with Stevens. After his appointment to the National Security Council he continued the relationship, and during the months prior to the announcing of SDI he met on several occasions with high-level LaRouche aides such as Uwe Parpart. They urged on him a plan for a beam weapons "Manhattan Project." He found merit in their ideas on the potential economic spin-offs. They offered to pay his way to conferences overseas, but he declined.

Pollock met twice with LaRouche at the prodding of National Security Adviser William Clark's right-hand man, Richard Morris. Morris was present at the first meeting, as was Helga LaRouche. They discussed German politics, and Pollock found LaRouche to be a "frightening kind of fellow." Pollock's recollection of the second meeting is that LaRouche explained his conspiracy theory of history. LaRouche in a 1984 deposition said they also discussed the "economic implications" of SDI. Pollock says he put LaRouche's views into a one-page memo and sent it across the street to the White House.

In 1986, LaRouche wrote that his personal contribution to SDI had been to demonstrate that it was affordable. Obviously the United States could pay for a "first-generation" system. The problem lay in the costs of deploying second-, third-, and fourth-generation systems if the Soviets developed countermeasures. LaRouche claimed that he had proven, via his LaRouche-Riemann economic model, that the "spillover" of SDI technologies into the civilian economy would produce profits fully offsetting SDI's cost. He had thus proposed "a 'crash program' . . . as the best way to cause this 'spillover' to occur." In other words, LaRouche had proposed that the Reagan administration adopt one of the key points of his own Grand Design: pay-as-you-go total mobilization.

The LaRouche organization chiefly contributed to SDI by publicizing and organizing support for it in Western Europe. They held numerous conferences and seminars in Paris, Bonn, and Rome, attracting many high-level military officers. The first such events occurred months before Reagan's Star Wars speech, with audiences being told something big was in the works. (This led many Europeans to subsequently regard LaRouche as a major player in SDI policy.) The LaRouchian effort was strongly supported by Colonel Marc Geneste, a French neutron bomb expert, and General Giulio Macri, a former NATO expert on high-technology weapons who ran for the Italian Parliament as a LaRouchian beam-weapons candidate. Several retired German officers joined with the LaRouchians to launch Patriots for Germany, a pro-Star Wars political party. A similar group was launched in Paris under the suggestive name France et Son Armée. In much of their propaganda, the LaRouchians presented themselves as allies of Defense Secretary Caspar Weinberger and Lieutenant-General James Abrahamson (USAF), the director of SDI. When Abrahamson went to Europe in July 1984 to build NATO support for his program, the LaRouchians boasted that their organizing efforts over the previous two years had prepared the ground for his favorable reception.

The success of LaRouche's European campaign hinged on maintaining an image of legitimacy. In this he received help from the highest levels in Washington. The State Department sent a priority cable bearing George Shultz's name to the Bonn embassy. Entitled "Anti-LaRouche Disorganizing Activity," the January 1983 cable quoted a complaint from a LaRouche aide that "certain U.S. embassy officials abroad" were trying to dissuade individuals in foreign countries from associating with LaRouche. The cable then reminded the embassy that negative characterizations of U.S. political figures "are not authorized" and that officials should "refrain from offering personal opinions while acting in their official capacities." (The cable was based on a DOS press guidance statement which *EIR* had quoted from the previous month.)

LaRouche's followers also promoted SDI in Japan, which they said could thereby be transformed into an "unsinkable aircraft carrier." Uwe Parpart and other FEF officials made several trips to Tokyo. According to General Yoshio Ishikawa, the Japanese defense attaché in Washington, these trips were sponsored by "several private associations concerned with defense." When a Japanese translation of *Beam Defense* was published in 1984, Parpart met with Liberal Democratic Party legislators in Tokyo, then addressed a defense industry seminar.

When Japan's Cabinet began formal consideration in 1986 of whether or not to participate in SDI, the LaRouchians staged a Tokyo conference to urge "full strategic commitment." In addition to LaRouche's usual gaggle of scientific experts, the speakers included a retired French general, a retired American colonel (who was receiving $2,000 a week from LaRouche as a consultant), an engineer from a California firm involved in SDI, and spokesmen for two Japanese research institutes. According to *EIR,* the conference was intended as an antidote to the "treasonous" influence of Assistant Secretary of Defense Richard Perle, who had visited Tokyo several weeks previously. *EIR* called him an agent of the "Mossad-linked Jewish Institute of National Security Affairs" and accused him of trying to undercut Japanese participation in SDI.

The LaRouchians also kept up a vigorous propaganda effort throughout the United States: signs at airports, FEF speaking tours, lobbying for pro-SDI resolutions in state legislatures, beam-weapons election campaign slates. They brought over General Macri and Colonel Geneste for speaking tours in 1984. Macri, who had previously urged American military officers to "begin to concern themselves with politics," was given an official Pentagon briefing on SDI. Geneste spoke at the U.S. Air Force Academy and met with Edward Teller. The Pentagon also furnished its own speakers for LaRouchian events. In May 1984 two top officials of the DOD's International Security Policy Division accepted an invitation to address a LaRouchian rally in Crystal City, Virginia. DOD spokesman John d'Amecourt said in September 1984 that the department regarded the LaRouchians as a "conservative group . . . very supportive of the administration in general." As LaRouche's notoriety grew, Pentagon officials became reluctant to speak at such events, but *EIR* continued to gain interviews with top brass (for instance, a 1985 interview with Supreme Allied Commander, Atlantic, Admiral Wesley McDonald).

In 1986 the Fusion Energy Foundation became the target of multiple criminal investigations. According to prosecutors, evidence showed that FEF fund raisers, along with those of other LaRouche front groups, were defrauding elderly persons in every region of the country by soliciting unsecured loans with no intention of repaying them. FEF officials were indicted for loan fraud in New York and Virginia, and for credit-card fraud in Massachusetts. (The LaRouchians denied the charges.) Federal authorities raided the offices and seized the assets of the FEF and other LaRouche front groups to collect fines levied by a federal judge after they failed to cooperate with grand jury subpoenas.

Despite these troubles, the FEF was not abandoned by its friends in the fusion and SDI community. The July 1987 issue of *Spectrum,* published by the Institute of Electrical and Electronic Engineers, carried a full-page ad signed by many scientists and engineers from Star Wars-linked corporations and laboratories protesting the government's shutdown of the FEF. The ad's signatories included twenty-two employees of Lawrence Livermore. Dr. Stephen Dean of Fusion Power Associates, which is supported by major Star Wars contractors, sent out a letter defending the FEF and calling the government's charges "quite far-fetched." Urging FPA members to take action, he suggested they contact LaRouche aide Carol White.

On balance, LaRouche's twelve-year campaign for fusion power, beam weapons, and SDI brought him more benefits than problems. His followers learned to operate in influential mainstream circles, not just among right-wing eccentrics. Many scientists and government officials found the LaRouchians useful and thus were willing to overlook their anti-Semitism and other unpleasant qualities. Some of these alliances of convenience lasted for years, involving frequent low-profile exchange of favors. LaRouche built up a pool of influential people whom he had compromised, and who thus had a vested interest in downplaying his extremism to avoid embarrassment to themselves.

Many SDI figures refused to have anything to do with LaRouche, others distanced themselves from him when informed of his background, and some, like General Daniel Graham of High Frontiers, publicly denounced him. Yet far too many SDI proponents quietly winked at his involvement in the politics of SDI. Such people wanted the American taxpayer to pour vast sums into building a supposedly invulnerable military shield against the Soviet Union, yet were themselves far from invulnerable politically and morally when a totalitarian movement appeared under their noses.

Many of the early claims for Star Wars were prompted by political enthusiasm and unsupported by scientific data. As in many historic cases of pseudo-science, the motives of critics were impugned to divert attention from theoretical and research flaws. This is where the LaRouchians played their most insidious role. In an atmosphere in which a scientist as important as Roy Woodruff could be demoted at Lawrence Livermore for questioning dubious data, hundreds of *Fusion* and *EIR* articles accused SDI critics—or persons such as General Graham, who advocated technological approaches different from Teller's —of being unpatriotic or worse. Although Teller himself denounced an especially nasty *EIR* attack on Graham, many SDI supporters continued to chat with the LaRouchians (for instance, Dr. Robert Jastrow, who told a *Fusion* reporter in 1984 that it would take a psychologist to explain the attitudes of anti-SDI scientists).

The use of the LaRouchians as SDI's cat's paw was a reflection both of the program's ideologically driven nature and of the cynicism underlying the ideology. But the LaRouchians were not merely pawns in all this. They had their own unique agenda.

# Ten

# Old Nazis
# and New Dreams

While speculating on total war in the late 1970s, LaRouche had to concede that an American-Soviet nuclear showdown was too dangerous. Between 120 and 180 million Americans would die in the initial exchange alone. This threatened his entire dream of world conquest. His solution was a multitrillion-dollar crash mobilization to build a space-based particle-beam missile shield. Naturally he said it would be a defensive system. The FEF's airport literature tables displayed "Beam the Bomb" posters. Dr. Steven Bardwell urged audiences to join the " 'higher' peace movement." But Bardwell quit the LaRouche organization in early 1984 and stated bluntly, in a letter to his former comrades, what many of them had known but ignored: LaRouche's goal was not a defensive system such as President Reagan's SDI, but a "first strike" system predicated on a denial of "the right of the Soviet Union to exist" in its present form. Indeed, Bardwell claimed, the LaRouchians had privately discussed "Doomsday weapons," such as "cobalt bombs with fans."

In the early and middle 1980s LaRouche utilized SDI and beam weapons to draw together the scattered forces of European and American neofascism to defend Nazi war criminals and promote revanchism. This effort was symbolized by a photograph of a four-pronged object, glowing with light, that appeared from time to time in *Fusion* and *New Solidarity*. Its shape was reminiscent of the swastika. A caption in a 1978 issue of *Fusion* said it was a plasmoid created at Lawrence Livermore National Laboratory in the 1950s, when a scientist supposedly collided four plasma beams to "form a rotating plasma structure whose dynamics are governed by a 'balancing' of forces." In later articles the object was identified as a model of a barred spiral galaxy. "The spiral geometry of many galaxies coheres with the spiral shape found in living biological processes," readers were told. Finally, in a LaRouche article urging total mobilization for SDI, the ghostly object represented "harmonic patterns" while SDI itself was said to be the precursor of a "hyperbolic flaring" based on "triply self-reflexive" spirals.

The reference to cosmic spirals in an article on advanced weapons systems was something which SS veterans in Germany could understand. During World War II the theory of spiraling expansion/conquest had been a staple of Nazi propaganda. As a 1942 tract put it, "The living space of the Third Reich can be enlarged only by moving out from a powerful territorial hub and by accomplishing this conquest progressively, step by step, following the accelerating movement of a spiraling dextrogyre."

In the postwar period, neo-Nazis developed various forms of swastika mysticism; for instance, the late James Madole of the New York-based National Renaissance Party, taught during the 1970s that the swastika represented "undefiled cosmic energy and hydrogen . . . flowing into the spiral arms of our mighty galaxy from the hidden galactic heart." But LaRouche developed a more sophisticated spiral mysticism embracing biology as well as cosmology, in which "manifold leaps" produce higher and higher stages of consciousness, racial types, superhuman species, and weapons systems.

The LaRouchians reached out to former Nazi scientists who had worked on V-2 rockets, jet aircraft, and the Nazi version of the atom bomb at research centers like Peenemünde. They also approached West German military officers, using a sales pitch which glorified "classical German culture" as the high point of world civilization while vilifying Russian culture. LaRouche developed a new version of the Grand Design featuring forced-draft development of SDI, underground factories on the moon, *Lebensraum* on Mars, and electromagnetic weapons capable of turning the Soviet Union into a vast microwave oven.

LaRouche and his wife, Helga, quickly developed a following among retired West German military men. Admiral Karl-Adolf Zenker, former head of the West German Navy and a World War II veteran, joined Patriots for Germany and met with LaRouche on many occasions. As a Navy captain in 1956 Zenker had created a furor by telling cadets they should respect Admirals Erich Raeder and Karl Doenitz, Nazi war criminals convicted at Nuremberg. Zenker said the two were blameless men who had merely done their "duty to their people." When La-Rouche was indicted for obstruction of justice in a credit-card fraud case in 1987, Zenker called him an "honest defender of a strong Western alliance."

Brigadier General Paul-Albert Scherer, former chief of West German military counterintelligence, also joined the bandwagon. After La-Rouche's indictment, he testified before a Schiller Institute-sponsored commission set up to prove that the U.S. government was violating LaRouche's civil rights. He praised LaRouche's warm heart, "gentle humor," and devotion to the Western alliance.

LaRouche's New Benjamin Franklin Publishing House issued a translation of *Modern Irregular Warfare* by Brigadier General (Reserves) Freiherr von der Heydt, a Bavarian professor and longtime ultranationalist. *New Solidarity* said the book presented a model of "total violent confrontation, involving the totality of the state and people." Suggesting this model might be useful in handling left-wing opponents of SDI, the NCLC newspaper urged the public to make bulk purchases "so that we can provide military, educational, and government institutions with the copies they need."

The list of those who endorsed LaRouche's various public appeals included a former Frankfurt police chief, a vice president of the Bavarian Soldiers Association, a Kiel University professor who had worked on Hitler's uranium bomb, and various ultrarightist generals in France, Italy, and Spain. The LaRouchians also cultivated former Nazi scientists brought to the United States after the war as part of the Army's Operation Paperclip to work on defense projects. They included the survivors of Wernher von Braun's team who designed missiles at the Redstone Arsenal in Huntsville, Alabama.

For decades the wartime deeds of these "old-timers" (as they call themselves) appeared to be a closed book. Former SS general von Braun became an American hero for his work on the space program. But in the late 1970s, after von Braun's death, the Justice Department's Office of Special Investigations (OSI) began to examine the records of alleged Nazi war criminals in this country, with the aim of deporting the guilty ones. When the investigators nibbled at the edges of the Paperclip crowd, the latter felt angry and betrayed. Had they not wiped the slate clean by their contributions to America's fight against communism?

LaRouche told them the slate never needed any wiping in the first place. In a 1981 *EIR* article praising Nazi Germany's work on jet aircraft, he distinguished between bad Nazi politicians and good Nazi scientists. "Although the Nazis commanded the German state," he said, "it was the German nation which deployed its non-Nazi resources to fight the war." The Peenemünde scientists were part of this healthy German nationalism. The crimes of the Nazi regime thus were "irrelevant" to any judgment of their wartime role. *Fusion* and *New Solidarity* published adulatory articles about how Peenemünde had paved the way for fusion energy and SDI. It was said to represent the "classical German tradition," the path to true progress as opposed to the degenerate science of the "British."

In November 1981 the FEF held a special dinner and awards ceremony for the University of Colorado's Adolf Busemann, who had worked at Peenemünde. In an interview with *Fusion* he criticized Hitler for not giving Germany's rocket scientists enough resources to do their job properly. When he died in 1986, *New Solidarity* urged its readers to "reflect on his life with joy" and bemoaned the fact that so few old-timers were left to "carry on the great traditions of the German scientific school."

The LaRouchians also developed close ties with Krafft A. Ehricke, a member of the von Braun team widely known for his visionary ideas on space travel. He had served in World War II as a tank platoon leader on the Eastern Front before being assigned to Peenemünde. Brought to the United States in 1947, he helped develop the Atlas rocket, America's first intercontinental ballistic missile. Retired and living in La Jolla, California, in the early 1980s, Ehricke dreamed of colonies on the moon. He wrote articles for *Fusion*, served on its editorial advisory board, and spoke at FEF and Schiller Institute events. In a 1984 phone interview shortly before his death, he praised LaRouche's followers as "open, clean-cut, and positive," in contrast to Jane Fonda and the environmentalists with their "African grass hut technology." He said he had spent many an evening with his friends Lyndon and Helga LaRouche discussing Star Wars and the Soviet Union's plan to become the neo-Byzantine "Third Rome." Ehricke said he agreed with LaRouche's assessment of the Soviet menace because of his own observation of their murderous qualities during World War II.

Another LaRouchian role model was Arthur Rudolph, the Paperclip engineer who developed NASA's Saturn V moon rocket. When he was accused by the Justice Department of working thousands of slave laborers to death at a V-2 factory in 1943–45, the LaRouchians and the old-timers launched a campaign to depict him as the innocent victim of a Communist plot. Yet his Nazi activities were extremely well documented. He had joined both the Nazi Party and the SA storm troopers in 1931, before Hitler came to power. After serving as an SA Oberscharführer and then as a Peenemünde engineer, he became production manager of the underground Mittelwerk factory in the Harz Mountains. Mittelwerk used slave labor from the nearby Dora-Nordhausen concentration camp. A third to a half of the camp's 60,000 inmates died from disease, starvation, and mistreatment. Approximately 5,000 died while working for Rudolph, who once stood by while SS men lynched twelve of his slaves. In 1945 a U.S. Army report called him a "100 percent Nazi, dangerous type" and recommended that he be interned. But after he joined Operation Paperclip a revised security report said he was "not an ardent Nazi." In the early 1980s, having long retired from NASA, he was investigated by the OSI. He admitted in a 1983 interview with OSI attorneys that he had been fully aware of the inhuman working and living conditions of the Dora-Nordhausen laborers. The following year he returned to Germany and agreed to give up his U.S. citizenship rather than face deportation proceedings. OSI prosecutor Eli Rosenbaum later described him as having an "almost unbelievable callousness and disregard for human life."

The FEF, the Schiller Institute, and the Huntsville crowd campaigned to restore Rudolph's citizenship. The old-timers were increasingly nervous because two more from their ranks, Dieter Grau and Günther Haukohl, had come under OSI investigation for their role at Mittelwerk. The FEF warned that "hundreds" of Operation Paperclip scientists were under investigation, but this was denied by the OSI.

An Old-Timers' Defense Fund was established, and a petition was sent to President Reagan asking him to help Rudolph. Major General J. Bruce Medaris (ret.), former chief of the U.S. Army Ordnance Command, Baltic and Ukrainian émigré groups, *The Spotlight*, and the neo-Nazi magazine *Instauration* all lent their support. A delegation from Huntsville met with White House communications director Patrick Buchanan.

Rudolph's most outspoken supporter was Friedwardt Winterberg of the FEF. A student of former Nazi physicist Erich Bagge after the war, Winterberg felt strongly that Rudolph was a victim rather than a victimizer. He launched his own investigation and sent letters of protest to Ed Meese and other administration officials on Desert Research Institute stationery. He also gave an interview to *The Spotlight* repeating the LaRouche line that an attack on Rudolph was an attack on NATO. Winterberg also sent handwritten notes (he called them "brainteasers") to OSI prosecutor Rosenbaum. With themes such as: Israel is guilty of Nazi-style crimes, Simon Wiesenthal was a Nazi collaborator, Zionism is a form of Nazism that has "infected" world Jewry.

*EIR* published an article by General Medaris: "Stop the OSI's Assault against German-American Scientists!" Editorials in *New Solidarity* described Rudolph as an American "patriot" and suggested that OSI prosecutors were Soviet agents and "traitors" who perhaps should be executed for treason. Their activities were said to be a plot to undermine the SDI by demoralizing and deporting America's brilliant cadre of Peenemünde scientists. The Schiller Institute expanded the list of patriotic martyrs to include John (Ivan the Terrible) Demjanjuk of Treblinka fame; Karl Linnas, the butcher of the Tartu death camp; and Tscherim Soobzokov, a Waffen SS mass murderer whose attorney, Michael Dennis, was also LaRouche's attorney. (Just why auto worker Demjanjuk, construction surveyor Linnas, and Paterson, New Jersey, ward heeler Soobzokov were vital to SDI was never explained.)

In 1985 the old-timers held their fortieth reunion at the Alabama Space and Rocket Museum beneath a giant picture of von Braun. Linda Hunt, a former Cable Network News reporter, recalled a darkened auditorium full of aging Nazis eagerly watching a slide show of the latest laser-beam weapons. She said that when the lights went on, the FEF's Marsha Freeman went to the front and delivered a tirade against the OSI to hearty applause.

This event was mild compared with the Krafft Ehricke Memorial Conference held that year in Reston, Virginia. Sponsored by the FEF and the Schiller Institute, it united support for SDI, defense of Nazi war criminals, glorification of Peenemünde, and a messianic vision of the conquest of outer space. *Fusion* boasted that participants included "military, scientific, and diplomatic representatives from four continents." Former top Nazi scientist Hermann Oberth sent greetings from West Germany hailing Ehricke's "vision of 'Homo Sapiens Extraterrestris,' " the New Man who would leave behind the "flaming harbors of the Earth." Speakers included Admiral Zenker and Peenemünde rocketeer Konrad Dannenberg. LaRouche gave the keynote address, entitled "Krafft Ehricke's Enduring Contribution to the Future Generations of Global and Interplanetary Civilization." Resolutions were passed calling on President Reagan to adopt LaRouche's crash program for SDI and halt the Justice Department's investigation of the old-timers. Since the only old-timers being probed were those who allegedly served at Mittelwerk, the FEF/Schiller Institute's hoopla about underground factories on the moon and the spirit of Peenemünde in space technology was suggestive, at the least.

Over the next two years LaRouche assumed Krafft Ehricke's mantle. He outlined plans for cities on Mars and in the asteroid belt—an extension of his earlier earthbound citybuilding schemes so reminiscent of the SS plans for Aryan colonies in occupied Russia. His prototype design for a space city was based on the geometry of cosmic spirals. He said his inspiration had come from the work of German scientists who, at the end of the war, while "awaiting reassignments" (presumably to the Redstone Arsenal) had amused themselves by drawing up plans for rebuilding the Ruhr.

While thus dreaming of a new Ruhr on Mars, LaRouche did not forget the Green Steppes of Earth. In a speech at a September 3, 1987, *EIR* seminar in Munich, he claimed that when he promoted SDI in the early 1980s he had intended it only as the first stage in the most awesome revolution in the history of military technology—the development of "mass-killing" weapons using the "full range of the electromagnetic spectrum." Such weapons would make possible the "true total war." Turned east, they could fry the entire Soviet population while leaving Soviet factories and railroads intact. LaRouche told his audience of military officers and Bavarian defense contractors that whoever develops microwave weapons first can "dominate this planet."

# Part Four

# Building
# a Movement

It was really a treat . . . to follow the perplexity and helpless-
ness of our adversaries in their
perpetually vacillating tactics.
. . . They called on their adher-
ents to take no notice of us and
to avoid our meetings. And on
the whole this advice was followed.

—ADOLF HITLER
on the rise of the Nazi Party

# Eleven

# More American than Apple Pie

In the mid-1970s the LaRouchians started to build a nationwide election machine. At first it grew slowly, hampered by their rhetoric about Rockefeller-CIA conspiracies and their hesitancy to run candidates in major-party primaries. But their percentage of the vote grew dramatically once they began to participate in Democratic primaries. They gained the financial support and even the organizational allegiance of thousands of discontented Americans. Like earlier far-right groups such as the John Birch Society, they attracted many senior citizens and economically troubled farmers and small businessmen. They also reached out to blue-collar workers and inner-city blacks. By 1984 the LaRouchians were fielding more candidates, gaining more votes, and raising vastly more money than any other extremist sect in America.

The LaRouche election machine contested almost 4,000 Democratic primaries and general elections in over 30 states between 1982 and 1988. Its fund raisers brought in tens of millions of dollars while its candidates attracted over 4 million votes, including voting percentages above 10 percent in hundreds of contests. In at least 70 statewide, congressional, or state legislative races, LaRouche candidates polled over 20 percent of the vote. At least 25 appeared on the general election ballot as Democratic nominees, either by defeating a regular Democratic opponent or by running in the primary unopposed. Although none was actually elected to any public office higher than a local school board, hundreds won Democratic Party posts (mostly county committee seats) across the country.

This election machine grew out of the U.S. Labor Party, an NCLC electoral arm founded in 1971 and disbanded when the LaRouchians entered the Democratic Party in 1979. Most of the USLP's youthful candidates and campaign workers were NCLC cadre with few ties to outsiders. They often sounded ludicrous with their warnings of imminent nuclear war, famine, and plague. But occasionally a USLP candidate would impress reporters with what appeared to be a sober grasp of economics. Paul Gallagher, who ran for governor of New York in 1978, issued a position paper on how the New York business community could take the lead in a "national export boom." He promised that if elected he would "defend the dollar."

In 1974 the USLP ran 33 candidates for major public office in 11 states, receiving 65,000 votes. In 1976 it sponsored 140 candidates in 21 states. Many were knocked off the ballot, but the number remaining was still greater than all other small leftist parties combined and greater than any single right-wing minor party. Although LaRouche received only 40,000 votes for President, the total vote that year for all USLP candidates running for major public office (Congress and up) was 154,000—more than any party of the radical left, but less than the right-wing American Party. In 1978 the USLP ran 72 candidates in 17 states, taking the total number of USLP candidates between 1974 and 1979 (including those knocked off the ballot) well over 300.

Most of this was the work of fewer than 500 NCLC local and regional cadres. In some cities virtually every NCLC member ran for office, year after year. Their compulsive electioneering was a source of amusement to other radical sects, yet the LaRouchians were gaining invaluable experience: They learned how to fill up nominating petitions rapidly, efficiently, and with a minimum of invalid signatures. They learned how to fend off petition challenges and, conversely, how to kick rivals like the Communist Party off the ballot. Their in-house lawyers and paralegals learned how to challenge local authorities over such issues as access to shopping malls and the right to use bullhorns on street corners. The USLP candidates mastered the tricks of campaigning on a shoestring budget. For instance, they submitted letters and op-ed pieces to local dailies and cadged invitations to appear on radio talk shows and cable TV. They also staged small but noisy demonstrations claiming that their candidates were being persecuted by the police.

When daily newspapers still ignored them, they went to neighborhood or ethnic weeklies, whose reporters sometimes were more desperate for a story or simply more gullible.

USLP candidates met with local trade union officials to request endorsements, something which most other radical groups rarely bothered to do.

In the 1970s radical sects such as the Communist Party and the Socialist Workers Party ran candidates chiefly for propaganda purposes, concentrating on the higher offices such as governor or mayor. Knowing they could not win, they rarely did much campaigning. But the USLP filed for minor public offices and campaigned seriously. A 1977 report from the Richmond, Virginia, USLP local claimed that its City Council slate had scheduled more than a dozen meetings with community groups and trade union officials, as well as appearances on three radio talk shows. The memo urged party members in other cities to field City Council candidates, since such contests furnish "virtually pre-set meetings for exposure of the USLP program."

Most USLP candidates were lucky to get 1 or 2 percent of the vote. Although voters will often give the benefit of the doubt to an outsider in the Democratic or Republican primary, they are reluctant to throw away their vote on a fringe party in the general election. Still the USLP did better than most fringe parties. A 1979 survey by the Manhattan weekly *Our Town* identified over two dozen races in seven states and the District of Columbia where USLP candidates picked up between 8 percent and 31 percent of the vote for everything from local school board to U.S. Congress. One Virginia USLP congressional candidate received over 10 percent in three successive elections.

These results did not reflect any ground swell of support for the USLP's politics. In most of the congressional races in which USLP candidates edged beyond the usual minor-party totals, their opponent was a Democratic incumbent with no Republican opponent. They would thus pick up the knee-jerk protest vote. Also they were often listed on the ballot as "Independents" rather than "USLP." The municipal and school board elections in which they did well were usually nonpartisan contests in which all names on the ballot were listed without party affiliation. Nobody told the voters who the USLP candidates were, or that they were extremists. Many voters pulled the lever for them at random.

In some cities the USLP attempted to exploit emotional public issues. During Boston's intense white ethnic opposition to school busing in 1974, the USLP fielded a congressional candidate in a district that included the antibusing stronghold of South Boston. After denouncing busing as a Ford Foundation plot, he received 10.7 percent of the vote.

Two years later the son of a former Ford Foundation vice president ran as the USLP's senatorial candidate in Massachusetts. Although he received fewer than 5,000 votes, *New Solidarity* boasted that he had done well in South Boston.

In Baltimore, USLP candidate Debra Freeman appealed openly to racist and anti-Semitic sentiments in her 1978 campaign against incumbent Congressman Parren Mitchell, chairman of the Black Congressional Caucus. Freeman, who is white, described Mitchell as a "house nigger" for Baltimore's "Zionists" and an example of "bestiality" in politics. Her campaign literature carried headlines like "End 200 Years of Zionist Slave Trading in Black Commodities." She won more than 11 percent of the vote, doing especially well in several white precincts.

In early 1979, LaRouche announced his second run for the presidency. He called himself the "candidate more American than apple pie" and toured the Midwest, speaking before chambers of commerce and civic clubs. He attempted to keep his rhetoric low-key, but his real views sometimes erupted. "If I had been President in 1973, and they had tried to do that [Watergate] to me . . . I would have smashed them," he told the Government Relations Roundtable of the Detroit Chamber of Commerce.

LaRouche began his campaign under the U.S. Labor Party banner, but by mid-1979 he recognized the futility of fringe-party electioneering and announced he would enter the New Hampshire presidential primary to appeal to the "silent Republican majority." Although he had not lived in New Hampshire since the age of ten, he called himself a "native son" candidate.

LaRouche's plan centered on his greatest asset—a devoted band of disciples who could be deployed anywhere in the United States on short notice to work sixteen hours a day without salaries while being housed and fed at minimal cost. Their legwork would compensate for his initial lack of a New Hampshire political base. To overcome his lack of name recognition he would start campaigning early, crisscrossing the state and holding "town meetings" in even the smallest villages. He would emphasize his French-Canadian descent, thus winning the sympathy of the state's largest ethnic minority. He would flood the state with campaign literature produced at low cost by the NCLC's in-house printing and typesetting facilities in Manhattan. The sum total of these efforts would invest the campaign with enough excitement—and the appearance of enough legitimacy—to attract local volunteers. Then, in the final weeks, LaRouche would bring in hundreds of NCLC members, including the entire national office staff. The result might not be as dramatic as Senator Eugene McCarthy's New Hampshire crusade in 1968, but LaRouche figured he could win 10 or 15 percent of the vote

—enough to gain celebrity status and a chance for financial backing from Texas oilmen.

In August, LaRouche sent in an advance team to open his Manchester headquarters. He made his first campaign tour in early September. At this point, most observers assumed he would enter the Republican primary, traditional magnet for right-wingers. Instead LaRouche declared himself a Democrat.

The decision was shrewd on both tactical and strategic grounds. The far right of the Republican Party was crowded with people who mostly disliked LaRouche. The Birchers in particular regarded him as a dangerous poacher and had repeatedly raised questions about his Trotskyist past. Most of the radical right in any case was supporting Ronald Reagan, and would have perceived LaRouche as an annoying diversion if not a spoiler. For his own part, LaRouche had no desire to harm Reagan's campaign. He already believed Reagan would be the next President, and hoped to gain influence with him.

By contrast, the Democratic Party lacked an organized right wing. LaRouche could have the territory all to himself—a domain of millions of conservative-minded voters seething with anger. These were conservatives of modest income and status, which is why they stayed in the Democratic Party rather than joining their more prosperous Republican brethren. They were the ones hardest hit by high interest rates, unemployment, and street crime. They had already revolted once to support George Wallace in 1968. Although most had returned grudgingly to the fold, the party leadership had lost touch with them during the following years. Nothing revealed this more clearly than the fact that all three major primary candidates in 1980—President Carter, Massachusetts senator Ted Kennedy, and California governor Jerry Brown—stood to the left of center. LaRouche thus could present himself as the voice of the party's forgotten wing, the proverbial common man. He could also use this guise to reach out to the mass of Democrats who were neither conservative nor liberal—the trade union members, small farmers, and churchgoing inner-city blacks whom his USLP had courted for years. By addressing their social problems in stark, angry rhetoric, he could perhaps nudge some of them into a new formation—a LaRouche wing of the party.

In New Hampshire, LaRouche attacked the liberals with gusto. The Democratic primary, he said, was a "Mad Hatter's tea party" dominated by Jane Fonda and her "antinuclear bacchanal" and by "Zen Buddhist governor Jerry Brown." LaRouche appealed to those sturdy "nation builders," the construction workers at the Seabrook nuclear power site. Vote for me, he said, and I'll build 2,500 nuclear plants by the year 2000. He also presented himself as a champion of "traditional" American values. "No one is going to grow a field of marijuana" in a LaRouche America, he said. "We'll spot it down to one stalk, and the next day we'll be in there with paraquat. . . . We can put this country on cold turkey."

LaRouche exchanged the academic bow-tie look he had affected during his 1976 campaign for three-piece business suits, yellow-tinted designer glasses, and a Texas Stetson. He dropped in on local VFW posts, spoke at Rotary and Kiwanis luncheons, met with leaders of the Franco-American community's Richelieu clubs. By November he had the second-largest campaign staff among Democratic candidates, with offices in eight towns. He bought newspaper, broadcast, and billboard advertising on the scale of a major candidate. His campaign events drew respectable crowds.

But the scheme had a major problem: The LaRouche organization was as cultish as ever, and LaRouche's personality continued to be volatile. To expect either the organization or LaRouche to maintain a strictly pragmatic stance even for a few weeks, to say nothing of an entire campaign season, was not realistic. Things began to unravel when New England newspapers picked up on a *New York Times* series about LaRouche's anti-Semitism and links to the Ku Klux Klan. Most articles reported this information in a low-key manner and without much detail. LaRouche could have simply ignored the charges and gone on campaigning for nuclear power. Or he could have issued a statement pointing out that many of his campaign aides were Jewish and that his contacts with the Klan were a legitimate part of his work as publisher of a political intelligence newsmagazine. Instead, his followers went into a frenzy, claiming there was a Zionist disinformation campaign afoot—the first stage of a plot to assassinate him. He marched into the Manchester *Union Leader* with armed bodyguards and threatened to "make it very painful" for a reporter. His guards took the hubcaps off his car as a precaution against bombs. His campaign workers made hundreds of harassing phone calls to New Hampshire state officials and Democratic Party leaders at all hours of day and night.

The LaRouchians also alienated public opinion by their almost gleeful exploitation of loopholes in the state's election law—including the absentee ballot provisions. LaRouche organizers rounded up low-income senior citizens in the industrial towns of southern New Hampshire and took them to the city clerk's office. There, they had the seniors fill out voter registration forms, get the forms properly certified, and then request and fill out absentee ballots on the spot. According to Manchester city clerk Joan Walsh, the LaRouchians even helped the seniors mark the ballots. Newspaper articles suggested that many who filled out the absentee ballots did so out of fear. Local police received several complaints about LaRouchian canvassers harassing and intimidating seniors. Meanwhile a LaRouche aide appeared at the office of the New Hampshire secretary of state to ask blithely for 3,000 absentee registration forms. When the request was refused, the LaRouchians printed their own forms.

By election day LaRouche's Grand Design for New Hampshire was in disarray. After spending over a million dollars, he received only 2,300 votes, about 2 percent of the Democratic primary total. Although this was more votes than Senator Robert Dole and former Texas governor John Connally received in the Republican primary, it devastated La-Rouche's followers, who had actually expected him to win. They charged that election officials had tampered with the voting machines to erase tens of thousands of LaRouche votes. Leaflets referred to New Hampshire as "Peyton State," the center of Yankee blueblood scandal and corruption. LaRouche went to court to demand a recount. When it was performed, he gained only 19 votes.

By mid-March, the LaRouchians had calmed down and were ready for more primaries. With the help of Teamster officials, LaRouche campaigned hard in Illinois and Wisconsin, sending Helga to Milwaukee to charm the German-American community. In Texas he held a press conference in front of the Alamo to call for a square deal for the nation's farmers. He told his followers to hang in there—he'd emerge as the dark horse at the national convention.

Most Democratic Party officials regarded the LaRouche campaign as a joke after New Hampshire. This view was not justified, for although LaRouche failed to gain a single convention delegate, he demonstrated his organization's electioneering skills and its potential for the future. He qualified for the primary ballot in fifteen states, including some with strict ballot access laws. He received 185,000 votes—over four times his 1976 total. In Connecticut he outpolled Jerry Brown by more than a thousand votes. He won endorsements and other campaign assistance from a number of trade union officials and farm leaders in the Midwest, Texas, and California. And, most important, he received over half a million dollars in federal matching funds—the first extremist candidate to get a penny.

LaRouche also gained name recognition. Millions of Americans viewed his half-hour network television ads in which he described himself as a Democrat in the mold of Franklin Delano Roosevelt. Daily newspapers published scores of articles about him. *People* magazine ran a full-page picture of LaRouche with pipe smoke swirling around his head, and said he had mounted what was possibly the "best-organized" fringe campaign in American history. Most of the media portrayed LaRouche as a mysterious figure who borrowed ideas from both the left and the right to express his anger about current economic conditions and his hostility to the Eastern Establishment—not a bad image for a man who aspired to capture the attention of the old George Wallace constituency.

When LaRouche requested floor passes for the national convention in New York, the party leadership turned him down, concerned as it was about possible disruption. Otherwise, the party leadership showed very little concern over his invasion of the party. His nominating petitions went unchallenged in most states and no one objected strongly to his calling himself a Democrat. In Texas he was allowed to address the state convention. The media continued to be unsympathetic and the party leadership contemptuous, but this was something LaRouche had already prepared his followers to accept and take advantage of: "an intensive 'soft' containment that is not an effective containment." The way to handle such a situation, he said, is to just keep plugging away, building up an intangible cumulative influence "on the other side of the containment wall." At the convention this took the form of seminars for delegates, appearances before state caucuses, a flood of position papers, a daily convention newspaper, and a coalition with the American Agricultural Movement to publicize an anti-Carter "Open Convention" strategy. Lyndon LaRouche had grabbed hold of the Democratic donkey's tail, and he was not about to let go.

# Twelve

# The Götterdämmercrats

Shortly after the 1980 Democratic convention LaRouche informed his followers that the NCLC was in the two-party system to stay. Having already disbanded the U.S. Labor Party, he now announced a "multi-candidate political action committee" that would work to eventually capture control of the Democratic Party. He called it the National Democratic Policy Committee (NDPC), a name falsely suggesting a link to the official party leadership.

The NDPC got off to a roaring start with a rally in Huntsville, Alabama, to Hang Paul Volcker (the chairman of the Federal Reserve Board and a favorite target of the ultraright). But before the LaRouchians could develop this campaign very far, they became preoccupied with figurative lynchings in their own ranks. First LaRouche declared war on his own chief of staff, Gus Kalimtgis, blaming him for the New Hampshire debacle. Kalimtgis and several other top NCLC members quit. Then LaRouche went after the Detroit regional leadership, accusing them of insufficient zeal. Virtually the entire Detroit membership resigned. In the midst of this, the organization was able to field only one Democratic primary candidate in 1981—Melvin Klenetsky for mayor of New York.

New York's Democrats could have taken vigorous action against this incursion, setting a nationwide example of how to handle LaRouche. Local leaders could have filed suit to keep Klenetsky off the ballot, on grounds that the NDPC's racism and anti-Semitism violated everything the Democratic Party stood for. They could have challenged his petitions. They could have denied him the floor at clubhouse candidates' forums. They could have urged the legitimate Democratic candidates not to participate in debates with him.

But none of this was done. As U.S. Senator Daniel Patrick Moynihan (D.-N.Y.) said, recalling the Klenetsky campaign in a 1986 speech about LaRouche: "To the disgrace of our party—the oldest political party on earth, and from the first a *democratic* party—*no* effort . . . was made to keep these fascists out of our ranks and off our ballot. To the contrary, rumor had it that in some circles they were welcomed: the more confusion, the better."

Moynihan was referring to the fact that Mayor Edward I. Koch's 1981 reelection campaign had regarded Klenetsky as a useful buffer between the mayor and Assemblyman Frank Barbaro, the main challenger. The Koch campaign encouraged Klenetsky's participation in public forums and debates to prevent the public from seeing the campaign as a one-on-one contest between Koch and Barbaro and to prevent the latter's criticisms of Koch from being given a serious hearing.

When Barbaro challenged Klenetsky's petitions, he received no help from Koch. When Barbaro protested against Klenetsky's inclusion in the debates, Koch insisted that Klenetsky be included. When Barbaro raised the issue of Klenetsky's membership in an anti-Semitic organization, Koch remained silent.

Koch could not claim ignorance. Reports of LaRouche's anti-Semitism had been widespread in the New York media for years. The Anti-Defamation League had denounced the LaRouche organization for injecting "anti-Semitic poison into the American political bloodstream." The Manhattan weekly *Our Town,* usually read carefully at City Hall, had published a twelve-part series delving into LaRouche's neo-Nazi proclivities. Koch's own police department had prepared several intelligence reports that carefully documented LaRouche's extremism.

Klenetsky was careful not to seem to be a tool of Mayor Koch. His campaign literature included the slogan "Stop Crazy Eddie—His Policies Are Insane." But in the debates and newspaper interviews his main role was to red-bait Barbaro, something that Koch hesitated to do on his own. The pro-Koch *New York Times* went along with this tactic to defeat real estate industry foe Barbaro. Although a 1979 *Times* editorial had denounced the LaRouchians as a menace, this fact disappeared into an Orwellian memory hole. Klenetsky was given what for a fringe candidate was an extraordinary amount of coverage, depicting him as almost a legitimate Democrat. The *Times* quoted him as warning New Yorkers that Barbaro's backers "include the bulk of the Socialist and Communist Party forces in New York." In an even lower blow, the *Times* reported two days before the election that Klenetsky had accused "some Barbaro supporters of anti-Semitism"! A pleased Mayor Koch then told the *Times:* "Klenetsky, he's not as bad as his rhetoric; Barbaro *is* as bad as his rhetoric." Klenetsky ended up with the votes of 25,000 New Yorkers—5 percent of the primary turnout.

The Klenetsky campaign set the stage for the national growth of the NDPC, by establishing the principle that its candidates could run in Democratic primaries as legitimate Democrats without significant opposition. It was a cynical LaRouche masterstroke: Use a Jewish follower to drive the opening wedge, and do it in the heart of enemy territory. Psychologically, LaRouche was operating from a position of strength—his utter contempt for the Koch machine as shortsighted "empiricists" who could be manipulated at will. Indeed, with Koch compromised, LaRouche received an additional bonus: the silence of the Jewish community. Not one mainstream Jewish organization spoke out against the legitimization of Klenetsky and the NDPC. In effect, many had acquiesced in the new dogma of neoconservatism: It's okay to ally oneself with fascists against the main enemy, the left.

In 1982 the NDPC sponsored several dozen candidates around the country. Klenetsky ran again, this time as Senator Moynihan's sole challenger in the New York primary. Moynihan, one of the Democratic Party's few intellectuals, took seriously the fact that the LaRouche movement represented a homegrown fascist ideology. Although Klenetsky was no threat to his reelection, he decided it would be a disgrace to sit back and allow the LaRouchians to gain further legitimacy in the party. He challenged every one of Klenetsky's 30,000 petition signatures, narrowly failing to remove him from the ballot. He also roundly denounced the LaRouche movement's anti-Semitism, and ended up spending $1.3 million on the primary.

Klenetsky waged a vigorous campaign. He obtained the endorsement of one of the state's most powerful labor leaders, John Cody, president of Teamster Local 282 on Long Island, as well as several Laborers International Union officials. He raised over $100,000 for newspaper, radio, and TV advertising, including a half-hour on New York City's ABC affiliate. In a half-page ad in the *Amsterdam News,* New

York's major black weekly, he accused Moynihan of racism (in spite of the LaRouche organization's own ties to the Ku Klux Klan) and listed endorsements by black ministers across the state. On primary day Klenetsky polled 162,000 votes statewide, of which 95,000 came from New York City. His statewide vote percentage was three times that of his 1981 mayoral primary campaign. His New York City vote total was four times his mayoral primary total.

Moynihan recalled being unable to get media help in unmasking Klenetsky. Most newspapers dismissed the LaRouchians as kooks, he said. Only two dailies in the state published editorials warning about what the NDPC candidate stood for. Compounding this media problem, Moynihan received a letter from the Committee on Decent Unbiased Campaign Tactics (CONDUCT) demanding how he could defend calling Klenetsky anti-Semitic. CONDUCT was concerned, the letter said, "that issues of bigotry would become an issue in anyone's campaign." CONDUCT was no LaRouche front organization but a coalition of prominent New Yorkers including R. Peter Straus, Rabbi Balfour Brickner, Bishop Paul Moore, Jr., and Howard Squadron, former chairman of the Conference of Presidents of Major Jewish Organizations. "It was bad enough to be running against a fascist," Moynihan said. "What if the respectable people of New York suddenly took the fascist's side?" Moynihan's attorney prepared a several-hundred-page brief, and CONDUCT finally exonerated Moynihan. (According to Straus, the watchdog committee also called in Klenetsky, questioned him closely, and found him to be "far off base.")

With the exception of Moynihan, Democratic Party leaders across the country ignored the NDPC during 1982. This contributed to strong electoral showings for several LaRouche candidates. Steve Douglas polled 19 percent in the Pennsylvania gubernatorial primary, coming in second out of four. A Minnesota NDPC congressional candidate—Pat O'Reilly, former state president of the American Agricultural Movement—picked up 32 percent. Debra Freeman, the terror of Baltimore's alleged Zionist slave traders, made her second congressional bid, this time against incumbent Barbara Mikulski. Freeman replaced Jew-baiting with lesbian-baiting, publicizing allegations of an affair between Mikulski and a staff aide. Freeman's radio ads featured a babble of monkeys, baboons, and hyenas, supposedly representing Mikulski's moral character. "Vote Freeman, Vote Straight Democrat," the NDPC's literature urged. With these tactics, Freeman polled 19 percent on primary day.

Only one major newspaper in the nation took the NDPC's 1982 gains seriously. The Baltimore *Evening Sun* published a hard-hitting series on

Freeman's political views and campaign finances. "We would like to hope," said a *Sun* editorial, "that even the 19 percent who voted for her were unaware of the dark impulses and exploitations that lurked behind her campaign." The voters got the message: In a race for Baltimore City Council President the next year, Freeman came in last of five, with only 2 percent of the vote.

LaRouche was heartened by the nationwide results in 1982 and decided to attract new blood into the NDPC via a grass-roots "candidates' movement." His followers advertised for and recruited hundreds of Americans with ultraconservative views to run for public office. These candidates—senior citizens, small businessmen, blue-collar workers, and, especially, farmers—were given quickie indoctrination sessions and thrown into the primaries. The NDPC didn't expect them to understand and defend the full LaRouche ideology, only simple points like the war on drugs, beam weapons, emergency aid for farmers. The NDPC had nothing to lose if some of the candidates proved unreliable. But if they remained loyal, LaRouche could take credit for their successes.

He carried his plan to the 1983 American Agricultural Movement convention in Nashville and a subsequent AAM rally in Georgia. Farmers were suffering through their worst economic crisis since the Great Depression, and thousands had lost their farms to the banks. LaRouche proposed his candidates' movement as a way to fight back: Farmers must "stop seeking out politicians and become politicians." They must "run early, run often, run for anything from dogcatcher to senator." The Eastern Establishment would try to stop the movement through media smears and vote fraud, but LaRouche had the answer to that: Just "keep adding candidates" until the Establishment's control mechanisms break down. LaRouche estimated that "one thousand candidates around the country" could provide the nucleus of a mass movement to alter the face of American politics.

By June 1983 the NDPC had recruited over 200 candidates. Many of them ran as "beam weapons" slates to promote President Reagan's new Star Wars policy. A Wichita, Kansas, woman decided this was God's will. She quit her job to run for the City Commission, to "open up channels to develop an 'E' beam in space." The movement attracted other obvious eccentrics, but it also attracted college professors, nuclear engineers, trade unionists, and scores of farm activists. By the end of the year the NDPC had fielded over 600 candidates in 27 states. According to NDPC chairman Warren Hamerman, they polled a total of 700,000 votes and 27 were elected.

Hamerman's figures were not as impressive as they sounded. Most of the candidates ran for Democratic county committee seats with no power or influence. Those who were elected mostly ran unopposed. Very few did any campaigning. In California an NDPC member was elected to a local sanitation board and another to a local school board. But the school board winner, an elderly man, later repudiated the LaRouchians. When the NDPC attempted to capture local school boards in New York and New Jersey, they stirred up a hornet's nest. Parents, teachers, community organizations, and local Democrats in upper Manhattan united under the slogan "Stop the Fascist Cult." Senator Moynihan supported the coalition and even dragooned Mayor Koch into co-sponsoring an anti-LaRouche press conference at City Hall. (Koch, clearly uncomfortable, edged away from the cameras after mumbling a one-liner, "They're the pits." He well knew the ability of LaRouche to exact revenge on bachelor political figures.) In New Jersey local newspapers conducted an intensive educational campaign against LaRouche's "beam weapons" school board slate. No NDPC school board candidates were elected in either state.

Incidents during the New Jersey contest suggest that the NDPC was sometimes recruiting candidates on a fraudulent basis. Bessie Mae Coleman, eighty-seven, told a reporter that the NDPC had never obtained her permission to enter her name as a candidate. Harding Evans, Sr., a fifty-four-year-old handyman, said that when the NDPC asked him to run, he thought they were ordinary Democrats. He and several other candidates dropped out when they learned the facts. New Jersey newspapers highlighted these incidents, but most of the 90-odd NDPC candidates stayed in the race, apparently willing to be associated with the LaRouche cause.

LaRouche ran for President again in 1984, selecting as his running mate a farmer, Billy Davis of Mississippi. Repeating his 1976 tactic, he encouraged the maximum number of grass-roots candidates who would work for his election while working for their own. The candidates' movement was rechristened the "NDPC's citizens' militia." According to *New Solidarity,* recruits were encouraged to attend "cadre schools" to learn the "science" of politics and listen to seminars on the "nature of the Russian empire."

The number of NDPC candidates in 1984 jumped to over 2,000 in more than 30 states. Once again the media ferreted out a few duds but ignored the fact that many well-educated people of apparently sound mind—people with careers and families—were willing to run on the NDPC ticket. These recruits were not all political novices. Some had prior experience in the major parties or in the American Party. They agreed with LaRouche on some things, disagreed on others, but were willing to call themselves LaRouche Democrats and support beam weapons. They also were willing to accept the risk of being LaRouche-baited in local newspapers.*

Although no surveys were conducted of the LaRouche candidates' movement, two Furman University professors did the next-best thing. In 1986 they interviewed a random sample of the thousands of La-Rouche campaign donors listed with the Federal Election Commission. Their survey found that LaRouche contributors tended to be "populist" conservatives, "profoundly uncomfortable with modern America and susceptible to conspiratorial explanations of their distress." To many, LaRouche's views offered "a plausible answer" to the question of who controls their lives.

"Nearly all," the report said, "now claim to be conservative, with half labelling themselves 'very' or 'extremely' conservative." Many expressed affinity not only for LaRouche but for traditional rightist groups such as the John Birch Society. There was a "uniform dislike" for Ralph Nader and the American Civil Liberties Union. Asked whom they regarded as especially dangerous, over half cited "figures prominent in conspiracy theories . . . such as communists, drug dealers, Jews, bankers, intellectuals and the mass media." Two-thirds were fifty-five or older, male, of Wasp or German extraction. Most were lower-middle-class people whose income and status lagged behind those of average donors to other right-wing causes. They seemed, the report concluded, "to be the remnant of the 'small-town America' of a generation ago."

This report was remarkable on two counts. First, it revealed a strong similarity between those surveyed and LaRouche's own parents. Second, it suggested that LaRouche had been successful in his long-range plan to reach precisely such people. In the mid-1970s he had begun to weave themes into his propaganda from the traditional rightist groups referred to in the survey, especially the John Birch Society and the

---

* *New Solidarity* articles and interviews in 1983–84 portrayed the NDPC grass-roots candidates as having a variety of political motives and fixations. An elderly woman in California complained that the Democratic Party had been turned into the "party of the giveaways." She had voted for Reagan in 1980, but when he was "turned around" by the Eastern Establishment she decided to support LaRouche as the man with "the ideas to guard our country." A Florida trade union official said he'd sensed there was a conspiracy controlling the country ever since Truman fired MacArthur. Then he bought a LaRouchian tract at an airport. "I felt like I had been granted my salvation; that somebody else was in touch with some of the same things I was." An Oregon school board candidate said that he'd always wanted to transcend the "banality" of his "backwater community" and fight the good fight against censorship, mistrust, cynicism, pessimism, prejudice, drugs, television, and thermonuclear terror. A North Carolina group home administrator was more down to earth: He just wanted to bring Star Wars R&D jobs to his hometown.

Liberty Lobby. His 1980 book, *What Every Conservative Should Know about Communism,* identified these people as a major part of his "constituency." They were the "patriotic conservatives" as opposed to phony conservative elitists like William F. Buckley. They were the "truly moral" conservatives who despised hippies, *Playboy* magazine, the Trilateral Commission, and the bestial advocates of "negritude." Many of these patriots, he said, were subscribers to *The Spotlight,* and a fair number had read W. Cleon Skousen's *The Naked Capitalist.* LaRouche called them the " 'Gideon's Army' of American nationalism today." He wrote about them affectionately, but without illusions regarding their intellectual limitations. He estimated their numbers at upward of a quarter million Americans—the "opinion leaders," he said, for a "similarly inclined population more than a scorefold larger."

As the 1984 primary season unfolded, it seemed as if the NDPC's grass-roots candidates were indeed beginning to establish themselves as opinion leaders to influence broader populist circles. The vote percentages for NDPC candidates rose dramatically, with dozens receiving over 20 percent in every region of the country. In Ohio the NDPC ran candidates in a majority of the state's 21 congressional districts. In the 7th CD the NDPC won its first contested Democratic nomination for major public office when family farmer Don Scott trounced the regular Democrat 23,000 to 15,000. This CD was heavily agricultural, centered on the small industrial city of Springfield. When *Newsweek*'s editors were seeking a typical American community to celebrate in their fiftieth-anniversary issue, this is the city they picked.

Scott, as described in NDPC literature, was as typical as the district: a "seventh generation" farmer, married with two daughters, a 4-H Club adviser, and member of the Covenant Lutheran Church, St. Paris Lions Club, National Farmers Organization, Knights of Pythias, and Champaign County Pork Council. The *Columbus Dispatch* noted that his victory "could go down in history as the first major step in legitimizing" the LaRouche organization. But the national media ignored the story. In the November general election the incumbent Republican spent $194,000 and Scott only $8,000, yet Scott received 46,000 votes— about 24 percent of the total. (By comparison, Mondale received 62,000 votes, or 31 percent, against Reagan in the same district.) Scott later was sent by the NDPC to Europe to speak before LaRouchian audiences.

Scott was not the only NDPC candidate on the Ohio ballot in November. In the 4th CD they picked up an uncontested nomination. And in the 8th CD, the NDPC candidate received 47 percent in spite of an effort by the regular Democrat to expose his extremism. Meanwhile, in North Carolina, the NDPC candidate for the U.S. Senate gained

127,000 votes (15 percent) in a three-way race, coming in second after former governor James Hunt. In Oregon the NDPC's U.S. senatorial candidate won 24 percent in a two-way race. In Pennsylvania the NDPC contested twelve congressional seats, receiving 46 percent in the 17th CD and over 20 percent in four others.

In California an NDPC congressional candidate won 49 percent in a two-way race. In Michigan the NDPC candidate in one CD received 26 percent in a three-way race, coming in second, while in another CD the NDPC candidate polled 33 percent in a two-way race. In Georgia an NDPC congressional candidate—an airline pilot—gained 24 percent in a four-way race, coming in second. He then won 34 percent in the runoff.

The NDPC later claimed that its candidates, apart from LaRouche himself, received close to two million votes in 1984, and that 280 NDPC members were elected to Democratic county committee seats in various states. However, most NDPC county committee members did not become active in the party, and nowhere did the NDPC build caucuses within the local party organizations. In Illinois's Du Page County, where dozens of LaRouchians were elected, the party leadership expected a major battle at the first post-election meeting. But the NDPC members just "sat like bumps on a log," according to Truman Kirkpatrick, a local party official. Most of them never came back.

The NDPC had more urgent concerns than building county caucuses. Its fund raisers were working around the clock to feed the maw of LaRouche's presidential campaign. Officially, LaRouche spent about $6 million on the campaign, including $500,000 in federal matching funds. It was later estimated that his organization raised over $30 million that year through various fund-raising entities.

As in 1980, LaRouche made heavy use of broadcast advertising by purchasing fourteen half-hour segments on network television as well as thousands of local radio and TV spots. In his network speeches, taped at his colonial mansion in Virginia, he called for sweeping economic changes to pay for a gigantic military buildup. He warned that "Henry Kissinger and his friends" were the cause of America's problems and that he himself had the solution. After an especially abrasive LaRouche speech that fall, TV stations around the country received close to a thousand viewer complaints.

LaRouche was on the ballot in 13 state primaries but received only 178,000 votes. The only primary in which he received a significant percentage was in North Dakota, where he and Gary Hart were the only candidates on the ballot. By that point LaRouche had been ruled ineligible for more matching funds, because of his failure to achieve 20 percent of the vote in any primary. He saw North Dakota as his one chance to restore his matching-funds eligibility. According to *New Solidarity*, LaRouche bought 998 radio spots, 127 thirty-second TV spots, and a full-page ad in a Bismarck daily. His ads also promoted the gubernatorial campaign of Anna Belle Bourgois, a farm wife and NDPC organizer, in an apparent attempt to piggyback off her wholesome image. The result was 12 percent (4,018 votes) for LaRouche and 12 percent (5,180 votes) for Mrs. Bourgois. It probably represented the maximum percentage of conscious votes for LaRouche ever. When he ran as an independent in 19 states that November, his total vote amounted to only 79,000. In the 1984 primary and general elections combined, LaRouche spent almost $25 per vote.

His failure at the polls did not discourage the NDPC grass-roots candidates. In 1985, an off year for elections generally, the NDPC claimed to have 500 candidates running for public office and Democratic Party posts. Once again Democratic Party leaders and local Democratic organizations prevaricated. And once again New York's Mayor Koch, facing another reelection campaign, attempted to make use of the NDPC. His aides urged various reporters to give coverage to the NDPC's Phil Rubinstein and Farrakhan supporter Fred Newman, both on the mayoral primary ballot. The *Daily News* produced a frothy piece, "Hey, Guys, We're in It Too," in which Rubinstein and Newman were described as offering voters "a breath of fresh air." Koch personally called for their inclusion in the mayoral debates, in the interest of "fairness." His obvious goal was to muddy the voters' choice between himself and his two major challengers, City Council president Carol Bellamy and Harlem assemblyman Herman Farrell. (Not to be outdone in the fairness game, Bellamy also expressed her hope that the minor candidates would be included.) But this time, the media didn't bite the bait. Koch didn't have a Barbaro to scare them with. Rubinstein remained a minor candidate and received only a minuscule vote.

The NDPC problem had receded in New York politics because LaRouche had moved most of his New York followers, including Melvin Klenetsky, down to Leesburg, Virginia, to run his new national headquarters. But the NDPC, unfought and unchecked, continued to grow almost everywhere else. It was only a matter of time before a combination of circumstances and the NDPC's hard work produced a major electoral breakthrough. That breakthrough came in 1986, in the heartland of blue-collar America, Illinois.

# Thirteen

## Tanks Down
## State Street

The Illinois Democratic Party received the greatest surprise of its history when, in the March 18, 1986, primary, followers of LaRouche won the nominations for lieutenant governor and secretary of state. The LaRouchians were no less amazed. Their Chicago contingent hadn't even bothered to watch the election polls that night, being too busy conducting a mock exorcism in front of the home of University of Chicago religion professor Mircea Eliade (they claimed he was an evil warlock). The following day, Janice Hart, thirty-one, the victor in the secretary of state contest, announced her plans for a different kind of exorcism targeting bankers and drug pushers: "I'm going to revive the spirit of Abraham Lincoln and General Patton. We're going to roll our tanks down State Street."

The Democratic candidate for governor, Adlai Stevenson III, announced that he would not run on the same ticket with Hart and the nominee for lieutenant governor, twenty-eight-year-old Mark Fairchild. He described them as neo-Nazis and said: "There is no room in the Democratic Party for candidates . . . who preach anti-Semitism, who cavort with the Ku Klux Klan, and who want to destroy labor unions." The following month Stevenson renounced the Democratic nomination and became the candidate of a hastily organized Illinois Solidarity Party.

The LaRouchian victory became the media sensation of the week. Janice Hart was interviewed on *Nightline,* and LaRouche almost made the cover of *Newsweek. Chicago Tribune* columnist Mike Royko called it "the strangest thing that's ever happened in an election in my memory." Syndicated columnist Max Lerner declared that "this is the face American fascism will wear." New York's Senator Moynihan spoke of a failure of the party's political immune system. LaRouche, in a speech before the National Press Club, described the Illinois victories as the will of the "forgotten majority." Farmers and blue-collar workers were turning to him as the new George Wallace, "the guy who's going to stick it to them in Washington."

The Democratic Party claimed it was all a fluke. Two political unknowns running an invisible campaign had won by narrow margins because voter turnout was low, because the media failed to warn the public, and because the regular Democratic candidates neglected to campaign vigorously. Also, Hart's Waspish name gave her an advantage over machine Democrat Aurelia Pucinsky among Chicago's black voters, who were angry at Pucinsky's father and other Polish-American politicians for dumping on Mayor Harold Washington. The name factor also may have helped Hart downstate, where many voters are suspicious of ethnic Chicagoans. But any further LaRouchian victories could be easily prevented with a little party vigilance and voter education.

It was to be expected the Democrats would assert something like this, for their aim was damage control rather than an objective postmortem. To perform the latter would have involved admitting that the party had allowed the LaRouchians to run amok in its ranks for over six years. If the Democrats already had a wimp image from the Mondale debacle, how would *this* appear to the media?

Undeniably a majority of the LaRouchian votes resulted from accidental circumstances. But the Democrats and the media ignored evidence that a substantial minority of these votes—a portion without which Hart and Fairchild never would have won—reflected various forms of conscious voter rebellion. Furthermore, no one examined the fact that the two victors were part of a statewide NDPC "Warrior Angel" slate, thirty candidates in all, running for everything from governor to precinct committeeman and adhering to a national NDPC strategy called, prophetically, Operation Takeover.

The vote percentages of these other Illinois NDPC candidates (none of whom faced Polish opponents) reveal the flaws in the only-a-fluke theory. The figures in statewide contests included 15.8 percent for U.S.

senator, 5 percent for governor, 22.3 percent for comptroller, and 14 percent for state treasurer. In congressional races the figures included 9.1 percent (3rd CD), 14.7 percent (4th CD), 35.8 percent (6th CD), 12.8 percent (8th CD), 15.6 percent (9th CD), 35.2 percent (10th CD), 15.1 percent (11th CD), 42.5 percent (12th CD). The total was over one million votes excluding the 13th and 15th CDs, where NDPC candidates won the Democratic nominations unopposed.

These vote percentages were commensurate with what an increasing number of NDPC candidates had gained in Midwest contests between 1982 and 1985. They also fit with what NDPC candidates would poll in later Midwest primaries that year and in Illinois primaries over the following two years. "How can anyone look at the record and say this is a fluke?" asks Chip Berlet, a Chicago journalist who has tracked the LaRouchians for years. "Flukes do not increment upwards in a steady pattern."

Michael McKeon, a pollster who specializes in the attitudes of blue-collar voters, warned of a possible LaRouche electoral breakthrough in Illinois over a year before it occurred. In open-ended interviews with trade union households in communities plagued by crime and unemployment, he found a growing willingness to vote for LaRouchian candidates. Those interviewed had little knowledge of what LaRouche really stood for, McKeon said, but "were fed up with the way they believed the two major parties were ignoring them." His January 1985 report was pigeonholed by state and national Democratic leaders who thought it was farfetched.

McKeon was willing to stake his reputation on an offbeat finding because of clear warning signs in grass-roots elections. In 1983, the LaRouchians managed to field 53 candidates in Chicago suburban school board races. Although failing to elect anyone, they bounced back in the March 1984 Democratic primaries, winning 57 suburban county committee seats, including all 31 of the seats they went after in Du Page County. Although three out of four of the NDPC candidates ran for uncontested seats, at least they were willing to run—the party machine couldn't find anyone. Meanwhile in the Will County auditor's race, the NDLC candidate defeated her regular Democratic opponent by over 3,000 votes. (Will County has an unemployment rate twice the state average. The county seat, Joliet, is a blue-collar town of failed steel mills. McKeon, who lives there, describes it as "everything Bruce Springsteen sings about.")

The Chicago dailies, which two years later affected so much amazement at the Hart and Fairchild victories, covered the 1984 victories in detail, with headlines such as " 'LaRouchies' Score Sweep in Du Page" and "LaRouche Party Victories Chill Du Page Democrats." But Democratic officials told the *Chicago Tribune* it was all a simple case of voter confusion—voters had thought the NDPC was the Democratic National Committee. One county chairman even suggested that the victories of the LaRouchian candidates weren't "necessarily all that bad" if they "really want to be part of the party and help build the party . . . if they are actually going to go out and support our nominees." Neither the Democrats nor the media bothered to ask how a tiny fringe group had persuaded ninety registered Democrats in a four-county area to run on its ticket for nonpaying, low-prestige posts while also fielding ten congressional candidates and several candidates for state and county public office. (The NDPC claims it ran 114 candidates in Illinois that year, garnering 220,000 votes.)

In 1986 the cornerstone of the fluke theory was the assertion that the LaRouche candidates did little or no campaigning. Michael McKeon disputes this: "They just weren't around where the media was," he said. "Most of the media was out of contact with the people." He observed the LaRouchians campaigning in Joliet months before the primary. "They knew their target area. They'd have tables by the K mart department store, where the people laid off from the steel mill shopped. Their literature was more easily available than Democratic or Republican brochures." Listening to their pitch, he sensed they would surprise everyone in March. As he later explained to *The Washington Post*, they had "taught themselves how to talk to Joe Six-Pack" and were "tapping into the feelings that are out here in blue-collar America." Working-class voters are "tough on crime and hate drug dealers. They'd like to see them all killed—Ramboed. This is what the LaRouche candidates have been saying too."

McKeon said that he received many reports of NDPC campaigning downstate. "They went around in information vans," he said. "They'd go to farms and talk to people for hours. This wasn't a fluke; they seized an opportunity."

Chip Berlet also received numerous reports. "I was called by Democratic Party activists all over the suburbs—from Joliet, Glencoe, Batavia. They wanted literature to counter them." Berlet criticized the Chicago media's analysis of the primary for ignoring the "cumulative" effect of LaRouche organizing over the previous decade. "This was never looked at," he said, "because it involved areas of politics that are usually invisible to the media." He noted their attempts to form antidrug alliances with black churches and mosques and with black weekly newspapers like the *Chicago Defender*. "They'd get rebuffed," he said, "but they kept coming back." In the late 1970s they formed ties with the Laborers Union in Chicago and downstate officials of the Teamsters union and the Cement Masons and Plasterers. Berlet also cited their year in, year out "nitty-gritty" work—fund raising, selling *New Solidarity* subscriptions, compiling phone lists of potential supporters, leafleting in downtown Chicago, manning literature tables at O'Hare International Airport seven days a week. He believes that "many thousands" of 1986 primary voters knew who the LaRouchians were, even if they didn't vote for them.

The first clear warning signal of their electoral potential came in 1980, when LaRouche received over 19,000 votes in the Illinois primary. Although this was only 1.1 percent of the total, it was half as many votes as California governor Jerry Brown received. It was far more votes than Howard Baker, John Connally, and Robert Dole received in the Republican primary, and almost as many as Illinois congressman Phil Crane. Most of LaRouche's votes came from the Chicago wards, where he received two-thirds the vote of Jerry Brown and more votes than six out of eight of the Republican candidates. Indeed, he received almost twice as many votes in the wards as George Bush. His slate of 49 convention delegate candidates, mostly in Chicago and the suburbs, received well over 75,000 votes. In the predominantly black 2nd CD on Chicago's South Side, LaRouche delegates received over 35,000 votes. "The LaRouchians had conducted a strong antidrug organizing drive in that district," Berlet said. "I attended rallies there in the summer of 1979. These were mass meetings, hundreds would show up." Over the next six years the LaRouchians continued to court black voters. Sheila Jones, a former Chicago public school teacher and perennial NDPC candidate, became widely known as their spokesperson in the black community. In the 1986 primary she received 70,000 votes in the Chicago wards (130,000 statewide) against incumbent Senator Alan Dixon.

When the LaRouchians asserted that they had indeed campaigned hard to win their 1986 victories, most of the media dismissed this out of hand. But months before primary day *New Solidarity* was already reporting details of the campaign. For instance, a January 1986 article described a weeklong tour of downstate Illinois by Mark Fairchild and the NDPC candidate for governor, Peter Bowen, to speak out on the farm crisis and unemployment. The article also revealed that the Illinois NDPC had purchased hundreds of sixty-second radio spots to publicize its positions on AIDS and the Gramm-Rudman bill.

Voters interviewed after the primary told the media they had not known who Hart and Fairchild were when they voted for them. Although the majority were doubtless telling the truth, the minority who *had* known had good reason not to admit it. Articles and TV news reports were calling their chosen candidates neo-Nazis, neofascists, extreme rightists, conspiracy theorists, kooks, cultists, white-collar crooks, crypto-Communists, and racists. As Chip Berlet observed: "Why should an unemployed steel worker or bankrupt farmer, already seething with resentment against the liberal media, 'confess' to some yuppie TV reporter and get looked at like he's dirt?"

Robert Albritton, a Northern Illinois University political scientist, analyzed the election returns county by county. He found a strong correlation in central and southern Illinois between the incidence of family farms relative to the population and voter support for Janice Hart and the NDPC candidate for state treasurer, Robert Hart. In the case of Robert Hart (Janice's husband), the relationship was especially striking. Democratic voters had three other choices, including an incumbent and a downstater. Unlike Janice's opponent, these candidates campaigned vigorously. Yet Robert Hart won thirty-five counties downstate. Most of these were economically depressed, like Johnson County in the state's far south, where an unusually large percentage of total family income came from welfare, unemployment, and other government benefits.

Dan Levitas, research director of Prairiefire Rural Action, monitored the NDPC's farm organizing in Illinois and other Midwest states for more than two years before the 1986 primaries. "They'd bring crews out of Chicago. They'd do a drive-through of the LaRouche vans with bullhorns where they had people running for Congress." Levitas said he'd listened in on weekly LaRouchian radio hook-up conference calls with farmers. "They'd take attendance," he said. "There were farmers at fifty to seventy-five locations, but the number influenced was much greater. You had Mom and Pop listening in, you had people making tapes and circulating them, you had neighbors gathering each week."

One center for Illinois conference call gatherings was a farm in Fayette County, where Janice Hart defeated her opponent by more than two to one. The couple who sponsored the gatherings, Elbert and Jean Finley, also organized in 1985 an NDPC rally, attended by about sixty farmers. Clem Marley, who operates a farm news service, signed the attendance sheet, and his wife later received a call from Hart.

LaRouchian agitation among Illinois farmers dates back to 1974, when the U.S. Labor Party candidates for governor and lieutenant governor toured southern Illinois. According to *New Solidarity*, they passed out leaflets explaining the "Labor Party Emergency Food Program," and learned firsthand about farmers' "bitterness and populist demoralization." Although the USLP was still too left-wing for rural America, *New Solidarity* continued to cover farm issues, gradually shifting its rhetoric into the populist mold. During the 1980 presidential primary, LaRouche sent his agricultural adviser, a Michigan grain farmer, on a tour of southern and central Illinois, where he was interviewed on TV and radio and met with many farmers. In June 1980, LaRouche invited farmers to an all-day conference at Chicago's O'Hare Hilton, where he talked about agriculture as a professional economist, downplaying ideology. A transcript of his extemporaneous answers during the lengthy question period reveals that he had thoughtful positions on a wide range of farm issues, which he expressed in colorful witty language. Meanwhile, his followers promoted a National Emergency Agricultural Declaration to maintain federal parity price payments at 90 percent. They formed an alliance with the American Agricultural Movement, which lasted through 1983–84 (LaRouche, as noted earlier, addressed AAM activists in 1983). Throughout the early 1980s—the worst years of the farm crisis—the NDPC organized farm rallies, participated in farm auction protests, ran farmers for public office, and sold LaRouchian publications across the rural Midwest.

Farm activists estimate that LaRouchian campaign activities in 1986 reached only a small fraction of Illinois farm families directly. But given the depressed economic conditions and political discontent in rural Illinois in the mid-1980s, that may have been sufficient to gain a significant protest vote. According to Susan Danzer of the Illinois South Family Farm Program, rural areas of the state were "riddled" with right-wing groups operating informally, without much high-visibility organizing. "Farmers in trouble talk to other farmers in trouble," she said.

Leonard Zeskin, the Missouri-based research director of the Center for Democratic Renewal, said that the interconnections of the various rural extremist groups make it possible to spread the word quickly about a candidate. Farmers active with the NDPC tend also to have ties with the Populist Party, Liberty Lobby, and Posse Comitatus. "One hand washes the other," he said. He noted that shortly after the primary, Populist Party leader Robert Weems (a former Klansman) announced his support for Hart and Fairchild in a front-page article in *The Spotlight.*

The murkiness of the LaRouchian relationship to Illinois farmers, and to downstate Illinois in general, was captured in a report by Tom Johnson, a freelance researcher for the American Jewish Committee, after a three-day swing through five central Illinois counties in late March 1986. He said no one would admit having voted for the LaRouchians, even though their highest vote percentages came from this region. He spoke to one of the NDPC congressional candidates, a farmer who said he was his "own man" but added: "You gotta have an organized unit to get enough people thinking the same way. . . . We're facing the big boys, not the politicians, but them who's running them." (This farmer later dropped out of the NDPC.) Johnson also talked to a Champaign County Democratic official who said Fairchild and another NDPC candidate had been "laughed at and greeted with anger" when they appeared at a forum for precinct workers. Yet Hart and Fairchild drew 57 percent and 52 percent, respectively, in the Champaign County primary. Although Johnson did not find much evidence of NPDC campaigning, he observed conditions that suggested a political tinderbox. "Town after town . . . appears to be a ghost town," he wrote. "In one small burg of 3,700 we saw ten 'for sale' signs on a single street."

A curious incident the day before the primary showed that the LaRouchians were well aware of this tinderbox. A contingent of NDPC demonstrators led by Sheila Jones invaded the lobby of the Federal Reserve Bank of Chicago. They unfurled a banner: "End the Bankers' Dictatorship—Jones for Senate." The NDPC had unsuccessfully sought major media attention during the previous week through a variety of stunts. In picking the Federal Reserve, a favorite target of right-wing populists, they knew exactly what they were doing. Thousands of farmers downstate would have received a powerful election-eve message if the demonstration had been reported on TV evening news.

In November's general election the majority of voters no longer could plead ignorance about Hart and Fairchild. For over seven months, the two had received extensive hostile press coverage and had been attacked by campaign literature of both Republicans and regular Democrats. But the NDPC candidates hammered away, albeit in bizarre language, with their message for the "forgotten majority": Halt farm foreclosures, reopen steel mills, form vigilante groups to crack down on drug pushers, prosecute banks for laundering money, quarantine AIDS victims.

By ordinary political standards, the LaRouchians suffered an overwhelming defeat in November. Hart received only 15.3 percent of the vote; Fairchild, only 6.4 percent. No Democratic nominees for major office had ever done so poorly in Illinois. Yet by the standards of vanguard extremist politics (in which winning public office is never the top priority) their campaign was a success. They drew a clear line between themselves and the political system, letting the public know they were at war with the existing order. They developed a reputation for an uncompromising spirit. And Hart received 478,000 votes, over 100,000 more than in March. She ran as strongly as the Illinois Solidarity Party candidate backed by Stevenson and the state Democratic organization. She received 226,000 votes in Cook County and about 25 percent of the vote in economically depressed St. Clair, Madison, and Rock Island counties. Her campaign evidently had tapped a substantial number of voters who knew who and what she was and weren't at all bothered by media warnings. Although her promise to send the tanks down State Street had sounded strange in March, it may have been the smartest move of her campaign.

Neither the Democratic Party nor the media, thinking only in mainstream political terms, drew any serious lessons from the Hart vote. Outside Illinois most newspapers reported only the vote percentages, not the totals. The Democratic Party announced that LaRouche had been defeated, and that was that. No one confronted the plain fact that in a state saturated with anti-LaRouche propaganda his candidate had received almost a half million votes.

The LaRouchian primary victories were the pivotal event in Illinois politics in 1986. Adlai Stevenson III, running on his third-party line, lost to Republican governor James R. Thompson by 400,000 votes. Democratic candidates in general were hurt by the ballot confusion: They had to warn voters to beware of non-Democrats running as Democrats, and to vote for "real" Democrats on a non-Democratic line. The Republicans meanwhile spent $200,000 in Cook County alone on ads with a simple message: If you don't know who the LaRouchian candidates are, play it safe by voting straight Republican. Thus did Lyndon LaRouche help deliver the nation's sixth most populous state to the Republicans for four more years.

# Fourteen

# After Illinois

Despite the nationwide barrage of anti-LaRouche publicity in the wake of the 1986 Illinois primary, NDPC candidates did well in subsequent primaries that year. According to the NDPC's own figures, it fielded candidates in 31 states, including 157 for Congress, 14 for the U.S. Senate, about 50 for state legislative office, and over 700 for Democratic Party posts (the last figure was probably inflated). Although none was elected to public office, ten made the ballot in November as Democratic nominees (four by winning primary fights, six by filing for uncontested nominations). Well over a million Americans voted for NDPC candidates in the post-Illinois primaries and the general elections.

The Anti-Defamation League compiled the percentage figures for 234 NDPC primary candidates, not including those for Democratic Party posts. It found that 119 received from 0 to 10 percent, 60 received 11 to 20 percent, 22 received 21 to 30 percent, 16 received 31 to 40 percent, 4 received 41 to 50 percent, 4 received over 50 percent, and 9 were unopposed. In other words, almost half received over 10 percent. Percentages of more than 20 percent were obtained in every region, from Idaho to Georgia and from New Hampshire to California.

Oklahoma's NDPC candidate for the U.S. Senate, farmer George Gentry, received 157,000 votes (33 percent) in a two-way race. This vote probably was influenced by the fact that Gentry lost his farm in a sheriff's auction shortly before the primary—an event widely reported in the local media. In Indiana the NDPC's senatorial candidate, Georgia Irey, campaigned hard in a two-way race against a regular Democrat who aggressively publicized Irey's LaRouche connection. When a Democratic official said the LaRouchians were like cockroaches who can't stand the light of day, Irey announced that she was adopting "La Cucaracha" as her theme song. Promising action to halt plant closings and farm foreclosures, she won 93,000 votes (26 percent).

In Iowa, Democrats and trade unionists were shocked when Juan Cortez, a former member of the Democratic state committee and a past president of Local 231 of the American Federation of State, County, and Municipal Employees, announced as the NDPC's senatorial candidate. In the face of strong attacks on his LaRouche connection, Cortez gained 17,000 votes, or 16 percent. Seventeen counties gave him over 20 percent. In no county did he receive less than 12 percent.

NDPC candidates gained significant vote totals in other statewide contests. In Ohio, farmer Don Scott challenged U.S. Senator John Glenn and received 96,000 votes, or 12.5 percent. In Texas and Georgia the NDPC candidates for state Agricultural Commissioner each won 18 percent—187,000 votes in Texas, 103,000 in Georgia. Both were farmers; the Texas candidate ran against a well-known and popular incumbent, James Hightower.

NDPC congressional candidates polled between 20 and 40 percent in 21 contests in California, Idaho, Illinois, Indiana, Massachusetts, New Hampshire, Ohio, Pennsylvania, and Texas. Also, two NDPC candidates picked up uncontested nominations in Ohio and Texas. But in New Jersey, where the Democratic Party conducted an especially strong anti-LaRouche voter education drive, the NDPC's 13-candidate congressional slate received only 15,473 votes combined.

On the state legislative level the NDPC won two Michigan state senatorial primaries. Both were in Republican-dominated districts where the Democrats had fielded weak candidates. In Idaho an NDPC candidate picked up an uncontested nomination for state representative, then polled 41 percent in the general election against the Republican incumbent. In Alaska an NDPC candidate won 19 percent in a state senate primary. In Texas an NDPC candidate gained an uncontested Democratic nomination for state assembly, then polled over 20 percent in November.

The NDPC claimed about 50 victories in races for positions within the Democratic Party, mostly county committee seats. In Pennsylvania's Bucks County an NDPC candidate won election to the Democratic state committee over four regular Democrats. In Texas the NDPC fielded over 150 candidates for party posts. Of the 16 who ran for county chairmanships, 12 received over 20 percent. Two months before the primary a newspaper columnist in Bexar County (San Antonio) warned that if the Democrats didn't wake up, the LaRouche candidate for county chairman, Donald Varella, would win. The columnist pointed out that another NDPC member had polled 40 percent in the previous Bexar County chairmanship race (1984). The local Democrats didn't heed the warning, and Varella came in first in the 1986 primary. The party was saved from further embarrassment only by the fact that Varella was not deeply committed to the NDPC. After unfavorable press coverage he dropped out of the race before the runoff primary, saying that he didn't really want to be county chairman and that he'd rather "follow the Man to the Cross than a man to Washington."

Varella was not the only NDPC candidate whose link to LaRouche was tenuous. The *Houston Post* polled 25 presumed NDPCers who were elected, mostly unopposed, as county committeemen in Harris County. Fourteen said either that they'd had second thoughts about LaRouche or that they'd been unclear about the NDPC's affiliations from the beginning. The same phenomenon was found in other states. Two NDPC candidates for Congress, nominated unopposed in Illinois and Ohio, disassociated themselves from LaRouche. Others, when questioned by the press, were hesitant to back LaRouche fully. "I am not a LaRouche follower," said a General Dynamics technician who won a Michigan state senate primary. "I like some of their ideas and they like some of mine."

But other NDPC candidates were less skittish. Major Robert Patton (USAF, ret.), a U.S. senatorial candidate in New Hampshire, told a local reporter that he backed LaRouche because whenever "evil rears [its] ugly head . . . LaRouche strikes with the written word, and it's effective." An Alabama NDPC candidate for the state legislature laughed off the media's attacks. "At first, we were 'followers of extremist LaRouche, neo-Nazis, blah, blah, blah,'" he told *New Solidarity* in mid-May. "Now, it's gotten to the point where—in the local media, more so than the national media—we're simply getting straightforward coverage."

Overall, despite the negative media coverage and the Democratic Party's anti-LaRouche mailings to voters in some states, the NDPC's post-Illinois candidates in 1986 did *better* than its 1984 candidates, who had faced almost no media or party opposition. But the Democrats made no serious attempt to analyze these results. They just noted that the LaRouchians weren't *winning* elections, as if this would make the hundreds of thousands of NDPC votes disappear. Democratic National Committee spokesman Terry Michael cited races in which the NDPC was held to under 30 percent as proof that the Illinois victories had been a fluke.

The truth was much more complicated. Although there was indeed a fluke factor in many NDPC contests, the high NDPC vote totals sometimes were also the result of hard work and clever demagoguery on volatile public issues. The fluke vote itself was not just a matter of voters pulling the lever at random. The LaRouchians were selecting their contests carefully, concentrating on Democratic primaries in staunchly Republican districts where the regular Democratic candidate was often as obscure as the LaRouchian one. The local party leadership didn't care much about the outcome, the voters didn't care, and the regular Democratic candidate merely went through the motions. Everyone knew the Democratic nominee couldn't win the general election anyway.

When NDPC candidates ran against well-known incumbents with no other primary challenger (e.g., Scott against Glenn in Ohio), they also picked up significant vote percentages with little effort. The incumbent couldn't lose, so again there was little incentive to wage a strong battle against an obscure challenger. Voters who didn't like the incumbent—especially conservative Democrats who regarded him as too liberal—could express their disgruntlement by voting for the NDPC candidate. They might not approve of the NDPC's extremism, but inasmuch as there seemed no danger of the NDPC candidate actually winning, they would seize the opportunity to "send a message," as George Wallace used to say.

These tactics involved conscious manipulation of weaknesses within the Democratic Party. But artful tricks do not explain everything. First, the LaRouchians did well in a number of multi-candidate elections which included well-known political figures. Second, their high 1986 vote percentages were mostly in low-turnout primaries. It is a rule of thumb in analyzing election returns that the lower the turnout, the higher the political awareness and socioeconomic status of those who vote. In other words, the LaRouchians were often getting support from the voters least likely to engage in fluke voting. Third, post-Illinois candidates like Georgia Irey in Indiana did well despite vigorous anti-LaRouche voter education specifically designed to counter fluke voting. Fourth, the LaRouchians were striking a chord with angry conservatives on the AIDS issue. In California they collected over a half million signatures in 1986 for an AIDS quarantine ballot initiative. It garnered 29 percent of the vote even after LaRouche's role was widely publicized.

In 1986–87 the LaRouchians were placed on the defensive for the first time—not in the political or ideological arena, but in court. Top LaRouche aides were indicted for credit-card and loan fraud. La-Rouche himself was indicted for obstruction of justice. It seemed for a while that this might be the end of the NDPC election machine. But that certainly wasn't the case in Illinois. NDPC candidates for city clerk and city treasurer in the 1987 Chicago municipal primaries received 47,000 and 50,000, respectively, while an NDPC aldermanic candidate received considerable support in a suburban district. Elsewhere, NDPC activity was muted as the LaRouchians reorganized their forces, but by early 1988 their machine was running smoothly again. LaRouche ran for President in more states than ever, including eleven on Super Tuesday. In California his followers recruited 205 registered Democrats in 45 congressional districts to run on his convention delegate slate. (They did this while also collecting 731,166 signatures to place a second AIDS initiative on the ballot.) LaRouchian fund raising also returned to normal, under the command of the very people who had been indicted. By June, LaRouche had gained over $650,000 in federal matching funds, more than in either of his two previous bids for the Democratic nomination.

As in 1984, he did poorly at the polls (receiving only 21,979 votes on Super Tuesday), but NDPC grass-roots candidates did well. In the 1988 Pennsylvania primary an NDPC candidate won the Democratic congressional nomination in the 5th CD by a vote of 10,670 to 9,298. NDPC candidates in the 7th and 10th CDs received 20 percent and 32 percent, respectively. In Pennsylvania's U.S. senatorial primary, NDPC leader Steven Douglas, running in a field of four, polled 146,050 votes, or 13 percent. Back in Illinois, the NDPC fielded a slate of twenty. Sheila Jones received 21 percent (115,000 votes) in the race for Cook County recorder of deeds, while NDPC candidates picked up 22 percent in the 4th CD, 38 percent in the 6th CD, 25 percent in the 13th CD. These Illinois results were achieved in spite of mailings by the party leadership to registered Democrats in the targeted CDs and a massive distribution of anti-NDPC brochures in Cook County.

The NDPC mounted a major effort in Iowa, with candidates for 16 congressional and legislative seats across the state (up from 4 candidates in 1986). Phil Roeder, the state party's communications director, told the *Des Moines Register:* "They are the political version of the 'Creature from the Black Lagoon.' They keep coming back to haunt us." The party leadership sent out anti-NDPC mailings and urged local party organizations to ban NDPC candidates from their candidates' forums.

Juan Cortez, the NDPC's 1986 senatorial candidate, was held to 11 percent in the 2nd CD and the majority of the NDPC candidates received under 10 percent. However, the NDPC candidate in the 1st CD polled 30 percent, and four NDPC state legislative candidates polled over 20 percent, with a high of 32 percent for a longtime LaRouche farm activist in House District 17. Prairiefire Rural Action in Des Moines did a county-by-county analysis. It found that a majority of the NDPC candidates received over 10 percent in one or more counties, with their best showings in rural counties and/or their home counties. It described as "surprising" the 14 percent vote Cortez received in his home county, where voters were especially aware of his LaRouche connection. The NDPC congressional candidate in the 1st CD received 40 percent or more in five of the sixteen counties; in three, he received over 45 percent. His best showing was in Wapello County, where "LaRouche operatives campaigned aggressively with door-to-door canvassing and literature distribution efforts." Comparing the 1986 and 1988 NDPC vote, the report concluded that although no "stable bloc" of LaRouche voters yet existed, the vigorous exposures of LaRouche in Iowa had not been entirely effective: "Far too many [voters] chose to support LaRouche-sponsored candidates in 1988. And, in the absence of continued vigilance, there is nothing to suggest that a significant number of Iowans won't make the same mistake again in 1990."

As in previous years, the LaRouchians took advantage of the flabbiness of local Democratic organizations in strongly Republican districts. Indeed, by concentrating on such districts they won more contested primaries in 1988 than in any single previous year. And they also picked up several uncontested nominations in districts where the regular Democrats simply didn't bother to field anyone. In Pennsylvania and Ohio, two NDPC candidates picked up congressional nominations unopposed. In Indiana, Georgia Irey, the NDPC's former U.S. senatorial candidate, gained an uncontested state assembly nomination. In Iowa, NDPC candidates harvested two state senatorial nominations without opposition.

The NDPC's surprise of the year was in Harris County, Texas (Houston). Although LaRouche received only 389 votes for President in Harris County, Claude Jones, a staunch LaRouche loyalist, was elected Democratic county chairman. He defeated the incumbent, Larry Veselka, by a vote of 54,394 to 51,318. In some respects the incident was a replay of Illinois in 1986. The local party leadership and the media again failed to warn the public about the LaRouche candidate, the regular Democrat again didn't bother to campaign very much, and everyone again ignored clear warning signals—the strong vote totals for local LaRouche candidates in several previous elections (for instance, the 26 percent obtained by Harley Schlanger, the leader of the LaRouche Texas organization, in a 1986 Houston congressional primary).

Although Jones had polled only 5 percent against Veselka in the 1986 county chairmanship race, LaRouche candidates had done well in other Texas county chairmanship races that year. In Houston, of all places, the Democrats should have remained vigilant. Harris County is the second-largest election district in the United States. It has 664 voting precincts and sends more delegates to the Democratic National Convention than many states do. Yet the ousted chairman, Veselka, defended his decision not to campaign vigorously: It had clashed with his duties as a trial lawyer, he said.

Houston Democratic leaders put most of the blame on the voters. "Jones is a simpler name than Veselka, so people went with the familiar," said the county committee's executive director. The argument was similar to that of the Illinois Democrats in 1986, that voters had chosen a Hart over a Pucinsky. Houston Democrats speculated that Jones had deliberately kept a low profile in order to keep the Democrats asleep at the wheel, so that he, too, could take advantage of the name factor. It was also pointed out that the record presidential primary turnout had included many voters unfamiliar with party officeholders—a theory far more plausible than the claim by Illinois Democrats that the Hart-Fairchild victories had been due to a *low* turnout.

The Democrats got off easy this time. The county Democratic leadership met three days after the primary and passed new bylaws stripping the county chairman of all powers, including the power to write checks and handle funds. When the full county committee met to approve the new bylaws, the NDPC could muster only a handful of protesters. Yet it was sheer luck that the LaRouche victory had occurred in an intraparty contest rather than in a race for public office—Jones, unlike Hart and Fairchild, couldn't hurt the Democratic ticket in November.

The LaRouchian electoral record from 1974 through 1988 shows that they have discovered and learned to exploit hitherto unnoticed weaknesses in America's two-party electoral system. And their opportunities for doing so apparently are expanding. An August 1988 *New York Times* article reported a national increase in the number of uncontested primaries and general elections, reflecting the growing clout of incumbency, the greater costs of running for office, and the closer press scrutiny of candidates' personal lives and finances. In the 1988 New York elections, the *Times* said, "at least one of every five members of the House and Legislature does not have a major party opponent and is thus virtually assured of re-election in November." Hence any extremist candidate who chooses to run on a shoestring budget can pick up a hefty percentage of the vote and in many cases an uncontested nomination.

Besides LaRouche, other ultrarightists and neo-Nazis recognize the growing potential for mischief. Robert Miles, America's leading old-style white supremacist, hailed the LaRouchians as "political raiders" after their 1986 Illinois victories. Comparing them to Hitler's SS, he said they had wrought "havoc" in the ranks of "ZOG" (the Zionist Occupation Government). "Well done, Lyndon, well done," he crowed. Former Klansman Robert Weems also praised the NPDC's feat in a front-page article in *The Spotlight.* Leaders of the Populist Party, electoral arm of the Liberty Lobby, called for a LaRouche-style strategy of infiltrating major-party primaries. David Duke, head of the National Association for the Advancement of White People, announced his candidacy for the 1988 Democratic presidential nomination. Like La-Rouche, he compared himself to George Wallace, entered the New Hampshire primary, and applied for government matching funds. Lacking a cadre organization such as LaRouche's, he failed to raise enough money to qualify for federal funds. But on Super Tuesday he received 41,177 votes in five states.

Pollster Michael McKeon believes that the electoral activities of extremists like LaRouche and Duke may "expand exponentially" in the next decade. Democratic and Republican Party leaders have failed to offer blue-collar voters credible solutions to the problems of drugs and street crime. Neither party has done much to reverse the decline of traditional smokestack industries or give long-range hope to America's remaining farm families. Meanwhile, the parties' traditional means of reaching the voter, network television, has been undercut by VCR technology. "The VCR means people can control information coming into their homes," said McKeon. "A lot don't listen to television news anymore. There's a lot of networking going on." McKeon believes that blue-collar voters are looking for ideas that mirror their frustration. "You've got couples working in low-wage or part-time jobs who used to make a good living at a plant that closed down. It simmers and simmers. Fred Flintstone starts picking up on all kinds of strange notions. When the Democrats and Republicans get together to tell him not to vote for a LaRouche candidate, he thinks: What have the Democrats and Republicans done for *me?*"

In this new political arena, the old standards of political measurement may prove inadequate. In mid-1986, pollster Mervin Field asked registered voters in California about LaRouche. Sixty-five percent had heard of him, and 55 percent had an unfavorable opinion of him. Field said the score was the lowest he'd ever found for a politician. Yet the following November, 2,039,744 Californians voted in favor of La-Rouche's AIDS quarantine initiative.

# Fifteen

## LaRouche and the Reagan Revolution

During his eight years of presidential press conferences, Ronald Reagan often took questions from *Executive Intelligence Review* correspondents. On August 3, 1988, the question and answer created a furor. *EIR*'s Nick Benton asked the President if he thought Michael Dukakis should make his medical records public. Benton was alluding to rumors spread by his own NCLC colleagues that the Democratic presidential nominee had sought psychiatric help for depression in the late 1970s. Reagan, grinning, answered: "Look, I'm not going to pick on an invalid." The remark elicited groans of dismay from the assembled reporters, and Reagan half apologized several hours later. Yet the President had managed to transform an unsubstantiated smear into a major international news story. *The New York Times*'s Anthony Lewis wrote that "anyone who thinks that crack was accidental must believe in the Tooth Fairy." Senator Daniel P. Moynihan used even blunter language, charging that the "Big Lie" of Lyndon LaRouche had "reached the Oval Office."

The LaRouchians had started their Dukakis rumors at the convention, with leaflets asking "Is Dukakis the new Senator Eagleton?" Afterward they called daily newspapers around the country, telling each that its competitors were already hot on the story. Fearful of being scooped, editors and reporters reacted predictably. Dukakis headquarters received a barrage of inquiries. Although campaign spokesmen denied everything and the LaRouchians offered no solid evidence, the rumors became newsworthy simply as rumors. The weekend before Reagan's "invalid" quip, a half-dozen important dailies reported the story. The Reverend Moon's *Washington Times* gave it front-page coverage with the sly headline: "Dukakis Psychiatric Rumor Denied." On August 3, a *Wall Street Journal* editorial noted "rumors about [Dukakis's] depression," which supposedly highlighted "how little the American people know about this man."

Dukakis called a press conference to deny the rumor, and within a few days it was overshadowed by the story of Dan Quayle and the National Guard. Syndicated columnists Rowland Evans and Robert Novak noted that the caper apparently had backfired by linking Bush to LaRouche more than Dukakis to the psychiatrist's couch. They charged that weeks before the story broke into print the "political apparatus of Bush campaign manager Lee Atwater was investigating the details and trying to spread the findings without leaving any vice-presidential fingerprints." The column suggested that Atwater's lieutenants had "asked outside GOP operatives" to do the dirty work.

There was a potential bombshell here, but most of the media showed the usual reluctance to cover anything relating to LaRouche. This emboldened his followers to escalate their smear campaign with a sixteen-page pamphlet on Dukakis's alleged mental problems, partiality for the "drug-sex counterculture," and support for "privileges for homosexuals." The initial press run was 100,000 copies, available for fifty cents each in bulk orders of 100 or more.

The press treated the original smear as an isolated incident, but the LaRouche organization had conducted scores of dirty-tricks operations against the Democrats (and occasionally against moderate Republicans on behalf of the Reaganites) over the previous twelve years. Almost totally ignored by the press except in the earliest and least harmful stage, this campaign is probably the largest and certainly the longest-running operation of its type in American electoral history.

The NCLC's wooing of the Republicans began in 1976, when LaRouche was running for President on the U.S. Labor Party ticket. Shortly after Jimmy Carter won the Democratic nomination, LaRouche shifted from seeking votes for himself to diverting votes to President Ford. NCLC defectors recall meetings that summer and fall to plan pro-Ford and anti-Carter activities. *New Solidarity* told the NCLC membership that the nation would face a "near-certain nuclear incineration" if they didn't launch an all-out "stop Carter" effort. On election eve LaRouche appeared on NBC-TV to warn the nation about Carter's alleged mental imbalance—the same charge as against Dukakis, although less artfully presented. The NCLC collected $96,000 on an emergency basis to pay for LaRouche's half-hour speech. *New Solidarity* said the money was raised "with the aid of a group of conservative Republican businessmen"—a statement which NCLC defectors say is true. Federal Election Commission records show large donations to LaRouche's campaign committee the day before the election. The reputed donors were NCLC members covering for the real donors. One conservative donor, who was a member of the board of directors of Ocean Spray, put up $15,000.

After the election, the Republicans joined with the LaRouche organization in Ohio, Pennsylvania, New York, and Wisconsin to challenge the election returns in court on grounds of vote fraud. The objective was to deprive Carter of his edge in Electoral College votes. Republican National Committee executive director Ed Mahe was in contact with the LaRouchians on this and encouraged support for their effort. He became involved at the urging of Representative Guy Vander Jagt (R.-Mich.), chairman of the Republican Congressional Committee and a close friend of President Ford. A spokesman for Vander Jagt told *The Washington Post* that "our Republican interest is similar to theirs on the one issue of voter fraud." In Oklahoma, a prominent publisher hosted a luncheon for a select group of Republicans to hear a pitch for money from LaRouche, while the state finance chairman of the Ford campaign also helped raise funds. A Denver stockbroker serving as director of LaRouche's so-called Citizens Committee for a Fair Election revealed that supporters of Ronald Reagan were also raising money for the suit.

Conservative journalist Morton Blackwell in *The Right Report* described LaRouche's success in wooing top Republicans that year as "a surprising success." LaRouche followers had contacted "literally hundreds of conservatives and Republicans." Their approach had been "unfailingly courteous." One LaRouche spokesman tried to ingratiate himself with Blackwell by saying, "You're committed to the ideals which created this country, as we are."

Many Republicans dropped the LaRouchians after major dailies reported on the curious alliance. But in some cases, the process simply went underground. NCLC defectors say that ongoing ties were established with several well-connected Republicans. One was Hal Short, a former Republican National Committee executive who operated as a political consultant in Washington. Another was Thomas Miner, president of Chicago's Mid-America Committee for International Business and Government Cooperation, who attempted to arrange meetings between LaRouche and several of his wealthy friends. In California, at least one wealthy Reagan backer became temporarily enchanted with the LaRouchians.

LaRouche soon recognized that Reagan was the man of the future. In May 1978 he issued an appeal to Reagan to take the leadership of the party away from flunkies of the "Judas-goat Kissinger" and to unite the party around an international strategy of export of "high technology capital goods." In a February 1979 *New Solidarity* editorial, LaRouche said that Reagan "is without doubt the best" among the potential Republican presidential candidates, exhibiting a "moral quality lacking in all the rest." George Bush was "totally unacceptable" to LaRouche, who said he was fulfilling a "duty" to the Republican Party by pointing this out.

By the summer of 1979, LaRouche sensed the impending conservative ground swell. "The giant nonliberal sections of the Democratic Party and the GOP are ready to bolt from the control of their national leaderships," he wrote. "Any presidential candidate who links up with this coalition will be 'piggy-backed' into the White House." But he expressed concern that Reagan might not move boldly enough to take advantage of the electorate's mood. *New Solidarity* urged Reagan to keep on a conservative course rather than plunging into the "mainstream." The latter strategy, it said, would be "fatal" to his campaign.

Meanwhile LaRouche announced his own candidacy for the Democratic nomination, to raise high the banner of American "nationalism" within the party most vulnerable to infiltration. His decision was encouraged by his pro-Republican friends in the Teamsters union. His New Hampshire campaign was managed by a Detroit businessman close to the Teamsters. Said Rolland McMaster, a top Detroit Teamster leader: "People like it he's a Democrat now." The Teamsters were the only major union in 1980 to support Reagan. Jackie Presser, the NCLC's most important Teamster ally, was appointed to Reagan's transition team and inauguration committee.

In the fall of 1979 LaRouche spent most of his time lambasting his liberal Democratic opponents—Carter, Kennedy, and Jerry Brown. But as primary day approached in New Hampshire, a curious shift in emphasis occurred. LaRouche focused his fire on Reagan's major rival, George Bush. A deluge of anti-Bush propaganda emanated from LaRouche headquarters, focusing on the type of conspiracy theories that John Loeb's Manchester *Union Leader* had long popularized throughout the state. LaRouche charged that Bush was a tool of the Council on Foreign Relations and the Trilateral Commission—a typical Anglophile one-worlder. He also alluded to the "bones in Bush's closet," his membership in Yale University's Skull and Bones.

Similar charges about Bush came from publisher Loeb, the John Birch Society, and Reagan's campaign aides. Reagan himself expressed concern over the Trilateral Commission's "undue influence" in government and politics, although not mentioning Bush's name. But La-Rouche spread the message most vigorously. He had hundreds of volunteers, millions of dollars, and his own printing and typesetting plants. Most important, he had nothing to lose. No intemperate or exaggerated statements could hurt him since he already was branded as an extremist.

It worked. During the final weeks of the primary campaign, Bush repeatedly was asked about the Trilateral Commission, and booed when he attempted to brush off the questions. *The Wall Street Journal* devoted a front-page article to his Trilateral problem, noting that it had become "a genuine, if unlikely issue."

LaRouche himself received only 2 percent of the vote on primary day, but *New Solidarity* suggested that he had helped Reagan to make "Bush's 'blueblood' connection to the Trilateral Commission . . . the key issue in the race." Supposedly the Reagan campaign and Loeb had borrowed their material from Citizens for LaRouche, and LaRouche's own attacks on the "silk-stocking crowd" had "set the tone" for the primary. This tactic had put Bush "on the defensive."

LaRouche was not so obvious as to eulogize Reagan while harassing Bush. In early January he wrote an article describing Reagan as "a man whose career was originally sponsored by Borax, and who is still selling the stuff." But he was confident Reagan would win in November, and fully intended to be on the winning side. He urged the Reagan campaign to continue on an aggressively conservative course. This could "make political mincemeat of the Carter administration," he said. For his own part, no sooner was the New Hampshire primary over than he shifted his main attack to Carter and spent the rest of the season pointing out that the President, like Bush, was a Trilateral Commission alumnus. The New Hampshire effect was not duplicated, but LaRouche did exasperate Commission member David Rockefeller. In a letter to *The New York Times*, Rockefeller complained about the outlandish conspiracy theories, citing specific charges made only by the LaRouchians. The *Times* accompanied his letter with an editorial deploring certain unnamed anti-Trilateralists.

That summer the LaRouchians met a veteran political operative who would become a mentor of sorts. Paul Corbin, a longtime Kennedy family retainer who had served Robert Kennedy as a specialist in sensitive operations, was working for Teddy Kennedy at the Democratic convention. LaRouche had long despised Teddy, entitling one of his political tracts "Beneath the Waters of Chappaquiddick." But at the convention LaRouche hoped to put together a coalition of Kennedy supporters, farm activists, labor leaders, and himself to stop Carter. Corbin was invited to LaRouche's convention command post at Regency House to discuss a deal involving delegates. He was amused to find that LaRouche had no delegates. However, he kept in contact with the NCLC. After Carter was renominated, Corbin was seething with resentment on behalf of Teddy. He offered his services to Reagan campaign manager William Casey, and was hired as an operative to report directly to Casey, James Baker, and Edwin Meese. (Corbin says he told Casey: "I'm not here for pay but I want to stop Carter. If Carter wins, the next nominee will be Mondale.") After linking up with the Reaganites, Corbin developed a relationship with the LaRouchians that lasted for years, although he never agreed with their politics. He attended many of their political events, had dinner with Lyndon and Helga, became fast friends with LaRouche's top Washington operative, Richard Cohen, and provided them with advice on how to gain influence within the Democratic Party. He also chatted frequently on the phone with Jeffrey Steinberg, the chief of LaRouche's security staff.

In 1983 the press uncovered that William Casey had surreptitiously obtained copies of President Carter's television debate briefing book prior to the October 1980 debate. The incident was dubbed "Briefingate." The Justice Department launched an investigation and a congressional committee made inquiries. Casey, who had become CIA director, revealed that he had received certain Carter campaign materials, although not the briefing book, from Paul Corbin.

The LaRouchians were anxious to stop the Briefingate probe, and put out a pamphlet calling it a Communist-liberal plot to undermine Reagan's Strategic Defense Initiative. The morning the story about Corbin hit the press, there was a lengthy phone conversation between Corbin and Jeff Steinberg, according to former security staffer Charles Tate, who took the incoming call. Asked about this in 1988, Corbin didn't recall the conversation but noted that Steinberg frequently solicited his opinion on fast-breaking political events. Corbin denied having anything to do with snatching Carter's briefing book and said he doubted the LaRouchians could have gotten close enough to Carter's inner circle to obtain it. But he speculated that Republican tricksters might be dealing with the LaRouchians against Dukakis. As to his own dealings with the LaRouchians, he said he had just been keeping an eye on them as a favor to another former Kennedy aide.

Shortly after the 1980 Democratic convention, LaRouche launched the National Democratic Policy Committee for long-range organizing and disruption among Democrats. Kenneth Dalto, a Detroit LaRouche follower and businessman with close ties to the Teamsters, was appointed executive director. NDPC literature announced that the goal was to organize a LaRouche-led "conservative" movement within the party, with the aid of the Teamsters and right-wing construction union leaders. This faction would seek national "bipartisanship"—that is, Democratic capitulation to the Reagan agenda. That autumn the NDPC functioned as an unofficial Democrats for Reagan movement attacking Carter nonstop. Two days before the general election the NDPC placed an anti-Carter ad in the *Detroit Free Press.*

After Reagan's election LaRouche tried to call in his chips. He went to Washington with aide Warren Hamerman, who later wrote in *EIR* that they met with "numerous officials of the Reagan transition team, a score of congressmen and senators, and various people with policy influence." (It was shortly after this that LaRouche began planning to move his headquarters to the Washington area.) In early 1981 the LaRouchians held policy seminars on Capitol Hill and provided *EIR* gift subscriptions to cabinet members and leading congressional figures. The most important administration contacts were handled by operatives such as Uwe Parpart and Richard Cohen, who knew how to push the right buttons and mouth the right slogans. They became known as strong supporters of administration policy on defense, the environment, and drugs. They kept their mouths shut about the LaRouche organization's peculiar views on the "Zionist-British organism."

The early stage of the "Reagan Revolution" was an ideal time for the LaRouchians to make inroads. Everything was in flux, and their extremism did not stand out. They seemed just another part of the mosaic of unorthodox ideas along with Ayn Rand's capitalist anarchism, Edward Teller's sci-fi weapons fantasies, and the Federal Emergency Management Agency's plans for emergency rule drafted by cronies of Edwin Meese. The LaRouchians crowed when Reagan stated in his 1981 West Point commencement address: "At Trophy Point, I'm told there are links of a great chain that was forged and stretched across the Hudson to prevent the British fleet from penetrating further into the valley. Today, you are that chain, holding back an evil force that would extinguish the light we've been tending for six thousand years . . ." In the heady atmosphere of the Reagan Revolution's springtime, the LaRouchians could actually convince themselves this was a coded reference to the six-thousand-year struggle between "humanists" and British "oligarchs."

*EIR* obtained interviews in 1981 with many high-level appointees, including Agriculture Secretary John Block, Defense Under Secretary Richard DeLauer, Commerce Under Secretary Lionel Olmer, Treasury Under Secretary Norman Ture, Assistant Attorney General Lowell Jensen, and the chairman of the President's Council of Economic Advisers, Dr. Murray Weidenbaum. In addition, Senator Orrin Hatch (R.-Utah), a friend of the President, and Senator John Tower (R.-Tex.), chairman of the Senate Armed Services Committee, granted interviews. LaRouche told *The Village Voice* in 1987 that all this was his reward for helping sandbag Bush, but in some cases there is a more pedestrian explanation. LaRouche spokesmen took the trouble to testify in favor of a number of Reagan appointees at Senate confirmation hearings, then called up for interviews. LaRouche himself cadged an invitation to have breakfast with Interior Secretary James Watt along with several other supporters of Watt's confirmation. LaRouche hoped for a consultant's post, but Watt recalls feeling "instinctively" that "something was off." (Within months, *New Solidarity* and *Executive Intelligence Review* began to attack Watt as a closet environmentalist.)

The most important LaRouchian inroads were at the National Security Council, where several LaRouche followers became frequent visitors, functioning almost as unofficial consultants. They met numerous times with Richard Morris, right-hand man to National Security Adviser William Clark. Other NSC officials who listened to them included Ray Pollock and Norman Bailey. (*EIR* has mentioned meetings with additional NSC officials, including one visit where Nick Syvriotis transmitted LaRouche's views to a specialist in Soviet affairs.) Morris met several times with LaRouche himself, as did Pollock twice and Bailey at least three times. After leaving the administration in early 1984, Bailey became an economics adviser to the Reagan-Bush reelection campaign, and traveled out to Leesburg for dinner and a political discussion with Lyn and Helga.

LaRouchian efforts in Washington were paralleled by a nationwide effort to serve the Republicans on the local level. Here the LaRouchians became specialists at smearing Democrats. This began well before Reagan's victory, but the first experiments were not very successful. When Jane Byrne won the Chicago Democratic mayoral primary in 1979, the LaRouchians published a scurrilous pamphlet about her, *The Plot to Steal Chicago*. Hundreds of thousands of free copies were distributed. Her Republican opponent repeated some of the charges, and when asked by reporters for proof, cited the LaRouchian pamphlet. Later he felt obliged to issue a sheepish retraction.

The following year the LaRouchians backed conservative Republican candidate Alfonse D'Amato for the U.S. Senate in New York against Congresswoman Elizabeth Holtzman. D'Amato held a joint press conference with LaRouche's National Anti-Drug Coalition, a group devoted to blaming the drug traffic on the Jews. The LaRouchians had attacked Holtzman for her role in founding the Justice Department's

Nazi-hunting unit, the Office of Special Investigations. The OSI, the LaRouchians charged, was a Zionist-British plot against America, and Holtzman was a traitor. They continued these attacks during the campaign, also calling Holtzman soft on drugs. D'Amato failed to publicly disassociate himself from the LaRouchian rhetoric at the time, although he held no more press conferences with them. Incredibly, Holtzman's campaign staff let slip the opportunity to score a major point with Jewish voters. D'Amato squeaked through to a narrow victory in November, riding the coattails of the Reagan landslide.

With the launching of the NDPC, LaRouche had the perfect cover for pro-Republican smear campaigns: One of his followers would enter the Democratic primary against the targeted candidate, disseminating the smears from within. This would soften up the target for the Republican nominee's post-primary onslaught.

In 1982 the LaRouchians used Red-baiting and sexual smears against former California governor Jerry Brown, who was running for the U.S. Senate. The material was issued by NDPC candidate William Wertz's campaign committee. It emphasized Brown's ties to Tom Hayden and Jane Fonda, presenting a wildly exaggerated account of the couple's leftist activities in hopes it would rub off on Brown. Fonda engaged in animalistic sexual behavior, one pamphlet said. Her movies promoted incest. Her mother had committed suicide. Her Malibu home had been the scene of "wild goings-on" prior to Sharon Tate's murder. She, her husband, and Brown were all part of the "Cult of Aquarius" plotting to deprive America of clean safe nuclear energy. The pamphlet advertised campaign bumper stickers: "Clean Up the Fruitflies—Spray Jerry Brown," "Don't Let Jerry Brown Pull Down Your Pants" and "What Spreads Faster than Radiation? Jane Fonda."

The Baltimore LaRouche organization smeared liberal Democratic congresswoman Barbara Mikulski in the 1982 and 1984 primaries, as noted earlier, but the softening-up tactic was best seen in 1986, when Mikulski became the Democratic candidate for the U.S. Senate. She was opposed by Republican Linda Chavez, a Social Democrat turned neoconservative who had served as the chief of President Reagan's public liaison office. The Republicans regarded the race as a crucial one in their battle to keep control of the Senate, and the LaRouchians obliged by lesbian-baiting Mikulski in the primary. NDPC candidate, Debra Freeman, urged Maryland Democrats to "vote straight Democrat." She continued this rhetoric beyond the primary season, calling Mikulski a "dike in the way of progress" and the "ugliest woman in Congress." *New Solidarity* quipped that there should be a prize for anyone "who can correctly identify Mikulski's sex." Chavez adopted a watered-down version of this, calling her opponent a "San Francisco-style Democrat" and warning that she could not "hide in the closet." Supporters also dredged up stories about an alleged affair between Mikulski and a staff aide. But many voters apparently were disgusted by the Freeman-Chavez act. Mikulski won a strong victory in November.

The LaRouchians intervened more successfully in a senatorial race two years earlier in North Carolina. It was a contest of national importance, with former Democratic governor James Hunt attempting to unseat Republican senator Jesse Helms, one of the most powerful figures on Capitol Hill. Former NCLC security staffer Charles Tate says he was told in early 1984 that work would be done on Helms's behalf. This was no surprise to Tate: he knew the security staff had been in touch with a top Helms aide for several years. (During the Falklands war in 1982, Helms had been the only senator to adopt the idea, also held by LaRouche, that the United States should invoke the Monroe Doctrine against "British imperialism" and in defense of Argentina's junta. The NDPC had issued a pro-Argentina propaganda pamphlet, including statements by LaRouche and Helms.)

Security staffers discussed sending an infiltrator into the Hunt campaign, but decided they could do the job best through undercover phone calls. Tate was present in the New York security office while a black NCLC member made calls to gay activists backing Hunt. The caller claimed to be from the *Chicago Metro,* a black weekly. Given Helms's notorious racism, the persons being interviewed all assumed the caller was anti-Helms.

Meanwhile articles linking Hunt to the gay community began to appear in *The Landmark,* a now-defunct conservative weekly published by Chapel Hill realtor Robert Windsor. *The Landmark* published excerpts from what apparently were taped conversations with various Hunt supporters in Chapel Hill, New York City, and elsewhere. The persons interviewed included gay activists as well as liberal socialites and civil rights leaders. The idea was to show that Hunt was getting substantial local and national support from constituencies disliked by many conservative Democrats. There were also articles suggesting Hunt was himself gay. "Jim Hunt Is Sissy, Prissy, Girlish and Effeminate," read one headline, followed by "Is Jim Hunt homosexual? . . . Is he AC and DC? Has he kept a deep dark secret in his political closet all of his adult life?" Hundreds of thousands of free copies of *The Landmark* were circulated throughout the state, especially in rural areas. Like any wily campaigner, Helms publicly disassociated himself from the false charges about Hunt's sex life (and there is no evidence that Helms personally knew of the LaRouchians' involvement), but *The Landmark*'s press run increased sharply right before election day. In the wake of Helms's narrow victory, many North Carolinians believed the smear campaign had tipped the balance.

At least some of the tapes used by *The Landmark* came from La-Rouche's security staff. In early March 1984, a LaRouchian phoned Virginia Apuzzo, director of the National Gay and Lesbian Task Force, pretending to be a news reporter. Charles Tate says he heard the call being made and "saw the tape recorder running." A transcript of Apuzzo's remarks appeared in the March 29 issue of *The Landmark*, which also included excerpts from a phone conversation with Lightning Brown, a gay activist in Chapel Hill. Brown says he received two calls. The first was from Grant Duay, a supposed reporter for a gay weekly, the *New York City News*. Brown said that Duay "asked about my fund raising for Hunt. The details ended up in *The Landmark* right away —it was frightening." Duay was in fact a notorious LaRouche operative who had previously used the *New York City News* as his cover for interviewing and taping political opponents of LaRouche. (In 1986 Duay would be arrested in Manhattan as part of a homosexual child pornography ring.)

Brown's second call was from the black LaRouchian. "I told him I felt sorry for the publisher of *The Landmark* and that I had prayed for him," said Brown, who is a Quaker. "My remark later appeared in *The Landmark*. It was supposed to prove I was a devil worshipper."

*Landmark* publisher Windsor was in close contact with the LaRouchians throughout that spring. He accompanied Tom Allred, Hunt's LaRouchian opponent in the Democratic primary, on a trip to Raleigh. "We toured the legislature and I introduced him to Liston Ramsey, speaker of the house, and many other people," Windsor wrote in a front-page article about Allred. In a 1987 phone interview Windsor said he had also attended an NDPC meeting held to recruit North Carolina conservatives to run on the LaRouche slate. Windsor claimed that a number of his conservative friends had contributed money to the NDPC, including one $50,000 contribution.

The LaRouchians' biggest effort ever was against the Democrats' 1984 national ticket. What they were planning was suggested by their attitude toward the party's May 1983 telethon. They called it a "disgustathon" and a cover for the laundering of drug money. *New Solidarity* gloated that "complaint and insult calls reportedly outnumbered favorable responses 9 to 1," and that party leaders believed but could not prove that someone "intentionally jammed their incoming lines." (The LaRouchians had scores of WATS line phones in their national and regional offices and had practiced jamming before.

That fall they went after Democratic front-runner Walter Mondale with insulting leaflets and carefully staged disruptions of his campaign appearances and press conferences. As against Bush in 1980, they used the Trilateral Commission issue, publishing a list of Mondale advisers said to be Trilateral members and citing his own membership as proof that he was a tool of "Kissinger and Rockefeller." At the time of the Grenada invasion they charged that Mondale foreign policy adviser Robert Pastor and former Carter aide Dr. Peter Bourne had been in cahoots with the ultraleft military regime overthrown by the invasion. In fact, Pastor and Bourne had merely provided advice to Bourne's father, who ran a medical school on the island, on how to steer safely through a dangerous situation. The LaRouchians circulated a pamphlet asserting that Pastor and Bourne had formerly been associated with the Institute for Policy Studies. When Mondale was asked about the Grenada allegations at an Oklahoma press conference, he complained about the smear campaign. But he never took any steps against the LaRouchians, and never raised the issue of their apparent ties to the Reagan administration.

The heart of the 1984 LaRouche operation was the NDPC candidates' movement, a spectacular eruption of approximately 2,000 candidates into Democratic primaries. This was not part of the normal electoral process within the party but a deliberate disruption orchestrated from without. Most of the candidates had no commitment to the party. Some were LaRouche cadre, others were senior citizens only dimly conscious of what they were doing. Many were longtime ultraconservatives well aware that the point was to help Reagan. The rhetoric of their campaigns was anti-Mondale, rarely criticizing the Republicans. They staunchly supported Reagan's key policies such as Star Wars. In effect, they were an extension of the Republican presidential campaign into the ranks of the Democratic Party.

The media as well as the Mondale campaign utterly failed to spot what was happening. Instead, they focused on a sideshow—the heckling of Mondale by conservative student activists who apparently were organized by Reagan operatives. No one probed LaRouche's hundred-times-larger operation.

In March 1984 NBC-TV's *First Camera* aired an exposé of LaRouche's ties to the Reagan administration and especially to the National Security Council. The report also described the NCLC's anti-Semitism, history of violence, and LaRouche's discussion of killing President Carter. Afterward, Democratic National Chairman Charles Manatt appealed to President Reagan to "repudiate" the LaRouchians and "order officials of his administration to cease all contacts with these extremists." White House spokesman Larry Speakes's reply was that the administration talks to "various people who may have information that might prove helpful to us. . . . Any American citizen, we'd be glad to talk to." In other words, there was to be no public repudiation of LaRouche. Later that spring, the Reagan campaign made much over the Democrats' failure to repudiate Jesse Jackson. Reagan spoke of the "insidious cancer" in the Democratic Party. "We have no place for haters in America," he said. He and Bush hounded Mondale about Louis Farrakhan even though the Democratic candidate had repeatedly and unequivocally denounced him. But in one sense Mondale merely got what he deserved. Although he could have shut up the Republicans by uttering the magic words "LaRouche" and "Nazi," he was curiously too timid to do it.

LaRouche filed a libel suit against NBC and the Anti-Defamation League regarding the *First Camera* show. At the trial in the fall of 1984, he called former NSC aide Richard Morris as a witness. Morris, who had moved to the Interior Department with Reagan crony Clark, was in effect the administration's voice at the trial. He studiously avoided any negative statements about LaRouche and praised him to the jury by affirming that he had provided "good intelligence" to the government. Roy Innis, the head of CORE and one of the Reagan administration's few black allies, appeared as a LaRouche character witness, telling the jury he didn't think his friend was at all racist or anti-Semitic. (Innis was a veteran at such denials. Back in 1973, after Uganda dictator Idi Amin called Hitler a great man, Innis had declined to criticize Amin, saying he had "no records to prove" that Hitler had ever been an enemy of black people.) Although Innis's support for LaRouche was in every respect the equivalent of Jesse Jackson's links to Farrakhan, Reagan praised Innis in a *New York Times* interview the following February for supporting the administration's social agenda. The jury in the NBC trial, however, was not fooled by Innis. They found the defendants innocent of libel and awarded NBC $3 million in damages on a counterclaim against LaRouche.

Although *The Washington Post* and *The New Republic* published in-depth probes that winter of LaRouche's White House ties, he continued to enjoy immunity from any open administration criticism. His fund raisers began calling elderly Reagan supporters all over the country. Their pitch was: Give us your life's savings to help President Reagan and keep America strong. This was how LaRouche rewarded the Reagan administration for not speaking out against him.

In 1986, as we have seen, the victory of LaRouchian candidates for lieutenant governor and secretary of state in the Illinois Democratic primaries guaranteed the reelection of Republican governor Jim Thompson. This was LaRouche's greatest service yet for the GOP (although an unplanned one). When Reagan went to Chicago to campaign for Thompson, he was asked his opinion on the LaRouchians.

His reply: "I'm not here to do battle with him [LaRouche]; but I don't believe I could find myself in agreement with him on just about everything."

In the following months the LaRouchians received amazing vote totals in state after state. The Democratic Party leadership tried to explain this away as a fluke or a failure to be "vigilant." But the Republicans knew better. They adopted the chief LaRouchian theme, support for SDI. Evans and Novak wrote in October 1986 that the "unlikely conversion" of SDI from an "outer space fantasy . . . to a highly positive political issue" had given Reagan a "potent last-minute weapon" in the congressional elections. They cited race after race in which Republican candidates were attacking Democratic incumbents for failing to back SDI. Reagan had served notice, they wrote, that "any Democrat who opposes strategic defense is fair game." Precisely the approach the LaRouchians had used in hundreds of Democratic primaries. LaRouche may not be the intellectual author of SDI, but he can lay claim to being the founder of SDI politics.

# Sixteen

# The Art
# of Scapegoating

In an October 1987 review of *Veil,* Bob Woodward's Iran-Contra book, LaRouche held forth on the subject of propaganda. "There is no morality, no truth," in a propaganda war, he wrote. "A choice is made to boost or to discredit this or that personality, group, issue, or policy, and the mechanics of the psy-ops [psychological operations] trade go to work without scruple to get the job done."

The statement referred to the CIA and the KGB, but LaRouche might as well have been talking about the NCLC. Few organizations have ranged the ideological map with such adroit inconsistency. First they attacked the U.S. government for being soft on communism, then they criticized it for giving aid to the Nicaraguan Contras. They praised the NAACP for its support of nuclear power, then they met with Ku Klux Klan leaders and bemoaned the decline of the white race. When they enjoyed access to the Reagan administration, LaRouche said Reagan was "touched by greatness." After the administration cut them off, LaRouche called Reagan a man of low intelligence, "pussywhipped" by the First Lady.

The inconsistencies sometimes reflect LaRouche's personal pique.

More often they arise from his dualistic view of politics—that all groups inevitably split into factions representing sharply opposed views. Thus, the LaRouchians condemn the bad Mafia of drug pushers but praise the good Mafia of redeemable patriotic labor racketeers. They rail against the bad Communists who, like Gorbachev, promote *glasnost,* but express admiration for the good Communists who adhere to old-fashioned Stalinist views. They distinguish between good and bad Freemasons, good and bad Knights of Malta, good and bad Klansmen. They also believe that the war of "humanist" vs. "oligarchical" tendencies is within the soul of individual world leaders, which makes it perfectly logical to praise Reagan one moment and savage him the next.

Underneath all this, LaRouche continues to pursue his anti-Semitic Grand Design through front organizations, coalitions with outside groups, election campaigns, pseudo-academic conferences, and what he calls the "naming of names." His propaganda methods are far more complex than those of the Ku Klux Klan and other extremist groups. He will start by selecting a legitimate issue such as AIDS, the farm crisis, or defense spending. Giving an appearance of sincere concern, his followers often research the issue thoroughly and come up with proposals that make sense. But they always announce that an evil plot is blocking implementation of their proposals and attempt to steer the campaign in an anti-Semitic direction. Sometimes they employ obvious euphemisms—"Zionist," "usurer," "shylock," or "cabalist." Other times, they refer to "monetarists" (as in moneylender), "Venetian bankers" (as in *The Merchant of Venice),* or "Our Crowd" (from the title of Stephen Birmingham's best-selling book about prominent New York Jews). They also use esoteric code words like "British," "Babylonian," "Whore of Babylon," and "Mesopotamian," which may puzzle the average person but strike a chord with anti-Semites of the old school.

Another tactic is to highlight well-known Jewish families or individuals. The Bronfman family (Seagram's), oil tycoon Armand Hammer, philanthropist Max Fisher, or investment banker Felix Rohatyn are either blamed for problems with which they have no connection or assigned a greatly exaggerated responsibility. If an individual happens to be a mobster or some other reprehensible type, the LaRouchians will emphasize his misdeeds to the exclusion of those of his Gentile associates. (To the LaRouchians, Meyer Lansky *was* the Mafia in his day; the Sicilians hardly counted.) LaRouche's publications also strive to hit mainstream Jews with guilt by association, through the use of semantic tags—e.g., "Lansky's ADL," "Lansky's Israel."

The list of those to be attacked includes many non-Jews, such as Senator Moynihan of New York or former Secretary of State Alexander

Haig. But the attacks usually focus on their support for Israel or their friendship with prominent Jews, and may allude to real or rumored Jewish ancestry. In a 1978 piece, LaRouche called Energy Secretary James R. Schlesinger an "imp of evil," born Jewish and "a convert to Lutheranism." While Schlesinger does come from Jewish ancestry, LaRouche's statement basically reflected a traditional practice of anti-Semites—call anyone you don't like a Jew. Slyly, LaRouche added that Schlesinger's alleged Jewishness was really "irrelevant" since his "morality is neither Jewish nor Christian." LaRouche failed to explain why, if it was irrelevant, he had bothered to mention it.

Through such tricks, LaRouchian propaganda blames the Jews for just about every problem facing the average American. The message is carefully tailored for different constituencies. Farmers are told that Wall Street "monetarists" are behind the agricultural crisis and the decline of the family farm. Teamsters union leaders are told that liberal Jewish foundations are behind the government's crackdown on union corruption. The AFL-CIO rank and file is told that its leaders are Zionist agents who don't really care about bread-and-butter problems. Black college students are told that Jews exploit black entertainers and that the Anti-Defamation League secretly funds the Ku Klux Klan. The public in general is told that Jews are inveterate conspirators who planned the slayings of Abraham Lincoln, John F. Kennedy, and Jimmy Hoffa, and are trying to assassinate LaRouche.

The LaRouchians weave into these charges a toned-down version of the "blood libel"—the belief, widely held in medieval Europe, that Jews kidnap Christian children and use them in ritual sacrifices. Various wealthy American and Israeli Jews are accused of pushing drugs to American youth, sexually molesting them, or teaching them immorality via rock music and Hollywood movies.

LaRouchian propaganda also tries to raise doubts about the patriotism of American Jews. When a Pentagon official, Jonathan Pollard, was arrested as an Israeli spy in 1986, the LaRouchians portrayed him as typical of Jews in the U.S. government. In March 1987, *New Solidarity* published on its front page a list of Jews in the Reagan administration, described as agents of a "subversive parallel government." These individuals, including Assistant Defense Secretary Richard Perle and Geneva arms negotiator Max Kampelman, were identified as Jewish via the label "JINSA operatives" (a reference to the Washington-based Jewish Institute for National Security Affairs). An *Executive Intelligence Review* special report described them as "not simply 'Zionist Lobby' activists, but hardcore Mossad operatives." A LaRouchian editorial urged a general "housecleaning" to get these associates of the Israeli "mafia" out of the U.S. government "once and for all."

The loyalty issue has been a standard anti-Semitic tactic ever since the French army captain Alfred Dreyfus was falsely convicted of treason in 1894. But the LaRouchians add another twist (as did Hitler in *Mein Kampf,* and Stalin in his polemics against Trotsky), claiming that the Jews are not just spies but political agents who secretly manipulate policy to weaken the nation's will to resist its enemies.

LaRouchian publications also depict Israel as providing the Soviet Union with intelligence culled from a vast network of Zionists in the U.S. government. It is said to be the "main intermediary country which Moscow uses in stealing U.S. sensitive equipment"—the United States gives Israel high-tech weaponry, and the Israelis pass it on.

Such themes go hand in hand with attempts to trivialize the crimes of the Third Reich. In 1978 LaRouche dismissed the Holocaust as mostly "mythical," while his wife, Helga, called it a "swindle." *New Solidarity* attacked the Holocaust curriculum in New York public schools as "viciously anti-German" and as "filth," saying that any teacher who taught it should be fired. When the television movie *Holocaust* was aired in 1979, *New Solidarity* denounced it. In the early 1980s, LaRouchian publications began to defend Nazi war criminals as innocent victims of persecution. The Justice Department's investigation of Tscherim Soobzokov, a former SS officer, was attacked as an "outrageously corrupt, KGB-modeled witchhunt." When he was seriously wounded in a 1984 pipe-bomb explosion at his New Jersey home, local LaRouchians called a press conference and accused the Anti-Defamation League and the Israeli government of complicity in the bombing. They demanded the appointment of a federal special prosecutor. When the FBI refused to take their allegations seriously, and Soobzokov died, *New Solidarity* published a cartoon of an FBI badge dripping with blood. "Blood on Hands of FBI, ADL," the headline said.

Austrian President Kurt Waldheim seems to be another innocent victim. When the World Jewish Congress produced evidence of his Nazi past in 1986, *Executive Intelligence Review* dismissed it as a "gigantic hoax." World Jewish Congress chairman Edgar Bronfman, *EIR* added, is a "Meyer Lansky-linked organized crime figure."

President Reagan's 1985 trip to the graves of SS officers at Bitburg in West Germany was no policy blunder in *New Solidarity*'s view, but a "courageous" action to strengthen the Western alliance. It gave the German people "a sense of pride in the historical importance of Germany's contribution to all mankind." Jewish leaders who opposed the trip such as Holocaust survivor Elie Wiesel, acted as anti-German "racists" and as dupes of Soviet propaganda. "There is no limit," *Executive Intelligence Review* wrote, "to the psychotic frenzy [Jewish leaders] can be driven to by guilt and [Soviet] blackmail."

Despite all this, LaRouche and his followers vehemently deny they are anti-Semitic. They say that the real anti-Semites are the Zionists, who keep the Jews in an inward-turned nationalistic frame of mind and use them on behalf of nefarious oligarchical political purposes. One of the supposed aims of the LaRouchians is to liberate the Jews from Zionism so they can lead fuller lives.

Zionism and the Jews are not the LaRouchians' only obsessions. They agitate around a variety of issues that appear innocuous and often intriguing: a crash program for fusion, a manned trip to Mars, new irrigation projects for the Rocky Mountain states. Yet there's always a catch to it. Support for space exploration becomes a crusade for a trillion-dollar government project necessitating centralization of the economy—an indirect way of promoting national socialist economics.

America's law-and-order problems likewise become a pretext for nudging the public toward accepting police-state methods. In 1978 LaRouche predicted a massive surge of domestic terrorism would soon hit America. The nation's survival would depend on "surgically precise" action against the controllers of the plot—e.g., the Zionists. When the terrorist wave failed to materialize, the LaRouchians simply linked the idea of extra-constitutional surgery to the drug problem, urging a mobilization of the armed forces.

In this they followed the basic principle of fascist agitation: Pick a problem that is real, highly visible, easy to understand, and, above all, charged with emotion, then offer a simplistic solution. They are attuned to such issues and the ever-shifting possibilities for demagoguery because of their constant dialogue with the public. LaRouche followers are at the nation's airports every day, all day, talking politics with quintessential middle Americans. Or they are on the phone for long hours as fund raisers, sounding out the views of potential donors. As candidates for public office, they fan out each primary season to working-class neighborhoods and farm communities across the country, not just to ask for votes but to engage people in serious discussions. Illinois pollster Michael McKeon has watched them at work at shopping centers. He observes that a LaRouche campaign worker may experience rejection from nine out of ten passersby, but the latter will often communicate the reason for their negative response. They will suggest new and more relevant issues even while flinging the leaflet back in the canvasser's face with a curse. The LaRouchians listen carefully to angry people, sometimes perceiving things about the public's mood before the pollsters and professional politicians do.

The best example is the AIDS issue. By the fall of 1985, LaRouche recognized that it was about to become the scariest issue of the decade. He concocted the slogan "Spread Panic, not AIDS!" The entire human race, he claimed, would face extinction if stern measures weren't taken immediately against gay people and mosquitoes. Offering himself as the only leader willing to act with the necessary ruthlessness, he picked California as his first battleground. In the summer of 1986 his followers fanned out through most of the state's fifty-eight counties. Operating through a committee called PANIC, they collected over 700,000 signatures for a ballot initiative calling for quarantine of AIDS victims. The signatures withstood all legal challenges, and the measure was placed on the ballot as Proposition 64. It received nationwide publicity and became a major issue in California politics. Congressman William Dannemeyer (R.-Cal.) championed it and became its respectable front man. Ironically, Dannemeyer had chaired the Republican Study Committee two years earlier when it produced a report warning conservatives not to be taken in by LaRouche propaganda and pointing out that LaRouche's intent was to "disrupt our democratic system." Dannemeyer now said, as did some other California conservatives, that he was supporting Proposition 64 solely on its merits. Gay organizations, the health professions, labor unions, and the Democratic Party launched a countereffort, warning the public that "political extremist Lyndon LaRouche" was behind the measure. (One of the anti-Proposition 64 groups was even called "Stop LaRouche.") Gay organizations charged that when LaRouche said quarantine he really meant concentration camps.

LaRouche's cadres were preprogrammed for the quarantine campaign. For years words like "faggot" and "queer" had peppered NCLC publications, along with allegations that child molesters, Satanists, and Communists control the gay rights movement. The articles also suggested that homosexuality is a characteristically Jewish condition and that rich Jews encourage it to undermine Western civilization. When the AIDS crisis erupted, LaRouche blamed the "shylocks" for being too cheap to pay for research crash programs.

His gay-equals-Jewish canard dates back to the 1970s, when *New Solidarity* raved against the "faggot politics" of "Zionist-supporting" gay activists. *New Solidarity* published a cartoon series in which prominent New York Jews were shown in Roman togas at a banquet sponsored by the "Emperor of Homohattan," Mayor Ed Koch. In the early 1980s LaRouchian publications accused prominent Jews and pro-Zionist Gentiles of being part of an international "Homintern." LaRouche wrote *Kissinger: The Politics of Faggotry,* a crude and defamatory leaflet on his longtime Symbolic Jew. According to LaRouche, Kissinger's alleged "heathen sexual inclinations are merely an integral part of a larger evil," and Kissinger is "psychologically" part of a "distinct species." In the context of LaRouche's biological-racial theories about the

Jewish "species," the equation of Jewishness and "faggotry" was unmistakable.

LaRouche also taught that the alleged pathology of the Jewish family, especially the mother's possessiveness, produces psychosexual aberrations in young Jews. A 1986 *New Solidarity* item, "Jewish Mothers in the Age of Aquarius," joked that homosexuality is the natural result.

That the Jewish oligarchy deliberately promotes homosexuality is suggested by LaRouche's references to "sodomic," "pederastic," and "lesbian" practices within oligarchy-controlled "cults" such as Freemasonry and the Quakers. In a November 1985 speech, he said AIDS was a "man-made evil" linked to these "cults out of Babylon." He further developed this theme in "The End of the Age of Aquarius?," a rambling discourse on AIDS that included attacks on the "Babylonians," the "British," "usurers," and "cabalists." His conclusion: "Homosexuality was organized in the United States. It wasn't something that sprang from the weeds . . . It was organized . . ."

In an article on government monetary policy, LaRouche claimed that the money for the necessary public health measures against AIDS could only come from funds currently being used to service the international debt. But the "shylocks" were blocking this: "Shylock demands his pound of flesh, and cares not in the least whether the collection kills the debtor." The implication was that anyone who opposed Proposition 64 was probably acting on behalf of powerful Jews. LaRouche lashed out at "Meyer Lansky's" Hollywood and a *New Solidarity* columnist joked that the Anti-Defamation League had launched a stop-LaRouche committee called "AiDsL."

LaRouche's AIDS propaganda bears a striking resemblance to Hitler's on syphilis as set forth in *Mein Kampf.* Syphilis, like AIDS, is sexually transmitted, and in the 1920s there was no cure. Hitler focused on it because of his obsession with racial purity and his fear that the Aryan bloodline was being contaminated. Just as he blamed the spread of syphilis on its victims, especially prostitutes, so LaRouche blames gays for spreading AIDS. Hitler believed that sexual promiscuity and prostitution were the result of "Jewification of our spiritual life and mammonization of our mating instinct" and thus called syphilis the "Jewish disease." LaRouche refers to AIDS as the "Babylonian disease."

Hitler's answer to syphilis was to call for a quarantine of prostitutes and other infected persons. "There must be no half measures; the gravest and most ruthless decisions will have to be made. It is a half measure to let incurably sick people steadily contaminate the remaining healthy ones. . . . [I]f necessary, the incurably sick will be pitilessly segregated—a barbaric measure for the unfortunate who is struck by it but a blessing for his fellow man and posterity." LaRouche, in "The End of the Age of Aquarius?," urges much the same solution for AIDS: "We've got to contain it, we can't find a miracle cure that fast; we're going to have to use methods of public health, which means we're going to have to put away every carrier until they can no longer carry."

The parallels continue. Hitler said regarding syphilis victims that there "is no freedom to sin at the cost of posterity." LaRouche says it's "nonsense" to be concerned about the "civil rights" of AIDS victims. Hitler criticized the authorities for not "summon[ing] up the energy to take decisive measures" and for their attitude of "total capitulation." LaRouche says the U.S. government is afraid to "estrange the votes of a bunch of faggots and cocaine sniffers." Hitler said that for people who refuse to fight to save their own health, "the right to live in this world of struggle ends." LaRouche says that unless the American people change their attitude toward AIDS and their "moral direction," they will "no longer [be] fit to survive morally, and will not survive."

*Mein Kampf* and "The End of the Age of Aquarius?" both express a concern for public health and describe quarantine as necessary in order to save lives. Yet Hitler clearly stated that his syphilis-fighting program masked a higher goal: The Nazi Party leadership, he said, must "succeed in representing to the people the partial goal which now has to be achieved, or rather conquered, as the one which is solely and alone worthy of attention, on whose conquest everything depends. The great mass of people cannot see the whole road ahead of them without growing weary and despairing of the task." LaRouche is equally candid, linking the struggle for an AIDS quarantine with the need for a new ideological "paradigm" in America. *New Solidarity* even suggests that AIDS might become the springboard for a nationalist revolution.

What America could expect in the wake of such a revolution is revealed in NDPC propaganda urging a roundup of prostitutes, gays, drug users—anyone who might have been exposed to the AIDS virus— and their incarceration in "special isolation hospitals, under prison guard if necessary." LaRouche's "Aquarius" article also discusses the possible need to "hang" or "burn" those responsible for spreading AIDS. Given the virtual equation of Jews and gays, Proposition 64 becomes simply an extension of earlier LaRouchian calls for an anti-Zionist Special Prosecutor's Office and for the "immediate elimination" of Zionists from American public life.

When two-thirds of California's voters rejected Proposition 64 in November 1986, the media depicted this as a defeat for LaRouche. Yet it actually was a major LaRouche victory. His measure received over two million votes in the teeth of an opposition that outspent the LaRouchians ten to one. In some rural counties it received the support of over 40 percent of the voters. Apart from these election statistics, LaRouche scored a major ideological breakthrough for neo-Nazism in America. He took a previously taboo idea—enforced isolation for the Scapegoat—and elevated it into a topic of legitimate discourse. He did this by reframing the discourse in pseudo-medical terms and targeting a minority less well organized than the Jews. Proposition 64's opponents, frightened by its implications but lacking a full understanding of LaRouche's ideology or of fascism in general, were maneuvered into appearing on talk shows with the LaRouchians, thus lending an aura of legitimacy to their extremist ideas.

As the campaign intensified, some opponents of Proposition 64 developed a strategy to cut through the smoke screen and expose the hidden political agenda. Howard Wallace, the coordinator of the San Francisco Labor Council's work against Proposition 64, stated in the SFLC newsletter: "The real purpose of this initiative has little to do with either AIDS or public health. . . . [The LaRouchian] purpose is to build their small corps of storm troopers into a larger one. . . . In the grand tradition of Hitler's Nazis, they're taking the path of least resistance: attacking those who suffer in some measure from social stigma . . ." But too much of the literature opposing Proposition 64 continued to be confused, jumbling together the political and pseudo-medical issues and dismissing the LaRouchians as kooks or cultists.

In the following year the quarantine idea became "respectable" nationally. Congressman Dannemeyer appeared on TV talk shows to discuss it as just one more proposal in the marketplace of ideas. Several other prominent New Right politicians expressed interest in the concept. In mid-1987 President Reagan's domestic policy adviser, Gary Bauer, when questioned about it, coolly commented: "I don't see any evidence *at this point* that a quarantine in the *traditional* sense would be *particularly* effective" (italics added). Thus does LaRouchian propaganda spread like ripples in a pond.

LaRouche meanwhile developed a more extreme solution for AIDS. Praising Western Europe's skinheads for beating up gays, he said they spontaneously expressed the "conspiratorial and other ethical characteristics" of a nationalist revolution. He suggested that lynching might be the next step—in Catholic countries they'd pick off the gays one by one, while in Protestant countries lynching would become a mass movement. The lynchers, LaRouche said, would perhaps be remembered as the "only political force which acted to save the human species from extinction."

From this, he passed over to the concept of an anti-gay Holocaust, stopping just short of advocacy. "The only solution" to AIDS, he said, "is either public health measures including isolation as necessary, or

'accelerated deaths' of carriers." He added: "The point of no return
. . . is coming up very fast. If the violence comes, the politicians, the
courts, and the governments will have no one to blame but themselves.
They left a desperate, terrified population no other choice."

Meanwhile, public concern over AIDS reached a high pitch. An
American Medical Association poll found that 50 percent of the American public believed all necessary measures should be taken to stop
AIDS "even if it means some people might have their rights violated."
LaRouche continued his inflammatory propaganda, claiming that AIDS
was spread by casual contact and that the majority of heterosexual
Americans would soon be infected if his draconian measures were not
adopted. His followers were on the phones at their telephone boiler
rooms in Leesburg, Virginia, night and day, calling thousands of Americans to warn them of impending disaster and to solicit funds to pay for
more propaganda. In California, LaRouche's PANIC committee, undeterred by Proposition 64's defeat, easily collected over 700,000 signatures to place a second initiative on the ballot, this time in the presidential primary election. LaRouche purchased a half hour on network
television to present his views on AIDS three days before the primary.
The initiative again failed to pass but received over 1,700,000 votes.

While this represented less votes than the first time (because of a
lower voter turnout), the percentage of supporters had risen from 29
percent to 32 percent. (In November 1988 a third AIDS crackdown
measure appeared on the ballot, this one sponsored by Congressman
Dannemeyer and other conservatives without LaRouche's direct involvement. Although polls in September indicated that it had majority
support, it failed to pass.)

LaRouche had demonstrated the vulnerability of the public, when
frightened and angry, to the lure of thinly veiled fascist measures. He
had desensitized millions to the idea of rounding up unpopular minorities. His California ballot initiatives had revealed that many Americans
with healthy biological immune systems have no political immune systems at all.

# Seventeen

# Get Kissinger!

On February 7, 1982, two LaRouchians met the Devil, not in a grave-yard at midnight, but in the well-lit terminal at Newark International Airport. They abandoned their literature table and rushed to exorcise him with a barrage of hostile questions. "Jesus Christ," muttered Dr. Henry Kissinger, their longtime hate figure. He and his wife, Nancy, kept walking toward the boarding area, en route to Boston, where he was scheduled to undergo triple-bypass heart surgery.

"Dr. Kissinger," shouted twenty-eight-year-old Ellen Kaplan, "is it true that you sleep with young boys at the Carlyle Hotel?" It was a standard LaRouchian accusation. Nancy Kissinger would have ignored it on other occasions, but she was distraught by the prospect of her husband's operation. According to her attorney, her hand reached out and came in contact, very lightly, with Kaplan's throat. Others assert that her actions were less restrained. Whatever the truth, Kaplan re-treated, and the Kissingers continued on their way.

A trivial event, one might say. Yet its consequences included a war-rant for Mrs. Kissinger's arrest, a heavily publicized assault trial, and a LaRouchian harassment campaign against Dr. Kissinger on four continents. This campaign, waged from mid-1982 through late 1984, is unique in the annals of radical protest against public figures. It involved a torrent of propaganda attacks in at least six languages, carefully planned disruptions of Kissinger's public appearances, the planting of defamatory rumors in the international press, scores of malicious pranks, and the expenditure of millions of dollars on network television ads denouncing him.

Some observers have viewed LaRouche's anti-Kissinger campaign merely as an example of irrationalism and cultism—the expenditure of enormous resources on an effort better suited to an insane asylum. Yet there were coolheaded pragmatic reasons for it. LaRouche had gained a measure of credibility with the Reagan administration over the previous year. He had to disguise his anti-Semitism better.

LaRouche's solution was to select a Symbolic Jew. Kissinger, with his thick Central European accent, "Semitic" features, rationalistic worldview, and reputation for secretive highest-level intrigue, was the perfect choice. The fact that he was Jewish was almost universally known—indeed, he was probably the most famous Jew in the world. What's more, he was a controversial one, disliked by many conservatives and by almost all leftists. Even many moderates had questions about his record as secretary of state. A campaign against him, no matter how nasty, could gain an unspoken sympathy across the political spectrum. Building on this dislike of Kissinger, the LaRouchians could turn it into a dislike of his alleged archetypal qualities.

The LaRouchians had attacked Kissinger on an overtly anti-Semitic basis throughout the late 1970s. When *New Solidarity* called for the "immediate elimination" of the "Jewish Lobby" from American public life, it said the first stage should be "the naming of names, such as Henry A. Kissinger." A subsequent editorial railed against infiltration of Washington by agents of the "Zionist-British organism." Heading the list was the "Israeli-British" agent Kissinger. When Kissinger's *The White House Years* was published in 1980, a review by LaRouche in *EIR* used *Mein Kampf*-style images of infection and contamination. America's moral "rot," he said, was due to "such alien 'Typhoid Marys' of immorality" as Kissinger. LaRouche then dashed off *The Pestilence of Usury*, a pamphlet sold at airport literature tables. Among the villains was Kissinger, said to be the servant of oligarchs "far worse than Hitler . . . nasty, evil."

America's traditional neo-Nazis and white supremacists recognized what LaRouche was doing. The Christian Defense League, a hate group based in Louisiana, developed its own line of anti-Kissinger pamphlets mimicking LaRouche's rhetoric. Robert Miles, the premier theoretician of the Aryan Nation/Identity crowd, stated in a 1984 arti-

cle: "We agree with LaRouche on . . . his efforts to dislodge the Kis-
singerites from positions of influence." Miles also praised LaRouche
for "exposing the neo-atheist materialism of Kissinger to the dismay of
the Talmudists."

LaRouche once again reframed reality so that his Jewish followers
could tell themselves that the anti-Kissinger campaign was "anti-Nazi."
He called it Operation Nuremberg, an effort to punish Kissinger for
alleged crimes a "hundred times worse than Hitler's." The government
would never punish Kissinger; only the NCLC could do it. The NCLC
might lack the power to exact the ultimate penalty, but it could psychologically torment Kissinger. LaRouche used his vaunted profiling technique to determine what Kissinger supposedly feared the most—ridicule. The NCLC set out to confront him with it, much like the
interrogator in *Nineteen Eighty-four* who confronted Winston Smith with
rats. LaRouche called this "psychological terror."

He framed his plan in such a way that no matter what happened, he
would look all-powerful to his followers. If Kissinger expressed anger,
this would be proof that LaRouche had freaked him out. If he ignored
LaRouche, this would be proof that LaRouche had frightened him into
silence. In either case LaRouche could claim that the trauma was fester-
ing and that Kissinger would sooner or later commit suicide or die of a
heart attack.

After the Newark Airport tussle the LaRouchians dispatched Ellen
Kaplan to criminal court to swear out an assault complaint. This tactic
had gained them media attention on earlier occasions, as when FEF
members filed assault charges against Peter Fonda after he ripped up
their poster at Denver International Airport calling for feeding his
sister Jane to the whales. The *New York Post*'s gossip page took note of
Kaplan's assault complaint, but the story would have stopped there
except for a simple mishap: The summons was delivered to the Kissingers' Washington home at a time when it was closed up. Mrs. Kissinger did not receive it in time to file an answer before a routine
warrant for her arrest was issued.

The LaRouchians were ecstatic. They called a press conference in
Manhattan. Kaplan briefly recounted her story, then NCLC regional
director Dennis Speed outlined the plan to psychologically harass Kissinger through ridicule. In an ideal world the press would have walked
out at this point. Instead, Kaplan and Speed's remarks—including the
canard about the Carlyle Hotel—were given national coverage.

On May 21, Mrs. Kissinger's attorney moved for dismissal in New
Jersey State Superior Court, arguing the case was "too trivial" for trial.
The judge denied the motion and set a trial date. An editorial in the

*New York Daily News* asked why the courts should be party to schemes that merely "add injury to the original insult."

When the non-jury trial convened on June 10, the media turned out in force. Kaplan took the stand and delivered a litany apparently designed for maximum quotability: Mrs. Kissinger "took her left hand and grabbed my neck. I was very scared. She sneered, bared her teeth, and I thought she was going to bite. . . ." Municipal judge Julio Fuentes found Mrs. Kissinger not guilty. Sometimes, he observed, it is "spontaneous and somewhat human" to assault someone.

Although press columnists denounced Kaplan as "swinish," "lowest," and "filthiest," LaRouche must have felt satisfied. First, he had escaped denunciation himself—most news accounts didn't even mention that Kaplan was connected to him. Second, the public had been exposed to a baseless charge against Kissinger, and it was inevitable the accusation would stick in many people's minds, in that twilight zone where people half believe something because they want to believe it. (Former NCLC security staffer Charles Tate says the Carlyle Hotel story came from a "demented" source who also purveyed hysterical rumors of nationwide homicidal conspiracies.)

The chief significance of the incident was on the level of archetypes: LaRouche had presented the media with a subliminal version of the medieval Christian blood libel—the belief that Jews kidnap and sacrifice Gentile children. In his Newark version, ritual sacrifice was replaced by the contemporary crime of sexual abuse. It was the perfect opener for Operation Nuremberg. In the summer of 1982, the LaRouchians announced the next step—an international campaign to draw the noose of psychological terror around the neck of "Fat Henry."

What followed was a multileveled effort by hundreds of LaRouche's followers. Most important was the planting of defamatory stories about Kissinger with overseas newspapers. This was easiest to achieve in Mediterranean and Third World countries where conspiracy theories are a basic part of the political culture, many intellectuals are anti-American and anti-Israel, and mass circulation dailies are subsidized by Communists and ultrarightists. LaRouche's intelligence staff concocted different stories for different audiences. Always there was a plot, and always it reflected anti-Semitic stereotypes. Kissinger and his friends were portrayed as plotting the assassination of prominent Gentiles, collecting usurious debts for the International Monetary Fund, engaging in real estate swindles, betraying America to its enemies, and encouraging moral degeneracy on behalf of a cosmopolitan value system. The supporting cast included, in one version or another, the CIA, the KGB, Mossad, the Mafia, the Freemasons, and a powerful homosexual cabal.

The LaRouchians held press conferences in various world capitals to release official-looking reports on behalf of Lyndon LaRouche, representing him as a leader of the U.S. Democratic Party, international publishing tycoon, friend of Giscard d'Estaing and Helmut Schmidt, and economist of world renown. Reporters for sensation-mongering newspapers often failed to check whether LaRouche's credentials were really what his followers claimed.

LaRouche's European Labor Party (ELP) presented a legal brief to the Italian government tribunal investigating the Red Brigade's kidnapping and murder of former Prime Minister Aldo Moro. The brief said Kissinger was behind not only the Moro murder but a wide range of terrorist acts—a "strategy of tension" designed to prevent Italian Communist Party participation in the government. A former Moro aide then told the tribunal about a 1974 conversation in which Kissinger, who was secretary of state at the time, told Moro that the U.S. government disapproved of his plan to bring the Communist Party into the government. The LaRouchians said this proved their case. The fact that Moro was kidnapped in 1978, when Kissinger was no longer secretary of state, didn't faze them at all.

This story obviously was aimed at the left, but the ELP also developed a version for the right: Kissinger was a member of the "Homintern," a secret gay brotherhood operating at the "highest levels of several governments." The KGB had learned about this and had blackmailed him into becoming their agent. Just why a KGB agent would have wanted to murder Aldo Moro and keep the Communists out of the Italian cabinet was not explained. The LaRouchians boasted that story number one (Kissinger/CIA) was picked up by Moscow's *Literaturnaya Gazeta,* while story number two (Kissinger/KGB) was supposedly reported in Italian, French, and Tunisian newspapers and on Venezuelan television.

The 1981 attempted assassination of Pope John Paul was also grist for the mill. To blame Kissinger fit right in with LaRouche's theory that the Jews controlled Europe in the Middle Ages through selective poisoning of popes. The LaRouchians also enticed the Arab press with a story that Kissinger had formed a real estate consortium to buy up the Israeli-occupied West Bank.

In mid-1982 the LaRouchians learned that Kissinger was planning a trip to Argentina, which was in political turmoil following the Falklands fiasco. A press statement was sent to Buenos Aires from the office of "U.S. Democratic Party leader" LaRouche reminding Argentinians that Kissinger had supported the British. The statement also accused him of murdering Aldo Moro, attempting to murder Helga LaRouche, and braining a Rumanian waiter with a whiskey bottle during a sex orgy in Acapulco.

*EIR* later claimed that the LaRouche statement was distributed by TELAM, the Argentine government press agency, and was printed under banner headlines in a Buenos Aires daily. A follow-up news release said that Kissinger intended to put the squeeze on Argentina for the usurers of the International Monetary Fund and would destroy any politician who opposed him. According to *EIR,* this release also was distributed by TELAM and printed in at least two Argentine newspapers. LaRouche's Mexican Labor Party joined the act with a demonstration at a Chase Manhattan branch in Mexico City to protest an upcoming Kissinger visit. Kissinger's name was again linked to IMF usury and threats to national sovereignty.

In late 1982 the LaRouchians set up a "special-operations 'Kissinger watch' " in Wiesbaden. This coincided with the arrival in Europe of LaRouche security aide Paul Goldstein (who according to FBI claims was hiding from a Manhattan grand jury investigating the NCLC's harassment of Roy Cohn). *EIR* boasted that the Kissinger Watch had "tracking capabilities extending from Ireland through the Middle East." In fact, security staffers merely called up Kissinger Associates in New York, posing as journalists, to obtain Kissinger's travel schedule.

The objective was to create a "controlled aversive environment" around Kissinger—schoolboy pranks, crank calls, demonstrations. When he was about to leave Munich for London to meet with British officials, an imposter called Britain to say Kissinger wasn't coming, then called Kissinger's hotel room to say the British had canceled. When he visited Milan, the LaRouchians released a banner supported by hundreds of balloons proclaiming that "Kissinger Killed Moro." When he traveled to Stockholm, Swedish ELP members disrupted his press conference and had to be removed by the police. *New Solidarity* boasted that this took place "under cascades of flashbulbs and television cameras," and that the story "reached as far as Singapore and Mexico via satellite hook-ups."

When Kissinger gave a speech in Worms on German-American Friendship Day, an ELP leaflet urged the audience to buy Seymour Hersh's biography of Kissinger, *The Price of Power.* According to *EIR,* a prankster dressed as Kissinger jumped up as the event began and shouted: "That man on the podium is not the real Dr. Kissinger. I am the real Dr. Kissinger. I will now tell you the truth about Aldo Moro . . ." *EIR* said that as the prankster was being carried out, a second one, dressed as Nancy Kissinger, jumped up to continue the disruption.

The campaign was no less intense in the United States. When Kissinger appeared on ABC-TV's *Nightline* in August 1982, the LaRouchians mobilized at the studio in Manhattan. Covering both exits, they pelted his limousine with eggs, forcing him to make his escape hidden in a catering truck. When he spoke at Georgetown University, they passed out copies of *EIR* containing an article entitled "How Henry Kissinger Will Be Destroyed." When his friends gave him a birthday party, the LaRouchians passed out a fake "medical alert bulletin" alleging that he had AIDS (again, the *Mein Kampf* theme: contamination). When he addressed the Anti-Defamation League of B'nai B'rith, picketers carried signs such as "It's Anti-Semitic to Call Kissinger a Jew."

LaRouche meanwhile issued a personal attack in *Kissinger: The Politics of Faggotry.* Circulated in leaflet form, it was a kind of manifesto of the harassment campaign, uniting LaRouche's loathing of Kissinger, Roy Cohn, gays, discothèque music, and the Roman Empire into a single extraordinary vision. To understand Kissinger's evil species-nature, LaRouche said, one must "think back to the Emperor Nero and his court. Think of Studio 54, then of Nero's court, and then of Studio 54 again. Think of Roy Cohn's parties . . . Think of Nero, and then of Kissinger, and then of Nero and then of Roy M. Cohn. That is the kind of faggot Henry Kissinger is." (Questioned about this quote in a 1984 deposition, LaRouche knew he was on shaky ground. He backed down and said Kissinger merely had the "personality of a faggot.")

LaRouche noted the tug-of-war in Washington between hard-liners on the White House staff and State Department moderates. LaRouche reasoned that given the bumbling moves of the hard-liners in foreign affairs, it was only a matter of time before the moderates, whose ranks included some former Kissinger protégés, would begin to exert a preponderant influence. By portraying this process as a Kissinger-backed conspiracy, LaRouche could inject his brand of anti-Semitism into the New Right.

A 1983 *EIR* special report accused Kissinger of "coordinating a drive to consolidate control of the Reagan administration for the Trilateral Commission wing of the Republican Party." When Reagan appointed Kissinger to head the White House Commission on Central America, *New Solidarity* claimed that "a wave of fear and foreboding is now sweeping through the United States." An accompanying article alleged "intense resistance among Reagan Kitchen Cabinet insiders to Kissinger involvement in administration policy making." (The LaRouchians were in contact at the time with Judge William Clark's assistant, Richard Morris.) But Kissinger was said to hold all the aces. He had supposedly obtained, via the "Israeli mafia," blackmail videotapes of top administration officials in bed with Alfred Bloomingdale's mistress, Vicky Morgan.

At this point the LaRouchians downplayed the theme of Kissinger the "British" agent, which always had been too esoteric for most Americans. Now the Symbolic Jew was given a guise the New Right could easily comprehend: a good old-fashioned Commie traitor like the Rosenbergs. *New Solidarity* announced that Kissinger, although still linked to the British, was also a "secure and long-term asset of the Soviet KGB." This charge was soon extended to other Jews in the U.S. government and to many Israeli leaders.

In 1984, LaRouche adopted the campaign slogan "Vote for the man that Kissinger hates the most." This was a variation on the 1980 campaign theme that LaRouche was the man the Zionists hated the most. LaRouche purchased fifteen half-hour spots on national television, incessantly attacking Kissinger as a traitor. Under federal law the networks had to sell LaRouche the time and could not censor his remarks, for he was a registered candidate. *EIR* boasted that LaRouche's television chats reached "up to 15 million people." When he referred to "Kissinger *and his friends*" and "Kissinger *and people like him,*" the real meaning was obvious to many viewers.

A LaRouchian internal briefing of March 7, 1984, reporting on the organization's daily round of telephone calls, alleged that the anti-Kissinger campaign was making headway in important circles. "Republican and military layers in the south and mid-Atlantic states are queasy about Kissinger," the memo said. It cited a "high level military contact who is a former astronaut." This individual supposedly hated Kissinger and believed "the Administration has been going 'downhill' ever since the removal of Clark from the NSC. He wants all our material on Kissinger." (It should be noted that internal briefings routinely exaggerated the NCLC's influence: High-level officials described as enthusiastic allies were sometimes just listening to them out of curiosity.)

The LaRouchian hysteria about Kissinger resulted in a strong indirect warning to him in July 1982. An *EIR* news brief quoted a prediction by an unnamed psychic that if any attempt should be made on the life of LaRouche, "a list of thirteen well-known political figures, headed by Henry Kissinger, Nancy Kissinger, and Alexander Haig, will meet sudden death by either massive heart attacks or strokes." Death fantasies about the Symbolic Jew thereafter became commonplace in LaRouchian publications. When Hersh's *The Price of Power* was published, *New Solidarity* reported that Kissinger was on the verge of a "potentially fatal coronary." *EIR* boasted that, as a result of Operation Nuremberg, Kissinger had become a "cardio-vascular risk" and might "choose [the] coward's way out" (i.e., suicide). When Jewish author Arthur Koestler committed suicide in 1983, *New Solidarity* suggested various ways in which Kissinger, his wife, and Federal Reserve Board chairman Paul Volcker (the arch-usurer, in LaRouche's eyes) could follow Koestler's example. In what could be read as an allusion to the Holocaust, the article asked: "Why should the worthwhile vast majority of the human race settle for attempts to solve its antisocial problems on a case-by-case basis? Why not get organized to settle with such characters all at once?"

The LaRouchians privately discussed various extreme measures. Former LaRouche bodyguard Lee Fick told *NBC Nightly News* that Paul Goldstein had asked him to put a bomb under Kissinger's car. Charles Tate recalls a security staff meeting on the lawn of LaRouche's Leesburg mansion at which members were told Kissinger must die. But this rage ultimately was just sublimated into more nasty leaflets and *EIR* articles. The LaRouchians had come to believe that really clever conspirators never carry out an assassination themselves, but simply spread hate propaganda about the targeted person which might trigger an attack by some disturbed personality or fanatic. That way, they can never be held legally responsible.

As a result of the menacing rhetoric, Kissinger wrote FBI director William Webster for advice in 1982. He was careful to emphasize that he was not asking the FBI "to interfere in any manner with LaRouche's First Amendment rights." When the harassment escalated, Kissinger sent a second letter. The FBI checked to see if there were grounds for prosecution under the federal statute pertaining to interstate obscene or harassing phone calls. There weren't.

When the LaRouchians obtained copies of this correspondence under the Freedom of Information Act, they immediately released it to the press in an effort to embarrass Kissinger. Jack Anderson, in an archly written 1985 column on the FOIA documents, made no moral distinction between victim and victimizer. He referred to a "decade-long feud" *between* Kissinger and LaRouche, as if Kissinger had been partly responsible. In 1987, James Ridgeway of *The Village Voice* rehashed this story, also affecting neutrality: LaRouche had harassed Kissinger, but Kissinger had an "animus" against LaRouche, Ridgeway said. The *Voice* illustrated Ridgeway's column with pictures of Kissinger, LaRouche, and Webster with the caption "The Three Faces of Evil." This type of press coverage encouraged the LaRouchians, when they came under federal indictment, to use the Kissinger-Webster letters as proof that the FBI and the prosecutors were motivated by a vendetta.

The press was not alone in displaying a curious blindness as to the true nature of the anti-Kissinger campaign. None of the major Jewish organizations spoke out, even in the face of blatantly anti-Semitic LaRouchian headlines such as "Kissinger Mafia Pollute the Holy Land." The Reagan administration also said nothing. Indeed, many administration officials continued to meet with the LaRouchians at the height of the anti-Kissinger campaign, all but egging them on. Kissinger was well aware of this. In a 1984 interview he called the administration's dealings with LaRouche "outrageous, stupid, and nearly unforgivable."

LaRouche's rhetoric against Kissinger sometimes became so wild that it ceased to be effective propaganda. But LaRouche was playing not just to the general public and Washington conservatives, but also to his own followers. On this level, what might have seemed demented to an outsider was often a highly effective tactic for manipulating the NCLC membership. For instance, when *New Solidarity* said Kissinger had organized a "multimillion-dollar special counterintelligence team" to combat LaRouche, this built up the NCLC's belief in LaRouche's status as an international figure—a man so important that even the famous Kissinger would stay up all night thinking about how to thwart him. It also helped to maintain the NCLC's siege mentality as an organization surrounded by innumerable enemy agents. Furthermore, the alleged machinations of Kissinger served as a convenient explanation for NCLC setbacks. When LaRouchian candidates did poorly in elections, it was because of vote fraud arranged by Kissinger. When an NCLC member defected, it was because agents of Kissinger had bribed him. When a journalist wrote a scathing article about LaRouche, it was because he was part of a Kissinger psychological warfare network. Thus, by a strange inversion, the setbacks became a proof of the NCLC's success, for Kissinger would only bother to do these things if the NCLC was a real and growing threat to the forces of evil.

Ultimately LaRouche's greatest gain from harassing Kissinger was in making an example of him. In powerful circles in Washington, New York, and Chicago, many people became aware of how much the attacks had upset Kissinger and disrupted his life. And these people recognized just how few options were open to him in fighting back. He couldn't sue: That would just give the LaRouchians an additional forum in which to attack him, as well as the opportunity to go rummaging through his financial records in pretrial discovery. He couldn't call a press conference about LaRouche: That would just be dignifying his insidious charges (besides, LaRouche would respond with new and nastier charges). He couldn't have LaRouche arrested, since the NCLC chairman acted mostly through intermediaries who either stayed within the law or engaged in telephone mischief too petty to prosecute.

Thus did Kissinger's ordeal become an object lesson for anyone in authority who might be tempted to stand up to LaRouche. Each leaflet and each demonstration helped to solidify LaRouche's public image as an unpredictable wildman who refused to play by the rules. The message—don't mess with Lyndon LaRouche—was received loud and clear. Along with his penchant for filing libel suits and collecting dossiers on his enemies, LaRouche's anti-Kissinger campaign helps to explain why, even in the late 1980s, he continued to enjoy a remarkable degree of immunity from public criticism.

# Part Five

# LaRouche's Private CIA

Every conspiracy collapses eventually, because . . . of the psychological likelihood that those who are superlatively clever at deceiving others become equally clever at deceiving themselves. Disinformation eats those who create it.

—ROBERT ANTON WILSON

# Eighteen

# The Billion-Dollar Brain

When indicted for obstruction of justice in 1987, LaRouche was well prepared. He had hired Bernard Fensterwald, Washington's premier attorney for wayward spooks. In addition to denying the charges outright, LaRouche and his codefendants decided to use the "CIA defense," as other Fensterwald clients (such as Edwin Wilson, the rogue agent who smuggled arms to Libya) had done. The argument went as follows: We thought we were operating on behalf of the government on instructions from high-level CIA officials. But dishonest elements in the CIA set us up, and now we are being hung out to dry. We can prove this to the jury if only the judge will order the CIA to turn over the relevant documents. The prosecution's response was to depict the LaRouchians' intelligence community ties as nonexistent. It argued that three nobodies from Reading, Pennsylvania, had pretended to be CIA agents to get consulting work from LaRouche. These hoaxsters simply invented government sources and wrote fictitious reports out of thin air.

The Reading trio did indeed operate a scam. However, the LaRouchians had a history of extensive dealings with the intelligence community dating back over a decade, entirely apart from this. The NCLC first offered its services to the CIA in 1976. A longtime CIA contract agent subsequently became LaRouche's security adviser and meetings with several retired high-level CIA officials took place. By the early 1980s the LaRouchians enjoyed a wide range of contacts at the CIA, the National Security Council, the Defense Intelligence Agency, the Drug Enforcement Administration, and the Federal Emergency Management Agency.

Admiral Bobby Ray Inman, former chief of the code-breaking National Security Agency and a consummate intelligence professional, received a steady flow of reports from the LaRouche organization while serving as CIA deputy director in 1981–82. He met personally with Lyn and Helga LaRouche in a little house on F Street in Washington to discuss West Germany's peace movement. After leaving the CIA to head an electronics firm, he talked frequently on the phone with LaRouche security staffers, who regarded him as their "rabbi" and hoped that someday he would become CIA director. Former LaRouche security aide Charles Tate, in his testimony as a prosecution witness in Boston, described taking the incoming calls from Inman to security chief Jeff Steinberg. Tate also claims to have chatted with Inman personally. (Inman's version is that he was merely the victim of a constant bombardment of phone calls from Steinberg, whom he did his best to evade. He believes the LaRouchians were attempting to use him to "establish their importance.")

Dr. Norman Bailey, senior NSC director of international economic affairs, met several times with the LaRouchians in 1982–83, including at least three times with LaRouche. After leaving the NSC he told NBC-TV that LaRouche had "one of the best private intelligence services in the world." Some people suggested Bailey was naïve, but he qualifies as a specialist in international politics as well as economics. Brought into the NSC by Richard Allen, he had some acquaintance with the world of covert operations. In the mid-1970s he acted as a supposed business consultant in the Azores when the CIA was preparing for a separatist coup if Portugal went Communist. As a scholar, one of his chief interests was political cultism. He wrote on the role of Opus Dei (a right-wing Catholic society that practices flagellation) in fighting communism in the Portuguese- and Spanish-speaking world. And certainly Bailey was well aware of the extremism of the LaRouchians, having sued them in the mid-1970s when they accused him of being a "fascist."

Richard Morris, executive assistant to Judge William Clark when the latter was President Reagan's National Security Adviser, met with LaRouche several times, and with LaRouche aides on numerous other occasions. He set up meetings for LaRouche with other top NSC officials, including Dr. Ray Pollock. Such meetings could not have taken place without Clark's approval.

In the mid-1970s the LaRouchians tried to cultivate General Daniel Graham, chief of the Defense Intelligence Agency, and General George Keegan, former chief of Air Force intelligence. LaRouche's ideology put them off, but they both recall his followers as being remarkably well informed. Graham cited an instance when the LaRouchians provided sensitive information on Angola and Mozambique that was unavailable from normal sources. Keegan noted their uncanny nose for the latest military technology.

LaRouche also impressed some European intelligence officials. Brigadier General Paul-Albert Scherer, former chief of counterintelligence for the West German armed forces, recalled in a 1987 speech how intelligence experts in the late 1970s were "amazed at his connections and his access to special information on terrorism, the drug scene, the intelligence services themselves, and on the details of developments in the East bloc countries and in the Middle East." Scherer said that when the LaRouchians asked him to work with them, he checked with "friendly intelligence circles" (apparently the CIA) to see if this would pose security risks. "The fact that I did take [the LaRouchians] up, and can speak publicly about it here, says enough," he pointed out.

Through the years the LaRouchians developed a reputation among investigative reporters as well as intelligence mavens for their access to occasionally stunning pieces of information. The best illustration is *Executive Intelligence Review*'s scoop on important aspects of the Iran-Contra affair in the spring of 1986, many months before the major media learned about it from a Lebanese daily. An *EIR* special report asserted in March that a journalist and National Security Council consultant named Michael Ledeen had visited Israel to negotiate a "massive expansion of Israeli arms sales" to unnamed "U.S. allies" whom the Reagan administration "feared to openly arm." Two months later, *EIR* predicted that a major scandal would soon break, implicating "the U.S. State Department, high Pentagon officials, top figures within the Israeli defense and intelligence establishment, and the Soviet government—in the arming of Ayatollah Khomeini's war machine . . ." The article provided three key names: Yaacov Nimrodi, an arms dealer and former Israeli military attaché to Iran under the Shah; Al Schwimmer, founding president of Israel Aircraft Industries; and Cyrus Hashemi, a New York-based Iranian banker.

Except for the reference to the Soviets, this was close to the target. The major media belatedly confirmed in November and December that Israeli involvement in the affair resulted from a 1985 meeting between

Prime Minister Shimon Peres and Michael Ledeen, and that Schwimmer and Nimrodi acted as the key Israeli intermediaries. As to Hashemi, it turned out that he had participated in early discussions with Iranian middleman Manucher Ghorbanifar and General Richard Secord's business partner, Albert Hakim. (In July 1986, Hashemi died under mysterious circumstances. U.S. Senate investigators have speculated that he was murdered because he knew too much.)

The NCLC's intelligence-gathering prowess of the mid-1980s was the fruit of hundreds of members working at it devotedly for over ten years. LaRouche had first raised the idea of an NCLC intelligence arm in meetings with his top aides in 1971. He proposed that it be set up "along the lines of a 'desk' organization of a major national newsweekly." What eventually emerged was a highly profitable weekly newsmagazine, a global spiderweb of confidential sources, and one of the world's largest collections of private political files and dossiers, compiled through novel but effective snooping tactics.

By 1976 the NCLC had established a smoothly functioning intelligence headquarters in New York, with branches in several European and Latin American cities. Three interlocking units emerged: the intelligence division proper, which mostly did telephone research and monitored the foreign press; the science unit, which operated out of separate offices through the Fusion Energy Foundation; and the security staff, which worked on sensitive matters such as the harassment of LaRouche's opponents.

The intelligence division was designed by NCLC member Uwe Henke von Parpart, a former West German naval cadet who claimed to have worked at NATO headquarters in the 1960s. In its early years it was more like a spoof of a government spy agency. The various "sectors" and "files" representing different regions of the world were crammed into a three-floor complex in a factory building on West Twenty-ninth Street in Manhattan. It was a rabbit warren of shabby offices, such as the "Southern Cone" room, where LaRouche disciples pored over newspapers from Argentina and Chile. When I visited in 1977, dozens of young people in rummage-sale clothing sat hunched over WATS line phones amidst a surrealistic clatter of the telex machine and typewriters. There was a smoglike atmosphere from chain smoking. When an ashtray became full, the contents were simply dumped on the floor. No one had swept up in days. The bathrooms were also in a state of neglect, and the walls were devoid of any decoration. One sensed that the members were so intent on their political tasks that they didn't even notice their surroundings.

The intelligence division was supposed to function with Parpart's Prussian efficiency. Each morning the sector heads deployed their underlings on the basis of instructions from the National Executive Committee. Many of them spent long hours on the phone with news reporters, government officials, Wall Street experts, or college professors to "profile" their thinking and pick up tips. A report on each conversation was filed and cross-filed for future use. Other members clipped newspaper articles, prepared translations from European papers, or conducted searches of the already voluminous files. The more enterprising scooted uptown to the New York Public Library to research the pedigrees of British aristocrats. The result was worked up as daily sector reports and further distilled into the daily "briefing" on the world situation, which was given final approval at the NEC meeting held each evening in the "war room" (a small conference room with a shabby carpet). This was turned over to the communications sector to be telexed overnight to all regional and overseas offices, so that a copy would be in the hands of every LaRouchian in the world the next day. "The ferocity with which they pursue intelligence is almost beyond the ken of outsiders," said a former NCLC security staffer, who described the organization as a "cult of intelligence."

Some defectors have said that LaRouche's brainwashing was what kept them in the offices twelve to sixteen hours a day. In part this was true. Members also endured a certain amount of psychological bullying from martinet types in the leadership. But many NCLC members had fun playing spook. LaRouche gave them titles like "intelligence officer," "sector chief," and "counterintelligence director." He told them they were part of a secret elite that would ultimately—indeed, soon—be called on to save the nation. Security staffers could thus imagine a five-minute phone conversation with a Pentagon public affairs officer as being Stage One of the global triumph of Neoplatonic humanism. They developed an extraordinary persistence and chutzpah: They would keep calling and calling a selected military officer or Wall Street banker until he agreed to talk to them.

The national intelligence staff's work was supplemented in a somewhat less organized fashion by the regional NCLC staffs, which sent to New York daily telex reports regarding their local organizing and snooping. When I asked a LaRouche aide in 1978 about the policies of the White House Office of Drug Abuse Policy, he referred me to an Ohio NCLC member, who had detailed information about the role of drug experts close to the administration in lobbying for a drug decriminalization bill in the Ohio legislature. The Ohio NCLC member referred me to a top Cincinnati police official, who confirmed the story and was as impressed with the LaRouchians' information as I was—he had gone to Columbus at their urging to lobby against the bill. (When I checked the story with the bill's sponsor, I found it was all true, and more.)

In 1974 three NCLC members incorporated the New Solidarity International Press Service (NSIPS), and the various LaRouchian intelligence offices in the United States and overseas were renamed as NSIPS news bureaus. This provided light journalistic cover—press passes and easy access to officials who otherwise might not have given them the time of day. The NSIPS invested in a telex network to link its offices and began publishing an intelligence newsletter to supplement the NCLC's *New Solidarity*. From the outset, this cost millions of dollars a year, and where LaRouche obtained start-up capital of this magnitude has never been adequately explained. As the money poured in, the newsletter was turned into *Executive Intelligence Review*, an attractively printed weekly newsmagazine along the lines envisioned by LaRouche in 1971. The NCLC intelligence director, Nick Syvriotis (a.k.a. Criton Zoakos), took the title of *EIR* editor-in-chief, and the various intelligence division sector chiefs became the *EIR* intelligence "directors" in their respective areas.

Field research was done by NCLC organizers (like the young man in Ohio) and by reporters for LaRouche publications. NSIPS gained White House press accreditation during the Ford administration, and both Carter and Reagan repeatedly took questions from them at presidential press conferences. *EIR* reporters sought interviews with public figures (and, even more important, with obscure experts) all over the world. The publication opened news bureaus in major foreign capitals, eventually establishing bureaus in thirteen cities from Bangkok to Stockholm which collected news as busily as their mainstream media competitors.

The effect was incremental. By the early 1980s, LaRouche operatives had been working the phones seven days a week for almost ten years, calling hundreds of contacts a day from New York headquarters and the regional and overseas offices. They had conducted hundreds of face-to-face interviews a year with influential people in Washington and around the world. Winnowing through this mass of names and faces, they had found individuals who, either because of naïveté, vanity, closet-fascist proclivities, or most often simply a desire to trade information, became part of the "briefing network"—a list that was phoned regularly for exchanges of gossip on a first-name basis.

Meanwhile, the security staff made thousands of undercover phone calls to the "enemy": left-wing activists, liberal Democratic Party politicians, and Jewish leaders. The reports on the most fruitful phone calls were filed away in what the LaRouchians called "raw and semi-finished files." Snippets of information from these files could then be traded with police detectives, investigative reporters, scholars, the Ku Klux Klan, and European and Third World intelligence agencies.

The LaRouche organization's effectiveness was not just a result of collecting masses of data. It also was a matter of intelligence analysis. Even prior to the Reagan administration, *EIR* developed an underground reputation on Wall Street and among some government people for its maverick focus on important issues which the major media were ignoring, such as beam weapons research and the international "debt bomb." Sooner or later LaRouche twisted every analysis to fit into his anti-Semitic worldview, but the original groundwork retained its validity, and *EIR* staff writers were skilled at keeping factual analysis and propaganda separate when necessary. LaRouche had launched his organization in the late 1960s by recruiting from the best and brightest on elite college campuses and among well-educated upper-class youth in Europe and Latin America. They might not have been streetwise, but they were probably smarter in an iconoclastic academic sense than their civil service counterparts at the CIA. They read a wide range of foreign languages, thereby giving the organization access to news reports generally unavailable to anyone outside the intelligence community or academic research institutes. They also knew how to squeeze the last clue out of research library special collections. Several possessed, like LaRouche himself, acute analytic minds. NEC member Fernando Quijano produced "The Coming Bloodbath in Chile," a 1972 *New Solidarity* article that explained with compelling logic how and why Salvador Allende would be overthrown. David Goldman and other members contributed research in the late 1970s on the IMF and the "debt bomb" which LaRouche synthesized into *Operation Juarez* to influence government officials and economists throughout Latin America. In the midst of the Falklands war in 1982, Uwe Parpart produced an analysis of Argentina's strategic blunders (based in part on Argentine government sources) that was far superior to the mainstream media's coverage.

According to LaRouche, revenues from *EIR* sales and other NSIPS activities reached $4 million in 1979. This presumably included *EIR*'s subscribers paying $396 for their annual subscriptions. (Some members of the briefing network received it free.) LaRouche was out to develop a select readership rather than mass circulation. *EIR* served basically as a come-on for more expensive spin-off products such as book-length special reports ($250 each), the weekly *Confidential Alert* ($3,500 a year), secret reports for individual clients (upward of $10,000), and annual retainer services (whatever the traffic would bear). LaRouche's West German organization launched the weekly

*Middle East Insider,* offering "reports from the Middle East and North Africa that no one else dares to publish."

The NCLC intelligence division would have been impressive enough if it had been simply a United States-based operation. But its work was duplicated by LaRouche groups overseas, working every bit as hard to build up briefing networks and compile their own files and dossiers, to which New York headquarters had full access.

In the early 1960s LaRouche had aspired to found a Fifth International to replace the Trotskyist Fourth International. What he ended up building was the International Caucus of Labor Committees (ICLC), a network including the NCLC, the Mexican Labor Party, the North American Labor Party (today the Party for the Commonwealth of Canada, dedicated to dumping Queen Elizabeth as ceremonial head of state), the Andean Labor Party with branches in Peru and Colombia, and the European Labor Party with branches in Italy, France, West Germany, Denmark, and Sweden. The combined membership outside the United States is probably no more than 1,000, yet these foreign LaRouchians are, like their American counterparts, talented, educated, and well funded. Each member organization has, like the NCLC, an electoral arm, propaganda organs, and local fund-raising sources. Each also has plenty of corporate shells and private bank accounts into which funds from the United States, brought over by courier, can disappear without a trace. Finally, each has its own intelligence division (the local *EIR* "bureau") which develops information-trading relationships with the local police and military, thus multiplying the amount of information available to the NCLC intelligence division whenever it is preparing a confidential report to impress some CIA or other government official.

Especially important is the Wiesbaden intelligence command center. Wiesbaden is the headquarters of the European Labor Party, and LaRouche has a villa nearby. Already in the early 1970s the ELP's German contingent began to cultivate military and intelligence officials. Defectors say that LaRouche aides met with the late Reinhard Gehlen, Hitler's Eastern Front military intelligence chief, who, after the war, founded the BND, West Germany's version of the CIA, and staffed it largely with former SS officers. Gehlen, already retired, reportedly was not impressed by the LaRouchians—they were still too left-wing. According to Charles Allen, a well-known writer on Nazi war criminals and German revanchism, the LaRouchians had more success with the BND after their swing to the right. They also nuzzled up to military counterintelligence, which was headed in the mid-1970s by General Scherer, today a close personal friend of LaRouche.

The director of LaRouche's German intelligence staff, Anno Hellenbroich, is the younger brother of Heribert Hellenbroich, chief of West Germany's Federal Bureau of Constitutional Protection (BfV) from 1981 to 1985. The BfV, West Germany's equivalent of the FBI, supposedly watches extremist groups, but removed the LaRouche organization from its list. Heribert told *Der Spiegel* that it wasn't extremist enough and besides, Anno had assured him it was not anti-Semitic.

From its inception the European Labor Party concentrated much of its energy on tracking, compiling dossiers on, and harassing politicians in Germany and Scandinavia who were critics of U.S. policy or advocates of Ostpolitik. They conducted a smear campaign against former Chancellor Willy Brandt, putting up posters depicting him in a Nazi storm trooper uniform with a swastika prominently displayed. (Brandt sued them and won.)

In 1982–83 the ELP went after Petra Kelly, leader of Germany's Green Party and a strong advocate of removing U.S. missiles from German soil. Various smear articles called her a Communist, a terrorist, and sexually promiscuous. An article entitled "Did You See This Whore on Television?" described her alleged affairs with married men. She sued the LaRouchians for libel in New York federal court. Her attorney, former U.S. Attorney General Ramsey Clark, said the LaRouchians had engaged in a "vicious campaign that made it difficult for her to appear in public. The campaign became physical at times. They cornered her on a train, they shoved her grandmother around. . . . They abused her most fundamental rights of privacy, dignity, physical integrity, and reputation."

The LaRouchians also built up a strong intelligence apparatus in Paris, where the ELP branch was headed by Jacques Cheminade, a former Foreign Ministry official. In 1984 the Paris ELP publicly disclosed a classified French cabinet memo discussing possible links between the LaRouchians and the KGB. The disclosure created a minor flap over government security, since the memo had been distributed to fewer than a dozen top French officials. Whoever leaked it had to have access to a wide range of government secrets. (According to a CIA memorandum on file in Boston federal court, LaRouche had boasted of his French presidential palace sources at a meeting at CIA headquarters a year before this incident.)

LaRouche came to regard himself as a spymaster of the highest skill. In a 1979 report he rated nine of the world's major intelligence services, distinguishing between what they really know and what they report to their nation's leaders. (In his view, which is probably accurate, spy agencies *always* withhold information from their own government leaders.) He claimed to take into account not just official agencies such as the CIA and the KGB, but each nation's total intelligence capability, "a mixture of private, official, and semi-official institutions," implicitly suggesting that the NCLC should be considered part of the team. He placed the NCLC's three great "enemies"—Great Britain, Israel, and the Swiss bankers—at the top in terms of quality of knowledge. In terms of quality of information released, he rated the United States at the bottom. Apparently he was suggesting a pressing need for his services and was petulant that the CIA was not reciprocating his flow of reports.

LaRouche tried to instill in NCLC members a sense of superiority over the CIA and other government intelligence agencies. He boasted that the NCLC often outperforms "those poor, plodding philistines, with their morose sense of a careerist's sort of duty, and their hunt-and-peck methods of deduction." The CIA thinks "arithmetically," but the NCLC reasons "geometrically." In general, CIA agents lack culture. A proper intelligence agent should be steeped in poetry, because intelligence *is* poetry. Agents should be "trained in Kepler, Leibnitz, Monge, Carnot, and the methods of Alexander von Humboldt's protégés at Berlin and Göttingen . . . Greek classics, music . . ."

LaRouche's most revealing article on espionage is couched in the form of a short story, "The Day the Bomb Went Off." On the surface, it is intended to indoctrinate his followers in cultish views, and the hero is LaRouche himself. But on a deeper level the story is a satire which makes fun of its author, his associates, his epistemology, the CIA, and the entire zany world of espionage. Whether or not the satire is entirely conscious is anyone's guess, but like LaRouche's writings on brainwashing, it suggests he cannot be dismissed as a paranoid kook in the grip of uncontrollable compulsions. Inside LaRouche there is certainly a mind of extraordinary cunning, laughing at all the suckers, including himself.

The story depicts an imaginary crisis facing the NCLC intelligence division. The security staff hears on the radio that a bomb threat has been received by the *Chicago Sun-Times* and that its offices have been evacuated. They call the Chicago police, nothing. They call the Federal Emergency Management Agency, nothing. They call each other, nothing. Then they call LaRouche. No one gives him a single fact to go on, but he uses his famous "hypothesis of the higher hypothesis." "Let us assume," he says, puffing on his pipe, "there is a suspect who signed a blackmail note . . . Let's assume he's a talented technologist . . ." LaRouche goes on to infer that this villain is suffering from "megalomania" and is "trying to reorder world events with the aid of some clever sort of infernal machine." Confirmation of LaRouche's theory comes weeks later, in the form of subtle inferences from a remark by a

CIA cutout to a LaRouche aide in Washington. Not only was LaRouche right, but Henry Kissinger was involved!

LaRouche then proceeds to his exegesis. There is a "special etiquette" in the intelligence "demimonde," where things function "by indirection, when not outright misdirection." What's really going on can only be known by inference, but is nevertheless a certainty. If the NCLC wants to transmit information to the CIA, all they have to do is mention it on the phone to some third party. The National Security Agency, which taps everyone's phone anyway, will record it and pass it on. Likewise, if the CIA wants to send a message to LaRouche, they will instruct some undercover spook to mention the item to a third party known to be in touch with LaRouche. The third party will not know he is being used as a cutout. Only the CIA chiefs and LaRouche will know what's really going on—the former through direct knowledge, and LaRouche through inference.*

One can instantly see the usefulness of this theory for NCLC morale. It invests the membership's daily toil with an invisible significance—something like the drudgery of medieval monks surrounded by invisible angels and devils. Lest the outside reader conclude that LaRouche is insanely serious, he appends a seemingly irrelevant note about quarks, those elusive particles of subatomic physics. "The most interesting thing about quarks," he says, "is that they do not exist. No physicist has ever conducted an experiment in which the effect of a quark's existence occurred. . . . The function which the quark performs is to fill a 'logical hole' in the schematic representation of physics . . ."

Once quarks infiltrate one's spy organization, Robert Ludlum and Richard Condon cannot be far behind (not to speak of L. Ron Hubbard and E. Howard Hunt). In fact, LaRouche and his top aides take spy novels seriously and *act them out* in the world of real spookery. LaRouche wrote in 1974 that the "best qualified CIA 'covert operations' planning executives are to be found among hack paperback novelists."

* LaRouche added an extra twist in later writings, presenting the indirect transmittal of information from and to the NCLC as having a deep operational significance. It was, he suggested, the means by which the organization participated directly, as a kind of switchboard, in secret deals between the CIA and the KGB and in all kinds of disinformation games, counterintelligence probes, and dog and pony shows. To play in this game, *EIR*'s staff members merely had to go about their daily routine and let the National Security Agency record what happened. But LaRouche changed his tune while preparing for his 1988 trial. His attorney made a Freedom of Information Act request to the National Security Agency for any records of electronic or other types of surveillance of the LaRouchians. The NSA responded that it had files on the Schiller Institute, but declined to turn them over on national security grounds. In spite of LaRouche's previous eagerness to be bugged, he now said it proved there was a government conspiracy against him.

A 1981 *New Solidarity* review of Ludlum's *The Bourne Identity* pointed out that "many espionage writers" write stories as "proposed scenarios for actual intelligence operations, or as 'disinformation' to cover up operations." Wall Street economist Michael Hudson recalls being told by a top LaRouche aide that Ludlum's fictional cabal of Corsican gangsters and Italian aristocrats in *The Matarese Circle* actually exists. LaRouche himself has repeatedly claimed that Edgar Allan Poe was a full-time intelligence agent and that Poe's mystery stories contain cryptic references to real-life operations. LaRouche's 1974 Christopher White brainwashing hoax was inspired in large part by Condon's *The Manchurian Candidate* and the movie version of Len Deighton's *The Ipcress File.* Former LaRouche followers have pointed out the uncanny similarities between his conception of the NCLC and General Midwinter's super-rightist spy outfit in Deighton's *The Billion-Dollar Brain:* Midwinter hires contract agents, devises a computerized system for planning operations, goes into competition with NATO intelligence agencies, and is put out of business by LaRouche's number one enemy, British intelligence.

The most startling parallels to LaRouche's operation are found in *The Intercom Conspiracy,* a novel by Eric Ambler, whose sardonic view of spookery generally resembles that of LaRouche. It is the story of two raffish NATO spooks who buy an *EIR*-type newsletter, Intercom World Intelligence Network, and use it to leak intelligence secrets embarrassing to both East and West. (Significantly, *The Intercom Conspiracy* first appeared in paperback in December 1970, only a few months before LaRouche announced his plan to found *EIR.*) After creating havoc for several months, the duo hold an auction to sell Intercom to whichever embarrassed agency will pay the most to stop the flow of information.

Ambler's satire is filled with terms that well fit the LaRouchians: "paper mill" (an organization specializing in disinformation and ideological slander), "shopping window" (a newsletter used to give hints of intelligence items for sale), and "play material" (low-grade classified information leaked through paper mills for various Byzantine purposes).

Whether or not *EIR*'s editors really have as much classified information as Ambler's two rogues, they like to give the impression they do. *EIR*'s international news briefs column often includes snippets similar to those in *The Intercom Conspiracy.* For instance, in the *EIR* dated May 12, 1981, an item from a "[Persian] Gulf intelligence source": "The British government is secretly extending offers to the Saudi Arabian government to sell the Saudis the British-made Nimrod radar aircraft system if the U.S. Congress forces the Reagan administration to back down on its offer to sell AWACS to the Saudis . . ." Or from the July

29, 1980, issue: "A secret component of the recent U.S.-British deal over Trident missiles involves the stationing of nuclear weapons on Diego Garcia in the Indian Ocean, according to confidential sources. Included in the Trident deal is an unwritten agreement by Britain to provide a 'supplementary Rapid Deployment Force' to back up Washington's RDF in deployments into the Persian Gulf."

But LaRouche's followers in the early 1980s went far beyond anything in *The Intercom Conspiracy* when they started publishing hot tips on how to make H-bombs and death rays in league with Dr. Friedwardt Winterberg, a character as odd as anyone in an Ambler novel. Besides his political activities as a nemesis of the Justice Department's Office of Special Investigations, Winterberg is also a brilliant research physicist. According to Edward Teller, he has "perhaps not received the attention he deserves" for his work on fusion. For the LaRouchians, he is a unique commodity—his value resides in what he lacks. What Winterberg lacks is a Q clearance. He therefore cannot be accused of leaking classified information. As a physicist, he can always say he rediscovered it on his own in his Nevada desert laboratory. In fact, he does indeed figure out the principles of secret weapons on his own. It is his hobby, just as other people breed hamsters. Winterberg sincerely believes that it is ridiculous to classify such matters, for the essence of science is the free flow of information. In 1981 LaRouche's *Fusion* magazine published Winterberg's diagrams of various devices, such as a "Nuclear X-Ray Laser Weapon Using Thermonuclear Explosives." Later that year, the FEF published his *Physical Principles of Thermonuclear Explosive Devices,* a how-to manual on H-bombs with the neutron bomb thrown in as a bonus.

Of course, the LaRouchians had been hinting at such knowledge ever since they set up the FEF in 1974. Predictably, they strove to develop ties with government desirous of becoming the next nuclear power: India, Iraq, South Africa, Argentina, Taiwan, and Libya. Government nuclear experts in at least two of these countries (India and Argentina) have met with FEF representatives, and the foundation and *EIR* have arranged speaking tours for Dr. Winterberg. In the wake of the how-to manual, *EIR* seminars in Washington and European capitals were well attended by appropriately obscure diplomatic clerks from various Third World embassies, with Mossad agents discreetly blending into the background.

# Nineteen

# Intrigue
# on Five Continents

According to Admiral Inman, the CIA suffered in the early 1980s from an intelligence "vacuum" in some parts of the world because of the Carter administration's cutbacks. This made it tempting to deal with private groups like LaRouche's. They were not the only such group around; the Unification Church was also in the private spy business, as were various rightist outfits supplying the Nicaraguan Contras. But LaRouche's snoops employed unusual techniques with especially intriguing results. "They are like ferrets," said the NSC's Norman Bailey, adding that they sometimes induced high-level foreign officials to "open up." Richard Morris also noted this. He cited LaRouchian reports to the NSC on meetings with government officials in Latin America and the People's Republic of China. For national security reasons, neither Bailey nor Morris would be more specific.

The "ferrets" were *EIR* correspondents who roamed the world interviewing hundreds of important persons each year. A subject would see a copy of *EIR* with an attractive cover and a masthead listing as many news bureaus as *Time* or *Newsweek,* and would assume it was an important American magazine. Many who rarely, if ever, had been interviewed by the U.S. media were glad for the opportunity to send a message to the American public. Some of those interviewed were susceptible to LaRouchian political views and would be particularly forthcoming with respect to such pet topics as debt repudiation. Others proved open to some kind of information-trading or consulting arrangement. They would be drawn into the NCLC's international briefing network as intelligence sources and/or "organic-humanist" allies. In a 1986 interview, LaRouche boasted of having such ties with governmental officials or members of the "Establishment" in about fifty countries.

During 1982 (when the CIA, according to Admiral Inman, was receiving a continuous "flow of materials" from the LaRouchians) *EIR* published interviews with former Venezuelan President Carlos Andrés Pérez, Argentine Foreign Minister Nicanor Costa Méndez, Vietnamese Foreign Minister Nguyen Co Thach, Spanish Defense Minister Alberto Oliart, Japanese industrialist and Mitsubishi Research Institute chairman Masaki Nakajima, and former Iranian Prime Minister Shahpour Bakhtiar (in exile in Paris). Other interviewees included the Foreign Ministers of Panama, Peru, Colombia, Ecuador, and Malaysia, the Brazilian Planning Minister, the president of Brazil's Senate, the head of Petrobas (Brazil's state oil company), the Bangladesh Finance Minister, the chief of Argentina's National Atomic Energy Commission, and the permanent secretary of the Latin American Economic System (SELA). *EIR* correspondents also met with hundreds of lower-level officials, trade union leaders, and businessmen—people that the local U.S. embassy or CIA might never have had contact with or who would be reluctant to open up with official U.S. representatives. A unique file of dossiers and profiles was thus compiled by the NCLC for its own use and that of its clients, including above all the intelligence agencies.

The LaRouchians strove for direct ties with the government of a targeted country, either on its home ground or through its Washington embassy or New York UN mission. If an embassy official liked their product, they would offer to provide various public relations and dirty tricks/smear services. They never bothered to register with the U.S. Justice Department under the Foreign Agents Registration Act nor did the Justice Department pressure them to do so. Defectors say the organization prepared research materials for at least a dozen governments, as well as Japanese multinational corporations. Besides the nuclear-bomb aspirants already named, the clients reportedly included French and Italian intelligence agencies, Iran (under the Shah), and Saudi Arabia. The name of the game was opportunism. While working for Panamanian strongman Manuel Noriega, they peddled antidrug trafficking reports in Colombia and Peru. While endorsing right-wing military terror in Guatemala, they provided information to Washington, D.C.'s left-wing Christic Institute for its lawsuit against LaRouche's longtime detractor General Singlaub, whom Christic attorneys accused of involvement in Contra terrorism.

Sometimes reports for foreign governments were prepared for cash, other times as a calculated political move to gain new contacts or a specific political favor. *EIR* operatives were able to arrange personal meetings for LaRouche with several chiefs of state as well as cabinet ministers, generals, and admirals. Over the years his catches included Mexican President López Portillo, Indian Prime Minister Indira Gandhi (twice), Argentine President Raúl Alfonsín, and Turkish Prime Minister Turgut Ozal. Although some NCLC defectors have suggested these meetings were merely a sop to LaRouche's vanity, he profited from them concretely. A report with photographs of the meeting would be published in *EIR* and other LaRouche publications in the United States to show wealthy but naïve senior citizens (the chief targets of LaRouchian fund raising) that LaRouche was truly a statesman of world stature.

If the LaRouchians were able to attract the attention of CIA bureaucrats, it was all the easier to gain the interest of the low-budget intelligence services of some developing nations. Information pyramiding was fairly easy. A LaRouchian might pick up an interesting rumor from a telephone conversation with a low-level diplomat at embassy A. He could then call up his contact at embassy B and tell him what he had learned. In return, he might receive another piece of gossip or conjecture. He could then move on to embassies C and D, multiplying his pennies like the lad in the pluck-and-luck story. One key was that much of the valuable intelligence floating around the world is neither classified nor secret, merely obscure. Whoever bothers to dig it out gains leverage *if* he can determine (as the LaRouchians apparently are able to do) which corporations or governments would be most interested in a given item.

LaRouche's conspiracy theories to a certain extent give him an advantage in peddling and collecting intelligence overseas. Such theories are an important part of the political culture in many countries. His followers are thus able to instinctively tap into moods and undercurrents which might be missed by an American Foreign Service officer who deals with people on a more rational and pragmatic level. Certainly an official in Saudi Arabia or Pakistan, where the anti-Semitic *Protocols of the Elders of Zion* have long been popular, is not likely to raise an eyebrow over LaRouche's arcane charges about British-Jewish bankers. Nor are Latin American daily newspapers, which often purvey tales of CIA machinations and flying saucers, likely to be altogether skeptical of wild tales about Henry Kissinger. And the public in, say, Colombia—where political and drug-related assassinations are frequent occurrences—could well believe that narcotics traffickers or terrorists were out to kill LaRouche.

The factor of sheer ignorance about the United States was manifest in a 1975 Iraqi request to the LaRouchians for a background report on the National Renaissance Party, James Madole's tiny New York storm trooper outfit. The Iraqis were considering funding the NRP as a propaganda asset. The LaRouchians reported back that the NRP was an isolated group unlikely to be useful. But the fact that a Middle East country could even consider working with the NRP revealed a profound naïveté about American politics.

The primary LaRouchian tactic in dealing with foreign governments was to tell them just what they wanted to hear. This was at the heart of LaRouche's agitation with regard to the Third World debt crisis. Nations such as Brazil owed the New York banks billions of dollars, and LaRouche's advice was simple (foreshadowing his own tactics with creditors in the mid-1980s): Don't pay, put them off with promises, threaten them with the debt bomb; after all, they're just a bunch of shylocks. LaRouche became known as an Important Economist, and government officials quoted *Operation Juarez*. As friends of "Ibero-America" his *EIR* intelligence profilers enjoyed an open door to high officials. Peru's President Alán García, already a populist on the debt question, even addressed a Schiller Institute delegation in Lima.

The LaRouchians also used flattery. Sometimes they praised the strongman of a government being courted (e.g., Noriega or Zaire's Mobutu). Usually they praised great achievements and men of a country's past. For instance, knowing that Arab governments are especially sensitive about racist Western stereotypes of their culture (camels, harems, and terrorists), the LaRouchians produced eloquent studies on the glories of medieval Islam, ascribing world-historical importance to the philosopher Avicenna. They launched an Avicenna Institute, staged an Avicenna conference, and published an Avicenna issue of *The Campaigner.*

Another variation was to appear to take sides in historic rivalries between selected nations or nationalities, as in supporting the Argentinians over the Brits in 1982, or the Hindus over the Sikhs. After Indira Gandhi was assassinated by her Sikh bodyguards in 1984, the *EIR* staff wrote *Derivative Assassination: Who Killed Indira Gandhi?* The book's footnotes listed numerous interviews with Sikh leaders in various countries which suggested that it was a spin-off from an intelligence report for the Indian government. In its published form it appeared in part to be propaganda to keep the Sikhs from gaining public sympathy in Canada, where they are an important immigrant group. It also appeared to be aimed at readers in India, especially Hindu nationalists who would read about the book's allegations in the daily press. *Derivative Assassination* described the Sikhs as tools of the Israelis and various rich Jews. It also said the assassination was organized by Israel's Mossad as part of a vast plot to sabotage Indian nuclear power plants. Given that Hindu rightists had run amok after Mrs. Gandhi's death, slaughtering hundreds of Sikhs—and that the country remained politically on a hair trigger—the book was a virtual invitation to further violence against Sikhs, not to mention a pogrom against India's tiny Jewish population.

A less sinister example was *EIR*'s cozying up to the Turks against the Greeks in 1987—an amusing choice, considering that *EIR*'s editor-in-chief was Nick Syvriotis and the LaRouche organization had long idolized the Renaissance Greek philosopher Plethon, apostle of total war against the Turks. But LaRouche has never let Neoplatonism stand in the way of opportunity. He traveled to Ankara to meet with Prime Minister Ozal, and afterward staged a press conference in which he accused Greek Prime Minister Andreas Papandreou of being an alcoholic, a Trotskyite, and a KGB agent. He also criticized the Reagan administration as "derelict" in that it wouldn't "supply this kind or that of military aid" (apparently meaning high-tech weapons for Turkey) as well as more economic aid. After conferring with the U.S. embassy, the Turkish government admitted it had been bamboozled by LaRouche. But he came out ahead, for his picture was taken with a NATO head of state and published by *EIR* to impress his contributors back home. He could use it along with the 1980 picture of himself chatting with Ronald Reagan in New Hampshire.

The LaRouchians have a special affinity for regimes that are tottering. It is as if the more desperate they are, the less closely they will look at LaRouche's credentials. In 1978, in the final months of the Shah's regime in Iran, they peddled information to SAVAK, his secret police. They also prepared a confidential memorandum for the Shah on how to save his Peacock Throne. Afterward, they maintained contact with the royal family and various Iranian politicians in exile. *EIR* staffer Robert Dreyfuss's *Hostage to Khomeini* (1980) blamed the Shah's fall on the British oligarchy and its alleged treasonous collaborators in Washington. The book appealed to the irrationalism frequently found among fallen elites, as for instance the anti-Semitic theories popular among czarist exiles in Paris and Berlin after the Bolshevik revolution. The Shah's widow, Empress Farah Diba Pahlevi, told the West German magazine *Bunte:* "To understand what has gone on in Iran, one must read what Robert Dreyfuss wrote in the *Executive Intelligence Review.*" *EIR* used this quote for years afterward in its advertising.

When Philippine strongman Ferdinand Marcos's regime was disintegrating in the fall of 1985, FEF spokesman Uwe Parpart and LaRouche's security chief, Paul Goldstein, rushed over to Manila to advise him. They took along Peru's former Prime Minister General Edgardo Mercado Jarrín as the nominal head of their Schiller Institute delegation, and the meeting with Marcos was widely reported in the Philippine press. According to LaRouche in a 1986 radio interview, his aides warned Marcos: "They're going to coup you." LaRouche claimed that if Marcos "had taken the kinds of actions we'd recommended . . . he would not have been couped." The evil force behind Marcos's problems was revealed by Goldstein in an *EIR* article shortly after the trip—Mossad and a cabal of Jewish businessmen.

When Polish Communist leader Edward Gierek was threatened by the Solidarity trade union in 1980, LaRouche prepared a document advising him on how to crush the "Trotskyite insurrection" of "British intelligence's . . . Judas goats" (i.e., dumb Catholics led by smart Jews). He told Gierek to crush the strikers the way American cops crushed the ghetto riots of the 1960s. "Use force to contain and separate groups of rioters from one another and from uninvolved areas of the population," he urged. "Isolate and neutralize the agents provocateurs as inconspicuously and quickly as possible, and let the dupes tire themselves back into a normal state of mind."

General Wojciech Jaruzelski's Soviet-backed martial law regime did just that in December 1981 when it rounded up and imprisoned tens of thousands of Poles. The regime became an international pariah, but not to the LaRouchians. They were the only enthusiastic Jaruzelski supporters in the West, save for a few small Moscow-financed CPs. *EIR* and *New Solidarity* published dozens of pro-Jaruzelski pieces, including the editorial "Don't Meddle in Poland," which claimed that Solidarity was linked to Western intelligence agencies. The AFL-CIO, which had attempted to aid Solidarity, was described as conducting "covert operations targeted against the Polish nation-state." Jaruzelski's "broad purge" was said to be a necessary move to get rid of "hardcore British intelligence protégés."

Some NCLC propaganda appears simply to be aimed at cleaning up the public image of regimes which have received negative U.S. press coverage. Jeffrey Steinberg, LaRouche security aide and *EIR* "counterintelligence" editor, traveled to Guatemala in 1985–86, accompanied at least once by a former Army intelligence officer working as a LaRouche consultant. They supposedly went with government troops on a raid to destroy marijuana plantations, and *EIR* published a special report co-authored by Steinberg, *Soviet Unconventional Warfare in Ibero-America: The Case of Guatemala*. It was a vigorous defense of Guatemala's brutal army, and urged total war against leftists, Maryknoll priests, and Indians in the highlands, all said to be involved in drug trafficking, gun running, and assorted other criminal and subversive activities. The report accused Amnesty International, which had lambasted Guatemala's human rights violations, of being a "support organization for Soviet-sponsored international terrorism." When Steinberg and his wife were indicted in Boston for obstruction of justice the following year, they obtained a measure of support from Guatemalan rightists. The daily *El Gráfico* carried an article on how "antidrug expert" Steinberg had been framed by a "drug money laundering mafia." As quoted in *EIR, El Gráfico* observed that "those democrats [in the United States] who have made so many campaigns about supposed violations of 'human rights' in other countries, had no qualms about violating the human rights of the Steinberg couple."

Perhaps the most clever foray of *EIR* staffers was into Israel in 1986. They conned prominent figures by affecting support for Prime Minister Shimon Peres's plan to bring peace to the Middle East via a multibillion-dollar Marshall Plan. This was just the type of grandiose scheme that the LaRouchians are most experienced at packaging and promoting, thanks to LaRouche's real achievements as the economist of total mobilization. *EIR* even hinted that Peres's plan might have been inspired by a 1983 LaRouche scheme along these lines. (LaRouche had traveled to Israel at least once to promote it.) *EIR* published several laudatory articles on the Peres plan, as well as interviews with Israeli officials. Then LaRouche was quoted in a London-based Saudi Arabian newspaper in support of the plan. *EIR* boasted that its "Israeli sources" regarded this article as "very significant." The stage was set for a ten-day trip to Israel in June by two *EIR* correspondents who gained interviews with Economics and Planning Minister Gad Ya'acobi, former bank of Israel governor Arnon Gafny, private foundation officials, and members of the Knesset.

The *EIR* representatives' apparent friendliness toward Israel was in blatant contradiction to the LaRouche organization's propaganda efforts in Washington that summer to use the indictment of Israeli spy Jonathan Pollard to drive a wedge between the United States and Israel (as by accusing the Israelis of working with the Soviets). But this wasn't the only apparent deception. The *EIR* correspondents while in Israel obtained interviews at the Armand Hammer Fund by presenting themselves as friendly journalists. Yet NCLC members back in Leesburg had just completed a massive dossier on oil tycoon Hammer, portraying him as a Soviet agent and an associate of mobsters. (In a 1988 letter to a journalist writing on Hammer, NCLC security staffer Scott Thompson claimed to have gained information for the dossier via a series of interviews with the late James Angleton, who for years was the CIA's liaison with Mossad. Thompson also said that an early version had been given to an unnamed foreign government involved in negotiations with Hammer's Occidental Petroleum.)

The LaRouchians sold the government of Thailand on their expertise in promoting grand economic designs. In this case it was a plan to atom-bomb a canal across the country at the Isthmus of Kra, so as to shorten the route for oil tankers from the Persian Gulf to Japan, and perhaps stimulate Thai industrial development along the way. The plan had long been under consideration by Japan's Mitsubishi Research Institute for its "global infrastructure fund." Powerful persons in Thailand became interested in LaRouche's version, thanks to the influence of a wealthy couple, Pakdee and Sophie Tanapura. Pakdee Tanapura was the son of a Thai magnate who owned vast tracts of land in the northeast. The Tanapuras had bankrolled LaRouche's European operation for years, and guaranteed an elite audience for LaRouche when he traveled to Bangkok in October 1983 for an FEF-*EIR* Kra Canal conference. The Thai Minister of Communications and top military officers turned out to hear him. According to *New Solidarity,* "the warmest welcome . . . came from the old Thai network" that "worked with the OSS in the region." Kevin Coogan, a former member of the NCLC Asia file, interprets this as a reference to associates of the CIA-military "old boys" who ran the Nugan Hand Bank—the kind of military officers LaRouche security adviser Mitchell WerBell would have worked with when he was in Thailand in the late 1960s on CIA assignment with the temporary rank of general.

In 1984 the Thai Communications Ministry co-sponsored a second FEF-*EIR* conference, and LaRouche again traveled to Bangkok to meet with military leaders. When General Kriangsak Chomanan and four colleagues were jailed in 1985 for alleged involvement in a coup d'état, the LaRouchians agitated for their release. *New Solidarity* claimed that they were being kept in jail by pressure from Henry Kissinger and other members of the so-called international oligarchy. But all was not lost. In 1986 *New Solidarity* announced that the chief of staff of the Thai Army had endorsed the Kra Canal project.

The best-documented relationship of the LaRouchians with a foreign government is with South Africa. In the late 1970s they met with South African diplomats in New York and Washington, staged a conference to promote investment in South Africa, and prepared intelligence reports on anti-apartheid groups for South Africa's Bureau of State Security (BOSS). At the time, BOSS was engaged in LaRouche-style dirty tricks in Europe. It also was conducting a secret influence-buying and propaganda campaign in the United States and Europe financed by a $74 million slush fund. This fund, conduited through the regime's Department of Information, was exposed in 1978 by South African opposition newspapers. The ensuing parliamentary scandal was dubbed "Muldergate," after the late Cornelius Mulder, the Information Minister, who was forced to resign.

Members of the NCLC Africa file approached Johan Adler, information officer at the New York consulate, in 1978. They wanted "to be friendly," Adler said. He sent an aide to the NCLC headquarters, and "they took him on a sort of grand tour—he got the impression they wanted to sell him something." Sure enough, the LaRouchians later tried to sell intelligence materials to the consulate. A similar approach was made to the Washington embassy's information officer, Karl Noffke, who said: "They wanted to alert us about certain forces they think are bad for South Africa—the British, the Wall Street bankers, and so forth." A LaRouche representative also approached Les de Villiers, a former South African information official whose name would feature prominently in Muldergate. De Villiers at the time was working for Sydney S. Baron & Co., a public relations firm which was a registered agent for South Africa. He said LaRouche's man offered to help boost investment in South Africa.

Adler, Noffke, and de Villiers all said they rejected the proposals and did not pay for the unsolicited materials they received. But the NCLC security staff struck a deal with BOSS by a different route. Defectors say they were assigned to call up U.S. anti-apartheid groups such as the American Committee on Africa and pump them for information while posing as sympathetic freelance journalists. The callers were told by top LaRouche aides that the reports were intended for BOSS. This was later confirmed by *The New York Times.* The reports included profiles of U.S. and British anti-apartheid groups.

The LaRouchians meanwhile sent a special report in early 1977 to John McGoff, an American newspaper publisher who was a close friend of Connie Mulder and a major figure in the slush-fund scandal. This report provided background on the National News Council, the now-defunct newspaper industry ethics committee which had been critical of McGoff, whom the LaRouchians were courting at the time. James Whelan, a former McGoff aide, recalled being "bombarded" with phone calls from them. After checking with McGoff, he humored them. He read over the National News Council report but found it worthless. (It said the NNC was part of a British plot.) Whelan denied that McGoff's Panax Corporation ever paid for it, but ex-LaRouchians who worked on it say that top LaRouche aides told them it was being prepared under contract and that several thousand dollars was to be paid on delivery.

In 1978 McGoff was named in South African parliamentary hearings as having received over $11 million from Mulder's secret fund. The money was to buy the *Washington Star* and the *Sacramento Union* and transform them into pro-South Africa organs. The plan never panned out, and McGoff came under investigation by the Justice Department for failing to register as a foreign agent. (After an investigation lasting almost a decade, charges were finally brought in 1986, but the judge dismissed the case, saying the time limit for prosecution had passed.)

The NCLC's most public pro-South Africa effort was the Conference on Industrial Development of Southern Africa, held in Washington in 1978 under Fusion Energy Foundation sponsorship. The conference was an attempt to head off disinvestment campaigns by offering an alternative strategy of massive investment in regional development. The FEF argued that this would create socioeconomic conditions for the "eventual" abolition of apartheid. (A former FEF official recalled that his associates, although willing to "court the Boers," had been too embarrassed to "endorse apartheid openly.") The conference speakers included Dr. William van Rensberg, former technical director of the South African Minerals Bureau and author of *South Africa's Strategic Minerals: Pieces on a Continental Chessboard,* published and distributed in the United States and Europe with money from Mulder's secret fund. A sprinkling of diplomats and corporate representatives showed up to hear van Rensberg describe the migrant labor system in South African mines. "While one may argue about the morality," he said, "it is not always appreciated [that] the mines provide these workers with certain basic skills and offer them, in some instances, their first contact with Western civilization."

A hint that the Pretoria government was appreciative appeared later that year in *To the Point International,* a South African newsmagazine. A full-page article by the magazine's managing editor paid tribute to LaRouche as an economic theoretician. It said he had "access to the thinking and plans of trans-Atlantic policymakers at the highest levels," and that "his semantics may be off-target but his message runs true." In 1979 a South African parliamentary commission revealed that *To the Point International* was one of Mulder's secret operations. Foreign Minister Pik Botha then confirmed that the magazine's financing had been handled by BOSS's chief, General Hendrik van den Bergh.

Articles and reports prepared by the NCLC Africa file throughout the late 1970s record its attempts to establish an ideological rapport with the apartheid regime. One report described a network of South African "humanists" who were said to share many of LaRouche's views. The report, prepared by David Cherry, cited Nicolaas Diederichs, a former South African President, now deceased. Cherry claimed to have been in correspondence with Diederichs and warmly praised his "humanism." In fact, Diederichs was a leading architect of apartheid and a Nazi sympathizer during World War II.

Another supposed member of the network was tycoon Anton Rupert, a major figure in the Broederbond, the Afrikaaner secret society which then controlled the ruling National Party. Professing to detect traces of a LaRouche-style philosophy in Rupert's business pep talks, Cherry praised him for allegedly maintaining the ethnic purity (no blacks, Jews, or British) of his corporate board. Cherry also expressed admiration for a scheme of Rupert and certain West German bankers to channel massive new investment into South Africa. (The 1978 FEF conference was partly an attempt to popularize this scheme.)

The most imaginative of the NCLC reports suggested that white South Africa's destiny is to bring the blessings of "humanism" to all southern Africa. It called for a massive expansion of the notorious contract labor system for purposes of cultural uplift. Included were maps of mineral deposits, railroads, and proposed energy grids for all of southern Africa. The linchpin of the scheme was to be South African domination of Mozambique. The choice of this Marxist nation which borders on South Africa was explained as necessary for "forcing" contract laborers "in the appropriate direction." Domination of Mozambique would create a "geometry" in accord with which anti-apartheid "terrorist networks" could be "mopped up." Strongly implied was that South Africa should invade and occupy its neighbors. But this plan proved to be too much for Dr. van Rensberg. In a 1979 telephone interview he called the NCLC "a bunch of dangerous crackpots." Besides, he added, their "maps were all wrong."

NCLC security staff defector Charles Tate says that the NCLC continued its relationship with the South African government into the mid-1980s. In 1984, he says, it received $5,000 to provide an updated report on U.S. anti-apartheid groups. Once again, undercover phone calls were made to activists. Tate says he personally edited the report, and that the contract was handled through a "cutout," a commercial research firm in Manhattan. "It was understood by everyone involved that the money came from the South African government," Tate says. But was money paid only for research? That fall the LaRouchians disrupted a Washington press conference held by seventeen U.S. Catholic bishops to protest apartheid. LaRouchian heckling "broke up" the event and "prevented questioning by genuine reporters," wrote Steve Askin of the *National Catholic Reporter*.

In 1985 LaRouche's Schiller Institute actively courted Bishop Desmond Tutu, the anti-apartheid Nobel Prize winner, who apparently had no idea of just whom he was dealing with. *New Solidarity* boasted that

Tutu had endorsed the Schiller Institute's "Declaration of the Inalienable Rights of Man." The following February, *EIR* reprinted a "historic" speech by South African President P. W. Botha claiming that apartheid had been abolished. More obfuscation followed: *EIR* published an interview in Durban with Chief Buthelezi, leader of the Zulus, but the commentary praised Botha and certain high-ranking military figures as "reformers." Reverting to its hard line, *EIR* praised South African "strike aircraft and commandos" for an attack on African National Congress bases in Zambia, Zimbabwe, and Botswana. It was the 1978 co-prosperity plan all over again—a "grand design" by which South Africa would become the " 'Japan' of the African continent."

In spite of the NCLC's ties with South Africa, Guatemala, and the CIA, many conservatives have suggested that the NCLC might ultimately be a KGB operation. Of course the NCLC denies the charges, and of the dozens of NCLC defectors interviewed for this book, including those who were high up in the organization, not one believes the NCLC is actually *controlled* by the KGB, or even that it is secretly still wedded to Communist ideology. However, most agree that the NCLC is capable of opportunistic dealings with governments across the political spectrum to further LaRouche's financial interests and his drive for power. The LaRouchians have acknowledged Soviet contacts on numerous occasions. Just as they found it useful to flirt with the Polish government in the early 1980s, so they found it rewarding to deal with the Soviets for almost ten years.

The Soviet connection began in 1974, when LaRouche aides met a Soviet UN mission official, Nikolai Logiunov, who passed them on to Gennady Nicolayevich Serebreyakov, a KGB officer attached to the mission. The latter met regularly with Gus Kalimtgis during 1974–75. LaRouche met twice with Serebreyakov, once at the Soviet mission and once at NCLC headquarters.

The same year the LaRouchians met Serebreyakov, they founded the Fusion Energy Foundation to work among scientists, including those engaged in classified work. The FEF zeroed in on researchers in plasma physics and fusion energy, areas with major military applications. Most of the scientists they called to pump for information were unaware that the FEF was a cover for the "science section" of the NCLC intelligence division. A January 1975 internal document sets forth LaRouche's plan for this elusive unit, which he has almost never referred to in any subsequent document. It would report directly to the NCLC's intelligence director, Nick Syvriotis. Its duties would include forming collaborative relationships with specialists at the Atomic Energy Commission's "CTR division, laboratories, universities, and so forth," using the FEF as a "vehicle" when appropriate. LaRouche suggested "ad hoc meetings of working discussion groups" in order to "accelerate the useful exchange of knowledge," but urged the science section to be very careful in its handling of these "sensitive relationships."

In 1975 a top FEF officer traveled to Moscow, supposedly to attend a scientific conference. He was welcomed, although the official line of the Communist Party USA and the Soviet press was that the LaRouche organization was controlled by the CIA. Meanwhile, LaRouche developed an elaborate espionage philosophy to provide an alibi for dealing privately with the Soviets. The NCLC was the "open channel" through which the KGB could pass "policy-relevant" information to the CIA, and vice versa. The NCLC didn't have to tell the CIA about these meetings; all it had to do was transmit the information over its telex lines. The National Security Agency monitored the lines and would automatically pick it up. As to anything secret the NCLC might learn from American scientists, not to worry—the NCLC was totally surrounded by government agents. Anything secret it learned would be something planted by the CIA because it wanted the KGB to get it through the open channel. Such information would be either disinformation or "policy-relevant."

Somewhere in this fantasy the idea of guarding national security secrets was entirely lost. It became permissible to transmit anything to anybody, because everything was just a dog and pony show. When two Soviet spies were arrested in New Jersey in 1977, *New Solidarity* declared them to be innocent and claimed that the NCLC had been dealing with them. The Soviet spies were not really spies but "conduits," and one of their "major functions" had been the "transmission of USLP/NCLC materials" to Moscow. This wasn't questionable behavior on the NCLC's part, for the materials had been "prepackaged by elements of the U.S. intelligence community as part of existing courtesy arrangements between the Soviet and U.S. intelligence services." Just why the Soviet spies were arrested if they were part of a "courtesy" channel was not made clear. But it is curious that *New Solidarity*'s extraordinary revelation did not lead to any trouble with the Justice Department, just as LaRouche's threat that same year to kill Carter led to no trouble with the Secret Service. Already the pattern was establishing itself that LaRouche could fantasize and do whatever he pleased without any fear of consequences.

An equally suspicious incident was described in a 1981 NCLC internal memorandum signed by LaRouche security aide Paul Goldstein. After referring to a "certain [Soviet] UN contact" and the need for "clear channels into the Soviets," the memo mentioned trips by FEF scientists to Moscow for "scientific collaboration." During one such trip an FEF representative, whom the memo identified only as "the man without shoes," prepared a ninety-page report for the Soviets "on the U.S. scientific community." The Soviets "found the information given to them quite useful." Although the memo expressed concern over a possible "national security problem," it boasted that "our open policy commitment to public cooperation with the Soviets on scientific and related questions makes our defense nearly airtight." In fact, there had been several FEF trips to Moscow following the 1975 opener. In December 1978, Chuck Stevens, well known among American fusion scientists for his wide-ranging gossip on research contracts, promotions, and job changes in the fusion (and later the Star Wars) community, attended a laser physics conference in Moscow along with another FEF representative. On another visit an FEF physicist was given a tour of the Soviet science complex near Novosibirsk in Siberia—and later gave a slide show on it at NCLC headquarters.

By the early 1980s LaRouche's scientific intelligence gathering and its possible Soviet links had become a cause for concern to Generals Keegan and Graham and the Heritage Foundation. Keegan warned in a 1984 interview that the LaRouchians had penetrated "every private and government organization in the United States" involved in fusion research. "I have observed with a sense of mounting shock," he said, "their success in eliciting what I thought was sensitive information." Keegan's view was echoed by John Bosma, editor of *Military Space*. He said that in 1981, when he was on the staff of the House Armed Services Committee, a LaRouche follower approached him seeking to find out the Cruise missile's odometer range, a closely guarded military secret.

The LaRouche organization's relationship with the Soviet Union ranged beyond military and scientific matters. Former NCLC intelligence staffer Kevin Coogan writes that in 1979 LaRouche met in West Germany with Julian Semenov, a Soviet spy novelist widely believed to be linked to the KGB. Semenov asked the LaRouchians to investigate the disappearance of a czarist treasure looted by the Nazis. The LaRouchians found no treasure, but they did publish an *EIR* teaser about it. They also published an article by Semenov on the Kennedy assassination. (He speculated Peking was involved.) Another key Soviet contact was Ioni Andronov, a correspondent for *Literaturnaya Gazeta*. Andronov frequently chatted with Paul Goldstein, whom he occasionally quoted as a counterintelligence expert. In one interview Goldstein told Andronov he thought the so-called Bulgarian role in the attempted assassination of Pope John Paul was a hoax. On this point he was probably right, but he went on to suggest that the CIA might have been involved—an allegation for which there is no evidence whatsoever.

According to Coogan, the LaRouchians met regularly with Soviet officials in Washington as late as 1983. The LaRouchians claim they provided reports on these contacts to Judge Clark's office at the NSC. Whatever the truth, LaRouchian publications until the death of Leonid Brezhnev expressed an affection for hard-line Stalinism because of its no-nonsense attitude toward Zionists and other dissenters and its commitment to central economic planning. *New Solidarity*'s obituary on Brezhnev praised him as a "nation builder" and avoided any mention of his invasions of Czechoslovakia and Afghanistan. Thereafter, as LaRouche became more heavily involved in supporting Star Wars and NATO, the NCLC line changed. Moscow became the "Third Rome," a center of unremitting Russian Orthodox evil. When Gorbachev took power, the LaRouchians said he was the Antichrist.

The Soviets in turn took serious note for the first time of LaRouche's West European political intrigues. In the wake of the 1986 assassination of Olof Palme, the Soviet press depicted the LaRouchians as the prime suspects. LaRouche countered that the KGB did it, a charge for which there was no more rhyme or reason than Goldstein's allegation's about the CIA and the Pope. Meanwhile, LaRouche claimed that the October 1986 government raid on his headquarters in Virginia was Soviet-inspired. According to LaRouche, when Reagan and Gorbachev met in Iceland, Gorbachev delivered an ultimatum: Either you get rid of LaRouche or there'll be no arms deal. In Paris, LaRouche sued the Soviet magazine *New Times* for calling him a "Nazi without the swastika." It was basically the same suit he had brought repeatedly without success in American courts. The Soviets chose to play by the Western legal rules: They mounted an aggressive courtroom defense, entering LaRouche's own writings as evidence. The Paris High Court rejected LaRouche's suit and ordered him to pay costs as well as damages to the magazine and its distributors.

LaRouche often pokes fun at those who would depict him as simply a pawn for East or West. "As long as some slow-thinking folk believed that we were CIA, and some other foolish folk believed that we were KGB, our mere continuing our own quality of independent intelligence-work kept the game on the field," he wrote in 1981. But even the most independent-minded ideologue is going to lean toward one side or the other. LaRouche's great dream was to rise to power in America with the support of the right. It was thus natural that he should put more effort into courting the CIA than the KGB.

# Twenty

# The Wooing of Langley

As LaRouche began his swing to the right in the mid-1970s a certain realism entered his thinking. Studying the failure in America of tiny "sect-like" storm trooper groups, he stated flatly that no such organization could ever grow into a "large-scale fascist movement" unless a "leading strata of capitalists and governmental agencies sponsor and direct such a development." He soon began to actively seek such sponsorship. Still influenced by leftist ideas, he turned to the agency that all leftists believe is the chief bankroller of anything and everything fascist: the CIA.

According to documents obtained under the Freedom of Information Act, NCLC members barraged CIA headquarters with phone calls in 1976 offering to provide briefings on international terrorism. They asked to speak with the director, George Bush, and even placed a call to his home. Commenting on these overtures, a CIA memo observed that LaRouche had "openly advocated the overthrow of the U.S. government" only two years previously, but that his organization appeared to be shifting its public posture "from one of violence to one reflecting more traditional, democratic values."

The late 1970s were an auspicious time for a private intelligence group aspiring to work with the government. The CIA was under a cloud of suspicion in the wake of Vietnam and Watergate, and had been forced to disband its domestic intelligence operations. Congress had quashed its efforts to halt a Marxist takeover in Angola. Carter's CIA director, Admiral Stansfield Turner, had fired several hundred covert action specialists. Many professionals were alarmed at what they believed were gaping holes in the nation's intelligence capabilities.

In 1977 *New Solidarity* began publishing attacks on Turner and President Carter for replacing deputy director E. Henry Knoche and firing the old boys. This culminated in LaRouche's "The CIA—Only a Caretaker Force," which claimed that "the once-feared premises at Langley have been degraded to a laundering agency for British and Israeli intelligence products. . . . British and Zionist agents generally have the run of the premises. . . . Menachem Begin runs Israel, and Moshe Dayan runs the United States."

The best solution, he suggested, was for CIA dissidents to put him in the White House. "I would pull together an effective overall U.S. intelligence capability within weeks," he promised. Just what he meant by an "effective" capability was already outlined in *The Case of Walter Lippmann*, his 1977 treatise on the need for a dictatorship in America. LaRouche advocated the centralizing of all U.S. intelligence functions under a single cabinet-level "Secretary for Political Intelligence." This super-CIA would be used for "auditing" the entire executive branch and would operate its own propaganda machine to smash the influence of the liberal media.

In 1977 the LaRouchians sought out Mitchell Livingston WerBell III, a longtime CIA contract agent and former arms manufacturer in Powder Springs, Georgia. "WerBell represented a group of former military and intelligence people, who we thought were patriotic and, therefore, would be very upset about the kinds of policies that would be coming about with the Carter-Mondale administration," said Jeffrey Steinberg in a 1984 deposition. "I went down and met with him at his home and for a period of time there was a sort of continuing discussion . . . in which he was reading and circulating our material . . ."

Apart from the security staff's hope that WerBell could become a political recruit, there was a more practical reason to cultivate him: If LaRouche was ever to gain any acceptance in the intelligence world, he would need a good public relations man with CIA ties. For WerBell the mixing of PR and spying was no novelty. He had once owned a PR firm in Atlanta, and he claimed to have done PR work as well as security consulting in the 1950s for Cuban dictator Fulgencio Batista. Ferociously right-wing and formerly involved in many anti-Communist operations, WerBell was just the man to dampen down the dust cloud of suspicion created by LaRouche's Marxist past. In addition, he was the ideal cutout for any future serious dealings between the NCLC and the CIA. The latter wouldn't have to risk embarrassment by dealing with LaRouche directly; everything could be done through WerBell.

Like the LaRouchians, WerBell had a fondness for grandiose schemes. In 1966 he became involved in a plot to invade Haiti. Having trained the invasion force, he brought CBS-TV to cover the embarkation. Federal agents swooped down and arrested the plotters. Shortly thereafter WerBell obtained a contract with Papa Doc Duvalier to retrain the Haitian security forces.

In the late 1960s he developed the Sionics silencer, the world's first efficient machine-gun silencer, which became extremely popular among drug traffickers, Mafia hit men, and Central American death squads. Needing start-up capital, WerBell went to Stewart Mott, the noted philanthropist and antiwar activist. WerBell told Mott the device could be used as a lawn-mower silencer to fight noise pollution. Mott invested a substantial sum.

In 1974 WerBell sold Nevada real estate mogul and Libertarian Party leader Mike Oliver on a scheme to invade the island of Abaco and declare it independent from the Bahamas. It was to become a tax haven run on libertarian principles. With Oliver's backing, WerBell began to train a handful of mercenaries, and sent his friend Walt Mackem to the island to organize the trappings of a secessionist movement. As with the Haitian scheme, the feds swooped down. WerBell was arrested along with his co-conspirators, but the charges against him were dropped.

WerBell engaged in media self-promotion with the zest of Buffalo Bill Cody. He succeeded because, unlike most intelligence professionals, he was willing to discuss his past. He befriended the journalist Andrew St. George, who called him the "Wizard of Whispering Death" and wrote a number of articles about his exploits. WerBell also opened up to writer James Hougan, whose best-seller on the private intelligence business, *Spooks,* contains many anecdotes about WerBell.

When his arms business failed, WerBell founded the Cobray International counterterrorism training school on his sixty-six-acre estate near Powder Springs, Georgia (called the Farm, after the CIA training center at Camp Peary, Virginia). He posed in a Scottish kilt on the firing range for *The National Enquirer*'s rival, *The Star,* attracted laudatory coverage from *Soldier of Fortune,* and gave himself a promotion to lieutenant general in the RFAA (Royal Free Afghan Army).

In Cobray promotional material, WerBell listed almost two dozen antiterrorist operations in which he supposedly had participated since the 1950s. He told *20/20* that Coca-Cola had hired him to take care of kidnapping threats against its Argentine executives during the urban terrorist wave in the early 1970s. He said he let out the word: "We'll kill you. We'll go after your wife. We'll kill her. We'll go after your children. We'll kill them. Your cats, your dogs, your pigs and your chickens." It didn't seem to occur to WerBell that the Argentine terrorists were upper-middle-class city kids who wouldn't know your pigs and chickens from their Gucci loafers. Nevertheless, he claimed there were no more kidnap threats against Coca-Cola.

If LaRouche and his followers wanted to meet some real live spooks, WerBell was willing to oblige. He arranged several meetings that included CIA personnel. "You're damn right he did—I was there," said Gordon Novel, a New Orleans private investigator who lived for several months at the Farm in 1977. Jim Hougan recalls attending two meetings in an apartment at the Crystal City Marriott near Washington—referred to as a "safe house" by WerBell—where the LaRouchians explained their theories about British control of the narcotics traffic to former and active-duty CIA men.

WerBell invited LaRouche and his top aides down to the Farm to regale them with stories about Vietnam and introduce them to more spooks. One of these contacts was Major General John K. Singlaub (U.S. Army), who had spent a large portion of his career assigned to CIA covert operations in Asia and had once been CIA deputy station chief in Seoul. He first met with them while stationed in Georgia. After his retirement in 1978 they showed up at his lectures around the country and at a ceremony where he and WerBell were given medals by the Taiwanese government.

Although Singlaub dropped the LaRouchians after learning of their extremism, some of WerBell's friends were less fastidious. Ex-CIA agent Mackem advised them on the international drug traffic in 1978 while they were writing *Dope, Inc.*, and continued to help them off and on. By 1986 they were paying him over $1,000 a month.

WerBell was a Liberty Lobby member and close friend of Willis Carto. His political views were thus in the same ballpark as LaRouche's on many questions. NCLC defectors recalled sessions where the two would chat away like old OSS cronies. (Although LaRouche had not served in the OSS, he had been a medic in Burma briefly at the end of the war.) Out of these conversations emerged a scheme as bold as the Abaco Revolution. In February 1979, LaRouche—once again decrying Admiral Turner's cutbacks at Langley—issued a call for "an outpouring of financial and political support" to establish a private intelligence organization to fill the vacuum created by the housecleaning at the CIA.

"What we propose," LaRouche said, "is a de facto augmentation of the resources of the [NCLC], thereby combining the core contribution to be made by the [NCLC] with the resources otherwise befitting a U.S. government intelligence service." He went on: "Such an agency, endowed by corporate . . . and other private sources, would immediately rehire those patriotic, trained former operatives of the CIA and related official agencies purged through British influence." LaRouche suggested in a follow-up article that certain trade unions (e.g., the Teamsters) should help finance this shadow CIA.

The idea of finding private sponsors for LaRouche's intelligence operation was shrewd. Some Teamster officials responded right away. But the proposal to merge the LaRouchians and various covert action veterans into a single organization was simply not workable. LaRouche's intellectualism didn't appeal to those who inclined toward traditional rightist groups. The Bay of Pigs veterans in Florida were interested in cocaine, not a coup d'état. The rogue element among the old boys was preoccupied with laundering heroin money or smuggling arms.

This left LaRouche essentially on his own, and with a problem galling to his vanity. The NCLC had impressive research capabilities, a telex network, a computer, and even a war room. But it lacked the crowning touch: its own "A-Team." LaRouche had learned during Operation Mop Up that most of his followers were klutzes, good only for ganging up on elderly Communist Party members. Even the toughest of his security staff were former college athletes with no military experience.

WerBell had a solution. Members of the security staff began trickling down to the Farm for a ten-day course (at $2,000 each) in "counterterrorism." *New Solidarity* boasted this was a "pilot project" for units to be attached to corporations and the Teamsters. WerBell, in a 1979 telephone interview, said it was simply training in "martial arts, pistol shooting, paramedical skills, the use of shotguns, rifle countersniper activity, countersurveillance, and the control of three-car caravans."

According to former NCLC members, the results were not very impressive. Although scores of LaRouchians took the training, followed by karate classes in New York, LaRouche himself had little confidence in them. For his personal security needs, he brought in professional bodyguards and moonlighting police officers. Nevertheless, the WerBell training provided a deep psychological satisfaction for LaRouche's followers. Here they were, pipe-smoking intellectuals hanging out with the world's deadliest anti-Communist he-men. First there was the "general" himself, adviser to death squads and owner of the world's largest private stockpile of automatic weapons. Then there was Colonel Drexel B. ("Barney") Cochran (USAF, ret.), a former unconventional warfare expert for the Joint Chiefs of Staff, who taught classes at the Farm on how to defend oneself using a hatchet or a ballpoint pen. Next came Bert Waldron, a sniper instructor with 113 confirmed kills in Vietnam, and Jason Lau, the resident martial-arts master whose "incredible expertise" (according to *Eagle* magazine) enabled him "to walk . . . across ceilings like a human fly, remain crouched in a motionless position for hours while waiting for his prey, jump higher than people's heads; and pause, bird-like, suspended in the air."

It is possible there was more than meets the eye in all this, and that WerBell was psyching out the LaRouchians for the CIA to see if they could become useful in some form. If so, nothing would have been better than to put them through a boot camp while keeping LaRouche well supplied with bourbon and ice on the porch. When *20/20* did its report on WerBell in 1979, it included footage of LaRouche's followers undergoing training. It also included an interview with General Singlaub, who said: "In every place where Mitch has operated it's . . . been either as a contract employee or with the knowledge of the local CIA, even if they couldn't officially support it." He added that WerBell specialized in handling situations where "to try to get this through the Congress, to try to get this through the approval of the American people, would be almost impossible."

Whatever his motives, WerBell began to exert great personal influence over the NCLC security staff. "I'm very fond of some of them," he told me in 1979. "They're smart as hell." Jeff Steinberg chatted on the phone with him almost daily. It became a sign of status within the NCLC to have met "Mitch" and taken the training in Powder Springs. However, the NCLC leadership also invoked his name in a vaguely menacing manner to keep members of the national office staff in line. One member, after dropping out, walked around for weeks worrying he'd be cut down by a silenced machine gun.

At the outset WerBell learned that being LaRouche's handler could be a nerve-wracking job. LaRouche was persuaded in August 1977 that German terrorists were out to kill him. WerBell sent a Powder Springs police officer, Larry Cooper, to Wiesbaden to reorganize LaRouche's personal security. Cooper sat in on a political discussion with LaRouche and several top NCLC members during which LaRouche suddenly brought up the idea of assassinating President Carter, National Security Adviser Zbigniew Brzezinski, NATO general secretary Joseph Luns, and David Rockefeller. It could be done, LaRouche argued, with remote-controlled radio bombs activated from public pay phones.

WerBell had told Cooper that guarding LaRouche was a CIA contract job, and that Cooper therefore would be serving his country. But Cooper now realized that WerBell had not told him the entire truth. He called the Farm in a panic, and said he was coming home on the next flight and contacting the FBI. Gordon Novel was in the room with WerBell, and recalls that "the general went through the ceiling, immediately started calling Washington and canceling a lot of things and generated a kind of propaganda story, a cover story, to completely suppress the affair." Indeed, WerBell had cause for worry—his name had been connected with a radio-bomb assassination scheme once before: During the Nixon administration he had worked with a secret Drug Enforcement Administration unit under Lucien ("Black Luigi") Conein that had planned to assassinate Latin American drug dealers. As a consultant, he had devised remote-control bombs and had provided a business cover for Conein's unit. The plan was scotched when Senator Lowell Weicker found out about it and called hearings. WerBell refused to answer questions before the committee, earning the nickname "Mitch the Fifth" in right-wing circles. Apparently LaRouche had taken this incident and transmuted it in his own spy novel-saturated imagination into something that could land them both in deep trouble.

WerBell decided he'd better get LaRouche into a "reality state" fast or there'd never be an "accommodation between the CIA and LaRouche," Novel said. Shortly afterward, Novel had a falling-out with WerBell and left Powder Springs. He says he told the FBI about the Wiesbaden incident, but they showed no interest. This was a curious apathy indeed: If a leader of a Communist group or the Ku Klux Klan had discussed an assassination scheme in the presence of a law enforcement officer, as LaRouche did, the government no doubt would have reacted instantly. The LaRouchians kept their White House press passes with Secret Service clearance. In 1984 Pat Lynch of NBC contacted Zbigniew Brzezinski about the incident; the answer from his office was "no comment."

The loose talk continued with impunity. According to a report prepared by former security staffers for *The New York Times*, a LaRouche aide briefed the national office staff in May 1979 on a plan for "selective assassination" of opponents. *EIR* later reported that an anonymous astrologer had named thirteen enemies of the NCLC who might die "within hours" of strokes and heart attacks if LaRouche was ever the victim of assassination or attempted assassination.

WerBell learned that one key to handling LaRouche was to provide him with illusory trappings of power. During his 1980 presidential campaign LaRouche was conveyed from the Atlanta airport to the Farm in a rented helicopter. Upon landing, he was warmly greeted by WerBell and some good old boys for the benefit of local Atlanta TV. They did all but play "Hail to the Chief." WerBell also provided guards for campaign events as a compensation for the Secret Service protection which LaRouche had been denied. But even when LaRouche was being manipulated on the psychological level, he somehow always manipulated right back on a level that really counts: His checks to WerBell began to bounce, and the Dooley Helicopter Company, whose services had been solicited using WerBell's name, went unpaid. WerBell dashed off a letter to LaRouche, together with a draft press statement which he threatened to release if LaRouche didn't pay up. "It is incredulous," WerBell said, "that an individual endeavoring to manage the economics and resources of a [Platonic] Republic is unable to cope with the finances of a small staff."

WerBell's importance within the LaRouche universe seemed to decline in the early 1980s, as the LaRouchians found other intermediaries for their intelligence community dealings. WerBell was suffering from cancer, and he and LaRouche continued to quarrel over unpaid bills. But when he died in December 1985, LaRouche penned an unctuous obituary saying that he owed his life to WerBell—a reference to the assassination plots his adviser had supposedly foiled.

LaRouche's efforts to cultivate ex-spooks, part-time spooks, private spooks, and even imaginary spooks reached an extraordinary range of people in the late 1970s and early 1980s. He met with former CIA director William Colby but failed to impress him. His followers befriended CIA deputy director Ray Cline, a research fellow at Georgetown University's Center for International Strategic Studies, and persuaded him to meet with LaRouche. Cline continued to chat with them throughout the early 1980s. An especially prized contact was former CIA counterintelligence chief James Angleton, who granted a series of interviews to a security staffer. Defectors recall Jeffrey Steinberg shouting to an underling in the midst of an office crisis in the late 1970s: "Quick! Go brief Angleton!" (The LaRouchians eventually turned on both Cline and Angleton, accusing the former of "genocide" and the latter of plotting against them.)

The nets were spread as widely as possible. LaRouche followers set up a literature table at a conference of the Association of Former Intelligence Officers (AFIO). They sent out a "Dear OSS Veteran" letter soliciting subscriptions to *Executive Intelligence Review*. They called former agents at home, asking them to sign Schiller Institute petitions, run for public office as beam weapons candidates, and donate money to save the NATO alliance. In 1984 Lieutenant Colonel Louis H. Atkins (U.S. Army, ret.), who had served in the CIA during the Korean War and was listed on the AFIO roster, was contacted at his home. Atkins listened politely, but when they importuned him for money and used his name on a list of endorsers without his permission, he became fed up. "I called the FBI," he said.

In the early years of the Reagan administration the LaRouchians established direct channels into the intelligence community. Admiral Inman appreciated their "flow of materials" to help fill the gap left by Turner's cutbacks. LaRouche was allowed to brief two aides to John McMahon, Inman's successor, at CIA headquarters in 1983. According to court papers, an aide to Federal Emergency Management Agency director Louis Guiffrida frequently met with the LaRouchians and even came to NCLC headquarters for a day's briefing. Jeffrey Steinberg visited the National Security Council eight to ten times between June 1983 and June 1984, according to his deposition in *LaRouche* v. *NBC*. Articles in *EIR* were peppered with quotes from unnamed "CIA Sovietologists" and "DIA analysts."

LaRouche's science adviser, Dr. Steven Bardwell, became convinced that the NCLC top leadership was prostituting itself to the CIA and the Reagan administration. Being himself a participant in several meetings with NSC staff members, he wrote an internal document sharply criticizing this trend shortly before his defection in early 1984. "At the point, nine months ago, that Reagan adopted an approximation of our policy [on beam weapons], our NSA/CIA/DIA 'connections' acquired a powerful hold over us," he complained. "We now began to bend our polemics, public statements, intelligence tasks, and terms of reference to suit our newly acquired clients."

The capstone of the new policy was the hiring of ex-Pentagon spooks and self-styled CIA operatives who claimed to have special high-level sources. NCLC security staff reports circa 1984 contain numerous references to "the Major," a code name for Anthony W. ("Danny") Murdock, a former Army Special Forces officer who worked from 1976 to 1982 as a civilian foreign intelligence specialist at the Army's Aberdeen Proving Grounds in Maryland. Murdock provided the LaRouchians with frequent security advice after leaving government service. According to Virginia law enforcement sources, he accompanied Jeffrey Steinberg on fact-finding trips to Guatemala. A June 1986 internal LaRouche memorandum says that Murdock received $3,000 a month in consulting fees and loans of tens of thousands of dollars, including a $12,000 loan that month.

In 1984 Murdock joined with Steinberg and Paul Goldstein to form a real estate partnership, Dan Bar Unlimited. (The "Bar" was Barney Cochran, who soon dropped out.) They purchased 4,500 acres of timber and farmland in Pulaski County, Virginia, and set up a firing range. According to Virginia authorities, paramilitary training for LaRouche security aides was conducted there beginning in 1984. A Vietnam veteran who lives nearby observed people in camouflage suits, their faces blackened "like for a recon assignment," training in a field. "I heard bursts of rapid fire, like an AR-15 on full automatic," he said. Another neighbor recalled frequent helicopter landings. Murdock had built a perimeter road around the farm and up to the top of the mountain, which was patrolled by jeep. The neighbors say that every Thursday night there would be a light on top of the mountain and a low-flying plane would come over. A 1986 LaRouchian memo mentioned transactions by courier totaling over $230,000 for the farm's expenses. The memo said these payments were being listed as "legal investigations," but warned this might not prove a very defensible position with the IRS. In 1987 court-appointed trustees seized the farm in partial payment of millions of dollars in fines levied on the LaRouchians because of their failure to comply with federal grand jury subpoenas.

By the mid-1980s the LaRouchians had over a dozen security-type consultants on their payroll, but the most assiduous were three men from Reading, Pennsylvania, who affected knowledge of vast intrigues. One said he was a CIA official and used a code name. The other two were known to the LaRouchians under their real names but claimed to be the cutouts for mysterious high-up people. Their ringleader was a man almost as brilliantly devious as LaRouche—Roy Everett Frankhouser.

# Twenty-one

# Night Riders
# to the Rescue

Roy Frankhouser is a roly-poly cigar-chomping little man with a glass eye and a taste for loud sport jackets. For much of his adult life he has lived with his mother in Reading, Pennsylvania. His late stepfather was a private detective, for whom Roy worked in the early 1960s. After that he usually worked as a department store salesman. Genial and polite, he is a difficult person not to like. He could be an officer of the local Rotary Club and a pillar of the community.

But Roy turns nasty in the twinkling of an eye. He has a recorded message on his telephone, which he changes every week. In early 1988 the messages were about Jesus Christ and the forgiveness of sins. But Roy was feeling the pressure from his financial and legal difficulties. The message changed to a shrill call for local Aryans to join the "Reading Night Riders." The Zionists, he said, are the "sons of Lucifer." It's time to send them "to the rope and telephone pole." It's time for a "Final Solution . . . a real solution for treason," and concluding: "You can smell the gas, can't you?"

Born in 1939, Roy has belonged at one time or another since his high school years to most of the important white supremacist groups—the

United Klans of America, the American Nazi Party, the Minutemen, the National Renaissance Party, the Liberty Lobby, the White Citizens Councils, the National States Rights Party. For years he was the Grand Dragon of the Pennsylvania Klan. He took the Fifth Amendment over thirty times during a 1966 congressional investigation of the Klan. In 1972 he demonstrated on Manhattan's Fifth Avenue in a National Renaissance Party storm trooper uniform to challenge a state law against wearing Nazi garb in public.

In his youth Roy participated in numerous cross burnings and street rallies and was arrested over two dozen times. He stockpiled guns and ammunition, and once ran a paramilitary training camp to prepare for the coming race war. He lost his eye in a 1965 barroom brawl. The American Nazi Party claimed a "Jew gang" did it. Roy sometimes claims it's a Bay of Pigs battle wound.

He operates the Mountain Church of Jesus Christ in a run-down Reading neighborhood, and lists it as his official residence. Some folks believe the electric cross in front is a Klan symbol. The church is the local arm of the Mountain Church in Cohoctah, Michigan, a neo-gnostic Identity church whose pastor is Robert Miles, one of Roy's closest "racial comrades" and a LaRouche ally for many years. ("Mountain" stands for Mont Ségur, the medieval fortress of the gnostic Cathars in southern France.)

In the late 1960s some of Roy's comrades began to suspect he was an FBI snitch. Roy says the FBI started the rumor as part of a plot to instigate his assassination. But in 1972 Roy did become an informer for the Alcohol, Tobacco, and Firearms Bureau's Reading office, using the code name "Ronnie." Special agent Edward Slamon, Roy's controller, reported to superiors that Roy had solemnly promised to sever "all relationships with other federal enforcement agencies" and work exclusively for the ATF. "This point was dwelled on and explored at length," Slamon wrote. "I informed Ronnie that at any time . . . I determined that he was dealing with any other agency and supplying them with the same information, our bargain was null and void."

Roy told Slamon that a Black September cell in Toronto was planning attacks on prominent American Jews. Earlier information from Roy had checked out, and the ATF asked the National Security Council in the White House for approval to send him to Toronto. The go-ahead was obtained by John Caulfield, the ATF's assistant director for enforcement, and Roy embarked on his very brief career as a foreign agent.

His reports of his Toronto adventures, as reflected in Slamon's own reports to superiors, suggest that the Black September cell, if indeed it existed, was composed of the world's most indiscreet terrorists. Barely acquainted with Roy, they were supposedly willing to tell him every-thing. Roy claimed to have picked the brains of one cell leader while they strolled around the city "visiting museums and public places." Roy said the cell was planning skyjackings and kidnappings with the help of Quebec nationalist bomb technicians and Czech diplomats. Roy was supposed to recruit a bush pilot to pick up ransom money, and also was assigned to "keep track of all visitors from Israel to America." The ATF finally became suspicious. Slamon met with Roy and asked him if he would be willing to return to Canada and discuss his story with the Royal Canadian Mounted Police. Roy "became visibly upset and agitated," Slamon wrote, and flatly refused, apparently knowing that the RCMP would see through his deception.

While working for the ATF, Roy seems to have tried to help out his friend and fellow Grand Dragon Bob Miles, who was facing a long prison sentence for masterminding the 1971 Pontiac, Michigan, school bus bombings to protest integration. Miles would serve six years in Marion for this crime, but at the time of Roy's ATF employment he was free pending the outcome of an appeal. Roy brought Slamon tapes of conversations with Miles and offered to set up a crony of Miles for a "controlled buy" of stolen explosives. Although Roy's maneuverings during this period are extremely murky, the best bet is that he was fishing for information about the Miles case and trying to compromise the feds so Miles could charge federal misconduct. Miles himself certainly believes this. He told journalist Martin Lee in 1986 that Roy "never really threw any right-wingers to the wolves" and that Roy was beaten up by ATF agents in reprisal. Roy says that he was indeed a double agent for the racialist cause, and that he was beaten by a motor-cycle gang in Berks County Prison at ATF instigation.

Roy landed in prison because, after the ATF rejected his plan for a controlled buy, he went ahead on his own with a real buy. In February 1974 he was arrested and charged with "aiding and abetting" the transportation of 240 pounds of stolen explosives to Michigan. At this point, the ATF washed its hands of Roy. His bail was set at $50,000, and he spent several months in prison before he could raise the money.

Finally out on bail and awaiting trial, Roy encountered members of the Reading NCLC as they sold *New Solidarity.* They had only just begun their swing to the right, and interaction was difficult at first. But Roy knew how to ingratiate himself with leftists from his experience infiltrating Socialist Workers Party meetings in New York in the early 1960s. (He claims he first met LaRouche then, but LaRouche denies it.) His approach to the NCLC was also facilitated by Nazi warlock Ken Duggan, who introduced him to security staffer Scott Thompson in New York.

Regarding his indictment, Roy told the LaRouchians he was an honest, dedicated government agent who had risked his life in the war on gunrunners, drug traffickers, and terrorists. He was being "hung out to dry" by the intelligence community because he knew too much about local cover-ups and corruption. The LaRouchians put him through an intensive grilling, and he thoroughly convinced them. They issued broadsides in his defense and sponsored a well-attended press conference at which he made numerous detailed allegations about unlawful activities by federal agents in the Reading area (for instance, directing him to commit burglaries and secretly tape conversations between the Pontiac defendants and their attorney). "My partner in crime was Uncle Sam," he said.

In a press statement aimed more at the NCLC than at the media, Roy claimed that while working for the ATF he had really been working for the CIA. He had been a CIA agent ever since the Bay of Pigs. He had perused a top secret White House Committee of 40 report. He had been drugged and brainwashed in Berks County Prison. Roy's account of his brainwashing was remarkably similar to LaRouche's account the previous year of Chris White's alleged ordeal: "strapped in a medical chair," "a sensation of receding into a tunnel," "an overwhelming sense of drowning," a lingering "disassociation reaction."

At Roy's trial, retired agent Slamon testified for three days. His account of the NSC-approved Toronto caper stimulated press attention, and Roy was glad to oblige with more details. The upshot was a deal whereby he pleaded guilty to trafficking in explosives and was given five years' probation, although he had originally faced a possible fifty-one years in prison. A Reading police official told me years later that he believed the intelligence community had intervened.

Roy's maneuverings during the trial apparently made a deep impression on the LaRouchians. He had shown that if you can get government agents to meet with you and give you money, then no matter what you do later, you can tell the court you were doing it for the feds. And if you happen to have observed any improprieties while working for the feds, you can use that for leverage. The LaRouchians would use similar tactics in Boston thirteen years later.

After the trial, Roy began to spend more and more time with the "comrades," as he called the LaRouchians. He exchanged information with NCLC security chiefs Jeffrey Steinberg and Paul Goldstein almost daily on the phone. He traveled to New York at NCLC expense on security assignments. While staying at the homes of Jewish members he was the perfect gentleman, never displaying any bigotry. For Roy, it was just one more manipulative relationship—to get money out of the

In speeches and "ego-stripping" sessions in the early 1970s, LaRouche warned his followers against CIA brainwashing, secret assassins, and the "pit creatures" of the unconscious mind.

These students from Philadelphia's Temple University were among the victims of Operation Mop Up, LaRouche's three-month-long campaign of violence against political rivals during 1973.

The LaRouche organization has sponsored literature tables at dozens of airports across the country since the mid-1970s. While promoting nuclear energy, Star Wars, and other high-technology causes, the NCLC members at these tables raise tens of thousands of dollars a week. Prosecutors charge that customers who pay by credit card are sometimes victimized by unauthorized additional charges to their accounts. They may also be contacted by telephone fund raisers.

The posters at this NCLC anti-Zionist rally reflect the organization's topsy-turvy form of anti-Semitism.

In 1979 NCLC members were greatly upset by articles in the New York City weekly *Our Town* that accused their leader of neo-Nazism. Carol White, LaRouche's former mistress, denounced *Our Town* at a rally in upper Manhattan.

LaRouche speaks at a Michigan Anti-Drug Coalition rally in May 1979. In the audience was one of Detroit's most notorious racketeers, Rolland McMaster, who afterward endorsed LaRouche for President.

LaRouche followers Janice Hart and Mark Fairchild stunned the nation by winning the March 1986 Illinois Democratic primaries for secretary of state and lieutenant governor, respectively. The media called it a "fluke," but surveys showed the LaRouche movement tapping into rural and blue-collar anger.

LaRouche's 171-acre estate, Ibykus Farm, in Loudoun County, Virginia.

Paul Goldstein, top LaRouche security aide, indicted in 1986 for obstruction of justice.

Roy Frankhouser, former Klu Klux Klan grand dragon and LaRouche adviser, convicted of obstruction of justice in 1987.

The late Mitchell WerBell III, reputed CIA contract agent who trained LaRouche followers in paramilitary skills at his Powder Springs, Georgia, compound.

Richard Dupont, prankster extraordinaire, who worked closely with Paul Goldstein and other LaRouche followers in an attempt to destroy the career of the late Roy Cohn.

Federal agents raided NCLC headquarters in downtown Leesburg, Virginia, October 6, 1986. Over four hundred boxes of financial records and intelligence files were seized.

LaRouche departs from the federal court house in Alexandria, Virginia, after pleading not guilty to fraud and conspiracy charges, October 1988.

LaRouchians and to persuade them to take political stances that would serve the fight against the pro-Zionist establishment.

The LaRouchians were chiefly fascinated by Roy because of his alleged intelligence community ties. When they indicated that they too wanted to hobnob with secret agents, he set about facilitating it to the mutual advantage of himself and various third parties. It was Roy who first suggested that the LaRouchians should link up with Mitch WerBell. Claiming to have worked with WerBell on CIA assignments, Roy helped them compile a detailed dossier on him. At the time WerBell was in trouble with the ATF and strapped for cash. His son, Mitch IV, had been arrested on charges of trying to illegally sell machine guns to an undercover agent. Although the charges against Mitch IV were dropped, the ATF forced WerBell out of the armaments business because of improprieties in his record keeping. An NCLC dossier suggested that the Rockefeller family and Interpol were behind this: "Roy believes that if we can pin down how the operation is being run against WerBell there is a possibility . . . he can be turned."

Months passed, yet no deal between LaRouche and WerBell was finalized, and it was time to prime the pump. When LaRouche went to Wiesbaden in the summer of 1977, Roy sent a warning from "Mister Ed," an alleged personage said to be linked to the CIA, that LaRouche might be in danger from terrorists. In previous months there had been several highly publicized terrorist assassinations and kidnappings in West Germany. On July 31 a band of anarchists linked to the Baader-Meinhof gang gunned down Jürgen Ponto, a banker much admired by LaRouche. Shortly before 5 A.M. on August 1, LaRouche received a transatlantic phone call from Roy, passing on an emergency message from Mister Ed: A hit list had been found in a terrorist safe house, and LaRouche's name supposedly was included. LaRouche panicked. In a news release later that day he announced the threat to his life. He did not specify the source, merely saying that it was "relayed . . . from high-level sources of the best qualifications." LaRouche immediately agreed to hire WerBell as his security adviser.

Roy's role as the cutout for Mister Ed became the centerpiece of his dealing with the LaRouchians. Mister Ed supposedly had asked him to open the channel because LaRouche's knowledge of terrorism had impressed many important people, including George Bush. (Roy knew the LaRouchians had called Bush's home in an attempt to brief him on terrorism.) Roy said that Mister Ed would be requesting reports from LaRouche on various questions, which would be transmitted to the highest levels of the CIA and the White House. Roy was careful not to neglect Steinberg and Goldstein. He said Mister Ed had assigned them the code names "Purple Haze" and "Honeywell."

Over a seven-year period Roy delivered to the LaRouchians dozens of "E to L" (Ed to LaRouche) memos. A typical memo included advice that LaRouche should try to work with Colonel Qaddafi, who supposedly was getting a raw deal from Zionist elements in the U.S. government and thus was being driven, against his will, into the Soviet camp. Roy also transmitted numerous verbal messages. LaRouche prepared the intelligence evaluations as requested, and his followers carried out the propaganda "assignments" suggested by Mister Ed. These assignments were often anti-Zionist, as when Roy told the LaRouchians that Mister Ed wanted them to spread the word that Israel had the A-bomb and was the main threat to world peace. Someone claiming to be Mister Ed also began to communicate directly with Paul Goldstein. Former NCLC members recall him rushing out of the office on West Fifty-eighth Street in Manhattan to answer the celestial ring at a street pay phone.

The identity of Mister Ed became a subject of endless speculation. Defectors from the security staff stated in a report prepared in 1979 for *The New York Times* that they believed he was former CIA deputy director E. Henry Knoche, whose 1977 firing by Admiral Turner had been denounced by LaRouche. The LaRouche leadership also claimed Knoche was Mister Ed in 1987 court documents. Knoche in a 1988 telephone interview denied ever meeting Roy or LaRouche or anyone that he was aware had any connection to them. "If I thought I was *ever* duped into dealing with those people I'd commit hara-kiri on the front porch," he said. Referring to LaRouche's trial, he added: "I hope they nail him."

Among journalists, Mister Ed became one of those unsolved puzzles —something like the tramps on the grassy knoll in Dallas. *Covert Action* editor Lou Wolf thought Mister Ed was "someone in Angleton's shop." Kevin Coogan argued that it was CIA renegade Ed Wilson, who was known in Libya as Mister Ed and held political views remarkably similar to those expressed in some of the E to L memos. Detroit journalist Russ Bellant thought it might have been one of Wilson's former superiors. In the mid-1980s the LaRouchians mocked such speculation with an advertisement in their publications for "Mr. Ed's Elephant Farm"—a Pennsylvania tourist trap—with a drawing of a charging elephant, presumably a rogue.

Some cynics theorized that Mister Ed was simply Roy. But the E to L memos, although anti-Zionist and extremely right-wing, displayed a conceptual grasp of international politics beyond anything Roy would have written on his own. This anomaly was explained, at least in part, by former associates of Roy who testified in court that the memos had been plagiarized from defense and foreign policy journals. Nevertheless, Roy claims there were a number of people—fifteen of them—who used the Mister Ed channel. Although Roy's word alone is dubious evidence, it makes sense that someone in the zany world of ex-spooks, contract spooks, and private spooks would have linked up with Roy (who *did* have contacts in that milieu) to milk the LaRouchians. After all, here was a multimillion-dollar international intelligence and propaganda network just begging to be used by anyone claiming to be from the CIA. In their eagerness to be accepted in the spy world, the LaRouchians would prepare massive dossiers at the drop of a hat, and publish the most outrageous disinformation and slander in *EIR*—as long as they believed the request was coming from "down the way" (i.e., from Langley). Apparently word of this circulated, and various people on the far right decided to use the channel to unleash the LaRouchians on personal or political enemies or simply to get a free dossier. There was little risk of exposure or embarrassment. Roy would take care of all direct dealings with the LaRouchians. And he himself had such a bizarre history that no one would believe him if he decided to expose the operation.

For years Roy's personal prestige with the LaRouchians was tied to his role as Mister Ed's messenger boy. If the LaRouchians wanted to talk directly with a real spook, they went to someone like WerBell. But with the decline of WerBell's health, Roy had his chance to emerge as a full-fledged security guru. He did not accomplish this overnight. In 1982, when LaRouche was living in a Manhattan town house on Sutton Place, Roy was brought in merely to provide backup security under his code name "Clay." Phil Perlonga, a retired New York City police officer, was working at the time for Metro Security, a professional firm hired by LaRouche. Perlonga recalled how Roy gave the Metro men KKK belt buckles as gifts. But Perlonga became annoyed when Roy tried to interfere in his work. Roy once took charge of whisking Lyn and Helga LaRouche out of a meeting. "He ran them into a locked door," Perlonga said.

Roy needed a sidekick with the physical presence and at least part of the expertise he lacked. He rekindled his acquaintance with Lee Fick, a Reading security guard who had been active on the far right. Fick had served in the Marines, mostly as an MP in California. When approached by Roy, he was unemployed and had a wife and children to support. He agreed to go to work for LaRouche as Roy's assistant, and Roy presented him to the security staff as an experienced operative.

For Fick it was a chance to play James Bond for $500 a week. He drove LaRouche's armored Pontiac Bonneville limousine, accompanied him to a meeting at CIA headquarters, and became the object of amorous advances from one of Helga's German Amazons. He and Roy cadged a free trip to Europe on the *Queen Elizabeth II* to overhaul LaRouche's security in Wiesbaden. Traveling on to Rome, they told the LaRouchians they would meet with the CIA station chief to arrange security for a LaRouche conference. "The Mediterranean climate offered us seven days of springlike weather which added great comfort to our tour," reported an unsigned article in *Dragonfire,* a rightist newsletter published by Fick.

When asked about Roy in a 1984 deposition, LaRouche described him as "an expert in security matters . . . he knows certain nasty people by sight or reputation . . ." LaRouche praised Roy's ability to keep his "pair of eyes" alert (so much for LaRouche's own powers of observation) and to "detect nasties by their wiggle." Roy's standing became even higher with the security staff. Steinberg and Goldstein marveled at his never-ending revelations from high-level sources inside the FBI, the CIA, the New York Police Department, and NBC-TV.

There was a good reason for Roy's success as a secret agent: He was making up most of it. "It was bullshit," Fick said. "Roy would make up a source A, then a source B, C, and D. I'd be sitting right beside him while he did it." Internal reports from LaRouche's security staff in 1984 confirmed Fick's story. They quote Roy as providing information from an alleged source inside NBC during its preparation of a *First Camera* report on LaRouche. The allegations pertain to incidents that the show's producer, Patricia Lynch, says never took place.

The LaRouchians asked Roy and Fick to provide them with a direct CIA channel in Reading. The two complied by introducing Paul Goldstein to "Nat" at a Reading motel. "Nat," a.k.a. "Nat Regnew," a.k.a. "Mister Nat," a.k.a. "N," was supposed to be Roy's control officer, a CIA covert operations specialist holding GS-15 or GS-16 rank. After Nat met with LaRouche, a flow of "N to L" memos began. Alas, Nat was just a neighbor of Roy's, actually named Monroe Wenger, who worked on an Army Corps of Engineers dredging barge. When the LaRouchians found this out years later, they naturally said the barge was a spy ship.

Meanwhile Roy and Fick began to supplement these memos and the E to L memos with weekly "COMSTA-C" reports from an alleged high official, much higher than Nat, called "the Source." Whatever the truth regarding Mister Ed, the provenance of the Source is known: Roy dictated the reports to Fick, making them up as he went along. Fick then took them to a local copy center in Reading to be typed.

Some high-level NCLC members, although not aware of the full depths of the deception, sensed that something was wrong, not just with Roy but with Murdock and all the other security consultants. Steven Bardwell noted in his pre-resignation letter that the NCLC's "susceptibility to any information presented in clandestine form through a covert (or apparently covert) source is a serious vulnerability. The amount of garbage we have retailed because it came from 'down the way' is quite remarkable." But this was a minority view. Most of the leadership believed that LaRouche had deep influence at Langley and that the Source was someone incredibly powerful.

Because they believed this, they decided they must be invulnerable to prosecution. Their real if limited success in gaining meetings with CIA and NSC officials helped to feed this view, but it also was stimulated by phony reports from consultants, such as the following from early 1984: "LaRouche['s] prestige [is] highest ever on economy and terrorism. White House collective view is we can no longer ignore LaRouche . . . LaRouche is now magnet for anti-Kissinger forces." In addition, the COMSTA-C reports provided apparent evidence, week after week, that LaRouche had friends and sympathizers in the highest places. The COMSTA-C reports were seen by only a few leaders, but the general attitude trickled down to the rank and file. In 1984 the NCLC's fundraising methods became wildly reckless, and many fund raisers and security staffers seemed to have no fear of the law. They ran the risk of indictment because they believed there was no risk.

Fick realized things were getting out of hand in the summer of 1984, when he and Roy were approached by Paul Goldstein with a deadly proposition. As Fick later described it to *NBC Nightly News*, Goldstein recommended "that we . . . go along with him and kill or assassinate Henry Kissinger." According to Fick, Goldstein said he knew where Kissinger parked his car in an underground garage, and that it would be "a relatively easy thing for us to do, to make a bomb, and strap it to his car."

Although Goldstein was probably just trying to impress them, the proposal unnerved Fick, and it apparently also worried Roy. Shortly afterward, I received a series of phone calls from Roy, posing as "Special Agent Phillips" of an unnamed federal agency. The calls were intended to interest me in investigating Goldstein. Roy did not mention the plot against Kissinger, but he did say Goldstein was a menace who must be stopped. He said his own hands "were tied," but if I would write an article on Goldstein or communicate Phillips's information to the federal prosecutor's office in Boston, then it could help to avert serious criminal acts.

In the fall of 1984 a federal grand jury was convened in Boston to probe allegations of LaRouchian credit-card fraud. LaRouche ordered Roy and Fick to go to Boston and conduct a counterinvestigation. Instead, they went to a *Star Trek* convention in Scranton, although Roy called the security office and warned them there were "feds all over" in

Boston. Jeffrey and Michelle Steinberg then asked Roy and Fick to contact E. Henry Knoche (whom they believed to be Mister Ed) and get him to "quash" or "fix" the investigation. How this was to be done, the Steinbergs weren't clear. But they felt the "cookie factory" (the CIA) owed them for their loyal services through the years. Fick's response was that if the CIA wouldn't go to the wall for Richard Nixon, it was unlikely to do so for LaRouche. Still the security staff believed the Boston investigation was an isolated and easily containable probe conducted by Kissinger-influenced FBI chumps. According to Federal authorities, the Steinbergs and other security staffers set about destroying records and arranging for NCLC members who might be subpoenaed to move to Europe—to hide out, as Michelle put it, "where the sun doesn't shine."

Roy encouraged these efforts to obstruct the grand jury's work. In a memo to LaRouche he noted that "paper burns at 451 degrees Fahrenheit." Fick wanted no part of this, and stopped working with Roy. Briefly he continued to do bodyguard work for LaRouche under the auspices of a New York private detective agency, but he still felt uneasy. He met with NBC's Patricia Lynch and then appeared on *NBC Nightly News* with the car-bomb story. As the Boston investigation heated up, the feds began to take his allegations seriously, and he became a key witness.

Meanwhile the LaRouchians blithely continued with their credit-card and loan schemes. They believed Roy's assurances of support from "down the way," the cumulative faith built up by a decade of transmissions from Mister Ed and the Source. When almost four hundred federal agents and state and local police officers swooped down on the NCLC's Leesburg headquarters in October 1986, the LaRouchians could blame it in no small part on the misleading advice of their Ku Klux Klan scout.

Roy was indicted for obstructing justice, along with several of LaRouche's security honchos. When I met him at a hotel near La Guardia Airport several months later, he was scared, and with good reason. He was already a convicted felon. He had avoided a prison sentence on his first conviction, but this time he'd end up with the Black Muslims and Five Percenters. Although he had sung "like a canary" (according to the FBI) the day after his arrest, the feds were no longer interested in cutting a deal. Roy had jerked them around, first promising to testify and then playing coy and claiming the feds had "tortured" him. The LaRouchians no longer trusted him, and wouldn't help with his legal expenses.

Roy told me that LaRouche had ruined his life, and that his mother would lose her home. Anything illegal that happened was the

LaRouchians' fault, not his. He'd never had anything to do with defrauding any old ladies. Indeed, the LaRouchians had ripped off his mother and his uncle for thousands of dollars behind his back. Fick, Wenger, and the Major meanwhile had all double-crossed him. The remark about 451 degrees Fahrenheit had merely been a literary reference to the Ray Bradbury novel; Fick had misinterpreted it because he was illiterate and stupid.

Roy plucked out his glass eye, wiped it on his shirt, held it up to the light, and regarded it with his good eye, like Hamlet gazing upon the skull of Yorick. "Life is more than bullet holes," he said. In December 1986 he went on trial in Boston federal court. After hearing prosecution witnesses Fick, Wenger, Charles Tate, and others, the jury found Roy guilty of obstruction of justice. He was fined $50,000 and sentenced to three years in prison.

# Twenty-two

## Join the Spooks and Stay Out of Jail

It would be all too easy to say that Frankhouser's manipulation of the LaRouchians proves them to be a band of naïve kooks. Undeniably, top NCLC security staffers believed Frankhouser's tall tales. But the idea that LaRouche himself completely shared his followers' gullibility ignores his ability to operate on both rational and irrational levels at once. Again and again, he has given vent to paranoia and delusions of grandeur, only to end up achieving useful pragmatic results from such behavior. He attacked Kissinger in an apparently demented way, but reaped the reward of sympathy on the ultraright, greater fanaticism among his followers, and a fearsome reputation among liberals. He accused a vast range of enemies of plotting to assassinate him during the Chris White affair, but also used the episode to consolidate his control of the NCLC.

Such behavior is not unlike that of many totalitarian leaders in whom madness and cunning have mingled inextricably. The seemingly paranoid Stalin accepted as truth the preposterous stories of his secret police about spies and saboteurs, but slyly used these concoctions to strengthen his power. It is easier to see this in a Stalin or Hitler, because they operated on a grand scale whereas LaRouche has been confined to a small stage.

LaRouche is quite aware of this type of slyness. In two essays on Soviet history written in the mid-1970s, he discussed Stalin's "hysterical" and "propitiatory" beliefs—his "nonsense-theses"—and how they were basically an "expediency" that enabled Stalin to handle his own neuroses while getting other people to do his bidding. Stalin's incessant discovery of plots was a matter of "fantastic lying"; it worked because of the "wishful credulousness" of the Communist rank and file. At certain moments, Stalin "might have reached the point of almost believing his own rhetoric," but remained in touch with the "contrary knowledge" within himself (i.e., the knowledge that his rhetoric was ultimately just a manipulative device). LaRouche argued (in effect) that Stalin's craziness served his cunning in the interests of consolidating his power. In his own behavior, LaRouche carried out a refined version of the formula: Craziness serves cunning in the interests of staying out of legal trouble if you're too weak to take power.

All this is well exemplified in his relationship with Frankhouser. From the very beginning in 1976–77, there were pragmatic reasons for LaRouche to accept and promote Frankhouser's "fantastic lying," whether or not he believed it. The NCLC had begun its first wave of white-collar scams: kiting checks, welching on loans, taking advantage of wire-transfer errors in order to rip off banks, filing fraudulent matching-funds applications with the Federal Election Commission. This was low-level stuff, but it was more than enough to make anyone nervous who had never before engaged in illicit activity. LaRouche began to speculate at that point on how criminals gain immunity from prosecution. The key, he suggested in mid-1977, was to become useful to the CIA. His apparent model was Mitch WerBell: An early 1977 NCLC internal report on WerBell showed that the LaRouchians firmly believed the CIA and other intelligence agencies had helped him out of legal difficulties on several occasions.

But LaRouche believed the successful use of this tactic hinged on the relationship of forces within the CIA or another protecting agency. He taught that the CIA was divided into opposing factions. The pro-"humanist" faction might protect a WerBell or a LaRouche, but what if the anti-"humanist" faction were in charge? LaRouche had the example of WerBell's 1975 indictment, when the Company *didn't* look after him. (We will examine this case later.) He also had the example of Frankhouser's indictment for transporting stolen explosives while working for the ATF. Both Mitch and Roy, and Bob Miles too, had been "hung out to dry" by antihumanist spooks (so the LaRouchians argued). What do you do when the antihumanists are out to get you? Or when the charges are so serious that even your allies can't intercede for you?

The answer is to adopt the "national-security defense" (also known as the "CIA defense"). Whatever you're charged with, blame it on the CIA or the White House. Say you thought you were following secret orders from high up and/or that you were framed because you knew too much about embarrassing operations. If you can prove you've *ever* been involved with the CIA, many people will believe the rest of your story. Possibly even the jury will go for it. LaRouche apparently figured this tactic had worked for WerBell in his smuggling trial (backed up by the fortuitous death of the government's key witness) and that it may have helped Frankhouser avoid a prison sentence in the stolen-dynamite trial.

But both WerBell and Frankhouser could establish that they had, indeed, worked for the intelligence community in some fashion. La-Rouche built a comparable record for himself. First, he offered the CIA his services and did everything he could to be useful (so they would *want* to protect him). Second, he compiled a detailed record of dealings with presumed agents. If he had to go into court, he could use this record to establish that whatever he did was done under CIA orders, at arm's length if not directly.

For the purpose of the CIA defense, it is not altogether necessary that one's dealings be directly with the CIA (since the agency won't reveal the identity of its agents anyway). The important thing is simply what a jury will believe. Thus, if one doesn't have a connection with real agents, one might as well use ex-agents, suspected agents, or even make-believe agents whom one can then staunchly maintain *are* real agents. Hence, the large number of spookish consultants, including Frankhouser, that LaRouche surrounded himself with.

Frankhouser and Fick both tell a revealing story about this. They would go to the Leesburg mansion to brief LaRouche on the latest scoop from the Source. But he never seemed interested. "He really didn't want to listen, he just wanted a captive audience," Frankhouser said. "Five minutes into the briefing, he'd cut us off and change the subject, doing most of the talking himself. He'd go into these amazing monologues, for hours, talking about a . . . lost civilization." Apparently LaRouche knew on some level that the reports were worthless, but went through the motions of meeting with Frankhouser and Fick anyway to build his record for his future CIA defense. (In 1987–88 his lawyers would tell the court in Boston that the LaRouche organization sincerely believed Frankhouser and Fick worked for the CIA.) Meanwhile, LaRouche would acquiesce in Roy's deceiving of his own Security staffers, since they would work twice as hard if they thought they were involved in deep operations with real cutouts and real spooks. In other words, while Roy thought he was scamming LaRouche, it appears that the NCLC chairman had actually figured out a way to get his money's worth out of Roy—by using him to keep the Security staff brainwashed.

Documents filed by LaRouche's attorneys prior to his 1988 Boston criminal trial shed much light on his multileveled approach to using alleged CIA connections to stay out of jail. First, they reveal that in early 1982 he was definitely thinking in terms of gaining outright immunity via CIA intervention. At the time he had special reasons for anxiety. Several civil fraud suits were pending, the Federal Election Commission was probing his campaign finances, and a New York bankruptcy court judge had ordered an investigation of the NCLC's alleged looting of a computer software firm. Furthermore, the Detroit NCLC, including several people with detailed knowledge of the NCLC's ties to organized crime, had resigned en masse. Frankhouser suddenly popped up with a proposal from Mister Ed: In return for LaRouche's not exposing an alleged CIA involvement in the Detroit defections, LaRouche and his loyalists would be given immunity from federal prosecution for any events occurring prior to January 1982. This immunity status supposedly would be worked out personally between the CIA director and the Attorney General!

Doubtless this was a hoax, but it shows that Frankhouser and/or Mister Ed had picked up on LaRouche's earlier writings on the CIA/ immunity question. As to the request that LaRouche shut his mouth about Detroit, this had a real basis. He was engaging at the time in indiscreet talk about the NCLC's Teamster/racketeer connections and an alleged joint venture in the financial printing industry. Many people would have wanted to use the "Mister Ed" channel to quash such talk (for instance, Bob Miles, who knew many Michigan Teamsters from the days when he handled their insurance). The suggestion that LaRouche keep quiet about CIA involvement in Detroit can therefore be read as a reference to mob involvement.

In the early 1980s, LaRouche appeared to have built a strong first line of defense by making himself genuinely useful to the intelligence community and the Reagan administration. He had personally met with Inman and several NSC officials. Yet he was not satisfied. In 1983 he requested a meeting at Langley with Inman's successor, John McMahon. Granted a half hour with two of McMahon's aides, he arrived like a head of state with Helga and an entourage of assistants and bodyguards. According to a CIA report on the meeting filed in Boston federal court, he had promised to reveal information on "drug trafficking, gunrunning, and terrorism." But instead of delivering the information promised, LaRouche came bearing a strange proposal for a mutually beneficial "continuing relationship" (i.e., regular meetings with no cutouts) between his organization and the CIA. He boasted of his good sources in the French presidential palace and among Spain's "old crowd." The CIA official (name redacted) who wrote the report was not impressed.

What was really going on here? LaRouche had a dozen channels for his "continuing relationship" without embarrassing either the CIA or his own followers.They had kept up contact with Inman after he left the CIA, and WerBell was still friendly. Why should LaRouche show up on Langley's doorstep begging for what was not necessary and, if obtained, would only undermine his value in the realm of arm's-length intelligence operations? One could say it was his vanity or his hunger for life in the Inner Ring, but a more tangible motive may also have been involved. At the time, his organization was embarking on risky new fund-raising practices, such as the nationwide solicitation of allegedly fraudulent loans from senior citizens. Being indirectly useful to the CIA might not be enough to prevent indictments. The LaRouchians needed a record of direct dealings with the agency that would allow them to claim in court that they were a genuine "proprietary" following the orders not just of a cutout but of high-ranking agency officials. More important, they needed leverage to *force* the CIA to protect them. What better weapon than the ability to hold a press conference at any time and "prove" the CIA was behind them? LaRouche believed this could create major problems for the CIA and within the executive branch generally. In his 1987 review of Bob Woodward's *Veil*, LaRouche said that if Casey had ever met with him and knowledge of the meeting had leaked out, the result would have been a "major political explosion." The request he delivered to McMahon's aides apparently was an attempt to plant just such a bomb.

How could LaRouche believe in 1983 that the CIA would fall into his trap? First, he was not as controversial then as before or since. Almost four years had passed since any major media had exposed him. His publications had become more artful in masking the NCLC's anti-Semitism, and Reagan administration officials who met with NCLC members in 1982–83 didn't seem worried about any fallout. Second, LaRouche had the example of Admiral Inman, who had compromised himself by agreeing to a seemingly unnecessary meeting with LaRouche while still CIA deputy director. Third, LaRouche knew that although he himself might be considered a kook by some CIA officials, several of his followers were respected for their intelligence analyses. (For instance, one of them gained consulting work from a prestigious Washington risk-analysis firm after defecting.) Fourth, the NCLC indeed had international sources such as LaRouche alluded to in the Langley meeting: He proved his boast about high-level French contacts by publishing a certain purloined letter a few months later. Given these factors, it was not beyond the realm of possibility for the CIA to decide to give LaRouche regular meetings as an easy concession to keep the flow of information coming.

The CIA did not accept LaRouche's proposal, being either too smart or too careful. But if the CIA *had* agreed to give LaRouche regular meetings or some kind of quasi-proprietary status, the consequences would have been interesting indeed. He would have had a much stronger "CIA defense" in his 1988 trial, and he also could have exerted real pressure on the CIA to rescue him prior to the indictments. For instance, he could have threatened to create havoc regarding the February 1986 assassination of Swedish Prime Minister and longtime LaRouchian smear target Olof Palme. Swedish police arrested a suspect shortly after the hit who was identified as a LaRouche follower (although LaRouche denied it). Lacking sufficient evidence to indict this suspect, the Swedish authorities embarked on a wide-ranging probe of possible LaRouchian involvement. (For at least two years, the LaRouchians remained under investigation, although in December 1988 a suspect totally unrelated to them was arrested.) If LaRouche had gained his "continuing" CIA relationship, he would have been in a position to bring automatic suspicion on the CIA for involvement in Palme's death. False as the impression might have been, anti-American and pro-nuclear disarmament forces in Western Europe could have used it. Although LaRouche's followers claim to be pro-NATO, they would have justified the leftist propaganda bonanza as being necessary to save LaRouche, who in their view is more important to NATO than a bunch of missiles anyway.

Much of the above is hypothetical (a hypothesis of the higher hypothesis, as LaRouche would say). But it is revealing to look at what happened when the Boston indictments came down. First, the LaRouchians retained Washington attorney Bernard Fensterwald, who had previously represented Ed (the CIA made me do it) Wilson, James Earl (the FBI made me do it) Ray, James (Nixon made me do it) McCord, Mitch (the DEA made me do it) WerBell, as well as the former employees of Task Force 157, a kind of predecessor to the NCLC in the parallel-CIA game. The LaRouchians then began to put together their "CIA defense" in detail. They couldn't directly prove they were acting under CIA control, but they could present a circumstantial case by simply describing their wide dealings with all kinds of people in, around, and on the fringes of the intelligence community. (They also could lay out dozens of conflicting conspiracy theories to confuse the jury and the press, with each of these theories the pretext for one or more of the scores of delaying motions filed by their virtual army of defense attorneys.)

A sanitized form of LaRouche's CIA defense was filed with the court "under seal" (pursuant to the Classified Information Procedures Act) by Fensterwald's law partner, Daniel S. Alcorn. Although full of details about the antics of Frankhouser and Fick, the twenty-six-page report curiously neglected to mention Mitch WerBell, Admiral Inman, James Angleton, Ray Cline, Paul Corbin, Danny Murdock, Barney Cochran, Walt Mackem, Tom Miner, Lucien Conein, or numerous other interesting contacts. Nor did it mention any of the alleged meetings of LaRouche underlings with CIA officials that they had boasted about to their NSC contacts.

*Loudoun Times-Mirror* reporter Bryan Chitwood thinks that LaRouche was doing a limited hangout. To use Eric Ambler's terminology, he was using his play material and signaling that if he didn't get relief fast he'd lay out something a bit heavier. Indeed, the report listed certain more sensitive matters that might be "raised during the course of Boston litigation" relating to "direct channels" between the CIA and the LaRouchians. What was briefly described appeared to be halfway between play material and reality. A bluff? Among the revelations promised was a detailed account of Jeffrey Steinberg's dealings with the Guatemalan Army and his alleged official debriefings by "CIA, Department of Defense, Drug Enforcement Administration, Joint Special Operations Command, Fort Bragg, N.C., and an official of the Vice President's National Narcotics Border Interdiction Service." Also promised was the history of the NCLC's alleged dealings with Colonel Frank Salcedo, an official at the time with the Federal Emergency Management Agency. Since FEMA, headed in the early 1980s by right-wing cronies of Ed Meese, already was known for its contingency plans for a martial-law America in event of nuclear attack, this promised to be fun indeed. The LaRouche legal brief said that the defendants had presented FEMA with a "series of proposals for the establishment under FEMA of a special government intelligence organization at the direct service of the President," apparently a kind of Meesean precursor of Oliver North's Project Democracy. Next, the LaRouchians promised to tell the full story of their relationship with the National Security Council and of how Judge Clark had supposedly been provided with "written reports and paraphrase transcripts" of LaRouchian meetings with Soviet officials "as per guidelines from 'E' " (Mister Ed).

The under-seal document was sent to the CIA and FBI, which both approved its release (not surprising, considering that the LaRouchians had precensored it themselves). The Justice Department, not wanting to give even the appearance of credibility to LaRouche's national security defense, made copies and passed them out to reporters under the eyes of stunned LaRouchians.

But this was by no means the end of the defendants' obfuscation. They knew that the NCLC's dealings with the intelligence community had left a paper trail and that some people in government were intensely suspicious of them. All they had to do was use subpoenas and the Freedom of Information Act to uncover incidents in which various officials had suggested that they be investigated. Indeed, they had been collecting FOIA documents for years, such as Henry Kissinger's letters to the FBI when NCLC members were harassing him. They could weave such items into a pastiche to "prove" a vast government conspiracy against them. LaRouche, like Roy in 1975, would emerge as an Agent Hung Out to Dry. Naturally they went after the documents in Oliver North's safe. Since they had begun exposing Irangate six months before anyone else, it was reasonable to assume North would have taken at least a passing interest in them. Sure enough, a memo from General Richard Secord to North was found: "Lewis has met with FBI and other agency reps. . . . Our man here claims Lewis has collected info against LaRouche." Lewis, it turned out, was Fred Lewis, a former Army sergeant major who had served in a Delta Force counterintelligence unit in the late 1970s and whose résumé said that he was "skilled in special sensitive low visibility operations."

Just what any of this had to do with alleged credit-card fraud at Boston airports was unclear, but it helped the LaRouchians drag out the trial and embarrass the prosecutors. When the defense attorneys demanded all CIA and FBI documents relevant to the case, the agencies were naturally reluctant to turn over materials that might compromise their security or simply set a dangerous precedent for future discovery motions in other cases. Thus they turned over some documents, withheld others, and simply failed to identify others because of the vast number of files that had to be searched. (Any half-clever defense attorney could have predicted this.) The prosecution had little choice but to accept the FBI's and CIA's solid assurances that they had fully complied with the discovery motions. Meanwhile the LaRouchians used the FOIA and various forms of snooping to turn up more documents (for instance, the one from North's safe). This created the appearance that the U.S. Attorney's office was involved in a cover-up. Relations between the FBI and the prosecutors became tense, with the LaRouchians demanding more documents and the FBI wanting to withhold one document even at the cost of jeopardizing the entire trial. (Strangely, the contents of this document were almost certainly innocuous.) The chief prosecutor, John Markham, asked to withdraw from the case during this altercation but later relented. The trial was held up for weeks while a search was conducted for more and more documents. The LaRouchians wanted millions of documents searched. Some of the press, smelling CIA blood, was verging on a certain sympathy for LaRouche, and articles about the trial focused on North rather than credit-card fraud. By this point the trial had dragged on for five months, and promised to continue for at least six more. Several jurors complained of grievous hardship, and Judge Keeton declared a mistrial. The *Boston Globe* subsequently quoted three jurors as saying they would have voted for acquittal, based on the government's withholding of evidence. (In a memorandum and order the following August, Judge Keeton delivered what in effect was a stinging rebuke to the Reagan administration regarding the disclosure problem. The prosecutors, he said, had been "limited in their ability to fulfill [their disclosure] responsibility by lack of adequate support and assistance both within and beyond the United States Attorney's office.")

Meanwhile, LaRouche, having planted doubts about the government's motives, came out with an accusation that best revealed his foresight in dealing with dubious former federal agents and/or informants through the years. Having once warmly welcomed them onto his payroll, he now depicted them as government moles who had intended all along to set him up. Ryan Quade Emerson, the Virginia-based publisher of a counterterrorist newsletter, proved to be the most useful example. In 1985, after the federal investigation had begun, the LaRouchians hired him as a part-time consultant. They knew he had once been an FBI informant, and they gave him $250 a week to tell them things they already knew. Bryan Chitwood, who has followed the investigation and trial more closely than any other reporter, states flatly that "the LaRouchians were setting a trap." Indeed, it was inevitable that the FBI would get in touch with Emerson. After he stopped working for the LaRouchians, he even made a visit to their offices at the FBI's request. Although he had not functioned as an FBI plant while on the NCLC payroll, his murky activities gave the LaRouchians a wedge to suggest government misconduct. "They used it to foul up the trial pretty well," said Chitwood. "They knew exactly what they were doing."

But during all the legal maneuverings in 1987–88, there was one factor LaRouche underestimated: The "CIA defense" is useful only if the judge rules it admissible. Markham, however, submitted a brief attacking the CIA defense at the root by pointing out that the CIA is not a domestic law enforcement agency. It has no power to grant immunity to citizens who commit crimes in furtherance of a criminal investigation. LaRouche's relationship to the CIA thus should be deemed irrelevant to the charges of obstructing justice and credit-card fraud. Concurring with this argument, Judge Keeton ruled that LaRouche's carefully prepared folderol about the CIA was inadmissible.

Probably the LaRouchians should have tried to pin things on a domestic law enforcement agency from the beginning, as Jackie Presser did with the FBI and Mitch WerBell with his alleged White House drug busters. But when the LaRouchians went back into court claiming they had been mistaken—that the evil force hanging them out to dry was really the FBI, not the CIA—it was too late. Judge Keeton wouldn't buy it.

No matter how much credit one gives to LaRouche's calculated maneuvers, there remains a substratum of naïveté in his dealings with both the real and make-believe intelligence networks around him. In part this was a result of his conspiratorial view of history which ascribes exaggerated powers to intelligence agencies in general and the CIA in particular. LaRouche appears to have really believed that the CIA director, if he wanted to, could simply pick up the telephone and tell the Attorney General's office to "quash" an investigation of LaRouche.

Also, LaRouche apparently believed at least a portion of the tips from Frankhouser and even more of the tips from the "General" and the "Major." But in this gullibility he was not unique. In the demimonde of informers, spies, cutouts, and control officers, even seasoned professionals get taken for a ride (for instance, ATF agent Slamon by Frankhouser in 1972). While Frankhouser and Fick were feeding reports from imaginary sources to the LaRouche organization in the early 1980s, an immigrant from El Salvador named Frank Varelli was running an even more elaborate scam on top FBI officials. Spinning tales of terrorist plots in return for $18,000 and a new car, he sucked the FBI into a five-year investigation involving thousands of man-hours in fifty-two of the FBI's fifty-nine offices. The target was a left-wing group that was agitating against U.S. policy in Central America but had no relationship to terrorism.

Furthermore, the various seemingly harebrained "Mister Ed" schemes that LaRouche became involved in during the late 1970s and early 1980s also had their counterparts in the world of government spookery. The closest parallel is seen in the late CIA director William Casey's Project Democracy. Just as LaRouche set up his private intelligence news service, as a parallel CIA to do what the liberals wouldn't let the real CIA do, so Casey set up Project Democracy. Just as LaRouche operated through the naïve Goldstein and Steinberg, so Casey chose the sappy Oliver North. Just as Goldstein and Steinberg believed in mystic spirals, so North belonged to a charismatic church whose members spoke in tongues. Just as Goldstein and Steinberg became entangled with the likes of WerBell, so North became entangled with General Secord (who was connected with some of the same rogue agents that WerBell knew). Just as the LaRouchians became involved with General Manuel Noriega, so did the Project Democracy crowd. Just as the LaRouchians spied on North and revealed his secrets, so North attempted to spy on the LaRouchians. Just as the LaRouchians raised money from wealthy old ladies to fight communism, so did North's networks raise money from the *same* little old ladies to supply the Contras. Just as LaRouche's ill-gotten fund-raising gains disappeared into a tangle of corporate shells, so did Project Democracy funds get "lost" in numbered overseas accounts. Just as LaRouche came under federal investigation, so did North. Just as LaRouche's aides discussed burning incriminating documents, so did North's secretary, Fawn Hall, shred documents. Just as LaRouche claimed his indictment was a plot by the Democratic Party and the KGB, so did North claim to be the victim of those who don't understand the dangers of communism.

One is forced to conclude that LaRouche is not just an aberration in the world of spookery. To a significant extent he is just one of the boys.

# Part Six

# The Security Staff

Of all passions the passion for
the Inner Ring is most skilful in
making a man who is not yet a
very bad man do very bad things.

—C. S. Lewis

# Twenty-three

# The School
# of Dirty Tricks

Every totalitarian movement needs a special cadre for secret, illegal, and often violent activities. Heinrich Himmler and his SS played this role for the Nazis during their rise to power in the early 1930s. Depending on circumstances, such a cadre may organize assassinations, rob banks, infiltrate the police, or carry out a variety of tasks aimed at protecting the movement and weakening the enemy's will.

When the NCLC shifted into a fascist mode in the mid-1970s, there was no class warfare raging in American streets. Hence what LaRouche needed as his special cadre were not storm trooper types but clever operatives skilled in primarily nonviolent covert activities, especially of the dirty tricks variety. To meet this need he set up a unit of "counter-intelligence agents"—the NCLC security staff (referred to as "Security" by insiders).

In a 1974 memorandum LaRouche explained the "psychological profile" of a good Security operative and how such a person can be controlled. This was ostensibly a discussion of CIA agents, but the description bore an uncanny resemblance to the elite security unit that LaRouche had already begun to create within the NCLC. Agent types, he wrote, are recruited out of university humanities and social studies programs "traditionally free of the obligation to demonstrate anything concerning reality in the outer world." (LaRouche recruited his original cadre among such students, chiefly at Columbia University.) For such individuals the CIA becomes an extension of academia where they can achieve "a sense of power without leaving the home and playground for the actual adult world." The typical agent thus lacks any "inner identity" except his dependence on the CIA. He is highly "suggestible" and plagued by "superstitious fears." Easily manipulated by arbitrary phrases and formulas, he has many features in common with a "synthetic zombie."

Of course this description bore little, if any, resemblance to real CIA agents, but it did fit the NCLC as a cult and the type of tricksters LaRouche needed for his security work—individuals who could totally immerse themselves in petty forms of intrigue in obedience to his will. Indeed, those he placed in charge of Security reflected the profile perfectly.

Security began in 1972–73 as a small karate-trained team to protect NCLC members from alleged Communist Party bullying. It organized Operation Mop Up and began stockpiling weapons, but soon turned away from any truly risky confrontations with the outside world. It was far safer to harass LaRouche's enemies from a safe range via smear leaflets, anonymous telephone calls, and legal frame-ups.

In the wake of the Chris White affair, Security took on the functions of an internal secret police. It watched members for signs of disaffection and harassed any dropout who publicly attacked the organization or tried to get others to leave. The members of Security developed a vested interest in discovering plots everywhere: The more assassins and other enemies they could report to LaRouche, the more power and prestige they gained. Former member Dan Jacobs writes that they effected a kind of "coup" within the organization, with LaRouche's blessings. Jacobs described this as the NCLC's "Thermidor Reaction."

NCLC organizational director Warren Hamerman defined Security's mission in 1976 as being "to detect and investigate enemy deployments against the organization, and to plan and execute offensive counterthrusts." The counterthrusts, generally called "counterpunch deployments," included attacks on public figures whom LaRouche accused of being part of the conspiracy against him, as well as genuine opponents such as journalists and members of rival organizations.

For years Security operated behind a reinforced steel door and bulletproof glass in the NCLC's Columbus Circle headquarters. The two Security chiefs, Jeffrey Steinberg and Paul Goldstein, maintained daily contact with regional Security officers in Detroit, Los Angeles, and other cities.

Members of Security were responsible for the NCLC's earliest propaganda attacks on Israel and the "Zionist lobby." Major General John K. Singlaub, after several visits from them in 1977, told *The New York Times* they were "the worst group of anti-Semitic Jews I've encountered." Former members say that Jewish Security staffers went out of their way to display the most fanatical loyalty—and engage in the nastiest harassment of outsiders—because they never knew for sure if they were really trusted by LaRouche and his top non-Jewish aides. Former Security staffer Charles Tate, a prosecution witness in the Boston trial, testified he never dared question NCLC policy in the presence of Steinberg and Goldstein. "They don't understand doubt. It's not a category that exists for them. . . . So you just don't—unless you want to get in a lot of trouble, you don't say 'I don't believe that' . . . to those people."

Security's duties included providing bodyguards and servants for Lyn and Helga. When the couple moved to the Riverdale section of the Bronx in the late 1970s, Security staffers were assigned to sit with a shotgun at the apartment door. Many had never handled weapons before and presumably knew no more than to point it at any intruder and pull the trigger. A frequent visitor recalled that "LaRouche was waited on hand and foot by Security. They cooked for him, they made his bed, they did his laundry."

LaRouche called for more and more protection during and after his 1980 presidential campaign. A multitiered system evolved, including off-duty and former police officers operating through a New York private detective agency, the Reading night riders, Mitch WerBell's mercenaries, and the Security staff itself. LaRouche claimed to be constantly threatened by such enemies as Mossad, the KGB, the Knights of Malta, the Yippies, the Freemasons, and Henry Kissinger. Helga decided that she too was a target of lethal intentions after a near traffic accident on an autobahn in Germany. The NCLC came to spend millions of dollars each year on the bodyguards who followed Lyn and Helga everywhere in both the United States and Europe.

Ultimately the Security setup was a good investment, for it kept the NCLC membership in the paranoid frenzy that LaRouche had learned was most conducive to maximum results in fund raising. But protection bred more protection, as the outside hired guns encouraged increasingly wild fantasies in order to get more overtime. Although believing these fantasies, Steinberg and Goldstein were also swept up in the profiteering fever. They established two corporations, SSG International and Cincinnatus Associates, to receive payments for campaign security services, as well as to recycle reports on LaRouche's enemies to multinational corporations.

When LaRouche moved to Loudoun County, Virginia, in 1983, he deployed as many as ten guards on each twelve-hour shift at his estate. Supposedly the guards, armed with Walther PPKs and MAC-10s, were prowling their respective free-fire zones under all weather conditions. But LaRouche didn't seem to really care how vigilant they were. In cold or rainy weather, they just stayed in the guardhouse. The electronic alarm was routinely ignored, for it tended to be set off simply by branches brushing against the fence in a breeze. Any enterprising hit man could have slipped under the barbed-wire fence that kept the neighbor's cows from fertilizing Lyndon's lawn. (Security precautions were tighter at LaRouche's villa in Stradecken-Elsheim in West Germany. It was surrounded by a ten-foot-high wall topped with barbed wire, television monitors, electric grids, and floodlights—the very model of a high-tech bunker.)

The major vendor providing guards with police backgrounds for the Leesburg estate was Metro Executive Protection and Security Consultants, Inc., a New York firm headed by former NYPD officer James Powers. According to Phil Perlonga, a former Powers assistant, LaRouche was the firm's principal client in the early 1980s. Its success in serving him helped it expand into other areas. For instance, it developed a clientele among Manhattan landlords by gathering evidence for eviction proceedings against tenants of rent-regulated apartments. (In 1986, Powers told *The New York Times* that his firm had prepared background reports on 5,000 tenants; many were for landlords planning co-op conversions.)

Shortly after the move to Leesburg, several Security staffers set up Premiere Services, Inc., a front for obtaining firearms permits. Among the firm's officers was Robert Kay, who claimed to be a graduate of WerBell's counterterrorist school, as well as the American Security Training Institute in Chicago and the Lethal Force Institute in Long Beach, California. According to Loudoun County records, some of the Security staffers were walking arsenals; for instance, Rick Magraw, who owned a Colt Commander 45, a Sig-Sauer P.380, a Browning 9 mm, and a MAC-10 submachine pistol.

When the permits came up for renewal in 1985, the sheriff's office was fed up with the NCLC's intimidation of local residents. Premiere Services said it needed the permits to protect LaRouche, but Deputy Don Moore told the court that the threats to LaRouche's life were "nebulous to the point of unreality," and "chiefly intended to promote a 'bunker mentality.'" Eventually the judge granted the renewals subject to restriction: LaRouche's armed guards would have to inform the

Sheriff's Department whenever they planned to accompany LaRouche outside his estate. (In 1987 their request for renewal was denied outright.)

Some members of Security were skeptical that LaRouche was really in danger from international assassins. But it was their job to provide the evidence, and they did so, for otherwise LaRouche would have removed them from their relatively cushy jobs and sent them back to field duty—the boring, low-status work of manning literature tables at airports or running boiler-room loan rip-offs. Charles Tate recalls often writing security reports or passing along rumors from informants that he knew to be nonsense, simply to avoid hassles. However, Steinberg and Goldstein spent long hours on the phone soaking up the latest preposterous tips from "Clay" (Roy Frankhouser), "the Major," "the General," "Leviticus," and assorted other paid "consultants."

However, Security's work was not just a game (although even the make-believe part served a serious function in maintaining the NCLC-controlled environment and motivating the membership to work hard). Security developed imaginative and effective techniques for gathering intelligence and harassing enemies. Most important was the undercover phone call or interview. Although there were many variations on this tactic, basically it meant a staff member calling or visiting an outsider (usually an enemy) under false pretenses or using a false identity. It was first employed in 1973 when the NCLC was at war with black nationalist Amiri Baraka. Paul Goldstein sent a directive to "all locals" urging them to set up meetings with "individuals of [the] Baraka type" in order to "pump them for information." He suggested posing as an "innocuous radical or interested sympathizer."

LaRouche himself, during his 1980 New Hampshire primary campaign, told the Associated Press that his followers used "all kinds" of covers and impersonation tactics to investigate their enemies. "Where a press is running a direct operation against us . . . ," he said, "that's an open target. We can impersonate them all we want to because they are doing it to us. It's just an open field." Charles Tate testified he saw his fellow Security staffers make hundreds of undercover calls in the early 1980s, often with tape recorders running without the callee's knowledge. "They were pretending to be priests, ministers, rabbis, newspaper reporters, doctors, lawyers, Indian chiefs," he said.

The late Canon Edward West of New York's Episcopal Cathedral of St. John the Divine was the victim of two LaRouchian imposters posing as freelance writers. They interviewed him and took his picture while preparing a dossier on the Knights of Malta. Later, they wrote an abusive article suggesting he was a homosexual and saying his office reminded them of "Dracula's castle." The reason for the abuse was obvious from the text of the interview. Asked what he thought of the LaRouche organization, Canon West denounced it as "terribly anti-Semitic" and added that "I have violent feelings about anti-Semitism."

The impostures sometimes were clumsy. Herbert Quinde called up *NBC Nightly News* producer Bob Windrem claiming to be "Herb Kurtz," a reporter interested in LaRouche. Windrem smelled a rat, and after meeting with Quinde was able to identify him from a *Hartford Courant* photo. (Quinde had run as a LaRouchian candidate in Hartford.) But Quinde once followed me onto the shuttle from New York to Washington, took the seat next to me, and convincingly introduced himself as "David Feingold," a fictitious AFL-CIO researcher.

In 1981 one "Jean-Claude Adam," an alleged French Defense Ministry official, gained interviews with William Bundy and Winston Lord at the Council on Foreign Relations. He also called several journalists who had written about LaRouche, trying to find out who their sources were. Photographed after one such meeting, "Jean-Claude" was identified as Laurent Murawiec, an *EIR* editor.

The most sinister undercover efforts were directed against anti-Klan groups. According to Tate, collecting this information was a "regular fixation" and reflected the Security staff's friendly ties with violence-prone white supremacists such as Bob Miles. In 1981 an NCLC member pretending to be a civil rights activist infiltrated an anti-Klan conference at Howard University. The LaRouchians then published a list of the attendees, which must have been interesting reading for the Klan. Tate said that a Security staffer was assigned to make undercover phone calls every few days to the National Anti-Klan Network in Atlanta to "get snippets which would be given to Roy Frankhouser." He recalled a "swap" in which "we gave Roy all our files on the Jewish Defense League and we got from him in return a batch of Klan publications." Tate said he personally Xeroxed the files on the JDL for Frankhouser. In general, Frankhouser (who was in constant contact with Miles) had unrestricted access to Security's files. "If he said 'our people need to see such and such,' he'd be given it," Tate said.

Security staffers sometimes claimed to be stringers for Intercontinental Media Service, with offices in the National Press Building in Washington. The service was run by Edward von Rothkirch, a friend of the Liberty Lobby. Charles Tate testified in the 1987 trial of Roy Frankhouser that von Rothkirch was called "the Baron" by Security, "would accredit somebody with a press card to appear as though he was a real reporter working for real newspapers so that he could do interviews." According to former Metro employee Phil Perlonga, the Security staff in 1982–83 had "stacks of blank press cards" from IMS. When a card was needed, Goldstein would sign von Rothkirch's name. Perlonga was given an IMS card and instructed to use it to gain entrance to Henry Kissinger's birthday party and serve legal papers on him. Perlonga took the card, but says he managed to evade serving the papers.

LaRouchian Security and intelligence staffers often have impersonated real reporters. In 1981, *U.S. News & World Report* filed a $1.5 million suit against *EIR* and *New Solidarity* after a LaRouchian posed in phone interviews as its White House correspondent, Sara Fritz. In 1983, pursuant to a settlement agreement, a federal district judge in Washington issued a permanent injunction barring staff members of *EIR* and *New Solidarity* from henceforth impersonating any *U.S. News & World Report* staffer. Jeff Steinberg later said the NCLC had stopped using this tactic. In fact, Security staffers gained interviews just as easily by using their own names and identifying themselves as freelance writers or college students working on a research project. Indeed, when they openly identified themselves as *EIR* reporters they sometimes received the same deference as members of the mainstream press. Some targeted persons would not have heard of *EIR* before and would assume it was a legitimate newsmagazine. Others would know of its LaRouche connection, but would talk anyway out of politeness or to demonstrate their broad-mindedness. (*EIR* gained a 1982 interview with Philip Klutznik, former World Jewish Congress president and Secretary of Commerce in the Carter administration; he commiserated with the interviewer over how people are sometimes unfairly accused of anti-Semitism.) Security staffers also openly called people they had previously harassed or were involved in litigation with. Such victims would stay on the phone, hoping to find out just what LaRouche was planning against them next.

A brash and hardworking Security staffer can conduct a phone "sweep" of LaRouche's opposition in a single day. He may openly identify himself as a LaRouchian, use a fictitious identity, or pretend to be a real person, depending on the targeted person's vulnerabilities. A frequent pretense in the early 1980s was to be Chip Berlet, an anti-LaRouche journalist in Chicago. Since Berlet was a freelancer who did not keep regular office hours, it was difficult for the callee to check this out.

By staying on the phone long hours and making one call after another with the speed of a telephone solicitor, Security staffers rapidly pick up large amounts of information—not only from what the victims say but from what they don't say. For instance, a May 5, 1982, Security document entitled "Harassment Networks" summarized twelve phone calls to alleged LaRouche enemies across the political spectrum, all apparently made by the same person. Among those called were Berlet, Dana Beal of the Yippies, Arch Puddington of the League for Industrial

Democracy, Jerry Eisenberg of the Jewish Defense League, Sheldon Ranz of The Generation After/Holocaust Survivors USA, Justin Finger of the Anti-Defamation League, and Fred Eiland of the Federal Election Commission. The list also included a National Jewish Community Relations Council staff member, Detroit financier Max Fisher's secretary, and a rabbi who deprograms Moonies. In most cases the caller elicited bits of information about the targeted person's whereabouts and/or current activities and/or contacts with other targeted persons—information which could then be "cross-gridded." When Berlet refused to talk, the caller gloated in his notes that "Berlet is currently paranoid as hell." In fact the encouraging of suspicious attitudes among LaRouche opponents was one of the benefits of the telephone sweeps. Some journalists simply would not discuss LaRouche with any caller unless they had time to thoroughly check his identity first.

The LaRouchians also used the telephone as a psychological assault weapon. In 1980, reporters in New Hampshire obtained a copy of a special LaRouche "New Hampshire Target List" of state political figures to be harassed. The names included the governor, the attorney general, the secretary of state, and the mayors and city clerks of several towns. "These are the criminals to burn—we want calls coming in to these fellows day and night," the instructions said. Attorney General Thomas Rath received about fifty phone calls at his home on the Sunday prior to primary day. The callers would say things like "We know where you live."

When the Federal Election Commission was investigating La-Rouche's 1980 campaign finances, the LaRouchians made threatening phone calls to Charles Steele, the commission's general counsel. In federal court testimony in 1987, former NCLCer Tate recalled the Steinbergs arriving late at the Security offices one morning. "They said that the reason . . . was because [Mr. Steele] had been receiving late-night phone calls and had received threats on his life very, very late at night; and that even though they were kind of late that day, they were sure that Mr. Steele's day was going to be even worse and that he had slept even worse . . ."

Another surrogate assault weapon is the LaRouchian printing press, which churns out smear leaflets and articles against journalists and other enemies, often featuring outlandish sexual charges. In this, La-Rouche and his top aides have much practice—they have routinely accused their own rank-and-file followers of sexual misconduct, repressed homosexuality, etc., ever since the ego-stripping days in the early 1970s. The first public smear sheets were directed against a faction that quit in 1974. They had naïvely discussed details of their sex lives during NCLC psychological sessions. Upon their resignation, *New*

*Solidarity* printed up a smear sheet that went into graphic detail. Much of it was taken from a "confession" written by a former member of the faction who remained with the LaRouchians and was pressured to prove his loyalty by tattling on his former comrades. Thousands of copies of the smear sheet were passed out on Manhattan's Upper West Side, where leaders of the faction lived.

As Security became bolder, it ceased to worry about obtaining "confessions" from anyone. It simply made up the smears out of thin air. Russ Bellant, a Detroit freelancer, came home one evening in the late 1970s to find that his neighbors had received invitations to a "gay coming-out" party at his house. Marcie Permut, a twenty-two-year-old researcher for NBC-TV's Chicago affiliate, was working on a LaRouche story in 1984 when leaflets appeared on car windshields on the block where she and her parents lived. The leaflets claimed she was a prostitute and gave her parents' phone number.

The cynicism behind such allegations was revealed most clearly in the 1984 deposition of Jeffrey Steinberg in *LaRouche* v. *NBC*. Steinberg was asked by defense attorney Phil Hirschkop for proof of NCLC allegations that William F. Buckley was a "sodomist." Steinberg alleged that he had heard it in the mid-1970s from Gregory Rose, a Security staffer who later defected and incurred LaRouche's wrath by exposing the NCLC in a cover story for Buckley's *National Review*. Hirschkop then peeled away Steinberg's pretensions as an investigator:

Q: In *New Solidarity*, are you familiar that Rose has been termed a "pathological liar"?

A: Sure.

Q: Would you agree that he is a "pathological liar"?

A: Yes.

Q: Why, then, would someone in your organization repeat the allegation made by Rose that Bill Buckley is a sodomist?

A: I merely cited Rose as one source . . . We wouldn't have even probably considered the issue if he hadn't originally provided lurid detail to that effect and proposed that as an area to be considered, but there is other additional material—

Q: What material?

A: Information from confidential sources.

Q: Name the sources.

Steinberg's attorney directed him not to answer this question on "national security" grounds. Hirschkop then continued:

Q: These sources, did they give that information directly to you?

A: No.

Q: To whom did they give that information?
A: To other people who maintained them as confidential sources.
Q: Which people have told you that Bill Buckley is a sodomist?
A: I don't recall.

What Steinberg didn't "recall" was that much of his information about Buckley actually came from the Liberty Lobby, which hated Buckley because of his strong stand against allowing anti-Semites to infiltrate the conservative movement.

The Security staff went beyond smear tactics in their 1980 attempts to intimidate Jon Presstage, then a reporter for the Manchester *Union Leader* in New Hampshire. LaRouche came to Presstage's office for an interview, bringing several bodyguards with guns. "They told me there were certain things I could not say in my stories," Presstage recalled on NBC's *First Camera*. LaRouche "told me that he would make it very painful for me if I wrote certain things. And I asked him, well, what do you mean by painful? And he kind of chuckled with the rest of the people there and said we have ways of making it painful beyond lawsuits." Presstage's family had three cats. "On successive days following the articles," he said, "the cats were found on my doorstep, dead."

To assist in Security's harassment campaigns the NCLC maintains a staff of in-house paralegals and has brought in "hired gun" attorneys to assist with aggressive lawsuits. The extralegal motive of such suits was indicated by a Security memorandum sent out to local NCLC offices in 1984 under the heading "Make the ADL [Anti-Defamation League] Pay Everywhere." It called for filing libel suits and complaints to government agencies against the ADL in every part of the country: "Go to your best and most political [sic] well-placed contacts and have them recommend lawyers who have a reputation for competence, meanness, and who like a good brawl." The memo then ordered that calls be made to local news reporters, giving them an ultimatum to either divulge the "ADL source" of their anti-LaRouche "operation" or else face a libel suit. The goal would be to build a "massive national dossier" on the ADL and tie it down defending itself.

Security waged elaborate counterintelligence campaigns (known among insiders as "damage control operations") to derail media exposés. When it found out *The New York Times* was preparing an article in 1979, Goldstein and an associate pretended to be defectors and arranged to meet with reporter Howard Blum. They brought along a concealed tape recorder and attempted to provoke Blum into saying something compromising. At the end of the conversation a third Security staffer snapped Blum's picture. The NCLC then called a press conference to announce that it would sue the *Times*. In fact, LaRouche did name the *Times* as a defendant in a suit he launched several weeks later against the Manhattan East Side weekly *Our Town,* which published a LaRouche series by me while the *Times*'s story was still in preparation. Security launched a wave of harassing phone calls to *Our Town*'s offices, while also attempting to jam lines at the *Times.* One caller to *Our Town* pretended to be a *Times* staff attorney seeking information about *Our Town*'s legal strategy. Smear leaflets about *Our Town* publisher Ed Kayatt were circulated throughout the East Side. *Our Town*'s advertisers and banks where the paper was distributed were threatened with lawsuits. A crude setup also was attempted: A man alleging to be an executive of LaRouche's computer company, Computron, dropped by the office and offered to sell the newspaper stolen financial records. The offer was declined.

For the next few years *Our Town* experienced mysterious acts of harassment, including bomb threats, the disappearance of office files, and visits from imposters requesting information about LaRouche. In 1983, after hard-hitting anti-LaRouche editorials, the offices were broken into, the typesetting and copying machines and other equipment were smashed, and acid was poured on the wreckage. Although Kayatt could not prove the LaRouchians were behind these actions, he knew of no one else with a sufficiently strong motive.

Security's trickery was used in tandem with legal action against NBC's 1984 *First Camera* report on LaRouche's ties to the Reagan administration. Prior to the show LaRouche filed a $150 million libel suit to delay or halt it. Security directed Roy Frankhouser to shadow NBC reporter Patricia Lynch around Manhattan, and picketers appeared in front of her office with signs and leaflets calling her a "KGB whore." While she was filming in the Washington, D.C., area, they found out she was scheduled to meet with Senator Moynihan. Pretending to be a Moynihan aide, a LaRouche follower called Lynch's researcher several hours before the interview—ostensibly to get background material for the senator—and probed for sensitive details about Lynch's sources. The LaRouchians then tried to intimidate Moynihan by threatening to publish defamatory material about his family.

LaRouche became worried that his former chief of staff, Gus Kalimtgis, might be cooperating with NBC. Charles Tate has testified that one day in early 1984 LaRouche "came downstairs to the security area in his home at Woodburn and he ordered members of the Security staff to call [Kalimtgis] at his home and threaten his life." Tate said the calls were made in LaRouche's presence by several staff members.

Kalimtgis has confirmed that he received several calls threatening himself, his wife and children.

The damage control operation against NBC is closely documented by several hundred pages of Security printouts and notebooks which Tate kept after leaving the NCLC. A dossier on NBC reporter Brian Ross described efforts to obtain information from former targets of his investigative journalism. "Calls [are] out to Teamster networks," it said.

LaRouche's suit against NBC, Lynch, Ross, and the ADL went on trial in federal court in Alexandria, Virginia, in October 1984. The jury found for the defendants and awarded NBC $3 million in punitive damages on a counterclaim relating to Security's attempt to sabotage the interview with Moynihan. (The judge later cut the award to $200,000.)

The outcome might have been quite different had an alleged Security attempt to buy a witness succeeded. One of the issues at the trial was whether NBC libeled LaRouche by reporting that he had urged the assassination of Jimmy Carter and other public officials in 1977. Lynch had several sources for the story, including New Orleans private investigator Gordon Novel. According to Novel, Jeffrey Steinberg offered him a large cash payment if he would recant his story and testify for LaRouche. Novel said he rejected the offer and promptly informed Lynch about it. Steinberg, in his deposition later that year, denied offering money, but said he did remonstrate with Novel over the phone, accusing him of telling a "bunch of lies." Although Novel had appeared on *First Camera* as an unnamed source with voice disguised, he was sufficiently incensed by Steinberg's tactics to allow the use of his name in a subsequent airing of the presidential death threat charge on *NBC Nightly News*. (Charles Tate, who served as the "liaison" between Security and LaRouche attorney Odin Anderson during the NBC suit, has testified that everyone in Security knew Novel was telling the truth about the kill-Carter incident.)

In the autumn of 1984 a federal grand jury convened in Boston to hear evidence of credit-card fraud by LaRouche fund raisers and shell organizations. Security began yet another damage control operation, but this time it resulted in obstruction of justice indictments of four members of Security's steering committee—Steinberg, Goldstein, Steinberg's wife, Michelle, and Robert Greenberg—along with erstwhile adviser Frankhouser and LaRouche himself. According to the 1986 indictment and courtroom testimony, the Security staff orchestrated a multilayered conspiracy to derail the investigation. This effort allegedly included destroying records, harassing prosecutors, and sending witnesses to Europe to duck subpoenas. At the Steinbergs' bond hearing, FBI special agent Richard Egan testified that Michelle Steinberg had boasted of hiding witnesses "where the sun doesn't shine." Egan said the defendants had engaged in "hundreds" of conversations to plan the conspiracy and had repeatedly asked Frank-houser and prosecution witness Lee Fick to get the case fixed through pressure on the government. Egan also said that authorities had seized Security staff files on William Weld, the former U.S. Attorney for Massachusetts, who had initiated the credit-card fraud investigation. Egan said the files took up "at least two file cabinets" and included lists of names of Weld's neighbors, information on his family and in-laws, and even information on guests at his wedding. Egan quoted an alleged statement by LaRouche that Weld "does not deserve to live. He should get a bullet between the head—between the eyes."

# Twenty-four

# Law and Order, LaRouche Style

The Security staff's approach to the FBI and local police in the late 1970s was similar to LaRouche's pitch to Langley. Just as the CIA had been weakened by media exposés and personnel cutbacks, the FBI had fallen on lean times because of the COINTELPRO scandal, a rash of citizen lawsuits, and a post-Watergate shift in legislative and judicial opinion regarding government snooping. In 1976 Attorney General Edward Levi issued guidelines prohibiting the FBI from conducting surveillance of domestic radical groups unless there was evidence that a crime had been or was about to be committed. By 1983 the FBI was investigating about 50 domestic security cases, compared with over 20,000 a decade earlier. Local police no longer could rely on the FBI for wide-ranging political intelligence data, and were increasingly limited by their own departmental guidelines.

Private organizations attempted to fill the vacuum. One was the Birch Society-linked Western Goals. Another was the NCLC Security staff, which crafted a synthetic law enforcement philosophy sharply opposed to its previous left-wing anti-police rhetoric.

To begin trading information with local police, private outfits needed their own base of raw intelligence data. Fortunately for Security, hundreds of LaRouchians had belonged to leftist groups before joining the NCLC. Many wrote up reports on their former comrades. A 1977 Security field report stated that a new member, Roger M., had just been recruited in Hartford, Connecticut. He previously had been active with the Venceremos Brigade (a now defunct Maoist sect in California) and had known its founder, H. Bruce Franklin. Roger would write up his experiences, the report said, and if necessary would come to Security headquarters for a full debriefing. However, while Roger informed on Bruce Franklin, another Hartford comrade would keep Security informed about Roger.

Many leftists, unlike Roger, were turned off by the NCLC's recruitment efforts. Even so, NCLC members would jot down anything derogatory they learned about these fleeting contacts. Reports from the Philadelphia office as early as 1974 included thumbnail profiles of trade union and peace activists. Often included were rumors regarding sexual, marital, psychiatric, or alcoholism problems.

The LaRouchians tried to keep their early efforts as police informers secret, but an NCLC telex intended for the NCLC midwestern regional office was sent by accident to the newsroom of a Minneapolis daily. Included in the transmission were instructions to "brief" various police officials.

In Seattle the LaRouchians took to preparing their intelligence reports on forms similar to those used by U.S. military intelligence, stamped "Classified," "This Form for Internal Agency Use Only," and "This worksheet contains information affecting the National Defense of the United States within the meaning of the Espionage Laws." A report obtained by the *Seattle Sun* stated that NCLC members had briefed the state attorney general's office on radical groups and would be briefing the Tacoma, Washington, FBI office. The *Sun* quoted the head of the Portland Police Department's Intelligence Division, who named a local NCLC leader as one of his best sources on local leftists.

Any pretense of secrecy was soon dropped. Jeffrey Steinberg admitted in a 1977 court case that he and his colleagues were in contact with police departments and FBI offices in dozens of cities. In 1978 they circulated a sample report on terrorism to police officers, together with a catalogue of reports selling for upwards of $25 on everyone from the Maoists through William F. Buckley. The catalogue also offered "Special Investigative Services" based on "extensive files of raw and semi-finished material built up over a nine-year period."

Security staffers were given sales quotas, which they met by calling up police departments and security-conscious nuclear power companies. They also set up literature tables at police and security-industry conventions. Jeff Steinberg attended the 1978 International Association of Chiefs of Police convention to circulate LaRouche's "National Strategy for Crime Control."

The NCLC material targeting police used "terrorism" as a code word for any kind of left-of-center social protest. This enabled the LaRouchians to discuss fascism and police-state methods without unduly embarrassing their audience. In a 1978 Security sales brochure, LaRouche advocated "surgically precise preventive action" against the controllers of terrorism. "It is essential . . ." he said, "to use the terrorism as justification for political penalties against the environmentalists," for in his view the environmentalists were part of the ideological "infrastructure" of terrorism. In a 1981 report he advised that the arrest and conviction of those who commit crimes is not enough for the "effective suppression" of crime. The problem is that under our "British" laws we can't arrest someone until he has actually committed the crime. What is needed is a system that can "control the crime before the fact," through "neutralization" of the infrastructure—"political machines, lawyers, support fronts and the like."

While calling for a state of siege, the LaRouchians were quick to benefit from the civil libertarian climate they decried. Many of them applied for their FBI files under the Freedom of Information Act. LaRouche and thirteen aides sued the Justice Department for alleged violations of their civil rights during the NCLC's leftist days. By the early 1980s, members of the LaRouche organization had filed scores of civil rights and ballot access suits against local and federal authorities in every part of the country.

In 1980 *Investigative Leads (IL)*, a newsletter for police officers, was launched as a spin-off from *Executive Intelligence Review*. It purported to give the latest scoop on terrorists, narcotics traffickers, Communists, environmentalists, black nationalists, leaders of Jewish-American and Arab-American organizations, and even elements in the Ku Klux Klan hostile to LaRouche's own Klan allies. Like *EIR*, it was an intelligence shopping window. Articles often included a list of the NCLC "reference files" consulted in preparing an article. The implication was that these files would be made available to interested police officers.

An *IL* house ad boasted that the intent was to build "a network of law enforcement and security professionals and others who are committed to the eradication of terrorism and narcotics trafficking." Ryan Quade Emerson, a writer on extremist groups who served as a part-time "intelligence analyst" for the LaRouchians during 1985–86, claims that *IL* editor Robert Greenberg had sources in "dozens of police departments." "It was his full-time job to cultivate them," Emerson said. "I'd hear the calls coming in, and I'd listen to his pitch. He'd call some guys every day with information and say, 'Call us collect if you have stuff for us.' He was trying to compromise them. Some fell for it, some didn't. But if [Security] hooked a guy, they'd try to brainwash him with their conspiracy theories."

One secret of the NCLC's success with police departments, as with Third World intelligence agencies, was the "pyramiding" of intelligence data. Through their phone sweeps Security members might find out, say, that the Revolutionary Communist Party was planning a demonstration in city X. They would call their favorite Red Squad detective in that city and offer him information from their files on the RCP. Next they would call a detective in city Y, pass on to him anything of interest they had learned from the detective in city X, and warn him that the RCP might be planning nationwide terrorism. Whatever this detective told them in return, they would swap along with the previous item to a third detective in city Z, thus rapidly building up their fund of tradable information without having to leave their desks.

This tactic sometimes worked because the LaRouchians were at least pretending to meet a real need. Police intelligence officers in, say, Portland and Chicago didn't have the time or resources to systematically exchange esoteric background information on radical sects. The LaRouchians thus could offer their services as a clearinghouse, pretending to have vast resources of their own.

When a civil liberties group sued the Los Angeles Police Department's former Public Disorder Intelligence Division (PDID), seeking to halt its alleged abuses, local NCLC members popped up as fanatical police supporters. They launched a smear campaign in 1980 against leaders of the Citizens Commission on Police Repression (CCPR), including its founder, Linda Valentino. The LaRouchians "made our lives miserable," she said. "They passed out, it must have been, a quarter of a million leaflets, accusing us of terrorism and drug pushing." The leaflets listed the home and work phone numbers of activists involved in the suit. "For days, we received harassing calls," Valentino said. "I got obscene calls at home in the early morning hours."

The leaflets were filled with blatant anti-Semitism, charging that the Israelis, the Lubavich Order of Hasidic Jews, the Jewish Defense League, Simon Wiesenthal, and a Jewish city councilman, Zev Yaroslavsky, were all in a plot to destroy the PDID so that "Israeli dopers" could take over. One leaflet bore the title "Smash the 'Kosher Nostra'—Defend the LAPD." Said another: "If your child's mind is eaten away by PCP provided to him by Meyer Lansky's drug runners, or if the mayor of your city has his legs blown off" by a JDL hit squad, "the person to blame is Zev [Yaroslavsky]." The leaflets were authorized and paid for by LaRouche's 1980 presidential campaign committee. Similar accusations were printed in *IL,* which solicited advance orders for an "in-depth special report" analyzing the backgrounds and motives of the plaintiffs in the CCPR suit. Meanwhile, Security prepared for the Los Angeles police a special dossier on Yaroslavsky, including attacks on other local and national Jewish leaders.

According to Jeff Cohen, the former ACLU attorney who represented the plaintiffs, the PDID had extensive direct dealings with the LaRouchians on intelligence matters. Cohen took the depositions of PDID officers who admitted that the NCLC's local Security man, Tim Pike, had given briefings at police headquarters. Cohen subpoenaed PDID intelligence booklets which included articles from *IL* and *New Solidarity.*

Detective Arleigh McCree, head of the LAPD bomb squad, met frequently with Pike in the early 1980s and also chatted on the phone with New York Security staffers. McCree, who died while attempting to defuse a bomb in 1986, told reporter Joel Bellman in a 1981 interview that he provided the LaRouchians with tips as well as receiving information from them.

A 1982 Security notebook, provided to federal prosecutors by Charles Tate, contains alleged tips about Israelis in southern California from a detective in the "Israeli mafia unit." The conversation is described under the heading "Calif. LAPD contacts." Mordechai Levy, a Jewish militant who infiltrated the LaRouche organization from 1980 to 1984, was working for Security in Los Angeles at the time. He says he examined copies of law enforcement files that Tim Pike kept in a cabinet in the NCLC's Vermont Street office. "Tim boasted he got them from the PDID," Levy said. The files related to radical groups of the 1960s and 1970s, including the May Day Tribe, the FALN, the Brown Berets, and the Jewish Defense League. "Pike had Xeroxes of the mug shots, surveillance logs, correspondence between the FBI and local law enforcement," Levy charged.

The LaRouchians wooed former Los Angeles police chief Ed Davis when he was running for the state senate in 1980. He spoke at a meeting of the NCLC's National Anti-Drug Coalition and gave interviews to LaRouche publications. An interview conducted by Jeffrey Steinberg appeared in *War on Drugs.* The headline called Davis the "Drug Fighter of the Month." He was quoted as saying that President Carter "philosophically was a drug pusher." Davis recalled in a 1988 phone interview that some California conservatives at the time regarded the LaRouchians as a "counterforce" against leftists. He said that a wealthy campaign contributor had urged him to meet with them, but that he cut them off upon realizing that they were not legitimate conservatives.

Chicago's police department was another major target. In 1979–80 the LaRouchians waged a smear campaign against Mayor Jane Byrne, who had launched a reorganization of the department. "The police work is moving along extremely well," said a memo from the NCLC's Chicago office, indulging in typical exaggeration. "There is a recognition of the [National Anti-Drug] Coalition as the vehicle to destroy Byrne from the standpoint of countering her police shakeup." The memo then cited a "series of conversations" with police officials, including a top Narcotics Division cop who supposedly "hates Byrne's guts." It also described efforts to organize support within the police unions and fraternal organizations.

The adopt-a-cop tactic backfired in New York City, where Security staffers sought out Detective John Finnegan of the Intelligence Division. Because of his reputation for dogged tracking of leftists in the 1960s, they figured he would be sympathetic to their rightward tilt. Finnegan recalled that "they'd like to talk to you all day, going back to the Renaissance . . . I used to meet with them at Police Headquarters." But while dutifully maintaining contact, Finnegan and other members of his unit (who remembered quite well the era of Operation Mop Up) prepared reports on the NCLC's new psychology, tactics, and goals, including its anti-Semitism. Their reports were far ahead of what other law enforcement agencies and the media were saying about the LaRouchians. As the years passed, Finnegan (now retired) became increasingly concerned about their activities. It was he who first persuaded Patricia Lynch of NBC's *First Camera* to focus on the LaRouchians in 1983–84. Lynch describes Finnegan as an "unsung hero" in the unmasking of LaRouche's conspiratorial network.

The LaRouchians in the early 1970s had the standard Marxist attitude toward the police. They were actually shocked when Communist Party members responded to Operation Mop Up's savage beatings by asking for police protection. *New Solidarity* said the CP represented "police socialism" reminiscent of Russia's Father Gapon during the 1905 revolution.

But the LaRouchians themselves began to seek police help during clashes with United Auto Workers members in several states in 1975. The violence was mostly the NCLC's own fault. In a basic scenario repeated over and over, they showed up at plant gates with leaflets naming union officials or rank-and-file workers as drug pushers, homosexuals, or Communists. One leaflet said of a Buffalo UAW member: "He can't go home to his wife with the smell of sperm on his breath . . . so he sleeps in parks . . ." The NCLC leadership claimed this was a powerful new technique to appeal to the workers' unconscious minds, but the only result was dozens of assaults on the leafleters.

In 1971–72 the LaRouchians had provoked similar assaults by stand-ing in front of Communist Party meeting halls and calling those who entered CIA agents, counterrevolutionaries, and "house niggers." La-Rouche had then goaded his followers into participating in Operation Mop Up to get even with their attackers. But the clashes at plant gates were something different: LaRouche hardly could mop up the giant UAW. However, his followers did the next-best thing by running to the police to get their assailants arrested. This was justified by the belief that the latter were all fascists, social fascists, CIA agents, drug pushers, and terrorists.

Robert Greenberg, later the editor of *Investigative Leads,* was allegedly involved in one attempt to set up UAW members for arrest. An affidavit filed by his comrade Theodore Held, in a lawsuit between the NCLC and the UAW, stated that when Held, Greenberg, and another NCLC member went to GMC Truck and Coach in Pontiac, Michigan, they expected trouble because of previous incidents. Held brought a cam-era. When several angry auto workers approached, "Greenberg mo-tioned to me . . . As the men stepped into the street I photographed them." Held then described how the auto workers chased them off, with one man delivering a "flying kick" to their car. "I then drove to the Pontiac police station," Held continued, "and filed complaint No. 393271 . . . I developed the picture I had taken of the men and Detective Peters took it to the plant the following Tuesday and made the identification."

Robert Greenberg and other Security staffers also developed a more sophisticated method for manipulating the police. They compiled hun-dreds of *Investigative Leads* articles, including false or exaggerated charges of illegal activity by their opponents. "They had this cynical attitude," Mordechai Levy said. "They thought, 'Why waste time going after an enemy when we can get the cops to do it for us?' A lot of what they put in *Investigative Leads* they knew was a total lie." In fact, it was just another example of LaRouche's hypothesis of the higher hypothe-sis, in which reasoning loses all touch with empirical reality in the service of a higher "natural law."

The earliest documented example of this false-witness tactic oc-curred in 1974. The LaRouchians approached the FBI with a fabricated story about an NCLC opponent, James Retherford, who had taken his small daughter from her LaRouchian mother and fled New York to save the child from being raised in a cultish environment. Hoping to manip-ulate the FBI into searching for them, the Security staff falsely claimed that Retherford was in contact with Weather Underground fugitives. Although the FBI failed to take this story seriously, the LaRouchians tried again, targeting other opponents. FBI documents released to

NCLC members under the Freedom of Information Act reveal that LaRouche emissaries made eleven visits or phone calls to FBI offices between May and July 1976 to present allegations about various leftists and that this was followed by further extensive contact. The FOIA documents, over 5,000 pages, proved so embarrassing that the NCLC went to court to get them removed from the FBI reading room. Yet the NCLC had to admit in court papers that it had "cooperated with the FBI and other federal and local law enforcement agencies" by providing information on the "terrorist activities" of persons associated with the Institute for Policy Studies, a left-wing Washington think tank, and the Repression Information Project, a research collective that had published a pamphlet critical of LaRouche.

In mid-April 1977, two weeks before a mass demonstration against nuclear power at the Seabrook nuclear reactor site in New Hampshire, two Boston area NCLC leaders—Larry Sherman and Graham Lowry—met with Lieutenant Donald Buxton of the New Hampshire State Police to outline alleged plans for antinuclear violence by environmentalist groups. Buxton filed a report treating the allegations as worthy of serious consideration and described the two LaRouchians as "very well informed gentlemen." A copy was obtained by the Clamshell Alliance and made public shortly after the peaceful demonstration. The NCLC also took its allegations about the Clamshell Alliance to the FBI. But an April 28, 1977, FBI memorandum said the NCLC had apparently "fabricated" the information in an attempt to disrupt the demonstration "and cause New Hampshire officials unnecessary problems."

The LaRouchians kept trying. One infiltrated a 1979 South Hadley, Massachusetts, planning meeting for another round of Seabrook demonstrations. He reported back to Security that it was "one of the most anal, turd-piling, hair-splitting New Left meetings it has been my displeasure to witness." Nevertheless, his report included a detailed account of the plans under discussion. Although the report contained no evidence of any plans for violence, the LaRouchians told the *Boston Globe* and law enforcement officials to expect violence. Once again, no violence occurred.

The LaRouchians used the false-witness tactic in 1981 against an enemy they hated even more than the environmentalists—the Yippies. To the LaRouchians, the Yippies were the symbol of everything evil— long-haired potheads who hung out at rock concerts, had no respect for Beethoven, and made constant trouble for LaRouche. They had picketed his headquarters with the banner "Nazis Make Good Lampshades" and on several occasions placed crank calls to Steinberg and Goldstein from pay phones. Aron Kay, the Yippie "pie man," was plotting to land a mushroom pie in LaRouche's face at the earliest opportunity. Security prepared a series of "Dope Dossiers" on Kay, Abbie Hoffman, and other Yippies. A *New Solidarity* editorial, "Cleaning Up the Filth," described them as "gutter scum" and announced that the dossiers were "being supplied to the New York City Police Department and other law enforcement agencies." The contents of the dossiers were oriented toward inducing the police to investigate the Yippies for possession or sale of marijuana. The LaRouchians were well aware that marijuana possession was low on the police list of priorities, but suggested that the police would thereby find evidence of Yippie involvement in terrorism and other serious crimes.

LaRouche already had developed a general philosophy about this. In a 1979 memo addressed to "key police and security-intelligence agencies" on how to deal with supposed "terrorists" in the "rock-drug counterculture" (an allusion to the Yippies), he claimed that such people are "highly vulnerable" to arrest inasmuch as they live "in significant part in either a criminal or semi-criminal mode of life." He suggested that their activities as protesters and NCLC opponents could be countered by using "arrests for drug violations" to "destabilize" their "political infrastructure" and gather "most useful material" about their political activities.

But in 1980 the tables were turned. A college student friendly to the Yippies decided to launch a one-man crusade to "destabilize" and gather "most useful material" about the LaRouchians themselves. Thus did the Security staff encounter Mordechai Levy, a kind of Prince of Provocateurs, who would cause it almost as much trouble as Roy Frankhouser.

# Twenty-five

# An Agent
# of Chaos

In the middle and late 1970s some NCLC members still worked at jobs in the outside world. Believing that it was dominated by the enemy, they naturally kept their eyes and ears open. Occasionally they gained useful information. A LaRouchian physician working at Lincoln Hospital in the Bronx in 1974 learned about earlier links between the Lincoln Detox Program—a drug-free acupuncture treatment facility for heroin addicts—and the Black Liberation Army. Subsequent NCLC reports on the BLA helped convince police departments that the LaRouchians might be worth listening to.

A woman in the organization gained a job in Drexel Burnham's international economics division. While trying to ferret out information about its links to the mythical Dope, Inc., she picked up valuable information on gold trading which was incorporated into NCLC economic intelligence reports. She also acquired a knowledge of Drexel's economic models, which LaRouche and his aides reworked into the so-called LaRouche-Riemann economic model.

Gail Goerner Kay, wife of Security staffer Robert Kay, used family connections to obtain a secretarial job with the Council on Foreign

Relations. To the LaRouchians the CFR was one of the world's chief sources of evil, and Kay was encouraged to stay in the job for several years while concealing her NCLC connection. Her greatest coup was to attend a meeting of the secretive Bilderberg Society, an organization of top European and American bankers and industrialists which, in the eyes of conspiracy theorists, is even more sinister than the CFR. When William Bundy, editor of the CFR's *Foreign Affairs,* learned that Kay was a Mata Hari for LaRouche, he was astounded. "It's like the CIA getting an agent into the Politburo," he told *The New York Times.*

But as life inside the NCLC became more tightly disciplined and prone to hysteria, it precluded any long-range infiltrations of the enemy camp. "Anyone who went undercover would be leaving the 'controlled environment,'" observed one former Security staffer. "LaRouche would lose his hold on them." Members gradually were withdrawn from outside jobs. Some top staffers became extremely nervous when the boss of the young woman at Drexel invited her to dinner. They feared he might be planning to turn her into a double agent by seducing her. Hysterical memos were circulated at NCLC headquarters, and she was removed from the danger zone.

Ironically, the LaRouchians began to function in the outside world—as long as they took it in small doses—more effectively than ever. Some visited the National Security Council and made favorable impressions. Some comported themselves well on radio talk shows. But this was done only while they wore the persona of an NCLC "organizer" or "intelligence operative." When they attempted to pose as ordinary people, they weren't very good at it. Furthermore, their paranoid belief structure made some types of snooping almost impossible for them. Although they were skilled at making undercover calls to the Yippies, they were reluctant to spend much time hanging out with people whose lifestyles were radically different from their own. Thus they had to build a network of paid and unpaid informers. This brought them into association with the likes of Mordechai Levy. They were on the lookout for such people.

Mordechai was a California State University undergraduate when he first encountered the LaRouchians in 1980. With a near-genius IQ and vivid fantasies, he was bored with his accounting studies. His great passion in life was to fight Nazis. At the age of thirteen he had joined the Jewish Defense League. He became a great telephone-booth crank-call artist, attempting to strike terror into the hearts of Klansmen and Nazis across the country. White supremacists complained incessantly in *The Spotlight* and other hate sheets about the dangerous "terrorist" Levy.

Soon after Mordechai began talking with the LaRouchians, they asked him to work for them as a secret operative. He jumped at the chance to become a mole in their ranks. Given the code name "Leviticus," he carried out various assignments in Los Angeles and made frequent trips to New York on direct orders from Steinberg, Goldstein, and West Coast Security chief Tim Pike. This relationship lasted for four years, with the LaRouchians paying tens of thousands of dollars for his meals, airfare, and hotel rooms. To maintain his cover, *New Solidarity* occasionally attacked him as a Zionist terrorist.

Mordechai was supposed to collect intelligence on LaRouche's enemies and run operations against them. What he actually did was compose fictitious information for Goldstein and Steinberg while passing along tips about LaRouche's plans to journalists, the ADL, and Jewish community leaders. The tips sometimes weren't worth very much, for in espionage textbook fashion the LaRouchians tried to feed disinformation through him. But Mordechai developed a shrewd understanding of their psychology and began to provoke NCLC security alerts with his warnings of imaginary dangers. In 1982 he cooperated with the Manhattan district attorney's office in an investigation of them. After dropping his double-agent role in 1984 he agreed to be a witness in the Boston prosecution of LaRouche for obstruction of justice.

The LaRouchians often pressured Mordechai for information on leftist sects. "I'd go off somewhere and pretend to make a phone call," he said. "Then I'd come back and tell them anything that popped into my head. I read a lot of leftist papers, so I could make it sound convincing." When they brought him to New York to run operations against various enemies, he set up a command post in a West Side hotel, then sat around chatting on the phone with friends under the guise of contacting "agents." He invited Yippie Aron Kay to the hotel for a free meal at LaRouche's expense. This was supposed to be a deep maneuver in an operation against the Yippies. Aron couldn't show up, but Mordechai let two Yippies crash in the hotel room. They had to leave at seven in the morning because Goldstein was expected at eight. Mordechai and Goldstein often met in Ratner's on Delancey Street or Bernstein's on Essex Street—the "mole" and his "control officer" plotting their next deployment against the ADL in a kosher restaurant!

Hundreds of pages of NCLC Security documents from the years 1980–84 describe debriefings of "Leviticus" and "Mark Levine." These documents confirm that the information he provided them was mostly innocuous or fictitious. He convinced Goldstein that he had a pipeline into Mossad, and told him to watch out for "Colonel Kiffel," "Henry Duvall," "Carlos the Jew," and other infamous assassins who had sworn to kill LaRouche. At one point he claimed to have seen a secret U.S. Defense Intelligence Agency report on Helga, allegedly concluding that she was an East German agent. His description of the document was extremely convincing, and for good reason. He often stayed at the Bleecker Street apartment of investigative journalist A. J. Weberman, who had several filing drawers full of old Pentagon and CIA documents obtained under the Freedom of Information Act. Mordechai studied these and his imagination did the rest.

Mordechai never met Roy Frankhouser and despised him as a racist. But he and Frankhouser inadvertently ended up in a curious indirect relationship as pranksters. According to Charles Tate's testimony in Frankhouser's 1987 trial, this was the result of their "bid[ding] up against each other about how much they knew." A Security staffer "would call Mr. Frankhouser and report what Mr. Levy had told them without saying it was from Mr. Levy. And Mr. Frankhouser, of course, in order . . . to show that he was not caught napping, would have to augment this fantasy with . . . yet more. If there were five assassins according to Mr. Levy's account, there had to be six according to Mr. Frankhouser's account. And this would go back to Mr. Levy, who would, you know, have a dozen." (This tactic was also adopted by "the Major," who apparently had figured out the magic equation: the greater the fear of assassination, the higher the consulting fees.)

Some Security staffers were skeptical of Mordechai's stories all along. After he told them an especially wild fantasy, they demanded he come to the New York office for a lie detector test. Mordechai went to a private investigator to learn how to beat the machine. The PI told him to eat five orders of Chinese mustard, take antihistamines to dry out his nasal passages, then stay up all night. But Mordechai never had to try this method: The LaRouchians canceled the test.

Mordechai's manipulation of Goldstein was the key to his success. It was Goldstein who bailed him out and restored his credibility whenever one of his stories didn't check out. Mordechai believed that Goldstein had "unconscious" doubts about the LaRouche organization and therefore needed him around as reassurance: "He would look at me, an Orthodox Jew with a yarmulke, and he would say to himself, 'If Mordechai can follow LaRouche, LaRouche must be okay.' "

In dealing with Goldstein, Mordechai learned to pick up cues and anticipate expectations like a vaudeville mind reader. The transcript of a 1981 debriefing which the LaRouchians passed on to the NYPD Intelligence Division contains a good example:

LEVY: And another [anti-LaRouche conspirator] named William . . .
GOLDSTEIN: Corey?
LEVY: Greenberg.

GOLDSTEIN: Greenberg, Maxwell Greenberg.

LEVY: Maxwell Greenberg, that's right. I said William . . . the guy who's in the police commission, very big. See, everything's on levels, it's layers, you know . . .

Mordechai was forced not only to juggle contradictory stories but to control his temper when LaRouche aides told him that only a million and a half Jews died in the Holocaust or that the "rich Jews" would have to go into camps after LaRouche's ascent to power. (Charles Tate says Mordechai was not exaggerating about Security's anti-Semitic atmosphere. "I heard the most execrable things about rich Jews," Tate said. "They'd say the problem with World War II was that the wrong Jews were gassed.")

In 1982 Mordechai broke with the JDL and formed his own Jewish Defense Organization (JDO). California newspapers published a photo of a scruffy gun-toting crew with Mordechai looking something like Captain Hook. He was soon too busy to continue his double life with the LaRouchians. In 1984 he revealed his deception and attacked them openly. This obliged Goldstein and Steinberg to settle ideological accounts with him, but they couldn't admit they'd been taken in so completely.

Their rationalization took the form of a published report, "Mordechai Levy: The Profile of Mossad Hit Teams," contained in a larger study of the worldwide "Israeli mafia" conspiracy. According to this report, Mordechai had been sent into the NCLC as an ADL agent, but Goldstein had succeeded in partially "turning" him by teaching him about Rembrandt and Heinrich Heine. Mordechai had thus started giving the NCLC genuinely valuable information until the ADL put him through "severe trauma" to turn him again. Once this happened, once Leviticus the double agent became Leviticus the triple agent, he became "extremely dangerous," a walking time bomb of fanaticism and psychosis. Yet earlier, Goldstein had shown almost superhuman skill as his control officer: "The ability of *EIR* counterintelligence personnel to detect and utilize Levy's psychological conflicts," the report boasted, "produced a higher . . . accuracy of information from Levy than any other law enforcement or intelligence apparatus—even the Israeli Mossad—could have achieved without the use of mind-altering drugs or torture." The example given of this accurate information was Mordechai's account of a multileveled assassination plot against La-Rouche, supposedly set for December 31, 1981, involving the Yippies, the ADL, the Israeli government, financier Max Fisher, a command post in London, and something called the AJEX/JWV Special Action

Committee, or Group 62. Supposedly by revealing this plot Levy had saved LaRouche's life.

But Goldstein showed a certain insight and even a hint of humor when he suggested that Mordechai could best be described as a "chaos agent." Goldstein listed the New York phone booths from which Mordechai supposedly made his crank calls. He pointed out, accurately, that the calls were mostly made from "booths in, or just outside," various kosher restaurants.

Security also managed to attract informers who were motivated by grudges or cupidity and who possessed, or were willing to gather, information of real substance. One example of these not so golden souls was Bruce Bailey, a tenant organizer well connected among New York leftists and anti-Zionists. According to former LaRouchians (including Charles Tate, who dealt directly with him), and substantiated by court records and internal NCLC reports, Bailey had numerous secret meetings and phone conversations with Security staffers between 1979 and 1984.

The principal target was me. I had worked with Bailey in community politics in the 1970s, but ended up on his list of ideological enemies. A February 6, 1984, report of an interview with Bailey conducted by Tate (entered into the NCLC computer under the access name "King, Dennis," ID 1044r, Code: Red, Sector: Security) suggests that once one becomes an informer it is difficult to restrict the range of one's informing. While discussing his grudge against me, Bailey ranged afield to gossip about various of his past and present acquaintances on the left. His nastiest sexual slurs were leveled at a woman who had testified against him in a civil fraud proceeding several years previously. He also offered sexual gossip about a woman who had helped organize a picket line in front of his Columbia Tenants Union to protest its anti-Semitism. One person mentioned was the well-known civil rights activist and folk singer the Rev. F. D. Kirkpatrick. Although Kirkpatrick was one of Bailey's closest political associates, the report accused him of belonging to a "touchy-feely cult" and described him as a "bejeweled and dashikied" figure who "likes to think of himself as a local celebrity." Bailey's information was passed on to "Clay" (Roy Frankhouser) by Paul Goldstein, whose report (ID 0625m) of his daily chat with "Clay" noted that Bailey's information "provides [the] basis for cross-gridding" various political activists.

Security also used the services of Grant Duay III, a writer of occasional pieces for the *New York City News,* an obscure Manhattan gay weekly. In late 1982, Duay first showed up at the League for Industrial Democracy, where I was working as a researcher. Duay asked to meet with the director, Arch Puddington, and showed him an article he had written attacking the NCLC as a right-wing political cult. Duay became a frequent visitor to the LID offices, and also showed up at a lecture I delivered on cult brainwashing, ostensibly to cover it for his newspaper.

Puddington and I became suspicious when we heard that Duay was making calls to journalists on the LaRouche beat all over the country. Our suspicions increased after Michael Hudson, a creditor suing the LaRouchians for racketeering in New York federal court, received a call from Duay (a total stranger to him) just before an important court appearance. Upon learning from Federal Election Commission records that Duay had made donations to several LaRouchian election campaigns, we stopped talking to him.

The full story of his relationship with the LaRouchians was later revealed by Charles Tate, one of whose Security duties had been to supervise Duay. According to Tate, Duay's assignments included interviewing LaRouche opponents under false pretenses, gathering background material on them, and monitoring anti-LaRouche public meetings. Tate said that although Duay had been mildly sympathetic to LaRouche's ideas, he had never been willing to work for free. "He'd bring in a tape recording, we'd give him twenty bucks," Tate said. This was confirmed by an NCLC Security logbook containing handwritten reports of conversations with informants in the spring of 1984. The notebook had Duay's name and phone number on the cover and contained a distorted summary of an actual phone conversation between Duay and Puddington.

In my own conversations with Duay he always seemed obsessed with uncovering what he said were secret links between various left-wing groups and the National Man-Boy Love Association (NAMBLA). But the truth will out. On March 23, 1986, he was arrested as an alleged member of a sex ring that produced, sold, traded, and distributed child pornography. His arrest occurred at Gay Treasures, a Greenwich Village porn shop where he worked as a clerk, after undercover agents from a federal and local task force purchased videotapes of men having sex with young boys. Duay subsequently pleaded guilty to obscenity in the third degree, receiving a fine but no jail sentence.

Members of the NCLC informer network, both fake and real, expected their identities to be kept secret, but the LaRouche organization demonstrated an utter disregard for their wishes. According to Tate, Bailey expressed a strong fear of public exposure, yet Jeffrey Steinberg (in a 1984 deposition in *LaRouche* v. *NBC*) gave away Bailey's name when it was clearly unnecessary to do so. (In the same deposition, he invoked "national security" to avoid naming several other sources.) Bailey became the target of newspaper articles that quoted from the deposition. Steinberg also neglected to protect Grant Duay's name. And LaRouche, in a subsequent deposition in the same case, blabbed about both Mordechai and Roy Frankhouser without forewarning them. Mordechai subsequently received physical threats from Jewish militants unaware of his double game.

Those who "traded" information with the NCLC also experienced problems. There were lax security procedures about the handling of confidential reports, so that copies of documents describing secret conversations with police officers in various cities kept falling into the hands of journalists such as Chip Berlet or me. Also, Security staffers felt no compunctions about double-crossing people they traded with, by peddling information on them to third parties. For instance, in the early 1980s Security staffer Ira Liebowitz cultivated contacts in the Church of Scientology's Guardians' Office for the alleged purpose of exchanging information on mutual enemies. (Scientology, like the NCLC, has a long history of aggressive tactics against its opponents.) Arnon Harari, New York director of Scientology's Office of Special Affairs (the new name for the Guardians' Office), recalled meeting at least twice with Liebowitz. Meanwhile *Investigative Leads* produced a special report on Scientology for police intelligence units, while *EIR* misquoted from a Liebowitz-Harari conversation to falsely suggest links between Scientology and narcotics trafficking.

The NCLC Security staff, through its remarkable range of deceptive tactics, has built up over a fifteen-year period one of the largest collections of private political intelligence data in the United States. According to defectors, these files contain blackmail-style information on public figures and details on the activities of both left-wing and right-wing political dissidents. Hundreds of thousands of Americans are mentioned in these files, and thousands are profiled in some depth. Much of the information is false, malicious, and defamatory, but some of it is accurate and potentially devastating to the lives of the targeted persons.

When the FBI and Virginia authorities raided LaRouche's headquarters in October 1986, they carted away more than 425 boxes of files. The media had the impression that these were mostly financial records, but the offices raided included those of the Security staff, and the files seized contained computer discs on which vast quantities of Security data were stored. The FBI thus came into possession of a major portion of the "LaRouche files." Apart from the details about political radicals and the rumors about the sex lives of public officials, these files contain evidence of extensive NCLC dealings with government and police officials and corporate executives throughout the country. Many of these individuals would be extremely embarrassed if their dealings with La-

Rouche should ever become a matter of public record. It is symptomatic of the media's curious blindness on the LaRouche issue that no one has raised the question of what the FBI intends to do with this intelligence bonanza. But whatever the answer, the seizure of these files represents a certain poetic justice. The LaRouchians set out to duplicate J. Edgar Hoover's infamous blackmail files, but their own files, once in the FBI's hands, led to the indictment of LaRouche himself for obstructing justice.

# Twenty-six

# To Roy Cohn, with Love

Security's most amazing operation was its smear campaign against New York attorney and power broker Roy Cohn. It was a classic case of Freudian reaction formation—LaRouche, the Red-baiter of the 1980s, going after Cohn, the former aide to Joe McCarthy; LaRouche, the propagandist for organized crime, going after Cohn, its attorney and fixer; LaRouche, who lives like a millionaire but last paid income tax in 1973, going after Cohn, who evaded the IRS through similar tactics for most of his adult life. No two antagonists ever deserved each other more.

The war on Cohn was triggered indirectly by an investigative series I wrote for the Manhattan weekly *Our Town* in 1979. These were the first articles to call attention to LaRouche's neo-Nazism. Former NCLC members say the series freaked out the national office staff. Especially affected were Jewish members, who had rationalized the turn to neo-Nazism via various self-deceptions.

LaRouche moved quickly to blunt the psychological effect on his followers and launch a counterpunch. The first step was to announce that the articles signaled yet another assassination attempt against him.

Previously, such announcements had led to security alerts and mobilizations, whipping up enough hysteria to keep his followers from thinking about things he didn't want them to think about. But for a security alert to be scary, the enemy must be scary—not just a neighborhood newspaper but a giant global conspiracy. Naturally that conspiracy had to include Jews and drug traffickers. In a broadside entitled "We'll Destroy the Zionists Politically," LaRouche announced: "I am a chief target . . . because I have had the guts to identify the enemy boldly and directly. Anyone attacking me in the way that the Zionist rag *Our Town* did is fully in cahoots with . . . Dope, Inc."

LaRouche filed a $20 million suit against *Our Town,* which retained Roy Cohn as its defense attorney. When Security discovered that Cohn had represented *Our Town* on several previous occasions, they blamed him for the articles. The NCLC issued a leaflet with a picture of Cohn and the caption: "Roy Cohn, the mobster who wants to see LaRouche dead." It described him as a major figure in Dope, Inc., and one of the plotters behind the assassination of John F. Kennedy. As the weeks passed, NCLC ascribed more and more importance to Cohn in their global conspiracies.

This propaganda was too hysterically worded to have much effect on the general public, but inside the NCLC it effectively diverted attention. By constant repetition LaRouche linked *Our Town*'s articles to the name, face, and odious reputation of Cohn. He even claimed Cohn had personally written the series. This was a trick LaRouche had described well in "Beyond Psychoanalysis" (1973): If one is faced with dangerous thoughts, one can "block the process of assimilation" by the "commonplace ruse" of slapping a nasty label on them. The *Our Town* articles called for a chain-reaction label: *Cohn, McCarthy, Mafia, Faggot.* This was effective because many of LaRouche's followers were former leftists with a gut hatred of McCarthyism, and Cohn was McCarthyism's premier living symbol. The NCLC members thus could regard themselves as the successors of the Rosenbergs, suffering jolt after jolt from Roy Cohn's *Our Town,* Roy Cohn's *New York Times,* and Roy Cohn's Anti-Defamation League.

On another level the anti-Cohn rhetoric reinforced the NCLC's anti-Semitism at the very moment when outsiders were harshly questioning it. One of the oldest ploys of anti-Semites is to focus on an individual Jew who is genuinely sinister, and to describe his crimes in a manner that suggests that criminality is an innate Jewish trait. The LaRouchians had frequently railed against Meyer Lansky, the financial wizard of organized crime, and long-deceased Jewish gangsters of the Prohibition era such as Bugsy Siegel of Murder, Inc. But such figures had always been too remote from the mainstream Jewish community to be convincing symbols. Cohn, however, was a power in New York politics, with ties to many prominent and respectable Jews. The LaRouchians thus could allege that he represented both a Jewish conspiracy and behavior patterns typical of rich Jews. (In fact, Cohn was an aberrant personality who could have come from any ethnic group. Neither of his two historic partners in demagoguery, McCarthy and J. Edgar Hoover, was Jewish, and his most sinister clients were Italians.)

Cohn's unrepentant McCarthyism, his homosexuality, his role in selecting judges in New York, and his notoriously unethical behavior before the bar all became grist for the propaganda mill, topped off by his media image as the meanest man in New York—an image he carefully cultivated to enhance the price of his legal services and the effectiveness of his courtroom theatrics. LaRouche transformed this into Cohn, the meanest *Zionist* in New York, the personification of the alleged inner meanness of Zionism itself. NCLC members then joined in the Cohn-hating much as the fictional denizens of George Orwell's *Nineteen Eighty-four* rallied for hate sessions directed at the scapegoat Emmanuel Goldstein. Critical thinking within the NCLC national office was almost completely blocked, and no defections occurred for over a year.

But LaRouche's troubles in the outside world were by no means squelched. *The New York Times* echoed *Our Town*'s findings in a front-page series, and the story spread to newspapers in New Hampshire, where LaRouche was making his Democratic primary presidential bid. He tried to counter the reports by claiming he was being libeled by Cohn and "the mob" as a result of his antidrug stance, but such protestations were not effective with the general public, and he received only 2,300 votes in the primary. He thus faced a new dilemma: He had built up Cohn as *the* enemy, but by the logic of this myth, Cohn had caused LaRouche's humiliating New Hampshire defeat. All LaRouche had been able to do to Cohn was fulminate. Some form of revenge would have to be extracted if LaRouche's reputation as a dangerous fellow was not to melt away.

A stroke of luck gave LaRouche the means to extract his revenge in an extraordinary manner, boosting his followers' view of themselves as a potent force and sending a message to the Establishment: Don't mess with Lyndon LaRouche if you have anything to hide. This lucky event was the convergence of the LaRouchians' rage with that of Richard Dupont, a former lover, business associate, and law client of Cohn's. Richard was the co-owner of Big Gym, a gay health club that had been evicted from its Greenwich Village quarters in 1979. Previously Richard had dreamed of purchasing the property, but it ended up in the hands of a real estate developer. Richard blamed this on Cohn's having made a deal behind his back, and he started to talk to anyone who would listen. He said that Cohn had been the silent partner in Big Gym, and that Cohn's personal assistant, Russell Eldridge, had been assigned to skim off cash and procure young men from among the club's clientele to service Cohn's insatiable sexual needs.

Through the years Cohn had double-crossed many clients, from rich elderly ladies through mobsters, and always with impunity. But in Richard he found a victim with an almost superhuman thirst for revenge and a cunning to match his own. Richard was determined to bring down his powerful betrayer, and was willing to run whatever risks were necessary. He contacted many of Cohn's past victims in preparation for a lawsuit. He waged a campaign of hundreds of crank calls to Cohn and various of his associates at their homes and offices. He wrote "Roy Cohn Is a Fag" up and down the sidewalk in front of Cohn's town house. He sent fire trucks and police on a false alarm to Cohn's Greenwich, Connecticut, estate, disrupting a dinner party that included Mr. and Mrs. Donald Trump, the Baron and Baroness di Portanova, and Mrs. S. I. Newhouse. When Cohn was in the hospital recovering from plastic surgery, Richard slipped into the room, wearing a white coat and with a stethoscope around his neck, to remonstrate with Cohn and give him a bouquet of wilted flowers.

Richard also developed a remarkable network of informants in Cohn's office and among Cohn's lovers. He knew where Cohn was at virtually every moment. Secretaries, switchboard operators, and business underlings all helped him, as did Cohn's lovers. His most important source was George Dowling, who ran the skimming operations at Cohn's porn theaters and parking lots. Dowling despised Cohn and provided Richard with information of the most sensitive nature. Richard then called up the head of real estate at the Rock Island Railroad in Chicago and told him how Cohn's associates were skimming off and double-ticketing approximately $350,000 a year from parking lots leased from the railroad. The Cohnheads promptly lost the franchise.

Said Kalev Pehme, a former *Our Town* editor who knew Richard well and often dealt with Cohn on news stories: "Richard had a profound understanding of Cohn's closet homosexual self-hate. He constantly preyed on this and on Cohn's vanity. It was the cumulative effect, one little thing after another, and suddenly you had this powerful figure breaking down because Richard sent him wilted flowers. Richard just kept hitting him like a prizefighter, little blows, you're woozy, then you're gone." Pehme attributed Richard's success in gaining the cooperation of Cohn's lovers to this same psychological understanding. "Richard would help them get over Roy. They were often innocent types, not boys, but men, with battered egos, no self-esteem, completely dominated and used by Cohn. Richard would commiserate with them in the most astonishing compassionate way. He developed tremendous rapport with them, and they told him everything."

In early 1980 a friend of Richard's was handed an NCLC anti-Cohn leaflet in front of Bloomingdale's. She passed it on to Richard, who asked Pehme about it.

Pehme warned him that the LaRouchians were a cult, but Richard figured any enemy of Cohn was worth meeting. He soon recognized that, cult or not, they had the resources to do what he and other Cohn victims had not been able to do on their own. As to the LaRouchian ideology, it simply was of no interest to him.

Over the next few months Richard met on numerous occasions with Paul Goldstein and other Security staffers, providing them with devastating information about Cohn's personal life, finances, and professional double-dealings. The result was collected and published in a magazine, *Now East*, whose two issues were devoted almost entirely to stories about Cohn and other attorneys at Saxe, Bacon, Bolan & Manley, as well as their clients.

Goldstein, Richard, and members of the *New Solidarity* editorial staff plotted out the first issue and its follow-up at Richard's apartment on West Eighth Street. Richard insisted that there be no anti-Zionist rhetoric, which he knew would destroy the magazine's effectiveness. Pornographic cartoons depicting Cohn in flagrante were drawn by a LaRouchian staff artist, while other cartoons were plagiarized and adapted from *The New Yorker*. (Richard supplied the captions.) The advertisements were taken without permission from legitimate gay publications. The entire production was written, laid out, typeset, printed, and paid for by the LaRouche organization, under Goldstein's direct supervision. Yet its masthead listed a fictitious editorial staff and the address of a telephone answering service used by Richard.

For Richard, it was sweet revenge. For the LaRouchians, it was a weird inversion of their experience with *Our Town*. The latter had dared to lay out the LaRouchians' dark secret, their closet Nazism. Now the LaRouchians were laying out Cohn's secrets.

As soon as the press run of the 52-page magazine was completed at LaRouche's PMR Printing Company, the bundles were whisked off to Staten Island and stored in George Dowling's garage. From there, they were distributed by Richard, his friends, and members of the Security staff. The first copies were passed out during New York's Gay Pride parade in June 1980. Copies of this and the subsequent issue were distributed to Cohn's clients and colleagues, to Manhattan's federal court judges, and to the city rooms of the metropolitan dailies. Stacks were left at East Side restaurants frequented by Cohn, such as "21" and

P. J. Clarke's. Charles Tate recalls being assigned to pass out copies at a meeting of a conservative Catholic group attended by Tom Bolan, one of Cohn's law partners.

The first issue's lead article was an "Open Letter to the Gay Community" bearing Cohn's name, in which he purportedly confessed his homosexuality and apologized for selling out Big Gym. Other articles provided details about the skimming operations at Cohn-linked businesses and a combination of real and fictitious stories about his glitzy clients such as Buddy Jacobson, Gloria Vanderbilt, Steve Rubell of Studio 54, Baron and Baroness di Portanova, and Gloria Steinberg, estranged wife of financier Saul Steinberg. In addition, *Now East* included the names of young men who allegedly had slept with Cohn, details about his health, and a drawing of a graveyard with his name on a tombstone.

The second issue followed in November, with a cover drawing labeled "Roy Cohn . . . Fairy." It included articles about a male model alleged to be Cohn's latest lover, Cohn's tax-evasion methods, and how he double-crossed several clients including an organized-crime boss.

Veteran Cohn watchers say that much of the information in the two issues was accurate, some was exaggerated, a few things were concocted. But even the false material bore an aura of believability (and hence a great capacity for embarrassing and humiliating Cohn) because of the skillful way in which it was interwoven with the factual material— the secrets that no one else had ever dared print about New York's vaunted "legal executioner." The reported incidents of professional misconduct were far more outrageous than those which led to Cohn's disbarment in 1986, shortly before his death from AIDS. In addition, the magazine discussed Cohn's silent partnership in a Staten Island parking lot skimming operation run illegally on city property by Enrico Mazzeo, former real estate manager for the city's Department of Marine and Aviation. Mazzeo already was the target of a Brooklyn federal strike force probe. In November 1983 he was found dead in a car trunk in Brooklyn, the victim of a gangland-style execution.

Cohn was desperate to stop the flow of information to Richard, but there were just too many inside sources. When John LeCarré's *Tinker, Tailor, Soldier, Spy* was dramatized on television, Dupont and the LaRouchians began to refer to these sources collectively as "Geraldine"—after LeCarré's "Gerald the Mole." Cohn went to his old antagonist Manhattan District Attorney Robert Morgenthau with a desperate request for help. In October 1980 Richard was indicted on thirteen criminal counts, mostly acts of petty harassment which, under ordinary circumstances, a district attorney wouldn't waste his time on. *The Village Voice* noted that Morgenthau and Cohn had seemed very chummy at a party the night before Richard's 6 A.M. arrest. The *Voice* believed the indictment said more about Cohn's power in New York politics than about Richard's criminality.

Morgenthau's office was well aware of the involvement of the LaRouchians with Richard. Assistant DA Harold Wilson called *Our Town* about them on several occasions in August and September 1980. Yet none of them were indicted. Richard's attorney, John Klotz, believes a political decision was made to let them off: "Just after Richard's arraignment I went to Wilson. I said, 'Let's work something out, we'll help you get LaRouche.' Wilson said to me, 'After I convict Dupont, I will immunize him and put him in front of a grand jury. I don't need your help.' "

That second grand jury was never convened. Former associates of Cohn and LaRouche say that an agreement was arrived at: LaRouche would stop harassing Cohn, and there would be no reprisals against LaRouche. *Now East* ceased publication, and *New Solidarity* scaled back its attacks on Cohn. According to Anne-Marie Vidal, a former member of the NCLC inner circle, LaRouche aides paid a substantial sum to Cohn to introduce LaRouche to important people and persuade the media to leave the NCLC alone. According to law enforcement sources, such a deal was indeed made, but Cohn never delivered what he had promised.

Dupont's trial in the summer of 1981 lasted five weeks. Wilson never once mentioned the defendant's LaRouche connection or the involvement of the LaRouchians in *Now East,* although its distribution was included among the charges against Dupont. This was an extraordinary omission. LaRouche's probable involvement had been mentioned repeatedly in *The Village Voice.* Bringing his name into the case could only have strengthened Wilson's hand, especially with Jewish members of the jury. Nevertheless, the prosecution maintained that Dupont published and distributed *Now East* alone. Defense counsel Klotz's questioning of Richard brought out that he was dyslexic, never graduated from high school, had no experience in newspaper layout or any other aspect of newspaper work, and could not have produced the magazine on his own. This left a hole wide enough to run a bulldozer through. All Wilson had to do was ask Richard who his accomplices were, and then claim that Richard, far from being a little guy seeking justice, was a sinister ally of the infamous LaRouche. But this was no ordinary trial. It was a political trial in which the *real* prosecutor was not Wilson but Roy Cohn, disguised as the star witness. And Cohn had gained a vested interest in keeping LaRouche's name out.

Everything about the wilted-flowers trial was potentially explosive: a homosexual *Dallas,* with Cohn as J.R., providing a window into the profoundly disturbed world of power in New York. But Judge Bentley Kassal's rulings, the prosecution's tactics, and Cohn's influence with the media kept that window mostly closed. If it had been opened, the public would have learned much about high-level New York political corruption, foreshadowing the Donald Manes–Stanley Friedman–Mayor Koch scandals of the mid-1980s. But editors at the metropolitan dailies allowed the trial only minimal play. Even *The Village Voice* only nibbled at the edges. There were no TV cameras on the courthouse steps. *People* v. *Dupont* disappeared into the Memory Hole.

The jury found Richard not guilty on both felony counts, but guilty of six misdemeanors. To convict him of crank phone calls to Cohn cost the taxpayers over $250,000. But when Michael Hudson, a victim of straight-forward loan fraud by the LaRouchians, went to the DA's office in 1982, he was told his complaint was too complicated (unlike the sexually-politically-psychiatrically entangled Dupont case!). Indeed no prosecutor seemed to be willing to take on LaRouche. In 1979 a *New York Times* editorial had urged a probe of his nonprofit Fusion Energy Foundation. But the State Attorney General's office, which is in charge of monitoring nonprofit organizations, took no action. It was one of the few times this publicity-conscious office ever ignored *The New York Times*.

Meanwhile, LaRouche's NCLC developed Manhattan-centered scams in the early 1980s that—according to subsequent indictments and civil RICO suits—would rip off the public for tens of millions of dollars. Even as this was beginning, *The Village Voice* and *Our Town* published articles pointing out LaRouche's financial improprieties and links to racketeers. Neither Morgenthau's office nor State Attorney General Robert Abrams' office nor the Federal Strike Force showed any inclination to look at this. The first real probe in 1984 had to begin in Boston. Abrams only went after LaRouche in the summer of 1986, when Roy Cohn was safely on his deathbed and several state attorney generals from Alaska to Florida were already on the case—investigating a conspiracy that began in Abrams' own backyard.

Charles Tate says the Security staff believed in the early 1980s that the soft treatment the NCLC received in New York—including Mayor Koch's speak-no-evil attitude toward LaRouche mayoral candidate Melvin Klenetsky in 1981—was due to a fear of NCLC smear campaigns. The NCLC's negative personal information about political figures, he said, was actually in files "in alphabetical order" in the Security office. Tate added that he personally interviewed an alleged former intimate friend of Brooklyn DA Elizabeth Holtzman and also received information on her from a paid informant. The aim was to make prosecutors and politicians think "they don't need an enemy of this type," Tate said.

In the 1987 Frankhouser trial, Tate testified that whenever LaRouche couldn't find damaging information "he would invent something." Indeed the LaRouchians followed an age-old smear tactic: Look at a person's lifestyle and figure what *might* be true, then publish your speculations as fact. A certain percentage of the time you will hit the bull's eye, and the victim will freak out thinking you know more than you do. If it isn't true, much of the public will believe it anyway, and the victim will heartily wish you'd just shut up. If you're doing this in an exceptionally corrupt political environment like Koch's New York, where most public figures have secrets to hide, you're guaranteed a large measure of immunity from libel suits. To gain a powerful intimidating reputation, you just have to be right once in a big way. The LaRouchians were right in a stupendous way with *Now East*, and after that no one in New York seriously went after them for years.

Following Dupont's trial but prior to sentencing, Judge Bentley Kassal received a letter from Roger Stone, regional director of Ronald Reagan's 1980 presidential campaign. Sent at Cohn's request, the letter was apparently intended to urge a stiff sentence for Richard. Stone complained that Richard had once called to ask him about his "personal relationship" with Cohn, then sent him flowers and several copies of *Now East*. Kassal delayed sentencing while ordering Richard to seek psychiatric treatment. However, the following June he imposed a sentence of four consecutive years for Richard's nonviolent prankish misdemeanors—a punishment virtually without precedent in such a case and regarded as incredible by some journalists who covered the trial. A few months later, Kassal was elevated to the Appellate Division.

While the case was being appealed, Richard was ordered to Rikers Island to begin serving his sentence. Believing accidents had been known to happen to enemies of Cohn, and that Rikers Island was a good place for such an accident, Richard went underground and spread the word that the DA's detective squad had better not come near him—he had AIDS. (This actually was not true.) Several months later Richard went to former U.S. Attorney General Ramsey Clark, who arranged for him to turn himself in. When the appeal came up, Kassal disqualified himself. The remaining judges agreed it was indeed peculiar that Dupont had been sentenced to jail for passing out a magazine on the street, a constitutionally protected activity. They dismissed that count, but let the rest of the conviction stand.

The Cohn-LaRouche war might have ended with Richard's conviction, save for Helga LaRouche's car being involved in a near accident in West Germany. The LaRouchians smelled an assassination attempt.

Frankhouser's Mister Ed gallantly offered to protect Helga and suggested that the CIA was taking the threat *very* seriously. Mordechai Levy
said that the infamous assassin "Henry Duvall" was involved and that
Roy Cohn was obviously behind "Duvall." The freak-out began when
Goldstein went to Richard to ask if he could find out anything from
inside Saxe, Bacon. Sensing an opportunity to resurrect *Now East,*
Richard confirmed Levy's story.

The LaRouchians were furious over Cohn's alleged "double cross."
They responded with an attack even nastier than *Now East*—hundreds
of thousands of copies of a bogus *New York Times* supplement, "Profiles
of the Times," designed to look like the Sunday book review section
but devoted to further exposing Cohn and his associates. Tate says it
was Richard's "brainchild," and that Richard devised "what to say and
how to say it." On a Saturday night in October 1982, two members of
LaRouche's Security staff took "Profiles" around to dozens of news-
stands in Manhattan and Queens in a rented van. Wearing dark glasses,
they represented themselves as *Times* employees and instructed the
newsdealers to insert the supplement in the Sunday papers. Before the
*Times* management could react, it had reached tens of thousands of
readers.

"Profiles" contained alleged quotes from former lovers of Cohn,
including three men who later died of AIDS. It also contained a fake
Barbara Walters interview with Cohn in which he purportedly admitted
his homosexuality and discussed in some detail his inner emotional life
and illegal dealings with various business associates. The piece was
written with subtlety and verve. After buying the *Times* that Saturday
night, I was halfway into the Walters-Cohn interview before it dawned
on me: Richard and the LaRouchians had struck again.

A later edition of the *Times* carried a disclaimer, and many of the
"Profiles" copies were never distributed. Yet the prank turned out to be
far more effective than *Now East*. It was reported on the wire services
and in daily papers across the country, raising the issue of Roy Cohn's
homosexuality with millions of readers. New York's daily papers on
Monday reported the indignant howls of eminent persons. Cohn declared "Profiles" a "total lie" and vowed to seek "every available" legal
remedy "to see that something like this does not happen again . . . to
someone less capable of self-defense." Republican gubernatorial candidate Lew Lehrman, himself a target in "Profiles" along with Mayor
Koch, said that "so outrageous a personal attack has never occurred in
an election in New York State politics." Leonard Harris of the *Times* said
that it was "the poison Tylenol technique applied to newspapers,"
while another *Times* executive, John Pomfret, promised that the paper

would "pursue vigorously an investigation of this outrage in consultation with law-enforcement authorities."

The *Times*'s veteran Nazi hunter Howard Blum was assigned to track down the LaRouche connection. Morgenthau announced the launching of an investigation by Harold Wilson and a team of detectives. A grand jury was convened to examine evidence that the LaRouchians had violated forgery laws.

But all this turned out to be mere bluster. Although the district attorney's detective squad raided LaRouche's printshop on November 16, it failed to simultaneously raid the type house, located at another address. When the police arrived at the printshop, a member of La-Rouche's legal staff was already there, forewarned.

Part of the story came out in 1986 in the Boston credit-card case, when FBI special agent Richard Egan testified regarding information on the *Times* supplement received from government informants. The NCLC Security staff had "managed to have some kind of leak of information from the district attorney's office which allowed them to destroy the [printing] plates" before the search warrant could be executed. Security chief Paul Goldstein, who was Morgenthau's chief suspect, had been sent on a "European vacation." Former LaRouche bodyguard Lee Fick had run into Goldstein in Wiesbaden, and Goldstein had told him, "Lyn wants me here because it's too hot in New York." LaRouche aide Jeffrey Steinberg had asked Klansman Roy Frankhouser to go to the printshop and "lean on" an employee whom Steinberg was worried might talk to the police.

Former police officer Phil Perlonga, a Metro employee who served as a LaRouche bodyguard in 1982–83, says that the LaRouchians asked him to shadow Richard, whom they were fearful might talk. "I followed him all over the fur district," Perlonga recalled. He also said the LaRouchians asked him to conduct surveillance of the DA's office to see if Dupont went in or out.

For several weeks, the LaRouchians were extremely jumpy. La-Rouche was living in a town house on Sutton Place. Perlonga, in charge of a security detail, recalls that someone phoned in with a report that Morgenthau's detective squad was on its way to arrest LaRouche. La-Rouche's in-house Security aides immediately "came downstairs, put on bulletproof vests, and checked their .45s. I took the Metro guys outside, and told them to stay there and if the police came, to tell them there were crazy people armed inside and that they should communicate through me. I then went back inside; I was prepared to blow LaRouche's guys away if they fired on police officers." But the DA's squad never arrived: The report was a concoction phoned in from Los

Angeles by Mordechai Levy. "I made it all up," Levy said. "It was part of my plan to drive them crazy."

In spite of their paranoia, the LaRouchians made some shrewd moves during the "Profiles" uproar. *New Solidarity* issued a threat as to what Cohn could expect if the case ever came to trial. The article began by noting that he had decided not to sue for libel. This supposedly reflected his "reticence to make himself and his business and sexual dealings the subject of what could only be one of the country's most highly publicized trials . . . especially given what this news service knows to be Cohn's many crimes." The article quoted LaRouche as saying that "Cohn has more enemies than a queen bee has eggs." If the DA ever brought the "Profiles" case to trial, the defendants would "drown [Cohn's] political career in a flood of publicity and gales of laughter."

The LaRouchians also targeted Morgenthau. Security notebooks from November 1982 show that they assiduously pursued negative information about the DA and his wife, former *New York Times* reporter Lucinda Franks. According to one notebook entry, a source at a drug treatment center told them a preposterous story that Morgenthau owned whorehouses. Another entry described an undercover phone call to one of Franks's colleagues. They then flooded downtown Manhattan with leaflets devoted to standard LaRouche charges—e.g., that Morgenthau was a tool of the "Israeli mafia" and that his wife was a "terrorist sympathizer." (She had indeed spent time with the Weather Underground, but for the purpose of writing a book about them.)

One leaflet, passed out in front of Morgenthau's office to make sure he received the message, contained a LaRouche zinger transcending the usual NCLC rhetoric. It alleged that Morgenthau had "sat on the biggest banking scandal of the past decade, American Bank and Trust's 1976 failure," and that he had "prosecuted clerk-level fall guys while top bank officers and manipulators . . . received immunity in a $45 million rip-off of depositors." Details followed, based in part on long-forgotten articles in *Barron's* and *New York* magazine by Richard Karp, a freelance financial reporter. Karp told me the LaRouchians had called him at the time and questioned him closely about the American Bank scandal and related matters. He recalled that they seemed extremely well informed.

The LaRouchians boasted in a December 10, 1982, *New Solidarity* article by Linda de Hoyos (who had been involved in the production of *Now East)* that they were engaged in an effort to "unnerve" Morgenthau and catch his office "off guard." A December 14 article by Security staffer Vin Berg in *Executive Intelligence Review* made the threat explicit: "Morgenthau has been involved in many covert operations against

LaRouche in the past, but this one is the riskiest, because it is being conducted openly . . . By stepping into the light of day in this way, Robert Morgenthau has made himself, his financial and political associates, and his record in office matters for intense public scrutiny."

By early 1983 the DA's office suspected that Goldstein and two aides were the chief culprits. Yet by December 1983 there was still no action. Harold Wilson, in a telephone interview, attributed the delay to a federal court lawsuit which the LaRouchians had filed against the DA that year. But the investigation may simply have been spiked. John Klotz says he approached the DA's office with an offer that Richard would give testimony in exchange for some consideration on his own sentence but the DA spurned the offer. Was the DA's office once again letting the LaRouchians off the hook to protect themselves and other powerful people from further embarrassment? Wilson claims that his office didn't make a deal with Klotz because they didn't believe Richard could give "direct, competent, truthful evidence." But this statement is belied by Richard's competent and truthful (if rambling) testimony about Cohn in his 1981 trial, as well as the extraordinary accuracy of his published information on Cohn. *The Village Voice* quoted Klotz shortly after the "Profiles" hoax: "The last investigation [the *Now East* one] was botched by Morgenthau's office because they didn't go beyond Dupont to look at the financing and publication of *Now East*. The New York Times is paying the price for that with this [second] reprehensible publication." Certainly the DA's double standard for big guy LaRouche and little guy Dupont bore more than a little similarity to the double standard in the American Bank case.

According to NCLC defectors and Security employees, LaRouche's top aides alluded to a new rapprochement with Cohn which supposedly resulted in the abandonment of the "Profiles" investigation. LaRouche and Cohn had associates in common who would have wanted this high-profile war stopped, even if Roy had to eat humble pie. Cohn was the attorney for Fat Tony Salerno, and Fat Tony, as would be alleged in a federal indictment in 1986, had his hooks deep into Teamster boss Jackie Presser, LaRouche's number one hoodlum ally. In fact, the La-Rouche-Cohn war ceased for good. There were no more major revelations, although *New Solidarity* would gloat over Cohn's AIDS a few months before the major media dared mention it. Goldstein returned from his "vacation" to continue his trickster campaigns with greater impudence than ever. Meanwhile, *The New York Times* abandoned its own investigation of the "Profiles." Nothing more than a brief item on the DA's raid was ever published. *The Village Voice* noted that the *Times* "seems curiously reticent on a matter so deeply offensive to its own integrity." But the *Times* had also been curiously reticent in covering the Dupont trial or, for that matter, anything relating to Roy Cohn's corruption of the New York political process in the late 1970s and early 1980s.

Nevertheless, LaRouche had played close to the edge with his "Profiles of the Times." Shortly after the DA's raid on the printshop, he packed up and moved to Virginia, although NCLC headquarters remained in New York for two more years. In a 1984 affidavit, he stated that he had not "travelled to New York since December of 1982 and will not travel to or visit New York City" because of the "security situation." However, he continued to dabble in New York political intrigues from the safety of his country estate. In 1983 a bitter enemy of Morgenthau, former New York City medical examiner Dr. Michael Baden, met with LaRouche in Leesburg. Baden had been removed as medical examiner in 1979 in part because of pressure from Morgenthau. The LaRouchians had championed Baden in several articles, depicting him as a victim of *Dope, Inc.* He was accompanied by his wife, Dr. Judianne Densen-Gerber, formerly of Odyssey House, who had spoken at LaRouchian anti-drug rallies, and by Dr. John Grauerholz, a former colleague of Baden's in the Suffolk County, New York, medical examiner's office.

That same year Grauerholz and other medical professionals allied with Baden became involved in a campaign to discredit Morgenthau and Baden's successor, Dr. Elliot Gross, over their handling of the death in police custody of a young black graffiti artist, Michael Stewart. Grauerholz served as a source for *The New York Times* in a series critical of Gross and was later honored at a dinner held by a political coalition that was seeking justice for the Stewart family. The *Times* and the political coalition suffered considerable embarrassment when the *New York Post* revealed that Grauerholz was a full-time follower of LaRouche. The campaign against Gross and Morgenthau meanwhile developed anti-Semitic undertones in the black community, thanks to the newsletter of African Activists in America. The LaRouchians did their bit by alleging that Gross and Morgenthau were part of an anti-Michael Baden conspiracy headed by the "Israeli mafia." An article by LaRouche's Upper West Side snitch Bruce Bailey was circulated, alleging that blacks were held in a Zionist "death grip." (After multiple probes on the local, state, and federal levels, Gross eventually was cleared of any wrongdoing in the Stewart case. In October 1987, Mayor Koch dismissed him from his post, citing administrative ineffectiveness.)

By June 1986 the LaRouchians were under investigation in over a dozen states for loan fraud. Many of the loans were solicited by New York NCLC members at a time when the NCLC's regional office was located right down the street from Brooklyn DA Liz Holtzman's office. But New York prosecutors, despite the strong sentiment against La-

Rouche in the Jewish community in the wake of his organization's Illinois campaign victories, lagged far behind states where public sentiment and the demands of justice were not nearly as strong. *Our Town* publisher Edward Kayatt ran an editorial calling for sacking both Morgenthau and Abrams if they didn't move on LaRouche. The untouchable Morgenthau ignored it. Abrams, however, spoke from the floor at a Jewish Community Relations Advisory Council gathering in Manhattan the week the editorial appeared, apologizing for his office's failure to exercise vigilance and asking anyone who had been ripped off by LaRouche to come forward. Shortly thereafter his office began contacting many victims of LaRouche's fund raising.

The LaRouchians figured they could once again use their embarrassing-revelations tactic. On August 4, *New Solidarity* published an article about how certain Abrams aides were involved in the gay rights movement. A week later an article by Michelle Steinberg and LaRouche's chief spokesman, Ed Spannaus, suggested that the NCLC might be in possession of potentially embarrassing information received from Cohn shortly before his death. Pointing out that Cohn had wanted on his deathbed to pass on some information about public officials, they speculated that this information was from Cohn's "blackmail files" and that "Cohn's knowledge of the homosexual weaknesses of some . . . as-yet-unnamed public officials was not academic." They boasted about the devastating quality of some of the NCLC's past insider information from circles around Cohn ("some of the very charges published in the 'Profiles' insert sheet were the basis for a series of civil actions that led to Mr. Cohn's ultimate disbarment"). They also alleged that in my forthcoming book (this one) I would demonstrate that "Cohn and LaRouche ultimately reached a coming to terms" and that "Cohn became an unofficial legal consultant to LaRouche." Finally they suggested that "some of the infamous Cohn files" might have "quietly slipped into the hands of some of Lyndon LaRouche's closest associates in rural Virginia."

But whatever information the LaRouchians possessed was not equal to quashing a felony investigation in the 1986 atmosphere in which New Yorkers wanted something done about LaRouche. It had been easy to evade indictment for pranks like *Now East* and "Profiles," but loan fraud running into tens of millions of dollars was no prank. In March 1987, Abrams' office indicted fifteen LaRouche aides. Among them were *Now East* writer Linda de Hoyos, who had boasted in *New Solidarity* in 1982 about unnerving Morgenthau, and Edward Spannaus, co-author of the August 11, 1986, article about the alleged "Cohn files."

# Part Seven

# Conspiracies and Code Words

If I were the head of the Illuminati, I certainly would not call it by that name . . . I'd call it the John Birch Society, and advertise it as an organization *opposed* to the Illuminati. That way I'd be able to rope in all the people who are against the Illuminati and use them as unwitting dupes.

This is such a plausible idea that if the Illuminati do exist, they must have thought of it already.

—ROBERT ANTON WILSON

# Twenty-seven

## LaRouche's Purloined Letter

American journalists are generally unaccustomed to dealing with the subtleties of extremist ideology. Electoral contests between Republicans and Democrats do not reflect the range of views found in, say, French or Italian elections, which span the spectrum from Communist to fascist. Even mainstream ideologies in the United States have become little more than pieties accompanying the TV glitz. It is thus hardly a surprise that American journalists have difficulty understanding what LaRouche is about. They assume he will use ideas and words in as straightforward a way as they themselves do. When he doesn't, they become confused and tend to dismiss his ideas as a "puzzle," a "mystery," or "difficult to characterize," although they concede that he appears to be some kind of "extremist." They conceal their confusion and intellectual laziness with jokes about LaRouche the kook who thinks the Queen of England pushes drugs, entirely missing the real meaning of his quip about the Queen.

LaRouche knows that his writings mystify most readers, but he provides little hints for them. For instance, he suggests that they approach his writings in the spirit of Edgar Allan Poe's famous detective, Monsieur Dupin. "The 'secrets' of my actions," LaRouche says, "are of the same order as the purloined letter of the Poe tale, or the open secrets of nature—it is a matter of knowing not only where, but how to look."

To learn how to look, one must begin with LaRouche's conspiracy theory of history, which highlights the role of deception and concealment in the transmission of ideology through the centuries. In "The Secrets Known Only to the Inner Elites," LaRouche claims that he and his followers represent a 3,000-year-old faction of "Neoplatonic humanists" locked in mortal struggle with an equally ancient "oligarchy." To avoid repression by the dominant oligarchy, the humanists through the centuries have concealed their ideas in much the way that an espionage agent conceals his identity. Indeed, the humanist is a combination of spy and underground organizer. LaRouche cites the example of St. Augustine, who supposedly adopted Christianity as his cover for organizing a united front against the oligarchy.

The concept of "cover" is also the basis of LaRouche's views on philosophy and literature. The wisdom of the humanist conspiracy supposedly is concealed in the writings of Plato, Dante, Machiavelli, etc. Their method is like a play within a play, using one philosophy as a smoke screen for another. The disciple *thinks* he is studying harmless philosophy A, but he is subliminally absorbing subversive philosophy B. By the time he gains full insight, he is so firmly hooked that he won't betray the truth to outsiders. Of course, many students never gain full awareness, and indeed these may be the most useful: In LaRouche's theory of espionage the best agent is often the one who is unaware that he is an agent—the zombie agent, the Manchurian candidate.

LaRouche believes poetry is especially useful as a means of communication among agents because it "disallow[s] any literal or ordinary symbolic significance" and "conjoin[s] predicates ambiguously so that only the preconscious transfinite for such conjoined elements can be intended." In plain English: If you use ambiguous language, you can always deny what you really meant when threatened with political repression. Meanwhile your message can reach the discerning few and you can continue to act on philosophy B while calling it philosophy A. As LaRouche, referring to his enemies, said in a 1978 speech: "It is not necessary to call oneself a fascist to be a fascist. It is simply necessary to be one."

But LaRouche's theory of ideological deception also asserts something more subtle. Through ambiguity and code words, it's possible to appeal to the reader or listener's "preconscious mind" and thus lead him gradually into ideas his conscious mind would otherwise reject. So when LaRouche wrote in 1979 about "Machiavelli's" success in outwitting the "donkey censors," the word "censor" was actually a pun referring both to political censors and to the censor (superego) of Freudian theory. A 1986 LaRouchian article, signed by none other than "Machiavelli," made this point clearly: Euphemisms or code words are "an artificial mechanism to avoid the moral shock of facing bestiality in its most degenerate forms." Although the author portrayed this as a method used by oligarchs rather than his favored humanists, the basic principle was in fact used by LaRouche in the mid-1970s to instill fascist ideas in his leftist followers. As most of them feared and loathed fascism, LaRouche could never have won them over without code words and ambiguity to short-circuit the moral shock they would have experienced if he had spoken frankly.

LaRouche was quite aware of what he was doing. "Words and syntactical forms," he wrote, have customary meanings. To elicit something *beyond* those customary meanings, to express an idea that is "genuinely new," one must add "a new meaning"—however subtle—to the "existing medium." LaRouche made this observation in *The Case of Walter Lippmann* (1977), which gave new meanings to many "customary" terms. For instance, "republican" was used over and over to mean "fascist." *Lippmann,* LaRouche's major theoretical work, also abounded in multileveled puns to slyly suggest various fascist and anti-Semitic ideas. For instance, LaRouche referred to the oligarchy as "nominalists." Nominalism was the medieval precursor of modern empiricism. For LaRouche, it is a synonym for "materialism"—the philosophy that anti-Semites accuse Jews of having developed as a weapon against Christianity and Aryanism. LaRouche's nominalism also designates materialistic values—the alleged money consciousness of the Jews and the alleged "bestial heteronomy" of the masses. On a deeper level the term refers to the "nominal Jews"—the "Jews who are not Jews." In addition, since the nominalist philosophy was closely associated with scholastic philosophers from England (especially William of Occam), LaRouche can use it to cross-reference his favorite anti-Semitic euphemisms: "British" and "British empiricist." Such puns aside, LaRouche has good reason to hate nominalism: It is a philosophy that argues that words are only signs for things and have no independent existence—it thus stands opposed to LaRouche's semantic tricks.

Ambiguity and puns are okay for some purposes, but a serious political conspiracy also needs ideological precision. LaRouche refers to "the 'codes' of the Renaissance intelligence and conciliar networks." These were not developed as a mere academic exercise, he says. "Certain qualities of ideas cannot be communicated in any other fashion." Here LaRouche is describing real history, although in a distorted way. For centuries political writers *have* used code words or euphemisms to avoid state repression. In the late nineteenth century, Russian revolutionaries employed an elaborate "Aesopian" language to evade the czarist censors. Poland's Solidarity trade union in the early 1980s used code words to criticize the Soviet Union. In the Soviet Union itself, dissidents have seized on Mikhail Gorbachev's term *glasnost* and transformed it into a euphemism for Western-style democracy.

In the United States, code language is a convenient tool for advocates of racism and anti-Semitism. They don't have to worry about being jailed for their ideas, but they do have to use caution in communicating with those outside their ranks. While laying out their argument they must avoid triggering a premature revulsion or feeling of embarrassment in their audience. They must also protect themselves against the backlash from their ideas—negative press coverage, social ostracism, or even physical assault from members of the targeted ethnic groups. Racists thus talk about "states' rights" in the South and "law and order" in the North. Anti-Semites call themselves "anti-Zionists." Naturally, not all advocates of states' rights or law and order are racists, nor are all critics of Israel Jew-haters. This is precisely what makes the code words so convenient.

West Germany outlaws overt neo-Nazi agitation. Yet hundreds of neo-Nazi, racial nationalist, and conservative nationalist groups have sprouted on German soil since World War II, each with an intense desire to communicate various forbidden or impolitic messages to the general public. They do so in large part through code words. Political scientist Kurt Tauber, in his 1,600-page *Beyond Eagle and Swastika*, describes the deceptive tactics of scores of such groups in the first two decades after the war. One militant youth league in the 1950s was called the Schiller Youth, although it engaged in activities more appropriate to the Hitler Youth. It is significant that LaRouche has founded a Schiller Institute, and his wife speaks of bringing a *Schillerzeit* to America.

Former LaRouche followers believe that the planting of code terms in NCLC publications is a means of signaling old-style fascists around the world (the "old humanist networks," as some LaRouchians call them) that the NCLC is sympathetic to their aims. One way this is done is by using occult buzzwords like "Atlantis" and "Thule" to allude to the Aryan race and the Third Reich. The practice springs from occult beliefs in Hitler's inner circle. Cryptic references to such beliefs are easily recognized in the secretive world of Western European and South American neo-fascism as well as in U.S. white supremacist circles.

LaRouche also has adopted various conspiracy theories of the Nazi and pre-Nazi era long forgotten by everyone outside of hard-core anti-Semitic circles. He uses these theories in a sly form, referring to the

"Babylonians" and the "British" rather than the Jews. This is not just sending signals; it is LaRouche's version of what he calls the Renaissance intelligence "codes." It enables him to evade the "donkey censor" to discuss in print the core theories of Nazism: that the Jews are the ancient enemy of the human race, that they are a separate biological entity, and that they must be crushed in a final cataclysmic struggle. Through this code language, he is able to promote a neo-Nazi ideology in all but name yet remain sufficiently respectable to gain meetings with high-level Reagan administration aides and raise tens of millions of dollars a year from elderly conservatives. LaRouche has shown his fellow fascists around the world how to have your cake and eat it too.

# Twenty-eight

## Babylonians
## Under Every Bed

LaRouche's conspiracy theory of history is not just a means of indirectly expressing neo-Nazi ideas. It is also a psychological device which serves to deepen the political paranoia within the NCLC and ultimately within the public the NCLC strives to influence. A paranoid belief system, if it is truly a totalitarian one, must be as all-encompassing as possible, since any holes in it are a potential escape hatch for the captive mind to liberate itself. The paranoid ideology, whether serving a cult or a totalitarian regime, must be a block of steel, not a slice of Swiss cheese.

This means that the conspiracy theory—the basis of political paranoia—cannot just concern itself with contemporary politics. Ideally it should extend into every field of thought and every period of history so that no matter what topic the captive mind thinks about, it can *only* think about it in paranoid terms of us versus them (with "them," of course, being infinitely evil).

LaRouche's theory of the struggle between two secret elites is perhaps the closest thing to a system of total multidimensional paranoia ever invented in the United States. It extends backwards in time tens of thousands of years, and also forward into man's future among the stars. It extends into every sphere of culture: music, art, poetry, philosophy, science—indeed, into every aspect of human existence. It descends into sexuality and the unconscious mind and even deeper into the genes and chromosomes, the level of racial struggle. It also ascends *above* history into a neo-Platonic supersensible realm. It has its source in the geometric structure of reality. If one is a LaRouchian, one's belief system literally cannot be escaped; the struggle is everywhere.

The lynchpin of LaRouchism, as of more primitive systems of paranoia, is the fear and hatred of an evil and secretive force. Although LaRouche calls this force the oligarchy, he really means the Jews. Given the total paranoia of the system, the fear and hatred veers into neo-Nazism. The latter is not an acceptable ideology in today's America and so must remain partially disguised to evade the "donkey censor." LaRouche's conspiracy theory therefore becomes a double system: First, it extends the NCLC's paranoia and hatred into every aspect of thought; second, it attacks the supposed forces of evil in a euphemistic manner. This dual nature of the theory should be kept in mind as we step by step "decode" the bizarre formulations in which it is couched.

If LaRouche had been a traditional anti-Semite, he might have based his conspiracy theory on the *Protocols of the Elders of Zion,* the infamous forgery that purports to document a nineteenth-century conspiracy to establish a Jewish world government through various diabolical intrigues. But the *Protocols* is too narrow in scope for the purposes of total paranoia and also is too thoroughly discredited by scholars for practical use among most educated people. LaRouche hesitated, however, to reject out of hand one of the most effective Big Lies of the first half of the twentieth century. So he compromised: The *Protocols,* he said, has a "hard kernel of truth" but is only of limited significance—it represents only a small piece of the *real* conspiracy of the "oligarchy."

LaRouche's oligarchy makes the Elders of Zion seem mild. It supposedly has dominated the world for tens of thousands of years with unremittingly evil motives. Indeed, LaRouche accuses it of periodically killing off a large portion of the human race through famines and plagues. Today it is supposedly plotting a New Dark Ages, which will include nuclear holocaust, the massive spread of AIDS, Zero Growth, and total bestial heteronomy.

Why the oligarchs should want a return to the Dark Ages when they obviously could accumulate more wealth and live more comfortably under conditions of modern capitalism is not quite clear. But LaRouche assures us that they destroyed all past societies they captured, from Atlantis through Rome. Three thousand years ago their headquarters was in Babylon. After they engineered its fall, they shifted their command post westward to Rome, then Venice, and finally to London. Again and again their poisons and daggers have defeated their valiant opponents, the "humanists," who champion productive investment, science, technology, and "citybuilding."

Unable to stop humanist networks, led by Benjamin Franklin and Friedrich Schiller, from launching the Industrial Revolution, the oligarchs struggled to slow it down through their control of Speculative Capital, which allegedly feeds like a vampire on Productive Capital. But the oligarchs today are extremely worried because Productive Capital has begun to link up with the powerful streamlined humanist conspiracy represented by the NCLC.

It is unlikely LaRouche believes all this, but it provides him with the necessary all-encompassing framework for his anti-Semitic mythology, giving it, even in a disguised form, a virulence far more intense than if he had based it on the *Protocols* alone. As to the true identity of the oligarchs, this is revealed in LaRouche's "Solving the Machiavellian Problem Today": They are the "anti-human bestialists" and "parasites" who "cooked up the hoax called the Old Testament." In a subsequent article he openly calls them the "Jewish usurers"—a "continuous and often dominant element" in oligarchical rule from Babylon through the Middle Ages. (LaRouche then throws up one of his characteristic smoke screens. Some people, he writes, have misinterpreted this dominant role of the Jews in order to promote anti-Semitism. Although he does not wish to be a party to spreading such misguided views, he can't help it that the hoax is bolstered by the "fact" that "some of the worst poisonings of the Catholic Church were accomplished by converted Jews representing such families of usurers"!)

"The Secrets Known Only to the Inner Elites" is LaRouche's most thorough account of his version of world history. Apart from his schema of oligarchs versus humanists, this work and other NCLC pseudo-historical treatises appear to borrow heavily from the anti-Semitic "classics": Houston Stewart Chamberlain's *Foundations of the Nineteenth Century* (1899), Oswald Spengler's *Decline of the West* (1918–22), Hitler's *Mein Kampf* (1925–26), Alfred Rosenberg's *Myth of the Twentieth Century* (1930), and Francis Parker Yockey's *Imperium* (1948), as well as assorted British and American Nazi tracts from the interwar years.

LaRouche's attacks on the evil "Babylonians," for instance, strongly resemble theories found in Chamberlain, who claimed that the Jews of the Babylonian Captivity rose to great influence over their captors, and that Babylon rather than Jerusalem was the real headquarters of the ancient Jews. Chamberlain even remarked on the "Rothschilds" of Babylon. This theory is popularized for American racists in pamphlets sold by the Louisiana-based Sons of Liberty—for instance, *The Merchants of Babylon* by Rev. Bertrand L. Comparet, which features a photograph of four bearded rabbis on the cover. When LaRouche denounces the "Whore of Babylon," the Ku Klux Klan knows exactly what he means.

LaRouche also rails against the "Persian Empire" and "Persian agents" who supposedly destroyed the ancient world. Again this is not new: Both Spengler and Chamberlain claimed that the Jews and the Persians were linked in a common conspiracy: Spengler said the Jews actually dominated much of the Persian empire, while Chamberlain described them as Persian puppets. In LaRouche's view the chief instruments of Persian-Babylonian infiltration of the West (Greece and Rome) were the Dionysian cults and Isis worship. (One LaRouche disciple wrote that modern Israel is the "Zionist bastard" of Isis.) Alfred Rosenberg, Hitler's "philosopher" who was executed at Nuremberg, brooded over Dionysius and Isis in a similar manner sixty years ago. The Dionysian cults, he said, were "racially and spiritually alien" to Aryanism, encouraging a frenzy based on that of the "insanely possessed" King Saul of Israel. As to Isis, Rosenberg associated her with Africa, sexual promiscuity, and race mixing.

Approaching modern times, LaRouche shows more originality. In the Middle Ages the center of power moved to Rome, whose "merchant-usurers" were Jews or converted Jews. Led by the Pierlioni family, they supposedly seized control of the papacy and squeezed Europe dry. Next the Venetian oligarchy took its pound of flesh during the Renaissance, after the decline of the Vatican oligarchy but before the rise of the "British."

Throughout these long centuries, LaRouche teaches, the humanist forerunners of the NCLC fought back continuously. Many famous thinkers and poets were secret members: Plato, Dante, Machiavelli, and Edgar Allan Poe, as well as Franklin and Schiller. But most important were the warlord humanists, the champions of the Grand Design. Not surprisingly, most of them marched their conquering armies east. The LaRouchians praise the legendary Pharaoh Sesostris, who supposedly marched east to subjugate evil Babylon; Alexander the Great, who marched east to crush evil Persia; and Timur the Great, who carried out an early version of the Final Solution against the medieval descendants of the ancient Persians and Babylonians. LaRouche also expresses reverence for the memory of Hassan ibn Saba, the "Old Man of the Mountain," who headed a medieval cult of assassins. Hassan didn't march east, but he did live in a castle called the Eagle's Nest—the same name as Hitler's mountaintop lodge in Bavaria. LaRouche wrote in

1978 that if only the Old Man of the Mountain were alive in Germany, he'd mop up left-wing terrorists in short order.

Of special significance in LaRouchian mythology is Frederick Barbarossa, the medieval German emperor who marched east against the Slavs (and in whose memory Hitler named his invasion of the Soviet Union "Operation Barbarossa"). The Wiesbaden branch of LaRouche's European Labor Party evoked Frederick Barbarossa's memory in its 1978 manifesto calling for a new type of state in Germany— *Der Rechtsstaat.* The translation of the manifesto in *The Campaigner* (the NCLC's theoretical organ) was illustrated by a map of Central and Eastern Europe, entitled "Frederick Barbarossa's Great Design." On the opposite page was a map of the entire area included in the European theater in World War II, with dotted lines going just about everywhere the Nazi armies went or dreamed of going. The caption underneath discussed the German *Drang nach Osten* (drive to the east), but identified it with the German emperors rather than Hitler. The dotted lines were said to be "European and Mediterranean Trade Routes."

LaRouche finds certain recurring patterns in history—the result of the oligarchs using the same strategy of control again and again. Ancient Babylon (dominated as it was by rich Jews) concocted the "synthetic" religion of the Old Testament, brainwashed the Jewish masses with it, then sent them back to Judaea as a strategic military colony. In the twentieth century, Britain (the new Babylon, also dominated by rich Jews) brainwashed the Jewish masses with the synthetic ideology of Zionism and sent them back to Palestine to serve as a garrison state.

Another case is the career of Alexander the Great, who was reared as a Persian agent but rebelled against his masters and took vengeance on them. Likewise, according to LaRouche, Hitler began his career as a "British" agent—and indeed, the German correspondent for *The New York Times*—but rebelled against the British and drove them to Dunkirk. Unfortunately, he lacked Alexander's humanist resolve to finish the job.

A final example is the medieval Jewish usurers in the Vatican. LaRouche says they charged such high interest rates that they drove Europe into utter penury. Weakened by starvation, the masses succumbed to the Black Plague. In the same manner, the London-controlled International Monetary Fund supposedly is driving the peoples of the Third World into starvation, causing them to succumb to AIDS.

In his gloomier moments LaRouche worries that Western civilization will suffer the fate of the Atlanteans, who supposedly showed great promise under the leadership of scientist-astronomers until being subverted and destroyed by the ancestors of the Babylonians, the evil magician-astrologers. Although LaRouche nowhere refers to the hapless Atlanteans as the "Aryan" race, he strongly suggests that this is who he means. They came, he says, from sunken lands in the North Sea, spoke a language akin to old Hessian, and roamed the Atlantic in "copper-sheathed" longships. A similar mythology was promoted by Alfred Rosenberg, whose blond and blue-eyed Atlanteans made their forays in Wagnerian "dragon ships." (Neither LaRouche nor Rosenberg offers scientific evidence for the existence of this lost civilization.)

It can be said that LaRouche's version of history not only begins with Nazi and proto-Nazi ideas (the Atlanteans from the North) but ends with them. His theory of the contemporary struggle between parasitic bankers and productive factory owners is suspiciously similar to the views of Hitler's early economics adviser, Gottfried Feder. The latter likewise urged the crushing and expropriation of speculative capital on behalf of industrial capital. Oswald Spengler, in a somewhat different version, hailed the "mighty contest between the two handfuls of steel-hard men of race and of immense intellect—which the simple citizen neither observes nor comprehends." Like LaRouche, Spengler claimed that the "battle of mere interests" between capitalists and workers is insignificant in comparison.

With all the above, it is still a long step to the conclusion that LaRouche's historical writings are genuine neo-Nazism. He does discuss the "British" as the racial enemy of humanity that must be crushed, destroyed, eliminated. But is he clearly referring to the Jews when he uses the word "British"?

# Twenty-nine

## Elizabeth,
## Queen of the Jews

When LaRouche says the Queen of England pushes drugs or that Britain is the chief enemy of the United States, he is not merely indulging in eccentricity or a Freudian dislike of female authority figures. These statements have a serious meaning to anti-Semites and neo-Nazis in West Germany and the United States. They are eccentric only to those who have not studied the history of modern anti-Semitism, in which the theme of Jewish-British race mixing and Jewish domination of the British Empire looms large.

The original Nazis popularized this theory. In *Mein Kampf*, Hitler complained that the Jews in England exert an "almost unlimited dictatorship" through their manipulation of public opinion. Heinrich Himmler speculated in his unpublished notebooks on the "Jewish blood" of the English and Scots. Alfred Rosenberg's *Myth of the Twentieth Century* discussed the alleged identity of the policies of "Jewish high finance" with those of Great Britain and claimed that the British government had "handed over control of all financial transactions to Jewish bankers such as Rothschild, Montague, Cassell, Lazard, etc." Expressing a theory that the LaRouchians later would repeat in *Dope, Inc.*,

Rosenberg said that England had "allowed the opium trade to fall increasingly into Jewish hands."

Once Nazi Germany and Britain were at war, the Nazis developed a more exaggerated version. *World-Battle,* an official propaganda organ, depicted "English high finance" as Judaism incarnate. England's aggression against innocent Germany, it said, was the result of the Jews buying Churchill with piles of gold. Meanwhile Hitler's propaganda chief, Joseph Goebbels, came to regard the Jews and the British upper classes as virtually one racial entity. He wrote in his diary in 1942: "Rothschild . . . took the floor [of the British House of Commons] and delivered a tearjerker bemoaning the fate of the Polish Jews . . . All members of Parliament rose from their seats as a silent tribute to Jewry. That was quite appropriate for the British House of Commons, which is really a sort of Jewish exchange. The English, anyway, are the Jews among the Aryans. The perfumed British Foreign Minister, Eden, cuts a good figure among these characters from the synagogue. His whole education and his entire bearing can be characterized as thoroughly Jewish."

The Jewish-British theme was popular among American anti-Semites as early as the 1890s. According to historian Richard Hofstadter, "anti-Semitism and Anglophobia went hand in hand" in populist writings of that decade. One tract included a map of the world with an octopus squatting on the British Isles, its tentacles stretching across the seas. The octopus was labeled "Rothschilds." Another tract denounced President Grover Cleveland as a tool of "Jewish bankers and British gold." Gordon Clark's *Shylock: As Banker, Bondholder, Corruptionist, Conspirator* (1894) accused the Rothschilds of bribing the U.S. government to deliver the American people *"into the hands of England,* as England had long been resigned into the hands of *her Jews."* The leading anti-Semite of the period, William Hope ("Coin") Harvey, called for war with Jewish-dominated England to "blot her name out from among the nations of the earth."

LaRouche's version most closely resembles *"War! War! War!,"* a Nazi tract published in 1940 under the pseudonym Cincinnatus to convince Americans that Hitler was right and that the United States should stay out of the war. (The pseudonym was apparently borrowed from the Society of the Cincinnati, an early American patriotic league named after Cincinnatus, hero of the ancient Roman republic.) Cincinnatus called the British Empire the "British-Jewish Empire." The United States, he argued, should not come to the aid of "a mongrel England, ruled not by Britons of the blood, but, largely, by a galaxy of Jews, half-Jews, and quarter-Jews." He added: "The England which . . . beseeches us to come to her rescue is little more than another segment of the Jewish 'nation.' " Just like LaRouche, Cincinnatus said that the real enemy of the United States is a "New York City, New England, Anglophile, Jewish plot."

There are many other parallels: LaRouche says the British are plotting to starve "billions" of people to death in the Third World. Cincinnatus said, "The starvation of men, women and children has been the most approved English method of warfare since the Jews became dominant there . . ." LaRouche says Henry Kissinger and Ariel Sharon are "British agents." Cincinnatus quoted the British anti-Semitic author Hilaire Belloc as saying "the Jew might almost be called a British agent upon the Continent of Europe and still more in the Near and Far East." LaRouche calls the British philosopher Bertrand Russell the most evil man of the twentieth century. Cincinnatus devoted several pages to Russell as the alleged purveyor of "Jewish" immorality. LaRouche claims that the British-Rothschild establishment (and the Queen) control the international drug traffic. Cincinnatus devoted a chapter to "The Chinese Opium Wars and British-Jews." LaRouche and his followers write about the alleged hereditary taint of the British aristocracy, its congenital brain damage, etc. Cincinnatus quoted Belloc: "[W]ith the opening of the twentieth century those of the great territorial English families in which there was no Jewish blood were the exception. In nearly all of them was the strain more or less marked; in some of them so strong that though the name was still an English name . . . the physique and character had become wholly Jewish and the members of the family were taken for Jews whenever they travelled . . ." With all of these similarities, it is not surprising that LaRouche's *New Solidarity* includes a column by one "Cincinnatus" (although the author of the 1940 tract is long dead) and that LaRouche's Security staff once applied for concealed weapons permits under the name of Cincinnatus Associates. (Of course the LaRouchians would claim they merely are identifying with the patriotic society of George Washington's day.)

The Jewish-British conspiracy theory is popular today with hate groups like the Ku Klux Klan. You can purchase dozens of pamphlets on this theme from the Sons of Liberty in Louisiana. Mostly written by British fascists in the 1930s, the titles include *The Jews and the British Empire, Our Jewish Aristocracy,* and *How Jewry Turned England into a Plutocratic State.* The latter says that the Jews regard "the British Empire only as a stepping stone towards a coming Jewish World-Empire" and that "the English government is only the British façade for the Jew . . . The English statesmen are the well-paid dummies of Jewish-English finance-capitalism." The pamphlet also describes the alleged "judaising" of the English aristocracy through intermarriage. Because of these "blood-ties," it concludes, "Jewish finance-capital is identical with British finance-capital."

In 1984 the Sons of Liberty republished *War! War! War!* with an introduction by Eustace Mullins, a scholarly anti-Semite who is friendly with the LaRouchians and attended their 1984 annual convention. The Sons of Liberty also launders LaRouche's neo-Cincinnatus doctrines into white supremacist circles via the pamphlets of the Christian Defense League's Dr. John Coleman. Scores of Coleman's pamphlets have titles similar to those of LaRouchian articles or books and contain identical analyses. They never mention LaRouche's name, yet the ideas are his. Mullins, who is a contributing editor of Coleman's *World Economic Review*, says that Coleman "claims to have mysterious connections in British intelligence, but for the last ten years all he's done is copy LaRouche's stuff." Thus does the LaRouchian message circulate in the swastika-and-bedsheet crowd, while LaRouche, the self-styled friend of the White House, is spared embarrassment.

LaRouche himself has admitted the true meaning of "British" on at least two occasions. In *The Case of Walter Lippmann,* in his discussion of the slave trade in early-nineteenth-century America, the word "British" is immediately followed by "Rothschild" in parentheses. In "Anti-Dirigism Is British Tory Propaganda" (1978) he expanded the "British" to embrace a *network* of wealthy Jewish families. "The policy-shaping kernel of the enemy forces centered in the British monarchy is a group of private banking families," he said. "These are notably the family interests of the Lazard Brothers, Barings, N. M. Rothschild, Hill Samuel, and other small private banking houses." He then added: "Britain—these same families' interests—has controlled the international opium traffic since early during the 19th century." Although LaRouche threw in a single non-Jewish family, the definition was essentially the same as Alfred Rosenberg's.

The British-Jewish theory was given symbolic expression in *New Solidarity* in 1978 by a Star of David with Queen Elizabeth at the top flanked by Henry Kissinger and economist Milton Friedman. The caption alluded to "satanic connections." Thus was made clear the real meaning of LaRouche's accusation that the Queen pushes drugs.

In "How to Analyze and Uproot International Terrorism," a 1978 tirade against the alleged British controllers of European terrorist cells, LaRouche discussed how the British oligarchy reflects the "national interest" and national "state of mind" of a network of wealthy families "embedded in various institutions of *each* nation." Traditional anti-Semitism regards the Jews in precisely this way: the cosmopolitan nation living parasitically off other nations. LaRouche implicated wide strata of Jews in the conspiracy. Around the Rothschilds and other leading families, he wrote, there is gathered a "secondary layer of plebeians. These . . . include leading intelligence and political families going back a generation or two, certain families with a legal professional tradition, and so forth . . . Around these there is an outer layer of agents, trusted, deemed useful . . . Around these strata, another layer of agents, and so down to the pathetically demented individual environmentalist and terrorist."

LaRouche was *not only* speaking of Jews; the secondary agent layers included non-Jews such as the Churchill family. But in LaRouchian propaganda Zionism is the chief international tool of the British, and Zionists are usually British agents. Since most Jews are Zionists, the implication is that most Jews must be British agents. In attempting to make this connection, the LaRouchians seized on General George Brown's infamous 1974 statement about the alleged excessive influence of Jews in Washington. In 1977 LaRouche wrote that it was time to "kick every *British*-loving son-of-a-bitch out of Washington." With a deft touch, the article took the form of an open letter to Defense Secretary Harold Brown but the picture was of George Brown. A *New Solidarity* editorial then accused the entire leadership and most of the membership of American Jewish organizations of being part of the treasonous British conspiracy: "Their loyalties lie not with the United States but with the Zionist-British organism."

Through the years, *New Solidarity* has fleshed out this theory in hundreds of articles. The first wave in 1978 included headlines like "British to Sell World Short," "Brits Run Spy Hoax to Push Cold War Clime," "British Launch Drive to Break Up the EEC," and "Expel Britain's Kissinger for Treason." When describing British machinations, *New Solidarity* referred to mostly Jewish names (Oppenheimer, Montefiore, Meyer, Weill, Warburg, as well as Rothschild). If the name wasn't obvious, they'd add a tag—e.g., "Lord Crewe, a Rothschild family cousin." When non-Jews in the British Establishment were mentioned, there was often a different kind of tag. Former Prime Minister Harold Wilson was referred to as a "Rothschild agent," while Conservative MP Winston Churchill III was said to live up to his grandfather's "reputation for sycophantic . . . braggadocio in the service of the Rothschilds."

The LaRouchians listed what they believed to be the key institutions of British power in the twentieth century—the Fabian Society, the Round Table group, the Royal Institute for International Affairs, the British Secret Service, etc. Each was said to be under "Rothschild" control. In a pamphlet on the British aristocracy, LaRouche aide Chris White wrote that the scions of the Rothschild family "preside over" the British organs of power: The "evolution of the Rothschild family and its outlook" has determined the "evolution and outlook of the British political system."

The LaRouchians concocted a pseudo-history of England to bolster this. The Norman conquest in 1066, they said, was instigated by converted Jews around the papacy as a flanking maneuver against the Teutonic peoples. (That the Jews were later driven out of England by the Norman kings was irrelevant to this theory. The oligarchy doesn't always need to rule directly on the spot. Indeed, it may sometimes *prefer* to rule from afar, using ideology as its control mechanism. Was not Oxford University in the Middle Ages a nest of bestial nominalists?)

The reestablishment of direct Jewish control of England began in the late seventeenth century when William and Mary allowed a few to settle in London. A Dutch Jewish banker, Solomon Mendoza, fastened on the Churchill family as the chief oligarchical agents for the centuries ahead. Ideological brainwashing of the English upper classes was accelerated through such mechanisms as the Anglican Church, the Freemasons, the Knights of Malta, Humean empiricism, utilitarianism, Fabian socialism, and most recently the Tavistock Institute. The vigorous English aristocrats of the Neoplatonic Tudor era were transformed step by step into effete puppets. Hence the frequent LaRouchian quips about homosexuality and genetic deficiency in the British royal family and top aristocracy: How can the British be real men if they've never stood up to the Jews?

# Thirty

# The War Between the Species

For an ideology of total paranoia to work properly, it must create an unbridgeable gulf between the forces of good and the forces of evil; they must be regarded as having nothing in common and as being in total antagonism. This state of mind is difficult to achieve. In the Cold War, for instance, the antagonists have never gone this far. Although sharply disagreeing on the questions of democracy and human rights, neither side totally denies the humanity of the other side. There is always the perception of a common interest—in preventing a nuclear war, if nothing else.

What LaRouche did in the late 1970s was to create an unbridgeable-gulf theory of extraordinary emotional intensity. Buttressed by the already existing NCLC paranoia, it stimulated the most fanatical of his followers to reject totally the humanity of a specific portion of the human race—the so-called British oligarchy. This created a state of mind—in theory if not in practice—akin to that of the Nazis. And as with the Nazis, it hinged on a racial doctrine. The enemy was defined as a separate species, totally alien, totally incapable of any common moral or intellectual ground with LaRouche's own Prometheans, totally hostile to the latter because of an inbred hatred going back thousands of years.

It was this viewpoint that enabled LaRouche to project his paranoid conspiracy theory into every aspect of his followers' thinking. The oligarchy, he taught, largely controls the world. This means it determines most of the science, philosophy, religion, art, and so on that we imbibe. But since the oligarchy is totally inhuman and hostile, anything it creates is hopelessly tainted. There cannot be any common ground between humanity and the cultural values of the oligarchical order. Their artifacts and ideas therefore must be combated wherever we find them—in the latest rock song, in the oldest medieval parchment, in our own thought processes. It is cultural war to the end, with no quarter possible. One side is totally right and the other side is totally wrong, and the wrong side cannot be won over because it is biologically incapable of understanding what is true and good.

LaRouche first expressed the racist underpinnings of this unbridgeable-gulf theory in *Dialectical Economics* (1975), published as a vanity-press textbook by D. C. Heath & Co. It portrays the American economy as a battleground between two breeds of capitalist—the industrial capitalist and the usurer. To LaRouche their struggle is not merely economic. The two classes are "primarily distinguished by methods appropriate to the differentiation of biological species." To explain this he adopted the theory of Stalin's agricultural czar, Trofim Lysenko, that an organism's heredity can change as a direct result of environmental stimuli. LaRouche gave Lysenko a racialist twist by suggesting that human intelligence is a result of a "general genetic alteration of the physiology of mentation after birth." His evidence was that the "quality of intelligence" differs from society to society.

So far LaRouche was merely indulging in speculation. But in "The Secrets Known Only to the Inner Elites" (1978), he asserted flatly that changes within a species can be "induced 'environmentally' without genetic variation." Thus, he said, the "hominid stock" can be artificially altered to produce a "new variety" (i.e., a new race). If the alteration is great enough, the new race will actually be a "new species."*

LaRouche argues that the "British" have been transformed by their

---

* LaRouche follower Carol Cleary, with an undergraduate degree in biology, tried to develop an underpinning for this. She argued in a 1980 *Fusion* article that evolution and mutation occur on the chromosomal level rather than the genetic level, but that the evil Darwinians had suppressed this fact. Cleary's article was denounced as "hogwash" in a letter from Professor James F. Bonner of the California Institute of Technology. *Fusion* printed Bonner's letter with an abusive reply from Cleary which essentially said that working hard for LaRouche will produce chromosomal changes resulting in a higher species.

ingrown social and cultural environment—bolstered by biological in-breeding—into precisely such a genetically separate "species." He suggests that this is nature's way of punishing them for engaging in usury and the opium trade, for it hereditarily cuts them off from the ability to grasp spiritual truths. "There is a higher reality, which the British are incapable of comprehending," LaRouche argues. It "exists beyond" the bestial "domain of deduction" to which the British mind is limited.

Essentially, LaRouche regards the British as having a relationship to the human race similar to that of parasite to host. In his own words: "The ruling British elite are like animals—not only in their morality, but in their outlook on knowledge. They are clever animals, who are masters of the wicked nature of their own species, and recognize ferally the distinctions of the hated human species." He has returned to this idea again and again: "I know the British mind very well—it is a lower order of mentality, which I can study as I watch the fish in an aquarium." It is the "mind of a species inferior to myself." The British are "a pack of animals" and "a different, alien species." They are the "avowed enemies of the entire human species" who "shamelessly declare war on the human species." As for their Zionist philosophy, it emphasizes the "sensual appetites of impulsions of a racial group, making that racial group self-defined as in moral likeness to a lower beast."

LaRouche disciple Chris White echoes these sentiments. The British are a "specific form of lower life," "not human," "the end product of a specialized process of genetic engineering" that produced "congenital deficiencies and brain damage" as early as the 17th century.

In "The Elite That Can't Think Straight" LaRouche portrays the biological struggle as a relentless personal contest between himself and the top oligarchs. Their "inner circles," he says, recognize him as "the ancient and feared adversary of their own evil species" and as their "potential destroyer." When they see the influence of his work, "they tense, growling such phrases as 'potential danger,' 'more dangerous than Hitler,' 'kill it before it succeeds in getting a real foothold in shaping events.' " Whether or not LaRouche actually believes himself to be the new Hitler as implied, he approved the publication of Chris White's *The Noble Family* (1978), which said just about everything left to be said: "Let us speedily expedite the urgently necessary task of freeing humanity from the grasp of that specific form of lower life before we are destroyed by them or enslaved by them. Let us joyfully ensure that the representatives of the British system are destroyed so that humanity might live . . ." And White concluded: "Those of us who should know better have been tolerant of such creatures for far longer than has been good for the rest of us. Let us, with ruthlessness, ensure that the job is done correctly now."

LaRouche's racialism, like Hitler's, doesn't just target the British. In a softer form it applies to most of the human race, whom LaRouche accuses of being mired in sheeplike bestiality and thus requiring close surveillance by LaRouchian shepherds. He professes great compassion for the sheep. Their subhuman state is the fault of the British. Once the latter are removed from the scene, the sheep's heredity can be changed, raising future generations to the level of true humanity.

LaRouche describes this process using terms from Plato's *Republic*, in which society is composed of an ascending scale of bronze, silver, and golden souls. But his ideas are very different from Plato's. To La-Rouche the bronze soul is a sensuous donkeylike wretch (or worse). To Plato the bronze soul was an upright moral citizen whose role was to build the wealth of society through craftsmanship and commerce. To LaRouche the silver soul is someone who has begun to accept political leadership from LaRouche or at least has developed an "organic" humanism parallel to LaRouche's (e.g., South Africa's white rulers). To Plato the silver soul was not defined by his ideology but by his specific function and talents—he was a member of the warrior class. To La-Rouche the golden souls are himself and those few lieutenants of his who have fully assimilated his intellectual method—the so-called "hypothesis of the higher hypothesis." To Plato the golden souls were the philosopher-statesmen who took care of government affairs and studied higher ethical and metaphysical principles to guide them in their work. These principles, as expressed by Socrates in Plato's dialogues, have little in common with LaRouche's ideology. Plato never theorized about a hypothesis of the higher hypothesis. Nor did he regard his philosopher-kings as a biologically superior race.

The misappropriation of Platonism as a buttress for modern fascism is not unique to LaRouche. In 1939, Dr. Otto Dietrich, the head of Hitler's press bureau, announced that Hitler's views on leadership were "in entire conformity" with Plato's "immortal Laws" which teach the "voluntary subordination of the masses, whilst at the same time bringing the 'wise men from within them to leadership.'" Platonic jargon was also adopted by Oswald Mosley, führer of the British Union of Fascists, and by members of South Africa's Broederbond during their rise to power after World War II.

When LaRouche begins to talk about specific ethnic groups, his humanist devotion to raising bronze souls out of their bestial mire suddenly disappears—apparently because they so stubbornly resist the values of his would-be golden souls. He adopts instead a relentless racism fit more for a master race than idealistic shepherds. For instance, the Chinese are a "paranoid" people who share, with "lower forms of animal life," a "fundamental distinction from actually human personalities." American blacks who insist on equal rights are obsessed with distinctions that "would be proper to the classification of varieties of monkeys and baboons." Puerto Ricans are intellectually impotent representatives of a culture based on " 'macho' pathology" and crazed blood oaths. Italians, also impotent, are obsessed with churches, whorehouses, and "images of the Virgin Mary" (whose "goddamn smile" LaRouche would like to remove from public view by closing Italy's churches). Irish-Americans are representatives of a backward Catholic "ethnic piggishness" and are responsible for a "hideous mind-and-body-eroding orgy of fertility." Tribal peoples, as in Brazil's Amazon Basin, have a "likeness to a lower beast."

These attitudes have definite implications for LaRouche's doctrine of world conquest. In discussing U.S. treatment of American Indians in the nineteenth century and the conquest of Mexican territories in 1848 by General Winfield Scott, LaRouche asked: "Was it . . . correct for the American branch of European humanist culture to absorb the territories occupied by a miserable, relatively bestial culture of indigenous Americans? *Absolutely.* Was it correct to absorb . . . the areas taken in the Mexican-American War? Historically, yes—for the same reason." And the underlying principle? "We do not regard all cultures and nations as equally deserving of sovereignty or survival."

How do the Russians fit into the LaRouchian racial theory? In the late 1970s and early 1980s, LaRouche tended to see the Soviet Union as being like the United States—a country influenced by networks of "British" agents but not fully dominated by them. For instance, these agents didn't dominate the great "nation builder" Leonid Brezhnev. But they have been present in Russia for many centuries as a conspiratorial force and are every bit as evil, in LaRouche's eyes, as Henry Kissinger or Queen Elizabeth. They are "morally subhuman," "incapable of creative thought," and addicted to "the lowest form of thought, Baconian swinish grovelling, rooting and sniffing of objects." They reek with the "hideous stench of subhuman Black Guelph breed." Ivan the Terrible should have wiped them out—he tried, but couldn't reach them all.

In 1984, LaRouche reworked his rhetoric against the Soviet Union's "British" agents into a form that attacked the Russian culture and people as a whole—apparently to bolster his argument for a crash program to develop SDI. The Russians, he said, have been completely dominated for over a thousand years by an evil culture, descended, like the British, from Babylon. The Russians developed by way of Byzantium and the evil Orthodox Church. Like their British cousins, they aim at a hideous world domination. They want Moscow to be the Third Rome, ruling all the earth.

Does the Third Rome theory take the Jews off the hook? Not at all, for the Jews and Orthodox Christians are really just two aspects of the same enemy: a single underlying racial-cultural bacillus. Here La-Rouche apparently borrows an idea from Oswald Spengler's *Decline of the West*—that there is a Semitic "Magian" culture common to Jews, Arabs, and Orthodox Christians, a culture of folks who like to hang out in caves (like Istanbul's Hagia Sophia and New York's Grand Central Station). Spengler regarded this culture as backward and superstitious in comparison with the cathedral-building Promethean/Faustian civilization of Germany.

LaRouche calls the Magians the "magicians." When he talks about the unspeakable evil of the Russian Orthodox Church, he is alluding to the theory that the Slavic peoples and especially the Russians are culturally an extension (thanks to the Orthodox Church) of the Magian culture—that of the "Babylonians" and "Persians" who wrote the Old Testament. This Magian culture is deeply engrained in the Russian soul. And it is a culture that ultimately comes, LaRouche suggests, from a specific racial type: dark-skinned Dravidians related to those who fled India at the time of the Aryan invasion and supposedly settled near Babylon.

If Russia has been under the domination of Magian Orthodoxy for the past thousand years, then according to LaRouche's cultural mutation theory the Russians—or at least the Russian oligarchy—must have evolved like the "British" into a separate species. The LaRouchians thrill to an almost mystical hatred of this ultimate enemy. And they can say about Mount Athos, the center of Orthodox spirituality: "It is about time someone bombed the Holy Mountain, its monks, its monasteries, and everything in it. Bomb it thoroughly, systematically, and completely so that nothing of its evil legacy survives." In context, the writer was referring to the Soviet Union, not Mount Athos.

On close inspection, LaRouche's racialist universe appears to have three species unknown to zoology: the Western oligarchs (the British-Jewish branch of Dravidian Babylon); the Eastern oligarchs (the Russian Orthodox branch); and the bestial masses. The *human* species, it would appear, is a fourth species composed solely of LaRouche and his followers.

Yet LaRouche dreams of a fifth species—the racial superman—the true goal of his life. The Platonic hierarchy of bronze, silver, and golden souls thus becomes a metaphor expressing the biological transmission of Acquired Characteristics. As LaRouche wrote in his autobiography, *The Power of Reason:* "The objective of my life is to contribute to bringing men and women out of the wretched condition of sensuous donkeys and incompletely human 'silver souls,' to contribute to making of our species a race of 'golden souls.' "

If the mutant race is to survive and prosper, however, the two Babylonian species have got to go. LaRouche would hasten their departure through the Grand Design described earlier in this book. The Grand Design and LaRouche's racialist theories, put together, include *all* the elements of Nazism.

# Part Eight

# LaRouche, Inc.: The Tycoon

One knows perhaps a child who, hand caught in the cookie jar and mouth full of cookies, will swallow quickly and insist with the "sincerest" of expressions, "Oh, you shouldn't have startled me. I just caught a mouse that had run into the jar; if you hadn't come in just now, he wouldn't have gotten away."

—LYNDON H. LaROUCHE, JR.

# Thirty-one

## The Root
## of All Evil

While dreaming in the early 1960s about becoming America's Trotsky, LaRouche had another dream—to become a capitalist. In a report on the shoe industry, he gave a hint of this ambition. The business world "has got to get back to management by tycoons"—that is, by strong leaders who will "manage the business as a whole" instead of viewing it "as a collection of semi-autonomous parts." In the true tycoon's conglomerate, divisions should dovetail into one centralized system. LaRouche thus conceived of a business empire much as his NCLC would become—in which money would be shuttled around from entity to entity, with no regard for ordinary accounting procedures, to meet the needs of the moment as determined by LaRouche himself.

In the following years LaRouche frequently railed against speculative capital. He contrasted Wall Street's "Levantine gnomes" with the upright patriotic "productive capitalists," the industrialists who make wheels turn. One therefore might infer that when he set out to make the NCLC into a money machine, he would have steered his followers into some kind of productive activity—machine tools, aerospace, or even hamburgers. Instead, he steered them into the least productive activity imaginable—a grotesque distillation of the speculative capital he so harshly denounced. He became a financial pyramider, only with a political twist: He built a web of political fund-raising fronts that fraudulently borrowed as much money as possible—by some estimates close to $200 million—from as many people as possible and then, according to law enforcement officials, simply refused to pay it back. None of this loaned money was invested in anything even indirectly productive such as stocks, bonds, or money market accounts. Instead it was mostly pumped into NCLC political propaganda to build up LaRouche's name recognition and create the conditions for yet more borrowing.

These loan scams were an extension of the systematic deceptiveness found in LaRouche's ideology, propaganda, electoral activity, and intelligence gathering. Operating as a combination NICPAC and junk-bond entity, his money machine targeted senior citizens and gullible professionals possessing liquid assets. Telephone solicitors appealed to their patriotism and conservative beliefs, and also promising 20 percent annual interest. Some lenders mortgaged or sold their homes and whatever other assets they possessed. But when the NCLC fund-raising entities inevitably defaulted on the loans, the lenders found themselves in an almost helpless situation, facing an impenetrable network of corporate shells, dead-end paper trails, and endless legal delaying tactics.

Ironically, the NCLC began in the late 1960s as a quasi-ascetic organization. The idea of making money seemed a diversion from the real world of ideas and revolutionary organizing. Yet step by step LaRouche urged upon his followers the role of cash in building a movement, and the necessity of raising as much money as possible by any means necessary. He steered them first into small deceptions, more unethical than illegal, then into individual acts of flagrant deception, and finally into actions that would lead to their indictment for large-scale white-collar crime.

LaRouche alluded to this transformation of his followers in a 1978 article dealing ostensibly with political cults other than his own. Such organizations, he said, "condition" their members to commit criminal acts, while also being on the lookout for recruits with preexisting criminal tendencies. Members are taught to view the outside world as "not real" and to treat its inhabitants as mere projections of the cult member's childhood emotions. Thus, the cult member becomes in some respects like a "disturbed but functionally effective" small child. In another article, LaRouche explained that this syndrome includes a "pathological lie pattern" as in the case of the child caught with his hand in a cookie jar.

This was not armchair theorizing. The conditioning of the NCLC membership for predatory acts had begun as early as 1974, with the leadership practicing rip-off skills on the rank-and-file members. The latter were pressured to turn over their savings and other assets. Several trust funds were netted from wealthy members, who overnight became poor members after turning over every penny in defiance of their parents' wishes. They were told this was for the socialist revolution, just as senior citizens would later be told their contributions or loans were for the Reagan revolution. Once all immediately available assets of the members had been looted, the leadership set out to exploit their credit—to get each member to borrow to the maximum of his or her credit line. Hundreds of members borrowed all they could from banks, finance companies, and via their credit cards or any other available source of credit, and turned the proceeds over to the organization. Some took out federal loans for college studies they never intended to pursue, knowing they would be able to evade repayment for many years, perhaps forever. Many borrowed heavily from relatives and friends. A favorite tactic was to tell their parents that they needed money for dental work.

According to a former highest-level LaRouche aide, at least 30 percent of NCLC operating revenues in the mid-1970s came from members' loans. The leadership was "like a pack of hyenas," he recalled. "Members would be induced to get one loan, then a second, then a third." The organization would promise to pay them back, but rarely returned more than token amounts. Although these practices netted millions of dollars, the real payoff was psychological: The membership was compromised ethically, and became inured to further sharp dealings. This made it easier to persuade them to bilk elderly widows during the 1980s. It also bound them tightly to the organization, for those who owed thousands of dollars to credit-card companies knew that if they ever quit the NCLC, it would never help them pay off these debts.

In the short run, most NCLC members didn't have to worry about credit collection agencies very much, because of their rootless lifestyles as political activists. They were moved from city to city, often housed in semicommunal apartments where the phone, mailbox, and lease were in someone else's name. Even when a creditor did manage to track them down, they had no assets to be seized, for they had already given everything to the NCLC.

But the cannibalizing of the members' credit soon reached a point of diminishing returns. They became known as deadbeats and were unable to obtain any further loans. Their parents and relatives became furious at them, and former friends avoided them. (This bound them all the more closely to their NCLC surrogate family and political friends, and to their surrogate father, LaRouche.)

If LaRouche couldn't get any more loans from them, he could get something even more valuable—their full-time labor. Many members were pressured to quit their jobs or drop out of college to work for the NCLC twelve to sixteen hours a day, seven days a week. Members assigned to the national office in New York moved into low-rent neighborhoods such as Washington Heights, where they survived on tiny stipends. Members not regarded as important enough to have stipends found part-time jobs as typesetters or proofreaders, but spent the majority of their time working free for the NCLC.

This type of labor exploitation was typical of cults in the 1970s. Newly recruited members of the Unification Church sold flowers on the street or worked on the Rev. Moon's fishing boats, while living in church dormitories and wearing used clothing provided by the church. LaRouche's version was the sale of NCLC literature at airports and other public places. New recruits were expected to undergo a testing period of up to two years in which they spent most of their time in this "field organizing." They were trained in adversary techniques to bind them more closely to the NCLC. When greeted with a less than friendly response from a passerby, they would insult him, often calling him a tool of Great Britain or Rockefeller. Occasionally the targeted person was intrigued or amused, and a sale would result. But more often he reacted angrily and walked away. Sometimes matters escalated. As a defector told *The New York Times:* "They get two inches from a person's face and [verbally] cut them to pieces. They can get anybody to hit them in a second."

After a long day of such confrontations and rejection, an NCLC field worker would internalize more deeply than ever LaRouche's vision of a Promethean elite besieged in a hostile world. Their anger would also increase—an important part of the conditioning. If one spends one's day insulting perfect strangers, it is not a large step to begin ripping them off.

LaRouche found it was not cost-efficient to keep a majority of his followers at the airports. Unlike the average flower-selling Moonie, many NCLC members had advanced degrees and highly marketable skills. LaRouche was able to utilize this extraordinary labor pool for a variety of ends. His intelligence news service and *EIR* were staffed by members with backgrounds in the humanities and social sciences. He founded the FEF and his computer software company, Computron, with those who had training in engineering, science, and business. Such members had sacrificed conventional careers and salaries but were nevertheless intensely ambitious and competed savagely with each other to rise within the NCLC's internal Chain of Being so as to get as close as possible to the Godhead (LaRouche).

LaRouche explained the economics of his business empire in a 1981 report: The NCLC membership's "voluntary and semi-voluntary labor" reduced the labor costs of the NCLC business fronts way below the equivalent costs in the outside business world. "If a person whose skill and activities are competitively worth $35,000 performs those services for $10,000," he wrote, "the activity has the implicit value of the same work done at $35,000." LaRouche cited members whose competitive worth would be $70,000 a year. "To sacrifice part of such income levels for a purpose related to a world-historical purpose," he said, "is morally acceptable, and worthwhile."

For Linda Ray, who joined the NCLC after dropping out of college in 1974, being "world-historical" meant working as a typesetter sixteen hours a day. "They'd pay me $100 a week, but if there was a cash-flow problem I'd get nothing," she recalled. One couple who worked full-time on the NCLC editorial staff had a combined 1982 income of under $5,500. They lived from hand to mouth, months in arrears on their semi-slum apartment rent and incessantly threatened by utility turnoffs while leaving a trail of bounced checks with neighborhood merchants.

Meanwhile, the NCLC's internal discipline became all-pervasive: Members were told what kind of music to listen to. Spouses informed on one another to the leadership. Wives who became pregnant were marched to the abortionist by the "coat-hanger brigade" (politically reliable women from the national office). Anyone who performed poorly at assigned tasks was denounced in psychological sessions. The cement holding this together was the frequent "crisis mobilizations" during which members were stimulated to work extra hours and raise giant sums of money to rescue the world from impending nuclear war or save LaRouche from the latest Zionist hit squad. The personal satisfactions were few and far between. To be allowed an evening off to sing in the NCLC choral group or listen to a lecture on Dante was the LaRouchian equivalent of a Caribbean cruise.

In the few moments available for reverie, many members felt desperately trapped. But their years of total dependence on the organization for their social life and livelihood had eroded their self-confidence to the point where they couldn't imagine living on their own or succeeding in the outside world. Breaking away meant losing their closest (and usually their only) friends. It meant having to learn all over again how to make decisions for oneself. So the majority remained, year after dreary year, developing to a fine pitch the specialized skills necessary to LaRouche's goals.

Under these conditions the NCLC intelligence staff, editorial department, printing and typesetting businesses, telephone boiler rooms, and field operations became a smoothly functioning profit machine. The national office "sectors" worked together to produce a wide range of books, magazines, and intelligence reports. LaRouche field workers sold them at major airports to affluent Americans waiting for a flight. Their tables were festooned with signs like "Feed Jane Fonda to the Whales"—a magnet for conservatives but a filter device to keep away all liberals except those spoiling for an argument. The books and magazines, such as *Fusion* and *Executive Intelligence Review*, had colorful, well-designed covers.

The field organizers accepted Visa and MasterCard, and hundreds of names were collected each day. Telephone solicitors at national headquarters and the regional offices followed up with calls urging the purchase of an *EIR* subscription ($396 a year) or a special *EIR* report ($250 and up). Purchasers also were asked to donate to LaRouche's campaigns or the Fusion Energy Foundation. In addition, the telephone fund raisers called people cold from lists purchased from conservative organizations.

By 1977 airport sales and telephone fund raising were bringing in over $40,000 a week. Defectors who left during that period recall having raised $300 a day on the phone. By 1980, according to a former top LaRouche aide, fund raising was producing $190,000 a week (about $10 million for the year). In mid-1981 LaRouche announced in a memo that he was upping the quota to "$225,000 weekly in organizing-income of gross sales." Anything less, he warned, would be a "disaster."

The airport tables were sponsored by the FEF, conveniently making the purchases tax-deductible for the customer and tax-free for the LaRouchians. Actually, the LaRouchians sent all the money to NCLC headquarters, not the FEF, where the finance officers put it in the accounts of any front group they pleased. Some businessmen bought *EIR* or *Fusion* subscriptions to humor the solicitor or as a gesture of support for nuclear power, writing off the purchase as a corporate expense. These purchasers included officers of major corporations such as ITT and TRW. By 1984 *EIR* claimed 11,500 paid subscribers— if true, this would have yielded $4.5 million. *EIR* also offered customized reports and "retainer-contract" intelligence service.

The publications were produced with state-of-the-art printing and typesetting equipment at the NCLC-controlled PMR Printing Company and World Composition Services in New York City and at Renaissance Printing Company in Detroit. Thanks to their low-cost labor, these firms were able to bid successfully for outside clients. In the late 1970s and early 1980s World Comp's clients included the United Nations and the Ford Foundation, while PMR handled jobs for Harper & Row, New York University, and the YWCA. Many clients were unaware of the LaRouche connection. Renaissance Printing worked for the Teamsters union, which *was* aware of the connection. It then expanded into financial printing, obtaining several Wall Street investment houses as clients. This gave it access to the type of confidential data that is sometimes used in insider trading, although there is no evidence that such information was misused.

Some LaRouchians began to dream of long-term business collaborations on a high level. Ian Levit of the NCLC Security staff went to Houston in 1980 to meet with oilmen who had been contacted through *EIR* and *Fusion,* and who supposedly had access to a "tremendous amount of venture capital." After drawing up profiles of some of the most promising contacts, Levit concluded that the trip was "proof that we can successfully mix our political and business activities directly" and thus "strengthen both dramatically." *EIR* and the FEF, he said, "can and must become the center of trade deals." The same attitude was seen in a 1979 letter from Chicago NCLC leader Mitchell Hirsch to Robert Malott, chairman of the FMC Corporation. It was carefully worded to suggest that the LaRouche organization was an integral part of the business community: "We [businessmen] face competition for key markets worldwide . . . Unless the decline of the dollar . . . is quickly reversed, we shall face a most dangerous international situation." The writer enclosed a copy of *EIR* and invited Malott to meet with LaRouche.

The most successful LaRouchian commercial business, Computron Technologies Corporation, grew out of a collaboration with Wang Laboratories. Computron was a software house founded by NCLC members in 1973. At its inception it received equipment, encouragement, and software development contracts from Wang, and later became a Wang turnkey vendor. Wang steered many of its own hardware customers to Computron for specialized software.

The chief founders of Computron were NCLC chief of staff Gus Kalimtgis and his close friend Andy Typaldos. Kalimtgis was the silent partner, although his wife was the office manager and signed the checks. In the computer world Computron seemed to be just another business, and Typaldos just another hustling salesman. But Typaldos was a member of the NCLC national committee, where he used the pseudonym "Andreas Reniotis." His wife, Rene, was one of the LaRouchians arrested for allegedly kidnapping Alice Weitzman in 1974. His sister-in-law, Janice Hart, later became famous as the LaRouchian candidate who won the Illinois secretary of state primary in 1986.

Computron established an excellent reputation. Many of its bright LaRouchian programmers received top-flight training from Wang but continued to work for Computron at salaries well below industry standards. Computron thus became one of the largest software houses in the New York area. By 1979, its revenues topped $5 million a year, and its clients included AT&T, Citibank, Mobil Oil, Colgate-Palmolive, Bristol-Myers, Weight Watchers International, and Benton & Bowles Advertising. Its NCLC connection was a carefully guarded secret from most clients and non-LaRouchian employees. Use of its computer facilities for political purposes took place at night, after the regular employees had left.

The secret was exposed by the Manhattan weekly *Our Town* in September 1979. When Computron denied it, *Our Town* published a second article showing that most top Computron executives were NCLC members and had made contributions to LaRouche's presidential campaign, and that LaRouche had lived in a company apartment and used a company car. Computron's LaRouche connection also was noted in a *New York Times* article. Wang, although well aware of these facts, continued its profitable association with Computron.

According to former Computron employees, upwards of 20 percent of the NCLC's operating expenses were covered by Computron in the late 1970s, when at least $750,000 was skimmed from company revenues at a rate of $5,000 to $10,000 per week. This skimming sharply increased to pay for the 1980s campaign. Computron also extended heavy credit to LaRouche's campaign committee for computer services. This was done although LaRouche had not yet paid back Computron's loans-in-kind to his 1976 campaign. (The treasurer of the 1980 campaign, Felice Merritt Gelman, was married to a top Computron programmer.)

Late in 1980, Typaldos and Kalimtgis protested that LaRouche was destroying the company with his incessant demands for cash. LaRouche called them KGB agents, forced them out of the organization, and ordered all loyal NCLC members at Computron to quit their jobs. Several executives and employees rebelled and sided with Typaldos and Kalimtgis, but most followed LaRouche's orders. LaRouche also circulated memos accusing the Computron chiefs of using NCLC funds to subsidize their firm. Kalimtgis argued that the opposite was the case, and that Computron's management had "repeatedly tried to sell off future business assets and business ventures" to meet the NCLC's needs. Kalimtgis warned LaRouche of possible "legal jeopardy" if he didn't shut up. "Unlike you, Lyn, I do not say to myself that 'even if I were put before ten grand juries I would tell them that I knew nothing . . .' "

In March 1981, Computron filed for reorganization under the Chapter 11 provision of the Bankruptcy Act, listing obligations of $3 million, including almost $400,000 owed to Wang. When the creditors' committee took the depositions of company officers, it learned that financial records for the period of LaRouche's campaign had disappeared. Subsequently the bankruptcy judge, upon receiving copies of the NCLC internal correspondence in which Kalimtgis and LaRouche accused each other of fraud, ordered the creditors' committee's attorneys to launch an investigation of LaRouche's alleged looting of the company. Several subpoenas were issued and depositions taken, but the investigation was terminated rather abruptly. An affidavit in the court record, signed by the accountant for the creditors' committee, states that Wang's Allen Vogel, chairman of the committee, "informed counsel that the investigation should be discontinued and that the committee wanted to get on with the plan [for reorganization]." Earlier Vogel had written that he strongly resented Computron trying to cover up problems with a "legal or political smoke screen." But now, Wang apparently feared the possible negative publicity from any airing of Computron's past, which would inevitably have called public attention to Wang's own dealings with the LaRouchian firm.

LaRouche had learned from the Computron split that his Neoplatonic humanism didn't mix too well with traditional capitalism. The problem, he decided, was that treacherous NCLC members had put business before politics, and private fiefdoms before the interests of the NCLC as a whole. He cracked down fast on PMR and World Comp executives who had displayed similar signs of "liberalism," but he was too late with Renaissance Printing in Detroit. In the fall of 1981 the entire staff and management quit the NCLC in one giant walkout.

LaRouche had to face the real problem—not treachery, but burnout. As he explained it to his loyalists: "Frightened people past thirty realize, 'I'm not a kid any longer.' Sexual anxieties become more insistent. The lure of 'inner psychological needs' and lusts of 'earthly paradise' become stronger in every person of middle years who has lost his or her moorings in the larger reality. Frightened people become 'little people,' and 'little people' are like rats, like the Jew in the concentration camps . . ."

Much of the burnout and associated discontent at Renaissance and Computron resulted from the 1980 campaign—the largest effort in the NCLC's history. In the desperate scramble to meet campaign needs, LaRouche and his closest aides turned to questionable financial practices on a bolder scale than ever before. They began to discuss the targeting of senior citizens for large loans, a practice that would flower during the subsequent 1984 campaign.

They also played fast and loose with federal matching funds in 1980, building on a scheme worked out during LaRouche's 1976 campaign. The law requires that a matching-funds applicant raise a minimum of $5,000 in each of twenty different states in contributions of no more than $250 each. The NCLC tactic in 1976 was to get a member to make a donation in, say, Oregon, often with money provided from one of the NCLC's many corporate shells. The donation would then be recycled by "expensing" it to one of the NCLC's in-house vendors, who would redonate it in Connecticut in the name of another NCLC member. The donor sometimes was not even an actual resident of the state, but an itinerant volunteer sent in for a few weeks. In the face of such abuses and bogus donations, the Federal Election Commission turned down LaRouche's 1976 application after conducting a thorough field audit. LaRouche's response was to sue the FEC in federal court, charging a conspiracy to violate his civil rights.

In 1980 LaRouche managed to obtain over $500,000 in matching funds. This was partly because he had moved to the right and thus could attract a greater number of legitimate donations than was possible in 1976. It was also because of false reporting of literature sales and FEF donations. According to Anne-Marie Vidal, who worked in the national office during the 1980 campaign: "A contributor would give money to the FEF to promote nuclear power. Unbeknownst to the contributor, the money would be listed as a contribution to La-Rouche." The Federal Election Commission audited LaRouche's campaign finances and ruled that he must pay back $112,000. LaRouche claimed political persecution by the commission, and again filed suit in federal court. He eventually paid a reduced assessment of $56,000, plus a $15,000 penalty, and the FEC refrained from recommending criminal prosecution. In 1984 and 1988, the FEC again awarded La-Rouche matching funds, making a total of over $1.7 million for all three elections.

What LaRouche had discovered was a virtually prosecution-proof scam. The FEC often sues for the return of money, but it almost never refers cases to the Justice Department for criminal prosecution because of the potentially chilling effect on the electoral process.

Also during the 1980 campaign the LaRouchians carried out several swindles targeting private citizens. The biggest was the alleged looting of Computron, which filed for Chapter 11 and thus forced Wang and other creditors to indirectly help pay for LaRouche's campaign. The LaRouchians also presumably benefited from an imaginative scheme involving an alleged Italian Renaissance painting. A LaRouche financial adviser, Stephen Pepper, who ran an art dealership on the side, persuaded several investors to put up $50,000 to purchase what Pepper said was a major work of art, Carlo Maratta's *Marriage of the Virgin.* Pepper promptly turned the money over to the campaign, leaving the investors to discover that their newly acquired asset was a fake having negligible value. They spent years in litigation chasing their money.

Pepper and several others, including LaRouche himself, cultivated a Wall Street economist, Dr. Michael Hudson, author of several works in economic history. They told him that their New Benjamin Franklin Publishing House would like to republish several important nineteenth-century economists that he had cited in his scholarship. They also asked him for money, offering 20 percent on a three-month loan secured by the publishing house and two top LaRouche aides. Hudson had his lawyer draw up the notes and with some trepidation turned over $75,000. But the only books that were published were by or about LaRouche. The latter met with Hudson two months later and asked him to convert his loan into stock in the publishing company, promising him an administrative post. When Hudson turned the offer down, his NCLC contacts dropped all pretenses of friendliness. They explained that LaRouche had told them he was politically unreliable. Franklin House defaulted on the notes, then sought to stretch out the payment period. Its checks bounced, and when Hudson demanded return of his principal, he was told that the money was needed to pay for LaRouche's bodyguards. If he persisted in asking for his money back, they would have to conclude he was part of the world plot to kill LaRouche. Hudson filed a federal racketeering suit and was promptly attacked by the LaRouchians in an article calling him a KGB agent. It took him four years in court to obtain a judgment against them, only to find there was no practical way to collect. Franklin House had been stripped to a bare shell.

When Hudson's legal efforts were discussed inside the NCLC, La-Rouche Security aide Michelle Steinberg said (according to FBI testimony at her 1986 bail hearing): "Piss on him. Fuck him. That's what he gets for lending us money." The victimizing of Hudson was the first well-documented case of fraud in what prosecutors allege was the defrauding of thousands of other lenders. And Hudson, for his part, cured of any illusions about the LaRouchians, became a prosecution witness in criminal proceedings against them.

In addition to overt loan fraud, NCLC corporate shells ran up huge bills with vendors. When the latter came to collect, they were usually offered stretched-out payments. But even these checks bounced. Plaintiffs found that the fronts had few fixed assets. For instance, they typically leased rather than purchased typesetting equipment and other machinery. New York County judgment dockets show that in the late 1970s and early 1980s LaRouchian business and political entities were hit with over a million dollars in judgments and tax liens, most of which have still not been satisfied.

NCLC bookkeeper Richard Welch described the practice of stiffing vendors as the " 'jettison' principle." He recommended it as a way to handle financial shortfalls. The trick was first to build up credit and then jettison the vendor for a new one. Welch suggested this be done with copying machine rental companies, telephone companies, landlords, and suppliers of office equipment, as well as with members' credit cards.

Defectors recall a variation on the jettison principle practiced at NCLC headquarters in New York in the early 1980s. Dozens of members began using a check-cashing business near the West Fifty-eighth Street office. Things went smoothly for a while, but suddenly one week all the checks (which were drawn on a NCLC payroll shell with no assets) bounced, leaving the check-cashing company holding the proverbial empty bag. Shortly thereafter, LaRouche's headquarters moved to Leesburg, Virginia.

Of course, not all vendors can be jettisoned or skipped out on. Sooner or later an organization heavily dependent on telephone fund raising has to pay the phone company. But there are still ways to delay payment and thus in effect get an interest-free "loan." When New York Telephone threatened to turn off the NCLC phones during the 1976 presidential campaign because of nonpayment, the NCLC filed suit, charging political harassment. It claimed the phone company was in cahoots with the FBI and the Rockefellers.

Not many people who receive a turnoff notice think of depicting it as a political plot. But LaRouche seemed to be learning from Third World countries, which use political rhetoric and demonstrations as a tactic to delay paying the interest on their bloated loans from "imperialist" banks. The NCLC suit against New York Telephone probably cost the company more in legal fees than the LaRouchians owed. Again, the principle is well known in the Third World: If American bankers know that IMF austerity will cause guerrilla warfare in country X and result in the United States having to underwrite an expensive counterinsurgency campaign, then they will ease off temporarily while trying to persuade Washington to help country X with its debt payments.

The LaRouchians supplemented their vendor stiffing with check kiting, a tactic which essentially works like this: You write a check to someone in New York drawn on an out-of-state account that has insufficient funds to cover it. Depending on whether or not the recipient of the check deposits it immediately, you have a shorter or longer period before sufficient funds must be present in the account to avoid the check's bouncing. This period corresponds to what the banks term "float." It can be extended several days by letting the check bounce, then asking your creditor to wait before redepositing while you check your records and/or straighten out a temporary unforeseen cash-flow problem.

Average citizens take advantage of check kiting whenever they write a check prior to depositing the money to cover it. But it does not become really profitable unless a business kites large numbers of checks on out-of-state banks. Companies that have specialized in this—say, by keeping an amount equal to their average kited amount in money market accounts they could not otherwise maintain—have made millions of dollars in profits before being prosecuted and having to pay heavy fines or make restitution.

An attorney who once worked for the LaRouchians says he brought up the question of float and check kiting with the NCLC finance sector in 1974 after having read a banking report on it. This was at a time when, to all appearances, the NCLC was still relatively unsophisticated about money. To his amazement, they not only knew all about float but described to him how they were kiting checks all over the United States using dozens of accounts. That this was continued and expanded is suggested by records of a 1984 suit by LaRouche's Campaigner Publications against Chemical Bank. In answering pretrial interrogatories, Campaigner furnished lists of hundreds of its checks that bounced over a three-month period that year. Most of the checks were written to individuals and companies in Virginia on a Chemical account in Manhattan. Of course, the LaRouchians blamed their problem on the bank's alleged negligence.

Today's NCLC has grown into a vast cash-in/cash-out business with tens of millions of dollars a year in revenue, most of which is kept in constant circulation. With hundreds of accounts all over the world, disguised under dozens of corporate names or held in the names of individual NCLC members, it has the ability to write checks against insufficient funds. This has the effect of a constantly self-renewed interest-free loan of huge proportions. The LaRouchians are getting interest-free use of the money of everyone around them—money which, with good luck and clever legal maneuvering, they may never have to repay.

# Thirty-two

# The Shell Game

How did LaRouche get away with so flagrantly defying his creditors and violating federal campaign financing laws? How did he and his followers evade scrutiny by the IRS? To answer these questions, one must understand the financial structure that LaRouche has built to protect himself: an interlocking network of over thirty entities, seemingly independent of one another but actually controlled centrally through informal mechanisms. This business-political "empire" is an elaborate shell game. Cash is always in motion from one shell to another, disguising questionable transactions and avoiding court judgments. The entities include corporations, partnerships, individual NCLC members operating under business names, political action committees (PACs), electoral campaign committees, and the tax-exempt (until 1987) Fusion Energy Foundation. At any given moment the money in the bank accounts of these various entities has little to do with their actual operating receipts and expenditures. Funds are shifted around to meet the needs of the LaRouche organization as a whole. Large amounts sometimes will be in the personal bank accounts of trusted but appropriately obscure NCLC members. Large reserves are reportedly held in offshore banks where

U.S. claimants and authorities cannot gain access. In the mid-1980s, there were well over one hundred bank accounts involved in these transactions in the United States alone, while LaRouche's European Labor Party had its own interlocking shells and cash was moved between the United States and Europe by courier.

At the center of this financial web sits an unincorporated political association, the National Caucus of Labor Committees (NCLC), of which LaRouche is the chairman. The NCLC has no assets, and keeps no bank accounts; in effect, it is judgment-proof. LaRouche controls it through a kind of politburo, the National Executive Committee, which meets almost every day. The most important financial decisions are made at these meetings, and LaRouche's approval is always required. Even when he is out of the country, he keeps in close daily communication.

To insulate LaRouche and prevent the entities from being liable for each other's debts, the NCLC denies any controlling role. Its leaders today describe it as merely a "philosophical association" which meets occasionally to discuss Plato's *Timaeus* and similar refined topics. But in 1974, LaRouche described it as a "vanguard political organization." And in 1976, the NCLC director of organization, Warren Hamerman, declared in a financial report that the "budget and deployment of funds" proceed from a unified strategy. His report used charts and figures to illustrate the flow of money to and from the various entities, including the nonprofit FEF. The NCLC's total resources, he said, are "centrally deployed internationally to achieve maximum concentrated political firepower."

From the beginning, all entities were headed by a tiny coterie of trusted LaRouche aides. The incorporators, officers, or directors usually included Nancy or Ed Spannaus and Kenneth or Molly Kronberg. Most entities shared the same offices, telephone switchboard, lawyers, computer services, bookkeepers, in-house payroll company, and printing and typesetting facilities. This made it extremely difficult for creditors of any entities to foreclose, unless their judgment was against several shells at once.

The personnel of the entities were as interchangeable as the equipment. Fund raisers would claim to be from the FEF one day and from Campaigner Publications or Caucus Distributors the next. The money raised rarely stayed in the account of the entity to which the check was made out. Indeed, weekly financial reports going back to the mid-1970s show the cash from all LaRouche's entities going into one kitty. Using CIA jargon, LaRouche referred to the NCLC's "proprietary" relationship to the entities. In a 1979 speech he called them the "predicates, the shadows, the footprints" of the NCLC. In a 1981 pamphlet he said the NCLC "participates as a 'mother' or significantly as a 'partner' component." The incorporation papers of Caucus Distributors, Inc.— the most successful of LaRouche's telephone fund-raising entities— affirm outright that its purpose is to promote the "political ideas and beliefs" of the National Caucus of Labor Committees.

Some of the entities are just fancy names for the NCLC's own internal sectors. For instance, New Solidarity International Press Service, Inc., is the NCLC intelligence sector in its guise as a commercial producer of intelligence in published form or as confidential reports for private clients.

Businesses run by NCLC members are expected to put the NCLC's needs first. Former LaRouchian Eric Lerner found this out when he and several comrades formed a company to promote a water desalinization invention. After leaving the NCLC, he stated in a 1979 lawsuit that NCLC leaders had pressured him to funnel the firm's profits to the U.S. Labor Party, the electoral arm of the NCLC, in violation of election laws. Lerner charged that this was standard policy with other NCLC-controlled businesses.

The practice extended to the nonprofit FEF with its multimillion-dollar annual revenues. Bank records show that in the early 1980s the FEF transferred large amounts to several profit-making LaRouche entities. Many large checks were simply made out to "cash."

The NCLC's policy of keeping no assets in its own name dates back to 1978, when a $90,000 judgment against the NCLC was obtained by the Bank of Nova Scotia. The NCLC simply shut down its accounts and transferred its assets to controlled entities. An NCLC internal memo boasted that these assets had gone "underground."

LaRouche handles his personal finances in the same way. He holds no property in his own name, maintains no personal bank accounts within the United States, and receives no salary, ostensibly living off the charity of his followers. His residences are always owned or rented by associates, so that he appears to be a guest in his own house. In 1984 he testified in a lawsuit that he hadn't paid a penny in income tax for twelve years, and had no idea who paid for his food, clothing, attorneys, and other necessities. "I have not made a purchase of anything greater than a five-dollar haircut in the last ten years," he said.

LaRouche's attorney, Odin Anderson, claimed that in living this way LaRouche was following the example of Mahatma Gandhi. In the early 1970s, when "Lyn Marcus" the Marxist ideologue lived in a small, run-down apartment, the comparison would not have been so absurd. But LaRouche's standard of comfort changed dramatically after he married Helga Zepp. The Sutton Place town house, a villa in Germany, hired bodyguards, armored limousines, frequent world travel all became necessities. Anne-Marie Vidal recalled the resentment that Helga's shopping sprees stirred up among NCLC women: "She'd put down more for a blouse than most members would spend on clothes in a year."

After Ronald Reagan became President, LaRouche and his top lieutenants discussed moving the organization to the Washington area. The first stage came in 1983, when LaRouche, Helga, and several top aides moved to Leesburg, Virginia, an affluent community thirty minutes from Washington in fox-hunting Loudoun County. They rented an estate with a three-story house and a barn for Helga's horse.

Moving hundreds of NCLC members and the national office to Virginia required massive sums. Homes and office space had to be found. Real estate had to be purchased as well as rented. All this coincided with LaRouche's 1984 presidential campaign, which included lavish plans for television advertising.

To cope with the heavier demands, the NCLC fund-raising system was reorganized in the spring of 1984. Until that time, fund raising had been left largely to the regional NCLC organizations. It was henceforth centralized at the national headquarters' telephone banks. Scores of NCLC intelligence and editorial staffers were reassigned to full-time fund raising. Anyone who balked was accused of elitism. A California NCLC leader, William Wertz, was brought in to oversee the revamped system.

According to federal court testimony, Wertz's philosophy was simple: There was no such thing as a loan, and money borrowed should not be repaid. An exception might occasionally be made for lenders who were politically important or threatened to launch a major legal battle. But that was for the NCLC leadership to decide. The rank-and-file fund raisers were expected to get on their assigned phones, work through their stacks of contact cards, and milk the lenders at top speed.

Soon the phones were being worked fourteen to sixteen hours a day by as many as 120 people in the national office and upwards of 300 people in the regional offices. Telephone fund raising became "the one and only activity for which people lived and breathed," according to federal witness Charles Tate, himself a former fund raiser. New York regional NCLC leader Phil Rubinstein supervised a telephone operation that floated like a crap game from apartment to apartment in upper Manhattan, the Bronx, and New Jersey, leaving a trail of victims. (While involved in this, Rubinstein ran for mayor of New York in the 1975 Democratic primary, promising to weed out corruption.)

The national office boiler room developed a boot-camp atmosphere. "There'd be a roll call in the morning," Tate said. "Wertz would call out each name. You were given these gargantuan quotas, and you were expected to work from 9 A.M. until you met the quota, even if that was eleven or twelve at night." Members who didn't meet their quotas were yelled at, denied any days off, or accused of homosexuality or drunkenness. When one party leader's wife failed to meet her quota, her husband beat her up. It worked—she became the most ruthless of fund raisers.

Wertz interrupted work twice a day for pep talks. "He would describe us as being like Patton's army," Tate testified. "If we didn't make the landing like at Normandy . . . all of civilization would come tumbling down." (Wertz also concocted little motivational poems, such as: "Here's to St. Martin, the Roman, who offered his cloak to a beggar. . . ." In a harsher frame of mind he wrote: "Armageddon is coming . . . if thou fail'st to act as the right arm of the Lord." And: "Killer instinct is needed in him who would wage righteous warfare . . . kill with the weapons of art.")

According to federal investigators, the LaRouche organization's income soared to more than $30 million in 1984. During a four-month period a single Manhattan bank account of Campaigner Publications handled credits of more than $4.5 million. This was only one of many Campaigner accounts, and Campaigner was only one of many fund-raising entities. Although a substantial portion of the revenues was legitimate literature sales or donations, investigators say that a large amount came from two intertwined scams: unauthorized charges to credit cards (prosecutors later learned of thousands of such charges) and the solicitation of loans which the NCLC had no intention of repaying.

Whenever airport travelers purchased literature or made a donation to the FEF or LaRouche's presidential campaign via credit card, they allegedly were at risk of additional, unauthorized charges. There was an art behind this, according to records in a suit filed by a bank against the LaRouchians. A fund raiser in the LaRouche boiler room would phone the National Data Corporation to verify how much could be charged. When told the requested charges exceeded the cardholder's credit limit, the fund raiser would call back requesting a lower charge, and repeat this process until the cardholder's credit limit was determined. The fund raiser would then decide how much to rip off, perhaps a small amount that might go unnoticed by the cardholder, or sometimes an amount that would clean out the account.

When the victim discovered the loss on his monthly statement, one of two things would happen. Sometimes the LaRouchians would apologize profusely, blaming it on a clerical error, and eventually return the money, having enjoyed an interest-free short-term loan. But more often, having withdrawn the cash through one of many LaRouchian credit-card merchant accounts, they stonewalled both the bank and the credit-card holder. Ultimately the bank would get fed up and freeze the merchant account, but the money in it would total only a fraction of the unauthorized charges. The bank would be out the difference.

Two banks hit hard were Chemical Bank and New Jersey's First Fidelity. After they froze the LaRouchian accounts they were sued for allegedly being part of a political conspiracy against LaRouche. First Fidelity eventually spent more on legal expenses than it would have lost by writing off the debt. In New Jersey, LaRouche's harassment machine went into high gear, with press conferences and hundreds of thousands of leaflets calling First Fidelity a Mafia money laundry. The bank responded with a federal court racketeering suit against LaRouche, twenty-one associates, and twenty organizations. (The suit, eventually settled out of court, produced detailed information about LaRouche's financial empire.)

Vendors who suffered included Sans Souci Travel in New York City. The LaRouchians paid for airline tickets via unauthorized charges to the American Express cards of people who had previously made donations or purchases. When these people protested, American Express invalidated the charges, for a loss to the travel agent amounting to $106,000.

Thousands of 1984 loans were solicited through LaRouche's two presidential campaign committees, which spent a total of $6.3 million. The FEC filings of Independent Democrats for LaRouche (IDL) listed almost 2,600 loans totaling over $1.2 million. By October 1985 almost all these loans were past due, and only $139,000 had been paid back. An FEC official described this as "highly unusual—I don't recall anything quite like it in any other filing." As of mid-1987 LaRouche's campaign debts totaled $2.6 million, more than any of the major 1984 candidates except John Glenn.

Additional loans were solicited in the name of Caucus Distributors, Campaigner Publications, and the FEF. Fund-raising quotas were set at $400,000 a week in 1984, then were upped to $500,000 and $600,000 in 1985 and 1986. Fund raisers increasingly targeted the most vulnerable people they could find—elderly widows living alone, stroke victims, and terminal cancer patients.

# Thirty-three

## The World's Most Expensive Glass of Sherry

Millions of senior citizens live alone. Often desperate for companionship, they are prone to manipulation by younger people who pretend to show interest in them. They also are easily intimidated or frightened. Some are in the early stages of senility, no longer able to make wise decisions about money, yet unprotected by a financial guardian. Others have clouded judgment because of illness or the recent death of a spouse. They may have substantial assets in the form of their life savings in stocks or bonds. They also may own their homes or other property, which can be borrowed against or even sold outright. They are thus ripe for the pickings, as LaRouche's followers perceived.

Anne Cresson, seventy-seven, of Princeton, New Jersey, lived alone when contacted in 1985. Her husband was in a nursing home with Alzheimer's disease, and her son lived in California. She was not wealthy, but from time to time she had donated to the Republican Party and various conservative causes. This put her on the New Right's fund-raising lists. The LaRouchians obtained her name from one of these lists and called her. They said they were patriots fighting for Ronald Reagan's policies. They asked her if she would like to personally help the President of the United States. They didn't ask her to donate money. Instead, they asked her if she had any property that could be used as collateral for loans.

Mrs. Cresson told them she owned a coin collection appraised at $75,000. A LaRouche fund raiser offered to pay her 12 percent interest for the use of it as loan collateral—seemingly a generous offer given the low loan-to-value ratio on coin collections. Mrs. Cresson consented, and a man from the LaRouche organization came to her house and picked up the coins. He gave her an unsecured promissory note—a printed form on the letterhead of Caucus Distributors. The address on the letterhead was the former NCLC headquarters on West Fifty-eighth Street in Manhattan, which by this time was an empty building slated for demolition. (The LaRouche organization had moved out several months earlier.)

Mrs. Cresson had second thoughts the next day. She called La-Rouche fund raiser Joyce Rubinstein and asked that the coin collection be returned. Mrs. Rubinstein refused, saying the coins had been sent to Chicago for appraisal, but offered to visit Mrs. Cresson to discuss the matter further. Mrs. Cresson happened to speak to her son on the phone that day and told him the story. He called the Princeton police. They arrested Mrs. Rubinstein at Mrs. Cresson's home. She was charged with theft by deception and held at the police station. It was one of the rare occasions when someone took a tough line with the LaRouchians. Several hours later, Mrs. Rubinstein's comrades meekly returned the coin collection to Mrs. Cresson.

Not all schemes had such happy endings for the intended targets. Margaret Beynen, eighty-three, of Berkeley, California, suffered more than a year of trauma to get back a portion of her money. LaRouche fund raisers began calling her in late 1985. They told her America's banking system was about to collapse. Her money would be safer if she lent it to them, and they would pay 10 percent interest. The loan would be used to fight drugs, which otherwise would destroy America. Then began the subtle intimidation: "Through long and frequent telephone calls," Mrs. Beynen later told the court, the LaRouchians "probed deeply" into her personal and financial affairs, pressuring her for money. Over a two-month period she made four loans to them totaling $60,000—a substantial portion of her life savings. They sent Federal Express couriers to pick up the checks.

Next, the LaRouchians began urging her to convert the loans into gifts. When she refused, they called her a selfish old woman. Interest payments on the loans, which had been intermittent, ceased altogether. In May 1986 she received a form letter from Caucus Distributors, Inc. (CDI), asking all its lenders to extend or forgive their loans. "If you have not been repaid according to schedule," the letter said, "you may be angry. You have a right to be angry." However, the letter suggested the anger should be directed at the Justice Department, the Eastern Establishment, and the drug lobbyists, who had launched "financial warfare" against LaRouche and CDI. The letter warned about certain liars who were going around saying that "LaRouche preys on old people." If any lender was contacted by such a person, they should alert CDI immediately.

Mrs. Beynen wrote to CDI requesting the interest due on her loan. Weeks passed before she received a brief reply: "We are winning the war—stay with us." But still no money came. In August she sent another letter. This time there was no reply at all. Mrs. Beynen realized that she might never see her money again and that she had jeopardized the financial security of her only heir, her blind and diabetic son.

A San Francisco attorney, Dan Bookin, was willing to take Mrs. Beynen's case pro bono, and filed a racketeering suit on her behalf in federal court. Mrs. Beynen eventually obtained a court order to seize the assets of two LaRouche front groups.

Thousands of elderly people have not been so lucky. Most cannot obtain free legal counsel, and even those who can afford a lawyer at the going rate are often too frightened, confused, or embarrassed to sue. Many are in such poor health that even if they did take legal action they probably would not live to see the suit and the collection process through to the end.

The amount of personal trauma has been enormous. As of mid-1987 Virginia state investigators listed 4,500 questionable LaRouchian loan transactions totaling $30 million in all fifty states and twelve foreign countries. Of the 3,000 victims in these transactions, about 75 percent are senior citizens. Virginia Commonwealth attorney Mary Sue Terry told CBS-TV: "We don't know of a single instance in which the terms of a note have been met in full by one of the entities that borrowed the money." (Federal investigators believe that the total amount bilked from the public may be much higher than $30 million.)

Occasionally a LaRouchian fund raiser hits the jackpot with a genuinely wealthy senior citizen. In 1986 the NCNB National Bank of Florida, trustee for eighty-year-old retired steel executive Charles Zimmerman, sued the LaRouchians to recover $2.6 million. Zimmerman had been induced to loan cash to the Fusion Energy Foundation and Caucus Distributors, transfer stock to the FEF, and purchase a limited partnership in a Maryland radio station controlled by the LaRouchians.

Some victims were disoriented by painful illnesses. Norman Flaningam, seventy-four, a Washington attorney dying of cancer, had turned over more than $100,000. In return, the LaRouchians gave him free

copies of *EIR* special reports and a box of chocolates on St. Valentine's Day, with a handwritten note "to a wonderful patriot." His daughter recalled coming into his room near the end and finding him in a distraught state, begging the LaRouchians on the telephone to return his money.

Carl Swanson, sixty-one, a stroke victim, was taken for $7,000 in credit-card charges. His wife and son told the Baltimore *Sun* how he had received calls from LaRouchian fund raiser Rochelle Ascher every five or ten minutes for hours at a time. His wife first learned about it when she discovered him "crying and trembling" on the phone. She picked up the receiver and heard Ascher tell him it was "his patriotic duty" to give money. Mrs. Swanson told Ascher not to call again, but Ascher persisted, disguising her voice and giving false names.

Elizabeth Rose, an eighty-four-year-old widow who lived alone in a Pennsylvania retirement village, was relieved of over $1 million, mostly in stocks. Her daughter, Nancy Day, explains that Mrs. Rose had made large contributions to Ronald Reagan's 1984 reelection campaign. In February 1986 the LaRouchians contacted her, saying they had gotten her name from a fund-raising list. They told her about the drug menace, the AIDS menace, the Soviet menace, and the various plots against Lyndon LaRouche's life. Soon they were at her doorstep with video-tapes of LaRouche's speeches. Cautiously at first, they induced her to donate money via her credit card, a thousand or two thousand dollars at a time. Don't tell your children, they warned her. Your children don't care about you, they just want to put you on a shelf. "It all happened very fast, in less than a month," said Mrs. Day. "They opened my mother up like a flower."

When the LaRouchians learned that Mrs. Rose was a major stock-holder in Church & Dwight (the manufacturers of Arm & Hammer baking soda), they induced her to turn over 92,000 shares that had been passed down in the family for generations. Her daughters found out and intervened. Although the LaRouchians had sold much of the stock as soon as they received it, the family was eventually able to retrieve about a third. "My mother clearly didn't know what she was doing," says Mrs. Day. "In the middle of all this I was talking to her, right in her bedroom. She said, 'All my stock belongs to you kids.' She was not aware she had given it away."

When Mrs. Day and her two sisters went to court in Bucks County, Pennsylvania, to seek a guardian for their mother, the LaRouche orga-nization urged Mrs. Rose to fight them. When the court case began, her behavior became increasingly erratic. "Some days I was a friend, other days the enemy," says her daughter. "She told me the LaRouchians had promised to send her to the moon and that she hoped to be the first grandmother on Mars." The LaRouchians introduced Mrs. Rose to a nationwide telephone support network of elderly LaRouche followers, all of whom were in conflict with their children regarding donations to LaRouche. "When the trial began, she got calls from old people as far away as Alaska," said her daughter. Mrs. Rose's attorneys called as their expert Dr. Judianne Densen-Gerber, the former Odyssey House director who had spoken at LaRouchian anti-drug rallies. She testified that Mrs. Rose was perfectly able to conduct her own affairs. The judge was unconvinced, especially after Mrs. Rose told the court her views on the Rockefeller family and dope dealing. He ruled that Mrs. Rose had been the victim of "designing persons" and appointed her daughters as guardians of her financial affairs.

The LaRouchians then sent Mrs. Rose on a tour of Italy, presenting her to the media as a victim of an American "reign of terror" against the elderly. NCLC literature described how happy she felt to give money to LaRouche. *New Solidarity* made her into a heroine with headlines like "Elizabeth Rose Inspires Audiences" and "Patriotic 84-Year-Old Begins Tour for Seniors' Rights."

Back from Italy, Mrs. Rose began her political career in earnest. She went to cadre school once a week, and counseled other elderly LaRouche contributors by phone. She testified before LaRouche's fact-finding commission set up to prove that he and other indicted members of the NCLC were victims of a political witch hunt. She went to a "thank you" reception in Leesburg where elderly donors were served sherry and allowed to chat briefly with LaRouche. Prosecutors in the loan fraud cases say that LaRouche's mansion serves "the world's most expensive glass of sherry."

"My mother used to have a great sense of humor," said Mrs. Day, "but she hasn't laughed since she met those people. They've filled her with hate. They told her we only want her money." In effect, the LaRouchians had become her mother's "surrogate children." Seducing her first with flowers and attention, they had offered her an illusory sense of personal fulfillment as an "organizer" of other vulnerable senior citizens. "They'd suck out her eyeballs if they could," Mrs. Day said.

NCLC defector Charles Tate, a federal witness in the Boston case, said the treatment of Mrs. Rose, Mrs. Beynen, and other senior citizens reflects an increasing recklessness within the LaRouche organization. Tate recalls the first months of the big fund-raising push in 1984. "It was crystal clear to every single member . . . that the organization would never be able to pay back [the] gargantuan amounts of loans . . . " he said. "And quite frankly, nobody really cared."

Internal NCLC memos seized by federal authorities in their October

1986 raid on LaRouche's headquarters reveal the predatory mentality of the fund raisers. A May 1986 memo described how a Louisiana oil worker took out a $90,000 mortgage on his home and lent the organization over $100,000 during a period when three LaRouche fund raisers were courting him. But he started asking for his money back because of the influence of his girlfriend (described as a "raving witch"). The memo examined ways to avoid full repayment. "If we are going to offer him a schedule which we can't keep," it suggested, "we might just as well call his bluff now and get it over with." It also speculated that it might be best to pay him $2,000 a week for several weeks just to cool him off.

The memos dealt with what were called "hardship" cases, such as a man in Alaska who "lent us his life savings and is dependent on us to a high degree," or the elderly woman "who did everything, including selling her house," and thus had "no means of support except our beneficence." In the Orwellian semantics of the NCLC, these victims were transformed into welfare loafers who should be grateful to the LaRouchians for grudgingly returning a tiny fraction of their money. Often there was a steely insensitivity to their plight. One woman who lent $60,000 was ridiculed as "the famous hardship case . . . going crazy as usual." A man who lent $17,000 and was having his wages garnisheed by the IRS was described as "going bananas." One destitute lender was said to have "nowhere to go besides us to cover living expenses and the mortgage on his house . . . He's hysterical." Another was called a "psycho" and a "troublemaker" because she demanded her money back.

Meanwhile, the massive sums raised were being used to build up LaRouche's real estate and other commercial holdings in Leesburg. The organization spent millions of dollars on industrial lots, a summer camp, a radio station, a weekly newspaper, and a 4,550-acre paramilitary training facility in the Blue Ridge Mountains as the bulk of the NCLC national staff of about two hundred people moved into Loudoun County in 1984–85. When Lyn and Helga decided they needed a larger estate, the organization persuaded David Nick Anderson, an Oklahoma oilman, to put up $400,000 and finance $900,000 for the purchase of Ibykus Farm, a 171-acre estate with a fourteen-room manor house. Three LaRouche fund-raising entities then kicked in almost $1 million for improvements, which included a swimming pool, riding ring, horse barn, and landscaping.

But the LaRouchians, with all their aspirations to public influence and eventual mass leadership, were unable to win many minds and hearts in Loudoun County. At first they provided jobs for local residents, but the paychecks soon began to bounce and many employees quit. Hundreds of checks to contractors and merchants also bounced. Although a few local ultraconservatives were willing to deal secretly with LaRouche, most residents were soon fed up. If the LaRouchians were not squabbling with the sheriff's office over their applications for concealed-weapons permits, they were battling with the local zoning board over their right to operate a children's day camp. Their newly founded *Loudoun County News* tried to whip up hysteria among local small businessmen over a nonexistent plot by county officials to drive them out of business. The LaRouchians threatened the life of a female attorney (who promptly fled town), sued a jeweler for libel, and published smears against families who had lived in the county for generations. The nadir probably was reached when LaRouche called the local Garden Society a nest of KGB agents.

The move to Leesburg turned out to be the biggest miscalculation the LaRouchians had yet made. In New York they had been protected by the anonymity of big-city life, their power over Roy Cohn, and the reluctance of prosecutors to tangle with them. But in Leesburg, population 8,000, their intimidation tactics and deadbeat attitude toward paying bills were much more conspicuous. "It was like they moved into a fishbowl and turned on the lights," says *Loudoun Times-Mirror* reporter Bryan Chitwood. Soon their antics were being questioned publicly by county board of supervisors member Frank Raflo and the *Times-Mirror,* while a wide range of citizens complained to the sheriff's office. Don Moore, the deputy sheriff in charge of the investigation, began to sense the nationwide and international scope of the swindles emanating from the NCLC headquarters in downtown Leesburg across from the colonial courthouse. A Vietnam veteran, he looked at the office building filled with LaRouche entities and thought that the time to take that hill had come. But he ran into the usual stone wall when he tried to interest the local FBI and other federal authorities.

The first breakthrough came in Massachusetts. In the fall of 1984 the Boston FBI had received complaints which suggested a pattern of credit-card fraud by organizations linked to LaRouche. A federal grand jury was convened in November. At first, its investigation proceeded slowly: The FBI and the U.S. Attorney's office had no idea of the magnitude of LaRouche's fund-raising operation or its bewildering network of corporate shells. The LaRouchians allegedly sent potential witnesses to hide in Europe, destroyed documents, and refused to honor subpoenas. But when LaRouche followers scored big in the 1986 Illinois Democratic primaries, newspapers around the country began to pay more attention to LaRouche's finances. Elderly victims and their relatives read these articles and came forward with complaints. Authorities in state after state launched investigations.

Meanwhile, First Fidelity Bank's civil racketeering suit against La-Rouche pierced his corporate veil, while U.S. Attorney William Weld in Boston appointed an assistant with special qualifications to prosecute the credit-card fraud case. This prosecutor, John Markham, had once represented in private practice a wealthy California cult, the Process Church of the Final Judgment. Markham knew how cults operate and how their members think. He also knew the key to cracking a case against a cultlike organization: Find defectors, offer them immunity, and get them to lead you to more defectors.

The LaRouchians seemed unaware that they had passed into the danger zone. After all, had they not outwitted the authorities a hundred times and always with impunity? Their sense of invulnerability was so brazen that when they brought a New Jersey attorney to Boston to defend them in the credit-card fraud investigation, they paid for his airline ticket via an unauthorized credit-card charge. (He resigned from the case when the Justice Department informed him of this fact.) In Leesburg every Wednesday evening, a shredding machine at LaRouche headquarters destroyed bank statements, canceled checks, and other documents—as many as ten thirty-gallon bags' worth each week. But no one thought to destroy the Security staff notebooks and financial memos which described and gloated over the NCLC's machinations in extraordinary detail. The NCLC leadership was preoccupied with rais-ing as much money as possible, as fast as possible, seemingly regardless of the risk. In an August 1986 briefing, Helga LaRouche ordered mem-bers to raise $750,000 in five days by focusing on "money questions as the absolutely necessary logistics" to defeat the evil oligarchy. "For us," she said, money represents "the bullets, the guns, laser weapons, and other kinds of weapons, which we absolutely need."

The LaRouche organization would need criminal lawyers more than laser guns. In October 1986, ten LaRouchians, including four of La-Rouche's top aides, were indicted in Boston federal court for credit-card fraud and obstruction of justice. Several more LaRouchians were subsequently added to the Boston indictment, and in February 1987, a Virginia grand jury indicted sixteen for securities fraud. In March, New York State indicted fifteen for securities fraud, grand larceny, and con-spiracy, including LaRouche's closest lieutenants, Ed and Nancy Span-naus. At least twelve states meanwhile obtained cease-and-desist or-ders against LaRouche fund-raising entities. On July 2, 1987, LaRouche himself was indicted in Boston for obstruction of justice.

The first conviction was obtained in December 1987: Roy Frank-houser, tried separately from the other Boston defendants, was found guilty of obstructing justice. That same month the main Boston trial began. Although it ended in a mistrial, a replay was scheduled for early

1989. Meanwhile, a federal grand jury in Alexandria was considering massive evidence of loan and tax fraud, and the LaRouchians themselves predicted it would hand down a "grand slam series of indictments." In October 1988, after a probe lasting almost two years, LaRouche and six followers (including Ed Spannaus and chief fund raiser William Wertz) were indicted on thirteen counts of mail fraud, income tax fraud, and conspiracy. The indictment charged them with obtaining over $34 million in fraudulent loans between 1983 and 1987 (they denied all charges, claiming that harassment and seizure of records by authorities prevented their repaying loans). If convicted, LaRouche faced up to sixty-five years in jail and fines of $3.25 million.

If LaRouche were the head of an ordinary criminal conspiracy, motivated simply by greed, he would have been washed up long before the 1988 indictments. His associates would have offered to cut deals with the prosecutors to inform on each other and the boss himself. But the LaRouchians are an ideological movement with an intense collective spirit. Such movements often function most vigorously when under attack, even when their top leaders are in jail or exile. By early 1988 most law enforcement officials no longer believed the LaRouchian leadership would collapse under fear of jail sentences. In an update report on the NCLC, the Anti-Defamation League of B'nai B'rith noted its "resilience" and "quick recovery." Whenever NCLC members were indicted, authorities found that within days many of the indicted people were back on the phones raising money. Their bravado was expressed in comparisons between their fund-raising methods and those of Benjamin Franklin and George Washington. The Founding Fathers, NCLC publications maintained, had resorted to a prototype of "credit-card fraud" to save the American Revolution!

The adaptability of the LaRouchians was also seen when the Justice Department brought involuntary bankruptcy proceedings against three entities which had refused to pay contempt-of-court fines of over $16 million. (The fines had been accruing daily for over a year, ever since the entities defied a Boston grand jury subpoena of their financial records.) A federal judge in Alexandria placed them under the control of interim trustees, but when U.S. marshals seized the firms' sixty-five known bank accounts, all but $20,000 was gone. And when the marshals seized the firms' offices and publications, the latter just reopened under new names: *New Solidarity* as *The New Federalist*, and *Fusion* as *Twenty-First Century Science and Technology*. In addition, the firms moved their telephone boiler rooms to private apartments also to operate under new names. In late 1987, federal authorities estimated the LaRouche money machine was still raising $2.5 million a month.

# Part Nine

# LaRouche, Inc.: The Underworld Connection

Inspector MacDonald smiled, and his eyelid quivered . . . "I won't conceal from you, Mr. Holmes, that we think in the C.I.D. that you have a wee bit of a bee in your bonnet over this professor [Moriarty]."

—*The Valley of Fear*

# Thirty-four

## The War on Drugs, So Called

LaRouche may not have originally intended to build an organization resembling an underworld enterprise, but he certainly took steps tending in that direction. First, he gathered a band of ruthless lieutenants, who acknowledged that he was the "boss" and defined their identities in terms of his approval. Second, he found out how the underworld actually works (money laundering and drug smuggling, for instance) from former government experts and by studying the careers of master criminals such as Meyer Lansky. Third, he constructed a good cover story that seemed to explain that what he was doing was quite legal. Fourth, he built up alliances with established organizations, such as the Teamsters union, which had the connections, resources, and expertise he lacked.

Like Sherlock Holmes's great adversary, Professor Moriarty—the fictional prototype of an intellectual underworld leader—LaRouche approached his activities with the mind of a strategist and grasped the key problem: how to develop an in-depth shield against prosecution, including a fail-safe system for times when the ordinary deceptions no longer suffice by themselves.

The solution he most favored was to associate himself with the U.S. intelligence community. It was well known that the CIA and other federal agencies had long collaborated with and protected crooks so long as the latter were useful in fighting communism (for instance, Santos Trafficante, Jr., against Fidel Castro). In *The Case of Walter Lippmann*, LaRouche observed that the most successful narcotics traffickers are those linked to government agencies responsible for investigating the drug trade. These agencies, to protect their criminal associates, use "the 'under investigation' fiction" to steer "regular, unwitting police agencies" away from any "interference with the drug-network operations." Although LaRouche buried this point in a critique of both the crooks and the intelligence community, he soon proceeded to hire as his adviser the often arrested but never convicted Mitch WerBell, who boasted of using his Langley connections to gain immunity. Years later, under investigation for credit-card fraud, LaRouche's followers would allegedly attempt a variation of WerBell's method—to persuade the CIA, through intermediaries, to get a federal investigation called off.

The development of a smoke screen for LaRouche's activities can be traced back to the founding of the National Anti-Drug Coalition in 1978–79. NADC's LaRouchian organizers talked tough. They were going to lead the American people in a campaign to "shut down the drug traffic" lock, stock, and barrel. They staged rallies and seminars at inner-city churches and high schools, lobbied state legislatures, held briefings for congressional aides, and published the monthly *War on Drugs*. The apparent sincerity with which they approached this crusade won them the respect of some law enforcement experts. An alliance was forged with Dr. Gabriel Nahas, the anti-pot expert who later became prominent in Nancy Reagan's crusade against drugs. *Dope, Inc.*, a 500-page book written by three LaRouche aides, became a kind of underground best-seller.

The anti-drug rhetoric continued into the 1980s, with LaRouche hurling the epithet "drug lobbyist" at any reporter who criticized him. This was his most audacious deception. For while conducting his so-called war on drugs, he and his followers sought alliances with individuals allegedly close to the heroin and cocaine traffic, including midwest racketeers and Panama's General Manuel Noriega. To facilitate such ties, the LaRouchians surrounded themselves with consultants, attorneys, business partners, and political allies form the underworld's fringes. For instance, when the Illinois attorney general began a probe of the National Anti-Drug Coalition's fund-raising in the early 1980s, the LaRouchians hired Chicago attorney Victor Ciardelli, reportedly at the recommendation of the late Roy Cohn. Ciardelli was later indicted along with over forty co-conspirators for his involvement in a vast cocaine- and pot-smuggling operation in the South and Southwest. He was accused of being in charge of laundering the profits, but received only a year in jail after turning state's witness.

To develop their own financial operations, the LaRouchians needed detailed background knowledge. In 1978 over a dozen NCLC members did library research for the authors of *Dope, Inc.*, studying the activities of criminal innovators such as Meyer Lansky and Robert Vesco, whose expertise included money laundering. But some things can't be learned from books and congressional reports. One of LaRouche's earliest gurus with direct knowledge of the drug underworld was WerBell. Although he was touted to the NCLC rank and file as a veteran government anti-drug fighter, this was a half-truth at best. His career as CIA contract employee, private spook, mercenary soldier, and arms dealer had brought him into tempting contact with criminal elements in the Caribbean and Southeast Asia's Golden Triangle. In the early 1970s he achieved notoriety as the manufacturer of the Ingram MAC-10, which became the preferred weapon of cocaine traffickers throughout the Western Hemisphere. In 1975 a federal grand jury in Miami indicted him as the kingpin of a conspiracy to smuggle 50,000 pounds of Colombian marijuana a month into Florida—to be distributed in Detroit, Cleveland, and Chicago. His co-defendants were John Nardi, a Cleveland Teamster official and crime boss; Morton Franklin, a Cleveland insurance man with close ties to organized crime; and two southern arms dealers, Gerald Cunningham, a Florida arms dealer, and William Bell, a former arms salesman.

The investigation began when Kenneth Burnstine, a major Florida cocaine smuggler facing a seven-year prison sentence, agreed to become a government informant and impresario of "sting" operations. Burnstine had formerly been an arms salesman for WerBell. He offered to sell WerBell his smuggling business in return for a $100,000 commission on each 5,000 pounds of pot. WerBell expressed interest, and Burnstine introduced him to DEA agents posing as smugglers with Colombian connections. Thus began a seven-month operation involving twenty-seven federal agents with planes and yachts.

Although the DEA collected fifty-five hours of audiotapes and videotapes linking WerBell and his cronies to the smuggling plot, the government case was undermined by the mysterious death of its chief witness. Only weeks before the 1976 trial, Burnstine was killed when his private plane crashed during a Mojave Desert air show. The FBI suspected Nardi, but couldn't prove it. Without Burnstine's sworn direct testimony, federal and state prosecutors had to drop over sixty marijuana- and cocaine-smuggling cases. The result in the WerBell trial was a ruling that most of the DEA's tapes of conversations in which Burnstine was a participant could not be played for the jury.

The defense conceded that WerBell had recruited William Bell, who in turn recruited Cunningham, who brought in Franklin and Nardi. However, the defense argued, the purpose hadn't been a smuggling conspiracy at all, but an anti-drug operation. The five defendants had played along with Burnstine in their capacity as drug busters for a government agency so secret that it had no name. (The LaRouchians used a variation of this defense in their 1988 Boston trial for credit-card fraud, claiming their activities had been directed by government agents so secret they were known only by code names.)

The brunt of the defense was borne by WerBell, whose connections with government agencies provided the hook on which to hang the drug-fighter argument. (His chief attorney was Edwin Marger of Atlanta, who would later represent LaRouche in a libel suit against Jack Anderson.) Franklin and Nardi offered no defense, preferring to rise or fall with WerBell. Former Nixon aide Egil Krogh was called as a defense witness, but testified that he'd never heard of the supersecret drug busters. Former CIA contract agent Gerald Patrick Hemming, called to attest to WerBell's commitment to the war on drugs, was himself arrested during the trial for allegedly smuggling cocaine and marijuana.

Still, the government fought a losing battle without Burnstine and the tapes. After ten hours of deliberation, the jury found the defendants not guilty. The drug-fighter defense was not the chief factor in this decision. As prosecutor Karen Atkinson told the jury: "There's not one scintilla of evidence that . . . any of these men were working for the U.S. government."

WerBell's attorneys said their client had been unacquainted with the Cleveland men prior to the indictment, but this argument was rendered dubious by a separate indictment of Franklin and Cunningham on gunrunning charges. The guns were Ingrams purchased from WerBell and were to be smuggled out of the country via a private Florida airstrip. Also indicted in the arms case were Cleveland mobsters Dominick Bartone and Henry ("Boom-Boom") Grecco. Bartone later became a suspect with Morton Franklin in an Ohio bank fraud case. Grecco, described in FBI documents as a "cold-blooded killer," was a close associate of Nardi.

In addition to Burnstine's death, an extraordinary amount of violence surrounded these two cases. One midnight in July 1975, while the sting operation was in progress, WerBell's partner in the arms business, retired Army Colonel Robert Bayard, was found dead in an Atlanta shopping center. He had been executed with a single shot to the head. The murder was never solved. In May 1977, Nardi was killed by a dynamite blast in the parking lot of the Cleveland Teamsters' joint council. Local media attributed the slaying to mob infighting. That same month Boom-Boom Grecco was gunned down in his car after visiting the Italian-American Citizens Club in Cleveland. (Convicted of the crime was Joseph Bonarrigo, who had killed Grecco after the latter declined to help him make a bomb to blow up a local businessman who had ordered a mob vending machine taken off his premises.) In 1984, Morton Franklin was arrested in Cleveland after paying $28,000 to an FBI undercover agent for a kilo of cocaine. Before pleading guilty to the narcotics charge, he forfeited bail because he allegedly attempted to hire a hit man to kill the FBI agent, offering to supply plastic explosives and a silencer as well as to pay $10,000. If LaRouche planned to associate with such circles, it was no wonder he felt he needed round-the-clock bodyguards!

A window on WerBell's Southeast Asian and Caribbean connections was opened in the early 1980s after the collapse of Australia's Nugan Hand Bank, the suspicious death of one of its two founders, and the disappearance of the other. Australian authorities launched several probes uncovering links between Nugan Hand and the CIA, organized crime and heroin traffickers. The March 1983 report of the Commonwealth–New South Wales Joint Task Force on Drug Trafficking listed twenty-six alleged traffickers, several of them former U.S. military officers and intelligence agents. Like WerBell, they had been active in the Golden Triangle during the Vietnam War.

When task-force investigators traveled to Washington they interviewed WerBell about a consulting fee he had received from Nugan Hand in 1979. WerBell told them he had met with Earl Yates, a retired admiral and president of Nugan Hand International. They had discussed a plan to resettle Meo tribesmen from Laos on a small island off Haiti. The Meo, famed as poppy growers and anti-Communist fighters, were to become peaceful fishermen. (Tom Naylor in *Hot Money* suggests they really would have become *gurkhas* for the cocaine traffic.) WerBell said he refused to get involved because the scheme was "unrealistic."

The LaRouchian inner circle was well aware of WerBell's checkered past. A 1977 Security staff dossier outlined his involvement with fugitive financier/cocaine trafficker Robert Vesco and speculated about his possible ties to Florida drug kingpin Santos Trafficante, Jr. The dossier described his smuggling trial and speculated that one of the attorneys had CIA ties. The Security staffers were doubtless well aware of the boast made by WerBell (after the government dropped an earlier case against him for violation of neutrality laws) that the Company looks after its own.

For the LaRouchians WerBell became a fount of tall tales as well as tips about the drug traffic. He also opened doors. On visits to his Georgia estate, they could meet key personalities of the violent, semi-psychotic world of gunrunners, drug smugglers, and CIA rogues—men like Gerald Hemming, who summed up the WerBell milieu to author A. J. Weberman as "nigger killers in bed with the Mafia and the Mafia in bed with the FBI and the goddamn CIA in bed with all of them."

In 1978 LaRouche commissioned the writing of *Dope, Inc.*, which purported to be a study of how the drug traffic worked. Over a dozen NCLC Security and intelligence staffers were assigned to the project, which furnished a rationale for gathering as much technical information as possible about smuggling and money laundering. WerBell personally provided much of the background on Southeast Asia. The LaRouchians also drew on the knowledge of Walt Mackem, a WerBell crony and former CIA narcotics expert. Mackem regarded the LaRouchians as crazy but was willing to take their money.

Another tutor in the late 1970s was Mafia drug banker Michele Sindona. After the collapse of his Franklin National Bank, he talked to many reporters about his woes. Members of the Security staff would stroll down the street from NCLC headquarters to chat with him at the Pierre Hotel, where he lived while awaiting trial. Vivian Syvriotis, La-Rouche's former mistress, was the NCLC member delegated to meet most often with Sindona. "To the [NCLC] leadership," writes Kevin Coogan, a former member of the intelligence staff, "Sindona was the very model of a 'pro-development banker.' They continued to tell us he was a good guy even when it became obvious he was involved in the heroin trade." (In 1980, Sindona was found guilty of fraud and embezzlement and was sentenced to twenty-five years in prison. Extradited to Italy on a murder charge, he died in his cell of cyanide poisoning. The Sicilian Mafia is widely believed to have ordered his death.)

The research for *Dope, Inc.* also enabled the LaRouchians to gather insights from law enforcement experts and to profile them in the process. One such source was Jack Cusack, former head of international operations for the Drug Enforcement Administration. Cusack had numerous meetings and phone conversations with the LaRouchians, especially with Marilyn James of the *Dope, Inc.* project, between 1978 and 1981. He recalled them as being "well informed" about the narcotics traffic, with excellent law enforcement contacts. "Sometimes they told me things I didn't know, but it turned out it was true," he said.

As a result of their research, the *Dope, Inc.* authors zeroed in on Resorts International, the leisure conglomerate best known for its casino in Atlantic City, New Jersey, and its Paradise Island resort in the Bahamas. "Resorts International equals big-time drug trafficking," alleged the 1979 first edition of *Dope, Inc.*, which also attacked Intertel, a

Resorts-linked private spook outfit headed at the time by rivals of WerBell. Some of the research was turned over to New Jersey state investigators. Willis Carto's *Spotlight,* which carried the NCLC findings in a series in 1978, boasted that the material had helped to persuade the state attorney's office to issue findings sharply critical of Resorts (although the LaRouchian allegation of links to the drug traffic were never substantiated).

When New Jersey authorities were considering a permanent license for the Resorts casino in 1979, the NCLC staged a protest rally in Trenton and vowed a statewide campaign. This effort petered out after the NCLC-controlled Computron Technologies Corporation landed a contract with Resorts to design software for its development division. A Resorts spokesman, contacted in 1980, said Resorts had been unaware of Computron's connection to LaRouche and that the contract was in no sense a payoff. Yet a number of individuals involved in the Computron contract (or their spouses) had previously been involved in the anti-Resorts publicity campaign and intelligence gathering. Gus Kalimtgis, founder and chief stockholder of Computron, was the senior author of *Dope, Inc.* and had been the keynote speaker at the Trenton rally. Yoram Gelman, the Computron systems analyst who wrote the programs for Resorts' Wang VS-2200 computer, was the husband of LaRouche campaign treasurer Felice Merritt Gelman, who co-authored a purported exposé of Resorts ("Organized Crime Goes Legit") in the December 12, 1978, *Executive Intelligence Review.* The article attempted to prove that Resorts controlled many top politicians in New Jersey. Mark Stahlman, a Computron vice president and its registered agent in New Jersey, was formerly the NCLC Security staff's electronics specialist. He was thanked in the acknowledgment section of *Dope, Inc.* for unspecified "contributions" to the book. Fletcher James, Computron vice president in charge of systems, was the husband of Marilyn James, Jack Cusack's contact. *Dope, Inc.*'s authors listed her as one of three key researchers who "supplied the core" of the book.

But the main benefit of the *Dope, Inc.* research perhaps lay not in finding out juicy facts about this or that corporation but in learning the methods of organized criminal activity—methods which could be useful in building a white-collar empire. For instance, the year after *Dope, Inc.*'s publication, one of its authors, NCLC staff economist David Goldman, published a *New Solidarity* article based on information not included in the book. It was a technical discussion of how drug money is supposedly passed "directly through the commercial banking system," and how the intelligence community allegedly participates in covering up such practices. "The international narcotics bosses' agents-in-place in the wire transfer and computer rooms of major banks 'switch' the funds into special 'dummy accounts' at these banks," wrote Goldman. He added that "we know the names of these agents at several large banks, but choose not to name them at this time."

Goldman described the techniques of wire transfer fraud as being "simple-mindedly easy." Curiously, the LaRouche organization had previously been sued by the Bank of Nova Scotia and Chase Manhattan because of mysterious errors in wire transfers between various LaRouchian accounts. In each case the decimal points had been shifted to the right, transforming hundreds of dollars into tens of thousands of dollars. The error happened twice with Chase in a four-day period. The litigation involved instances in which the LaRouchians withdrew the money from the receiving account before the bank discovered the error, then refused to return it. An affidavit by LaRouche aide Warren Hamerman indicated that many such wire transfer glitches had occurred to LaRouchian accounts across the country. Hamerman said the NCLC should not be required to repay the money, because the errors were really donations by individuals who did not wish their identities known. He also charged that the lawsuits were political warfare against his organization instigated by powerful persons. The political wrapping to LaRouche's financial manipulations was already coming in handy.

# Thirty-five

## Las Vegas in the Sky

Former Socialist Workers Party member LaRouche's entrée into organized crime began appropriately with the Teamsters union, which the SWP had helped to build into a powerful force in the 1930s. As usual, LaRouche developed a cover story: He wanted to organize a "grand coalition" of America's industrial producers to smash the power of the "monetarists." Who better could qualify as industrial producers than America's truckdrivers—those Teamster rank and filers whose forebears were the foot soldiers of the SWP-led Minneapolis General Strike in 1934? But LaRouche targeted Teamsters who hadn't done an honest day's work or led a legitimate strike in years—for instance, Jackie Presser, the bloated boss of the Cleveland joint council.

Presser was a close associate of Mitch WerBell's co-defendant in the pot trial, John Nardi. Their dealings went back decades. Nardi had backed the rise of Presser's father, Ohio Conference of Teamsters president William Presser. When slain, Nardi was the secretary of a vending machine local in the Cleveland joint council. His son, John Jr., was on the books of the younger Presser's Local 507.

The LaRouchians were aware of Nardi's links to both Presser and

WerBell. In an attempt to reframe the NCLC's view of Teamster corruption, LaRouche argued that Teamster leaders such as Presser and Nardi were not what they appeared to be, but constituted a "traditionalist" faction in organized labor, a faction of patriotic "nation builders." If they were under attack from the Justice Department/media cabal, it was because they, like the LaRouchians and WerBell, were seen as a threat to the power of the monetarists. *New Solidarity* thus took issue with the mainstream media's depiction of Nardi's slaying as mob-related. *New Solidarity* said it was an FBI hit. (Later that year Presser told author Steve Brill that Nardi's murder was probably drug-related.)

LaRouche warned his followers that Presser and other traditionalist labor leaders were not yet fully conscious of their factional destiny. It was up to the NCLC to tutor them. If a LaRouche follower was sitting in an Italian restaurant with some hoodlum and wondered "What am I doing here?" he could just close his eyes and imagine his dinner partner as a potential convert to Neoplatonic humanism. However, such mind games weren't always necessary. Many LaRouchians were thrilled to associate with tough guys. The New Left of the 1960s had discovered its ultimate fantasy in the guns, bandoliers, and glistening biceps of the Black Panthers. The LaRouchians found something similar in the flowery shirts, diamond rings, and blowtorches of Teamster organizers. Although Operation Mop Up had failed to dispel the self-image of LaRouche's followers as wimps and nerds, associating with the Teamsters provided a vicarious super-masculinity, like being the towel boy for the high school football team. Meanwhile, some Teamster officials may have found a balm for their own insecurities. For the first time, these despised and reviled outlaws of organized labor were getting respect from smart college boys, just like Cesar Chavez.

In 1977–78 the Teamster leadership was facing one of its periodic sieges by the Justice Department and the media while also under fire from rank-and-file reformers. Trucking deregulation meanwhile loomed in Congress as a threat to the union's bargaining power. The LaRouchians told the Teamsters that it was all one big Establishment plot and suggested they take the offensive. Jackie Presser had similar ideas, although not as grandiose, and this provided the LaRouchians with their opening wedge. *New Solidarity* urged the Teamsters to get behind Presser. NCLC members showed up at highway off-ramps and busy intersections in several cities to sell *New Solidarity* and pass out fliers attacking Teamster reform groups. Often they gave out Presser's phone number and urged truckers to call him with their grievances.

In the April–May 1977 *Ohio Teamster*, Presser adopted the LaRouchian rhetoric. "For years we have ignored our enemies," he wrote. "We now find that we must counterattack because it is becoming increasingly clear that these attacks . . . are part of a cleverly orchestrated campaign. . . . We can only assume that it must be those radical forces who seek to destroy democracy and responsible capitalism. We are beginning to see curious alliances among those who attack the [International Brotherhood of Teamsters]. Alliances between self-proclaimed social reformers and self-confessed socialists and powerful money interests including tax-protected foundations. Recall if you will that it was foundations that were revealed as frequent conduits for 'dirty money' from the CIA . . ." Presser's complaint about CIA money can only be regarded as bizarre in light of the Teamsters union's cooperation in the early 1960s in CIA plots to assassinate Fidel Castro.

Presser's connection to the LaRouchians soon became widely known. The Teamsters for a Democratic Union (TDU) newspaper, *Convoy*, repeatedly criticized it. Teamster vice president Harold Gibbons, now deceased, complained both inside the union's highest councils and to the press. In a 1979 telephone interview, he said the circulation of LaRouchian literature in the union was mostly Presser's doing. Two years later, he told *Mother Jones* the alliance was still in place and that Presser seemed to "admire" the LaRouchians. At the 1981 Teamster convention in Las Vegas, Presser openly associated with NCLC guests in defiance of his critics. For their part, the LaRouchians dismissed reports of Presser's organized-crime ties as enemy propaganda. When former mob enforcer Aladena T. ("Jimmy the Weasel") Fratianno testified in the trial of a San Francisco Teamster leader that Presser took orders from "La Cosa Nostra," *New Solidarity* assured NCLC members that this was a total lie.

The LaRouchians also fostered illusions about Presser's father, a twice-convicted felon who had been forced to resign in 1976 as trustee of an IBT pension fund after taking the Fifth in response to questions about alleged loans to mobsters. When the elder Presser died in 1981, *New Solidarity* stated that "the Teamsters not only lost a great leader but this country lost a great man . . . Young people in and out of the labor movement should look to him and his life for inspiration." *New Solidarity* doubtless had an eye to influencing Jackie, whose idolization of his father was well known. But the obituary was also useful in boosting the morale of NCLC members. Bill Presser, it was reported, had dedicated the last months of his life to saving America and the IBT pension fund from the forces of evil. The implication was that he had virtually become a LaRouchian. Although untrue, it reflected a new scheme the LaRouchians had begun discussing in 1980—to "borrow" money from senior citizens. This meant *any* senior citizen, even a racketeer. The rumor spread within the NCLC that Helga had been given a racehorse by an elderly Detroit mobster.

Jackie Presser gained a measure of respectability by backing Reagan for President in 1980. He served on the presidential transition team and inauguration committee—honors which facilitated his rise to the union's presidency in 1983. But the IBT's corruption was simply too visible to be ignored. The Justice Department continued to probe Presser's activities, and in 1985 summoned him before the White House Commission on Organized Crime, where he took the Fifth Amendment fifteen times. (Among the questions ducked was his relationship to an official of a LaRouche-linked Teamster local on Long Island.) The commission's report, released in March 1986, described Presser as having an "extensive record of organized crime associations." Two months later he was indicted in Cleveland on embezzlement and racketeering charges, including the theft of $700,000 from the union to pay "ghost" employees, including John Nardi, Jr.

In November 1986, Anthony ("Fat Tony") Salerno, former boss of the Genovese crime family and reputedly one of the nation's leading heroin traffickers, was indicted in New York. The government charged that he had conspired in 1983 to select Presser as Teamster president. (Presser's predecessor, Roy Williams, had resigned to begin serving a fifty-five-year bribery sentence.) A Salerno associate had met with the heads of organized crime in Cleveland and Chicago to seek their approval. Salerno allegedly had then influenced Teamster officials from the New York metropolitan area and elsewhere to support Presser.

By 1987 the Justice Department was so fed up with Presser and his Mafia friends that it announced a civil racketeering suit to remove the entire Teamster national leadership and place the union in trusteeship.

Presser was by no means the NCLC's only Teamster friend. La-Rouche emissaries in the late 1970s dealt with Teamster officials on all levels, from the locals and joint councils up to the general executive board and the office of then IBT president Frank Fitzsimmons. For instance, there was the connection to Joint Council 73 in New Jersey, controlled by Genovese crime family captain Anthony ("Tony Pro") Provenzano. In September 1977, on the eve of Tony Pro's trial for the murder of a union rival, the Joint Council 73 newspaper published a summary of a New Solidarity International Press Service report on how the Teamsters were being victimized by evil forces. The clear implication was that Tony Pro was also being victimized. When he was found guilty and sentenced to life imprisonment, he continued to control his union fiefdom through his brothers Nuncio and Salvatore ("Sammy Pro"). *New Solidarity* listed Sammy Pro as a sponsor of an NCLC call for a pro-nuclear power demonstration in Trenton. An NCLC member was invited to speak against Teamster reform groups at a local in Jersey City, with no questions from the floor allowed. According to NCLC defectors, LaRouche emissaries met several times with top New Jersey Teamsters to explore deeper cooperation and solicit financial donations. The Provenzanos were urged to guarantee no work stoppages at the construction site of Princeton University's Tokamak experimental fusion reactor. Fusion energy, the LaRouchians told them, was vital to the fight against communism.

A key attraction for many Teamster leaders was the NCLC's propaganda pamphlets. The most popular one, *The Plot to Destroy the Teamsters*, alleged that Wall Street bankers and liberal foundations controlled the TDU and another Teamster reform group, the Professional Drivers Council (PROD). *The Plot* was circulated in locals from Florida to Oregon. According to *New Solidarity*, 46,000 copies had been sold by late 1977. A map purported to show bulk purchases by twenty Teamster locals in twelve states. *The Plot* was followed by *The Deregulation Hoax: The Conspiracy to Destroy the Trucking Industry and the Teamsters*, allegedly written to order for officials of the Southern Conference of Teamsters. Both pamphlets depicted Senator Edward Kennedy as a major villain.

The TDU and PROD carefully traced the circulation of NCLC smear literature. They recorded scores of incidents in which *The Plot* or other NCLC publications were displayed at union hiring halls, passed out at union meetings by business agents, or mailed to members with a cover letter from a local official and/or using union mailing labels. PROD staff attorney Steve Early went to Alaska in 1979. "You know there's no U.S. Labor Party [electoral arm of NCLC] in Fairbanks, Alaska," he said. "But guys were getting up at meetings or calling in to radio talk shows to ask me questions like 'What is your relationship to the Baader-Meinhof gang?' "

The NCLC reported with glee on alleged incidents of violence against reform leaders. An August 1978 *New Solidarity* gloated that "a PRODite was annoying workers at a nuclear plant construction site . . . The Teamsters circulated a petition . . . stating that they didn't want him around because of his 'anti-American, anti-union activities.' The workers' enthusiastic explanations of their just grievances left the PRODite befuddled at the bottom of a garbage pail." A later article suggested a "necktie party" for TDU national organizer Ken Paff.

The most widely circulated pamphlets disguised the NCLC's anti-Semitism behind such euphemisms as "Wall Street speculator" or "British banker." But the NCLC also produced overtly anti-Semitic literature for the Teamsters, apparently unconcerned that Presser was Jewish and that his wife sold Israel bonds. In *The Gang That Killed Hoffa*, circulated in many IBT locals in 1978, LaRouche professed to have solved the mystery of the former Teamster chief's disappearance: "We may not know the names of the thugs sent to do the killings [sic], but we know who sent them . . . The guys who did the hiring are walking around . . . as the 'most respected persons' of the international Zionist community." The pamphlet depicted Jews as inveterate plotters: "The rituals of entry into the synagogue . . . include elements of a conspiratorial 'password' system."

Teamster officials typically played a peekaboo game with the LaRouchians. As one Teamster dissident explained: "You hear about a business agent passing out [U.S.] Labor Party literature—you even have eyewitnesses—but when you ask him, he denies it." And TDU's Paff said: "It's an old tactic. The union leaders don't want to look bad, so they get outsiders to come in and conduct their smear campaigns for them, calling us Communists, drug pushers, homosexuals. When the people who are being smeared complain, the union leaders simply disclaim any responsibility." What Paff described the Teamster bosses as doing was exactly what the Reagan administration and the Star Wars lobby would do: Make full use of LaRouche's talents, but deny it when accused.

In the fall of 1977, Frank Fitzsimmons began weaving LaRouche's Rockefeller conspiracy theories into his speeches, and even considered working with the LaRouchians directly. His reasoning was eminently practical: These highly effective smear artists were Presser's creatures. If Presser could use them against union reformers, he also could use them against Fitzsimmons. The Teamster president thus proposed to co-opt them to be his own propaganda hit squad. When the Teamsters' staff attorneys learned of this scheme, they were dismayed and brought in Chicago journalist Chip Berlet, one of the authors of *Brownshirts of the Seventies,* an anti-LaRouche pamphlet. "I went right up to Fitzsimmons' floor to the legal section," said Berlet. "I spent hours with the attorneys laying out *everything.*" The attorneys were then able to convince Fitzsimmons that the LaRouchians were too volatile to be relied on. Fitzsimmons also received complaints from members of the IBT general executive board and from the TDU. In January 1978 the board passed a resolution disclaiming any association with the NCLC, although Presser continued to work with them.

Even apart from Presser's attitude, Teamster reformers were skeptical of the sincerity of the anti-LaRouche resolution. *Convoy* (April 1978) speculated that the executive board had simply wanted the resolution on record in case anyone filed a libel suit regarding the contents of *The Plot.* However, Fitzsimmons' staff issued its own 22-page attack on the reformers that spring, repeating many of *The Plot*'s allegations. Former PROD research director Bob Windrem speculated that the LaRouchians had written it. Teamster communications director Duke Zeller, who distributed the piece, claimed not to know who had written it.

The LaRouchians set about proving they could snoop as skillfully as they could smear. After infiltrating the June 1978 national conference of PROD, they prepared a 32-page report for Fitzsimmons. The document described the conference in detail, and included "background interviews" elicited under false pretenses with PROD leaders and Justice Department organized-crime strike force officials. Containing only modest doses of LaRouche's ideology, the report recommended a strong IBT counterattack against PROD and other enemies, along with overtures to the NAACP to construct a grass-roots coalition for jobs and economic development.

One by one, the Teamster executive board members forgot about the anti-LaRouche resolution. International vice president Louis Peick's home local in Chicago used LaRouchian smear literature to fend off an election challenge from a reform slate. According to PROD's *Dispatch*, Peick recommended the LaRouchians' services to other locals. As high-level Teamsters in other cities also recommended them, they became a fixture. Whenever mob-linked union incumbents were threatened by an insurgent slate, an NCLC "truth squad" was always on call to brief the membership on the alleged conspiracy of Communists, PROD, TDU, Ralph Nader, and Jewish liberal foundations. "Their propaganda was very, very effective," said Bob Windrem. "They mimicked our [PROD's] style of using specific documentation. Their facts were usually wrong, but some guys believed them. We had panic calls from a lot of our supporters." Often, the NCLC provided campaign literature for incumbents. A federal district judge in Oakland, California, ordered a new election for Local 70 after a trucking school owner linked to the local's president purchased and distributed thousands of copies of NCLC pamphlets calling members of the reform slate dope pushers and terrorists.

On Long Island, the NCLC helped the leadership of Local 282 fend off a challenge by PROD members. The local's president was John Cody, a four-time-convicted felon and a friend of the late Mafia boss Carlo Gambino. One official of the local was Harold Gross, a former Murder, Inc., associate who had worked closely with Santos Trafficante, Jr., in Florida in the 1950s. An NCLC truth squad briefed Cody and his cronies, helped them produce smear leaflets, and addressed a union educational meeting a week before the election. After the insurgents were defeated (in an election marred by several acts of intimidation), *New Solidarity* quoted Cody as saying to the truth squad, "You gave us the ammunition to win." The local's leadership then purchased a $500 subscription to NCLC's *Executive Intelligence Review* to be sent to Cody. When the PROD members found out about this donation they filed a complaint of election irregularity with the U.S. Department of Labor.

An investigator went to NCLC/U.S. Labor Party headquarters in Manhattan, but was not allowed in. The matter was dropped after USLP attorney David Heller denied that there was any connection between his client and New Solidarity International Press Service, the publisher of *EIR*. In fact, these entities shared the same offices and telephone switchboard, the same attorney (Heller), overlapping personnel, and a common source of control—the NCLC National Executive Committee.

While campaigning to reelect hoodlums, the NCLC also launched the Michigan Anti-Drug Coalition, the first of several state organizations that would merge into the National Anti-Drug Coalition. Former smuggling defendant WerBell sent a message hailing the founding conference as a "profound step towards restoring this nation to health and prosperity." An officer of Cody's Local 282 co-signed a telegram pledging "100 percent support to your coalition's efforts to clean up the drug trade." The hypocrisy reached its height when Teamster general organizer Rolland McMaster showed up at a Michigan ADC conference in May, after meeting privately with LaRouche. McMaster called on IBT officials across the nation to support their local anti-drug coalitions, and he endorsed LaRouche as the anti-drug candidate for President.

The NCLC hailed McMaster as "one of the most respected . . . voices in all of organized labor." In fact, McMaster was one of Detroit's most notorious hoodlums. In 1959 he had taken the Fifth Amendment more than fifty times before the McClellan Committee. He later went to federal prison after being convicted of thirty-two counts of labor extortion. When he met the LaRouchians, he was, among other things, the power behind a truckers' local in the Meli crime family-dominated steel-hauling industry.

Dan Moldea's *The Hoffa Wars*, the definitive study of midwestern Teamster corruption from the 1950s through the 1970s, describes McMaster as having been Hoffa's top leg breaker and an associate of some of the nation's most notorious crime bosses. The book devotes more attention to McMaster than to any other living Teamster hoodlum, describing numerous beatings, bombings, and other acts of mayhem carried out by his associates. Moldea cites the statement of Edward Partin (the former IBT official responsible for Hoffa's jury-tampering conviction) that McMaster was "a personal Hoffa liaison to Meyer Lansky, Santos Trafficante, the Dorfman family and the syndicate in Chicago, and the Genovese mob of New Jersey and New York."

According to Moldea, the earliest contact between McMaster and heroin overlord Trafficante was in 1957, when Hoffa sent McMaster to Miami to set up Local 320. The local, headed by Harold Gross, "served as a front for many of the mob's gambling and narcotics activities. Trafficante . . . occupied a small office in the union hall."

McMaster later became the head of Local 299, Hoffa's home local, where his depredations prompted dissidents to adopt the slogan "Take the Hood out of Brotherhood." In 1972 he was picked by Fitzsimmons to head up a Central States task force to organize steel haulers. According to a series in the *Detroit Free Press,* the organizing drive was little more than a shakedown racket employing ex-cons and other thugs armed with blowtorches and dynamite. It cost the IBT treasury $1.3 million, but organized fewer than 800 drivers.

The NCLC regarded McMaster's endorsement of LaRouche as a major coup. They circulated his statement throughout the Midwest in hundreds of thousands of leaflets and launched a "Teamster Committee to Elect LaRouche President." The officers of TCELP, as listed with the Federal Election Commission, were Detroit NCLC leaders, not members of the IBT. Teamster Joint Council 43 in Detroit, led by enemies of McMaster, promptly passed a resolution condemning LaRouche. Frank Fitzsimmons had to join the denunciatory chorus after a TCELP leaflet speculated that he too might endorse LaRouche. The speculation was not entirely wacky in light of Fitzsimmons' prior dealings with the LaRouchians, his aides' telephone chats with them, and candidate LaRouche's visit to IBT headquarters earlier that year. ("It took place; I was there," McMaster said in a phone interview.) Yet Fitzsimmons was angered. He sent a letter to the LaRouche campaign calling the leaflets "false and misleading" and demanding that it stop using the Teamsters' name. His letter was printed in *The International Teamster* for union members at large to read.

LaRouche's campaign committee sent Fitzsimmons an unctuous reply: "We applaud your decision and that of the Honourable Executive Board to refuse to endorse any presidential candidate at this time . . ." The letter gently suggested that loyal Teamster ally LaRouche be considered on his merits at the appropriate moment. When this elicited no response, LaRouche followed up with an open letter to Fitzsimmons implying that he fully understood the strong pressures being exerted on the IBT from "the White House, the Kennedy machine, and [Texas] Governor Connally" to stay away from the LaRouche campaign. LaRouche advised Fitzsimmons not to succumb to this divide-and-conquer tactic. Were not the IBT and the NCLC in the same boat as victims of the liberal establishment's "lying defamation and vicious persecution"?

With his typical audacity, LaRouche invited the leaders of America's largest union to give up their illusions about placating the power structure and join him in the fight for a new political order in which they would be safe forever from organized crime strike forces. He described the IBT as the "potential backbone" of this "American System": "When the IBT leads the way on issues of fundamental importance to this nation and its people, the building trades and other unions will follow—some quicker, some slower, but they will move. With such a nucleus of organized forces, farmers, entrepreneurs, minority forces, and others will group themselves together with such a force." The ultimate payoff would be "thousands" of executive posts for Teamsters in a LaRouche administration.

It is not recorded what Fitzsimmons thought of this plan for a Greater Las Vegas in the sky, but LaRouche's letter did suggest an interesting vision of McMaster's goon squads transformed into a secret police to shake down the entire economy, not just a few trucking bosses. *New Solidarity* had earlier suggested that the Jews were the main stumbling block to such a plan. One article called for a national network of "traditionalist American System-oriented" trade union leaders to fight against AFL-CIO leader Lane Kirkland "and other Anti-Defamation League linked circles . . ." Another article criticized union officials who hesitated "to come to grips with the Social Democratic and Zionist lobby traitors" in labor's ranks. (What LaRouche had in store for the so-called Zionists had already been spelled out in *New Solidarity* using such terms as "immediate elimination.")

# Thirty-six

## Fishing for Piranhas

No sooner was the ink dry on Fitzsimmons' letter in *The International Teamster* than the peekaboo game started again. The Local 299 leaders in Detroit who had supported the anti-LaRouche (really, anti-McMaster) resolution continued to allow stacks of *New Solidarity* in the union hall and copies of *EIR* in the waiting room of the business office. McMaster continued his support of LaRouche, although in a low-profile way. In a January 1980 telephone interview, he described LaRouche as "the most intelligent of all the [presidential] candidates." As for Fitzsimmons' letter, McMaster said that "individual locals can support whoever they like . . . The Teamster union is one of the most democratic goddamn outfits in America." He claimed that some locals were considering an endorsement of LaRouche and that he personally had discussed it with union officials in Florida. "People like it that he's in the Democratic Party now," McMaster explained, referring to La-Rouche's decision in the fall of 1979 to jettison the U.S. Labor Party and enter the Democratic primaries.

McMaster's support for LaRouche may have had self-interested motives. A Federal Election Commission schedule of receipts and expenditures filed by Citizens for LaRouche (CFL) shows that a few days after opening LaRouche's New Hampshire campaign headquarters in September 1979, CFL began making payments to Project Consulting Services Co. of Southfield, Michigan. The firm was headed by John R. Ferris, McMaster's closest friend and—according to *The Hoffa Wars*—his reputed business partner in several ventures. CFL paid Project Consulting over $96,000 during 1979–80 to oversee LaRouche's New Hampshire primary bid. One of the experts sent in by Ferris was a former Michigan state senator, Edward J. Robinson, who had just been sentenced to six months in federal prison for his role in a $3 million Florida land swindle. While appealing his case (he lost the appeal in 1981), he directed CFL's volunteer operations and handled press relations.

Ferris says he was reluctant to get involved with the LaRouche campaign but they offered him a fee so high he "couldn't say no." He previously had done consulting for other candidates, but set up Project Consulting exclusively to work for LaRouche. However, the latter adopted tactics that alienated the voters instead of following Ferris' pragmatic advice. After New Hampshire, Ferris stopped working for LaRouche. He said that CFL owed him $200,000, although he doubted he would ever collect. (The CFL's FEC filings never listed this debt.)

Ferris and Robinson were not the only colorful characters attracted to the New Hampshire campaign. According to a former top LaRouche aide, the NCLC leadership paid $100,000 to Manchester businessman George Kattar to attempt to fix the election in Dixville Knotch, traditionally the first place in the state to have its election returns reported. The FBI regards Kattar as a leader of organized crime in New Hampshire. At a U.S. Senate hearing in 1971, a witness identified him as a loan shark and said that his business was nicknamed the "Piranha Company."

LaRouche later referred to the vote-fixing idea as the "have a hundred-dollar bill" plan, and blamed its failure on an aide. NCLC defectors say it had to have been LaRouche's own idea, pointing out that no policy decisions were ever made in the NCLC without his approval. The cash to pay Kattar supposedly came from a Bank Bumiputra Malaysia loan involving several LaRouche business fronts. In 1981 the bank filed suit in New York State Supreme Court after the LaRouchians defaulted on the notes—just the beginning of what would be a decade of loan defaults. Kattar was interviewed about the incident for NBC-TV's *First Camera* in 1984, and acknowledged that the LaRouchians had asked him for help in the primary. He said two of his employees worked for LaRouche for a month, but quit when they were not paid the full amount promised. He denied personally receiving any money from

LaRouche. In 1986 Kattar was indicted in Boston on extortion charges; the victim, ironically, was the cultlike Church of Scientology. The FBI then raided Kattar's home and office as part of an arms-smuggling probe, seizing ammunition and weapons.

The Federal Election Commission audit division reported in 1981 that LaRouche had overspent his allowable maximum in New Hampshire and should pay back $112,000 of his matching funds to the U.S. Treasury. Several matters regarding LaRouche's campaign financing were forwarded to the FEC's general counsel for further investigation. Citizens for LaRouche (CFL) counterattacked with a suit in federal court in Manhattan seeking to stop the FEC from questioning LaRouche contributors. CFL's attorney in this action was Mayer Morganroth of Southfield, Michigan. According to *The Hoffa Wars,* Morganroth is a former business partner of Ferris and has represented McMaster in legal matters. In the mid-1970s Morganroth and Ferris (with McMaster allegedly as a silent partner) owned Leland House, a Detroit hotel which provided living quarters and part-time jobs for two of McMaster's muscle men during the months of fierce Teamster infighting prior to Hoffa's disappearance.

In 1977 Morganroth's name surfaced in connection with a Miami Organized Crime Strike Force investigation into a dubious loan by the mob-controlled Teamsters' Central States Pension Fund to the Indico Corporation, a financially ailing Florida real estate firm in which Morganroth was a principal stockholder. This investigation was a spin-off from a strike force probe into the business dealings of the Southeastern Florida district council of the Laborers International Union. (One upshot of the Laborers probe was a racketeering indictment of Santos Trafficante, Jr., and fifteen co-conspirators, including a Miami lawyer who had helped arrange the Indico loan.) According to *The Wall Street Journal,* Morganroth was also under investigation in 1977 by the Detroit Strike Force, as part of a probe into "alleged organized crime proceeds being funneled from Canada into the U.S." He denied any wrongdoing.

Morganroth became one of the LaRouche organization's chief lawyers. He defended them in the 1983 anti-racketeering civil suit brought by creditor Michael Hudson, helped them incorporate a number of fund-raising fronts, and was part of their defense team in the Boston credit-card fraud trial in 1988.

Apart from the "Southfield, Michigan, advisers," as LaRouche called them, a number of Teamster officials continued to work with LaRouche. The president of an Illinois local was reported by *New Solidarity* to have run on LaRouche's delegate slate in the state's 1980 Democratic primary, and a "Special Teamster Edition" of CFL's *Campaign*

*News* that spring showed a picture of LaRouche with Bill Bounds, president of Illinois' Joint Council 65. Bounds was quoted as saying, while introducing LaRouche to a monthly council meeting: "I want you to meet my dear friend Lyn LaRouche, who's been a friend of labor and of the Teamsters for years . . . He deserves your support for the Presidency." The back of the newsletter contained a picture of Rolland McMaster and the full text of his May 1979 endorsement.

LaRouche also sought campaign support from the mob-dominated Laborers Union. In his initial approach he addressed the legitimate economic worries of the Laborers and other construction unions, as well as the special problems of indicted leaders. As in his support for the Teamsters on the question of trucking deregulation, he seemed to make sense in a demagogic way. He talked about the slump in housing starts due to high interest rates (chairman of the Federal Reserve Board Paul Volcker's fault) and the slowdown in nuclear power plant construction (the fault of hippies, Yippies, Quakers, and Communists). LaRouche suggested he'd string up Volcker, crush the environmentalists, and build hundreds of nuclear plants. Several weeks before the Democratic convention, a group of California building trades officials, including several from the Laborers, announced their support for LaRouche and launched a campaign committee. *New Solidarity* reported a similar committee being formed in Ohio. This triggered a memo from Alexander E. Barkan, national director of the AFL-CIO's Committee on Political Education (COPE), to union leaders around the country. Noting the reports that "some local union and local council officials not only have attended meetings convened by LaRouche, but have permitted their names to be used," Barkan warned that the LaRouche organization was "anti-labor, anti-Catholic, anti-Semitic and anti-minorities."

However, LaRouche had a way to get around Barkan by coming to the aid of indicted labor racketeers whom the AFL-CIO had washed its hands of. In 1980–81 the Justice Department closed in on a number of top labor leaders from coast to coast. Building trades officials, including Laborers president Angelo Fosco, were indicted, as were a number of the most notorious Teamster leaders. In New York, International Longshoremen's Association vice president Anthony Scotto was indicted and convicted. The bribery sting operations code-named Brilab (bribery-labor) resulted in indictments in the South and Southwest of union leaders, public officials, and major crime lords such as Trafficante (Florida), Carlos Marcello (Gulf coast), and Anthony Accardo (Chicago). This gave LaRouche an opportunity to expand his connections. His followers could do publicity work for the defendants—encouraging a political fight-back against sting operations on civil liberties grounds—and also cadge investigative assignments to probe the backgrounds of federal witnesses and prosecutors. According to ex-NCLC members, some LaRouchians began to talk not just to Teamster hoodlums but directly to the organized crime families. They had now established their calling card.

# Thirty-seven

# How to Win Friends and Influence Hoodlums

To maintain contacts with persons linked to organized crime, La-Rouche had to justify it first to his own followers. This turned out to be not very hard to do: LaRouche simply announced that "many of the persons and circles which are reputed to be associated with the Mafia are good people." These "good" mobsters, he explained, personally disapprove of the drug traffic but are infected with a pragmatism that causes them to continue to make deals and keep peace with the Zionist ("Drug Mafia") wing of organized crime. LaRouche claimed to have met with a "top official" of the Laborers Union to convince him to break with the Zionist drug pushers, but without success. This official and other members of the "good" faction refused to understand that the Brilab prosecutions were an attempt by the "bad" Mafia in alliance with the government to destroy the good Mafia and take over the latter's empire. The good Mafia could defeat this Zionist plot only by taking the offensive—by turning the courtroom fight into a political fight. But because of its pragmatism, the good Mafia was reluctant to do this. The NCLC therefore would have to do it for them. Indeed, the NCLC was their "last political bastion of resistance." If it should fail in its historic task, then the "honest trade-unionists" linked to the good Mafia (e.g., the Laborers and Teamsters) would "be picked off by [Justice Department] task-forces like flies."

This was all for internal NCLC consumption. Doubtless the proposition was put to the organization's new "Sun Belt allies" in a more businesslike fashion. Certainly in the NCLC's public attacks on Brilab there was no mention of good or bad Mafias, only of honest trade unionists. This was most noticeable in the two cases involving really big organized crime figures: the New Orleans indictment of Marcello for conspiring to bribe public officials and the Miami indictment of Trafficante, Accardo, Fosco, and thirteen co-conspirators for labor racketeering. *New Solidarity* carefully avoided mentioning the names of Marcello, Trafficante, and Accardo. Instead, it mentioned only the indicted union officials, whom it described as victims of "the most widespread witch-hunt ever attempted against American labor."

Once again, LaRouche was using code language—"labor" for Mafia, just as earlier he had used "British" for Jewish—to sanitize a morally repulsive message. He was also borrowing Jimmy Hoffa's old tactic of depicting racketeering prosecutions as an employer attack on the labor movement, akin to strikebreaking and lockouts. This pseudo-militant dodge used class-against-class rhetoric to divert the labor movement's (and the public's) attention away from the real issues at trial.

In March 1981, New Jersey Teamster boss Tony Provenzano's brothers, Sammy and Nuncio, went on trial in Newark federal court for racketeering. Despite the massive evidence of Mafia control of many New Jersey locals, and irrespective of Tony Pro's multiple convictions for murder, extortion, and racketeering (he was serving a life sentence), *New Solidarity* portrayed all three brothers as labor martyrs. The trial of Sammy and Nuncio was a "shocking farce." The Justice Department was "attempting a classic frame-up." The jury was presented with the "spectacle" of "bought-and-paid-for" witnesses. When Nuncio was convicted, this was proof of the "near impossibility" of labor leaders receiving a fair trial in the face of the Justice Department's "politically motivated" vendetta. (Nuncio was sentenced to ten years. Sammy Pro was found guilty in a subsequent racketeering trial and sentenced to four years. In 1984, federal judge Harold Ackerman ordered that their Local 560 be placed in the hands of a trustee. The Provenzanos had engaged, he said, in "a multifaceted orgy of criminal activity.")

Another of *New Solidarity*'s alleged witch-hunt victims was Frank Sheeran, president of Teamster Local 326 in Wilmington, Delaware. This was the same Frank Sheeran who, according to federal investigators, drove to the Pontiac, Michigan, airport on the morning of July 30, 1975, the day Jimmy Hoffa disappeared, to pick up three Genovese crime family enforcers. In September 1979 a Philadelphia grand jury charged Sheeran with two murders, four attempted murders, embezzlement, and a bombing, naming Pennsylvania crime bosses Russell Bufalino and Angelo Bruno as unindicted co-conspirators. Although Sheeran was acquitted in this trial, he was indicted shortly afterward in Wilmington on labor racketeering and mail fraud charges. *New Solidarity* denounced the Delaware prosecution as a "frame-up attempt" and the chief government witness as a "rat." Failing to inform its readers of the substance of the charges in either the Philadelphia or the Wilmington case, *New Solidarity* hailed Sheeran as "a labor leader committed to policies of growth and development for the United States." Sheeran and NCLC Baltimore leader Larry Freeman held a press conference. After complaining about the alleged frame-up, Sheeran gave Freeman the floor to attack the International Socialists, a small non-Communist sect active in the TDU. Freeman accused the group of plotting with the government to undermine Sheeran and other "respected and traditional labor leaders." But in October 1981 a federal jury found Sheeran guilty on eleven counts, including conspiracy, labor racketeering, mail fraud, obstruction of justice, and taking bribes from an employer. He was sentenced to eighteen years in federal prison.

While engaging in this dubious propaganda campaign in 1981, the LaRouchians were gaining *Executive Intelligence Review* interviews with cabinet members and top Republican lawmakers in Washington. *EIR* obtained an interview with Senator Orrin Hatch (R.-Utah), chairman of the Senate Labor Committee. The interviewer asked Hatch leading questions about Brilab in an attempt to elicit answers that could be useful to the anti-Brilab campaign or that would show that the LaRouchians had clout with the senator. But Hatch artfully ducked the questions and gave innocuous answers.

The NCLC launched the Committee Against Brilab and Abscam (CABA) to solicit funds from people with a vested interest in stymieing the federal strike forces. (Abscam, short for "Arab scam," was the code name for a series of FBI bribery sting operations targeting members of Congress and utilizing an FBI agent dressed as an Arab sheikh.) A press statement by the Detroit-and-Houston-based committee announced that a "prestigious roster of labor leaders" had joined CABA's advisory board. The list was headed by Rolland McMaster, followed by IBT Joint Council 65 leader Bill Bounds (who later said his name had been used without permission) and several construction union officials.

The advisory board's "Statement of Principles" included an affirmation of support for a CABA "Trust" which would solicit funds to provide defendants with legal assistance and to "research background material and provide investigators for attorneys and publications."

(The "investigators," naturally, were to come from the NCLC Security staff in New York and the McMaster-linked Detroit NCLC.) The first public advocacy pamphlet was entitled *Brilab-Abscam: Union-Busting in America.* Filled with vigorous denunciations of "snitches" and "stool-pigeons," it warned that Brilab was part of an undeclared war against the "American System," orchestrated by the Trilateral Commission and other Eastern Establishment forces. "The targeted victims . . . are America's unionized workers and their friends in business and politics—the machinery that makes America work," the pamphlet claimed, adding that "no crime in America . . . is more organized than that run by the U.S. Justice Department [and] its 13 Organized Crime Strike Forces." Ironically, this pamphlet was a reprint from *Investigative Leads,* a newsletter produced in the same offices as the National Anti-Drug Coalition's *War on Drugs* magazine. The editor of *Investigative Leads* at the time, Michelle Steinberg, doubled as an editor of *War on Drugs.*

One of CABA's first public activities was an October 1980 press conference in New Orleans, a city where the LaRouchians had never been active before. The event can be seen as a gesture of support for Marcello, the most important local Brilab defendant. NCLC member Tim Richardson told reporters that CABA already had raised $35,000, mostly from national labor unions. He declined to say if any of the New Orleans defendants had accepted the group's offers of aid, but apparently they had, because a second New Orleans press conference was staged in March 1981. Richardson was again the spokesman, and called on President Reagan to end Brilab. He also called the Justice Department's principal witness a "pathological liar." The following August a federal jury found Marcello guilty of conspiring to bribe a public official to gain millions of dollars in state insurance contracts. He was sentenced to seven years in prison. *New Solidarity* complained that he had been "entrapped."

Marcello's co-defendants included his longtime friend I. Irving Davidson, who was acquitted on all counts. Davidson, a self-described Washington "door opener and arranger," had been in touch with the LaRouchians since the mid-1970s and was regarded by them as a key contact. But he recalls being surprised when they showed up in New Orleans. "I never introduced them to people there," he asserted, adding that neither he nor Marcello became involved with the Brilab committee, which he said was financed by "a certain branch of the Teamsters." Davidson said his own frequent meetings with the LaRouchians were merely to pick their brains and purchase intelligence reports. He admitted that Mitch WerBell had occasionally been present at these meetings, but only in a security capacity.

Although Davidson denied ever introducing the LaRouchians to anyone big, he was a useful contact simply to chat with. He knew the Teamsters well, having been Jimmy Hoffa's public relations man. In 1959, he joined with Hoffa and Bill Presser to sell arms to Fulgencio Batista on behalf of the CIA. In the 1960 presidential election, he served as Hoffa's emissary to top aides of Richard Nixon and Democratic vice presidential candidate Lyndon Johnson. He later received a $13.5 million real estate loan from the Central States Pension Fund.

The LaRouchians also offered their services to Brilab defendants in Houston. An indicted Operating Engineers Union official accepted, and his attorney told the *Houston Post* that information gathered by CABA against a prosecution witness would be used in the defense. Other defendants turned them down. A spokesman for the Harris County (Houston) AFL-CIO denounced CABA as the tool of "cheap muscle people." By the summer of 1981, CABA's Houston phone number was disconnected and the group henceforth was run solely out of Detroit, where its phone number was listed under the name and address of one Larry Sherman, an NCLC leader who had just moved from Boston. Sherman was a strange choice to lead a campaign against alleged government frame-ups and vendettas. Four years earlier, the Boston media had exposed how he tried to frame members of the Clamshell Alliance, an antinuclear group, by feeding the New Hampshire State Police reports of nonexistent terrorist plots.

The Detroit NCLC began publishing the *American Labor Beacon*, a pro-CABA newsletter. Edited by Sherman, the first issue was mailed free to Teamster and AFL-CIO locals throughout the country. Union leaders were then called and asked to subscribe. The *Beacon* asked its readers to donate to CABA. It said that although direct contributions to CABA could not lawfully be made from union funds, such funds *could* be applied to the purchase of "educational materials." Potential contributors were assured that CABA was *"not* obligated to report donors" to the government.

The *Beacon* featured a "Rat of the Month" column targeting prosecutors such as Thomas Puccio of the Brooklyn Organized Crime Strike Force and various witnesses from the Federal Witness Protection Program (collectively referred to as "slime from the gutter"). The newsletter also announced a "Rat of the Decade" award for Walter Sheridan, former chief investigator for the McClellan Committee. Quoting Jimmy Hoffa, the *Beacon* called Sheridan a "slimy, sleazy rat."

CABA and the *Beacon* were closely linked to Renaissance Printing, the Detroit firm incorporated by the NCLC's local leader, Kenneth Dalto, and two associates. For several years Renaissance had done printing work for the NCLC and the Michigan Anti-Drug Coalition, as well as the Teamsters and other outside clients. Gradually, the Detroit LaRouche network had been drawn into the activities of Rolland Mc-Master, developing what *New Solidarity* would later allege were an "array of mafioso connections." The various McMaster-Dalto-NCLC forays into Teamster politics were the surface manifestation of this alliance. The president of Renaissance, Scott Elliot, had been the treasurer of the "Teamster" Committee to elect LaRouche President, which circulated McMaster's 1979 endorsement of LaRouche. Elliot later worked with Larry McHenry, a McMaster sidekick, on a scheme to get TDU leader Pete Camarata expelled from Local 299 for allegedly violating its bylaws; they succeeded in getting him placed on probation. The two also appeared on local television to attack the TDU.

In 1980, Renaissance obtained a major infusion of capital which LaRouche later alleged came from organized crime. Elliot and his associates then launched a national financial printing operation under the name Computype, with headquarters at Renaissance. They opened branches in seven cities, leased state-of-the-art equipment for facsimile transmission, and began soliciting business from energy companies in the South and Southwest. Like other financial printers, much of their work included circulating confidential drafts of tender offers and stock prospectuses to principals involved in the transactions.

As of 1981, Renaissance claimed 150 accounts, but its growth proved to be a disaster for LaRouche. It gave Dalto and his associates a large degree of independence from the NCLC national office. They began to chafe under political directives from New York that seemed always to clash with their new interest in getting rich. They bought new cars and affected the flowery shirts popular among Teamster officials. They studied books on franchising. Elliot even asked his attorneys for a crash course in offshore banking.

LaRouche became suspicious in the summer of 1981. He had cracked down on Computron six months previously for placing profits before politics, and he now had some probing questions to put to Dalto and Elliot. The latter could see the handwriting on the wall. They planned to break away from the NCLC before LaRouche could drive a wedge between them and the Detroit rank and file. It is not known if McMaster provided them with advice based on his vast experience in the Byzantine world of Teamster politics. But so well did the Detroit faction plan its revolt that LaRouche and his vaunted Security staff were taken totally by surprise. In late October, LaRouche received a letter signed by almost the entire membership of the Detroit organization and by Computype employees in Chicago, Atlanta, Houston, and Boston—a total of 117 NCLC members—announcing their resignation from the NCLC and "all other LaRouche-affiliated organizations."

LaRouche responded with a flurry of internal memos intended to whip up his loyalists for a counterpunch against the Detroit "country and western" faction, so named because of their alleged fondness for popular instead of classical music. He claimed that the split was instigated by Jewish financiers and mobsters, above all the Detroit financier Max Fisher. The "Fisher-centered banking apparatus" had sunk its "dope-soaked teeth" into the Dalto group. Also blamed was the Anti-Defamation League of B'nai B'rith: "We know how the ADL officials and others have been playing the game . . . We now know exactly how to proceed to crush this murderous filth."

LaRouche's memos that fall included amazingly indiscreet revelations about the 1980 New Hampshire campaign and the alleged mob role at Computype. LaRouche mentioned the hiring of Ferris in New Hampshire, the scheme to influence voters through a policy of "have a hundred-dollar bill," the pressure on the NCLC of " 'advisers' in Southfield, Michigan," and alleged contacts with " 'wise guys' assets" in Atlanta. He also discussed how the NCLC had deliberately developed a " 'Mafia Connections' self-image" during the 1980 campaign and had used threats of Mafia violence to keep the membership in line. LaRouche said this policy had been a mistake, but he blamed it all on Dalto and Gus Kalimtgis. (NCLC defectors say it really was LaRouche's idea.) LaRouche was a bit nervous about the long-range consequences: "Under no circumstances discuss . . . the use of the 'Mafia Violence' aura outside of the ranks of the membership . . . ," he instructed NCLC members. "If you were to discuss this publicly, we would prematurely trigger [the] possibility of legal action."

However, LaRouche and his followers continued to use the very rhetoric he was criticizing. An NCLC memo boasted of a scheme to make trouble for Dalto with the Mafia. "It has been learned," the memo said, "that . . . Dalto was keeping a double set of [Computype] books to rip off a business contact in Chicago." The latter was described as a "so-called Mafia boss" and Dalto's "partner." LaRouche himself said: "Let the 'Mafia' rub out Ken . . . Naturally, we shall not be reticent in mentioning to certain circles certain facts now documented in our possession. Let the creep sweat. Let him run. Let him choose his hiding place."

Associates of Dalto say the double set of books was a LaRouche fabrication, although they worried at the time that LaRouche might have concocted false evidence. No physical harm came to Dalto either from mobsters or from the LaRouchians. Yet there can be no doubt of the ferocity of LaRouche's fantasies as reflected in various jokes included in the NCLC daily briefings. In one joke Dalto ends up committing suicide. In another the "Chicago Mafia" plants a bomb under his

"Lincoln Continental." In a third he arrives at the gates of Hell "wearing a new, custom-fitted pair of cement overshoes."

LaRouche also warned his loyalists that they'd better stay loyal: "Anyone who opposes my orders will, in the moral sense, be shot on the spot for insubordination . . . I am the 'boss.' " The statement confirmed the observation by NCLC defector Dave Phillips, in a document earlier that year, that LaRouche, with his emphasis on personal "fealty" and " 'ecumenical' . . . Sun Belt ventures," had transformed the NCLC into a comic-opera version of a "Sicilian family business."

The Dalto faction's enterprises flourished after the split. Renaissance expanded to almost a hundred employees and attracted Drexel-Burnham and other Wall Street investment firms as clients. It also continued to print Teamster smear literature, although no longer a unionized shop. Dalto and his partners bought out "Frank Edwards" (the Chicago investor) but McMaster remained as a behind-the-scenes influence. Renaissance executives went on vacations with him, and the firm eventually moved into a building he had purchased, where he kept his eye on the accounts. But there were also problems. Elliot and two other former LaRouchians sued Dalto for control. Two satellite offices had to be closed. Finally, in 1985 Renaissance entered Chapter 11 bankruptcy, laying off a majority of its staff.

The Dalto faction found it difficult to break with the old habit of compulsive deceptiveness, since, indeed, it was as much a habit of their hoodlum friends as of the NCLC. When the *Beacon* editors received a letter from a building trades official asking them to "clarify" their relationship to LaRouche, their answer, published in the first *Beacon* issue after the split, blithely ignored their ten-year history of participation in the NCLC. "The *Beacon* has been dedicated to defending labor from its enemies within and without," they wrote. "After investigating [!] the LaRouche organization for a period of time [!], we have come to the conclusion that he and his organization fall into the category of 'enemies without.' "

Soon thereafter close cronies of Dalto began to feed investigative reporters tidbits about LaRouche, but avoided any revelations about their own faction's past. Although they claimed they were through with extremist politics and only wanted to operate their commercial enterprises in peace, they continued to run smear campaigns against union reformers. These activities were conducted through a variety of pre-split and post-split fronts: the Beacon News Service, Inform America, Environmental News Service, the Parity Foundation, Union Communications, and Intellico (the latter a self-styled private intelligence organization).

In 1982 Larry Sherman prepared an Intellico report for United Mine

Workers Union president Sam Church regarding the latter's opponent in the upcoming union election, Richard Trumka. Purportedly based on a trip through the coal district and interviews with people in and around Trumka's campaign, the report included unsubstantiated allegations that he was linked to Communists. The report helped Church gain support from gullible outsiders, including the Moral Majority and *Penthouse* publisher Bob Guccione. A major role in soliciting this outside support was played by Michael Doud Gill, a member of the Republican National Committee and a prominent Washington power broker. Meanwhile, Senator Orrin Hatch announced an investigation of charges (apparently Intellico's) of alleged subversive influences in the UMW and other unions. All this had no impact on the union rank and file, which gave Trumka a resounding victory.

The Dalto group became involved in Detroit Teamster elections in 1983, when international vice president Robert Holmes, a former rival of Rolland McMaster, faced a stiff election challenge from the TDU for control of his power base, Local 337. Holmes hired Richard Leebove, a Dalto/McMaster crony and former NCLC member, as a thousand-dollar-a-week "communications" aide. Leebove's specialty had always been the heavy-handed smear. In the late 1970s he had traveled around the Midwest delivering tirades against the TDU at Teamster local meetings. He had also displayed his talents as the spokesman for Citizens for Chicago, a LaRouchian front group that circulated scurrilous leaflets against Chicago mayor Jane Byrne in 1979–80 (the leaflets accused her of being controlled by the mob and of being married to a gigolo).

Leebove's role in the 1983 Teamster elections showed that the Dalto faction was still practicing LaRouchism without LaRouche. Smear articles appeared in the *Local 337 News* repeating previous NCLC charges against the TDU—for instance, that it was funded by the Rockefellers. One article implied falsely that Senator Hatch intended to launch an investigation of the TDU for subversive activity. Indirect attacks were leveled against the local's secretary-treasurer, TDU member Jerry Bliss, who was denied equal space to respond. Forged handbills appeared in Local 337 shops purporting to be from the TDU but containing material intended to embarrass the TDU candidates.

The hiring of Leebove underscored the opportunism that was always at the root of the Teamster/NCLC connection. In 1979, Holmes, as head of the Teamster joint council in Detroit, had supported the resolution condemning McMaster's so-called Teamster Committee to Elect LaRouche President, in which Leebove had been active. Now, in a situation in which Leebove's usefulness appeared to outweigh any potential embarrassment, Holmes was willing to deal.

# Thirty-eight

## Senators, Cabinet Members, and Dictators

LaRouche's message that racketeering is twentieth-century American-
ism was useful to stroke the egos of Teamster officials. It might also
have been read by Mafia dons as a signal that LaRouche wanted a niche
in organized crime. But it was hardly the stuff of which effective publicity campaigns are made. For that, he needed something more subtle—
an issue that could give a veneer of legitimacy to his "hands off the
mob" propaganda.

He found this issue in Abscam's civil liberties implications. FBI undercover agents had solicited bribes from congressmen who, unlike the
Brilab defendants, had not previously engaged in a pattern of illegal
activities. Targets such as Senator Harrison Williams (D.-N.J.) were
widely perceived as victims of prosecutorial tactics outside the legitimate mandate of law enforcement. Williams had a distinguished legislative record and staunchly maintained his innocence. Although a jury
found him guilty in May 1981 on nine counts of bribery and conspiracy,
he had the potential to gain public sympathy—something a Carlos
Marcello or Frank Sheeran could never hope to achieve.

In the fall of 1981, when Williams' case was on appeal and he was facing expulsion from the Senate, the LaRouchians adopted him as their latest victim of political persecution by evil FBI agents. Lacking support from his fellow senators, Williams was ready to grasp at straws. When LaRouche's National Democratic Policy Committee launched a petition campaign among trade unionists to stop the Senate expulsion proceeding, Williams consented to be interviewed for a half-hour NDPC-produced videotape that was later shown at gatherings of labor officials and politicians in New Jersey. The NDPC also sponsored a fund raiser for Williams at New York's Statler Hilton. A Williams aide commented to the Passaic *Herald-News* that the NDPC had "a rather broader following than is generally thought," especially among "auto dealers and construction people." As the expulsion vote approached, *New Solidarity* claimed that the NDPC was rallying the Laborers, Teamsters, and other unions to defend Williams. NDPC speakers had been sent, the paper said, to Democratic clubs and union locals around New Jersey to "explain the broader threat to the Constitution and to labor and constituency organizations . . ."

In February 1982 the NDPC joined with officials from the Teamsters and the construction trades to found the National Labor Committee to Defend Harrison Williams. The LaRouchians promised to launch an "immediate lobbying mobilization across the country to press for a full investigation of Abscam illegalities." The founding meeting was held in Atlantic City. The committee's statement of policy suggested that the defense of Williams was really a cover for defending FBI-targeted labor racketeers: "We . . . regard the case of Sen. Harrison Williams . . . as being a turning point for the labor movement. We either rise to his defense in a unified fashion, across the nation, from the bottom to the top of labor, or we ourselves should not be surprised to hear the knock at the door saying we're next." Support for this statement came mostly from local New Jersey union officials. The AFL-CIO leadership refused to have anything to do with it. *New Solidarity* then accused AFL-CIO chief Lane Kirkland of being pro-Abscam. In fact, Kirkland spoke out strongly against the sting operations, as did many civil libertarians and trade unionists totally unconnected to LaRouche's committee.

The high point of the NDPC's campaign to defend Williams was a Washington rally at which a message, supposedly from the senator, was read out: "I think that the entire American people will one day thank and commend Lyn and Helga LaRouche . . . for bringing to light the facts of police state methods, and organizing the resistance to them . . . Our tradition is not to give in to Gestapo methods but to fight them."

Another beneficiary of the LaRouche organization's crusade against FBI entrapment tactics was auto tycoon John DeLorean, indicted in

1982 on charges of cocaine trafficking. According to Gordon Novel, who worked as a private investigator for the defense, LaRouche aide Jeffrey Steinberg provided research materials on how the British government allegedly was out to get DeLorean. Former NCLC security staffer Charles Tate recalls: "I wrote a big paper on Jeff's instructions. I was told I'd get to meet with the DeLoreans but that fell through." Former NCLC security consultants Roy Frankhouser and Lee Fick also say they were assigned to this project. DeLorean, who was acquitted by a jury in 1984, has said that he received information from the LaRouchians but never paid them any money.

The LaRouchians also attempted to help out beleaguered Labor Secretary Raymond Donovan when a federal special prosecutor investigated allegations that his firm, Schiavone Construction Company in Secaucus, New Jersey, had paid bribes to labor racketeers and that Donovan was himself an associate of organized crime. According to LaRouche defectors, a Teamster-linked attorney asked the NCLC's Security staff to gather information on behalf of Donovan and Schiavone. LaRouche's Security chief, Jeffrey Steinberg, personally handled the investigation. A June 18, 1982, *Investigative Leads* memo from Steinberg to Morris Levin, Schiavone's house counsel, outlined the progress of Steinberg's work and mentioned plans for a meeting with Robert Shortley, a private investigator also working on behalf of Schiavone. Levin recalled this memo in a 1984 phone interview and said he had talked to Steinberg "from time to time." He also said the firm's president, Ronald Schiavone, had met with Steinberg.

Copies of the Steinberg memo and other private investigative documents were obtained by a University of Oklahoma graduate student, Frank Smist, from Robert J. Flynn, a Washington attorney who had been hired by Schiavone to find out who was spreading the allegations about Donovan. In 1984 Smist turned the documents over to the Brooklyn Organized Crime Strike Force. This set off an investigation of whether unauthorized disclosures from government sources (suggested by the documents' contents) might have triggered the murder of Fred Furino, a former official of Tony Pro's Local 560. Furino, whose body was found in a car trunk in mid-June 1982, had been a prospective federal witness regarding alleged Schiavone payoffs to the mob. He had appeared before the grand jury several months previously.

The Steinberg memo, written several days after Furino's disappearance, mentioned that the Teamster official had been a topic of conversation between an NCLC staff member and an NBC television reporter. The NCLC member pumped the reporter to find out if he knew anything about the contents of the not yet released special prosecutor's report. Steinberg claimed his associate learned from the reporter that the special prosecutor's office had given Furino a polygraph test.

In 1984 Ronald Schiavone told *The New York Times* that he had hired private investigator Shortley to find out who on the Senate Labor Committee staff was spreading allegations about himself and Donovan. NCLC defectors say that Steinberg and other members of Security did research on similar lines. In fact, *Executive Intelligence Review* published at least two articles in 1981 by a Steinberg assistant purporting to describe a conspiracy by Senate Labor Committee staffers to embarrass the Reagan administration by bringing down Donovan.

Although the special prosecutor's report concluded that there was "insufficient credible evidence" to indict Donovan, an investigation subsequently launched by the Bronx district attorney's office resulted in the September 1984 indictment of Donovan and seven others, including Levin, Schiavone, and Genovese crime family member William ("the Butcher") Masselli. The defendants were charged with 137 counts of larceny and fraud in relation to contracts on a New York City subway tunnel. It was the first time in American history that a sitting cabinet member had been indicted on criminal charges. Donovan resigned after taking a leave of absence. *New Solidarity* said it was all part of a plot by the KGB, Henry Kissinger, and the AFL-CIO to take over the Labor Department. (As matters turned out, Donovan and his co-defendants were all found innocent in 1987 after an eight-month trial.)

LaRouche's allies in Teamster Local 282 on Long Island were also feeling the heat. Business agent Harry Gross, McMaster's old associate, was indicted in 1981 on charges that included extorting a no-show job from Schiavone Construction for his chauffeur. Local 282 president John Cody was indicted for racketeering in January 1982. That spring *The New York Times* published a series on corruption in the local construction unions. A major problem, the series charged, was Cody's conduct as head of Local 282, representing 4,000 building supply truckers. Rushing to Cody's defense came LaRouche follower Mel Klenetsky, a candidate in the Democratic primary against U.S. Senator Daniel Patrick Moynihan. Klenetsky issued an appeal to the labor movement to unite behind Cody. He also printed up copies of a letter from a prominent builder taking issue with the *Times*'s criticisms of Local 282. Cody's name subsequently appeared along with those of several Laborers Union officials in an advertisement in New York City's *Amsterdam News* endorsing Klenetsky. In October 1982 Cody was convicted of seven counts of racketeering and income-tax evasion. One contractor testified he had handed Cody $100,000 in a shoe box. The guilty verdict was obtained in spite of the disappearance of several witnesses, including Carpenters Union chief Ted Maritas (federal investigators believe Maritas was murdered). When Cody was sentenced to five years in prison, *New Solidarity* said this was more proof of selective prosecution. The case was simply a "frame-up engineered by *The New York Times* and its organized crime gestapo," allegedly to punish Cody for supporting LaRouche. "The word is that the *Times* wants to see John Cody dead, because he dared to oppose their friends," said the LaRouche paper. A subsequent article by Klenetsky said the Cody case demonstrated the need for a "national citizens' mobilization to strip the FBI of its funds until its lawlessness is checked." The LaRouchian arguments regarding the Cody case were quite similar to those LaRouche himself would use in his 1988 trial for obstruction of justice.

The LaRouchian relationship to the national Teamster leadership had its ups and downs in the early 1980s. Roy Williams became IBT president in 1981 after Fitzsimmons' death. Jackie Presser moved up to number two, and was widely expected to soon replace Williams, who was indicted for bribery shortly after assuming office. To demonstrate his capacity for aggressive leadership, Presser decided to go after the TDU and isolate it as thoroughly as possible prior to the 1981 national convention in Las Vegas. A wave of bogus TDU fliers and other forgeries began to circulate in the union. The TDU's newspaper charged that the NCLC was producing them. The nastiest was a letter purporting to be from the National Right to Work Committee, an antilabor lobbying group, to TDU leader Pete Camarata. "Pete, you are going to have the NRWC's total . . . support in your upcoming effort to disrupt the Teamsters' Convention," the letter said. Copies were mailed to Teamster locals in plain envelopes with no return address. The TDU promptly denied any connection between Camarata and the NRWC, and pointed out the preposterous references in the letter to such LaRouchian bugbears as the Mont Pelerin Society and the Heritage Foundation. However, many Teamster officials used it, just as they had used *The Plot to Destroy the Teamsters* in 1977–78. Reports began to pour into the TDU national office from rank-and-file Teamsters who had received copies of the letter. The president of an Alabama local mailed it to members at union expense. It was also distributed by local officers in St. Louis, Toledo, San Antonio, and other cities. "It is clear," the TDU's *Convoy* said, "that a national distribution of the Big Lie is underway."

Meanwhile, Presser set up two paper organizations, TRUTH (Teamster Ranks United to Help) and BLAST (Brotherhood of Loyal Americans and Strong Teamsters), spreading standard LaRouche smears about "Commie-Rat-A" (Camarata) and "Ayatollah Mel" (TDU trustee Mel Packer). Goons claiming to be from TRUTH and BLAST created an atmosphere of intimidation at the convention, roughing up Camarata while LaRouche intelligence operatives roamed the floor with guest passes from midwestern locals.

The LaRouchians struck out, however, with Roy Williams. They denounced his indictment with the usual litany about witch hunts, frame-ups, squealers, and Gestapos, but Williams, the creature of Kansas City crime lord Nick Civella, showed little interest. This coolness and Rolland McMaster's continued friendliness with the Detroit defectors apparently were the reasons for a 1982 editorial in *New Solidarity* entitled "Teamster Stupidity." For once, the LaRouchians revealed their true feelings about their blue-collar allies. The Justice Department, the editorial argued, could be "easily defeated" if the IBT would organize its nearly two million members for a political counterattack based on LaRouche's ideology. "Unfortunately for this nation," the editorial complained, "the leadership of the Teamsters has thus far proven itself to be of two types when it comes to acting upon this reality: corrupt or stupid." Yet when Williams was convicted of bribery, the LaRouchians commiserated. It was, they said, "nothing less than Nazi justice."

When Presser ascended to the Teamster presidency, the LaRouchians finally seemed on the brink of becoming the brain trust of labor's hoodlum wing, in spite of their setback in Detroit. Presser continued the aggressive posture against the TDU that had given the LaRouchians their initial entrée to the union leadership. When a TDU convention in Michigan was violently disrupted by thugs in October 1983, Presser stated at a Cleveland joint council meeting: "We should be doing more of that . . . I'm not going to let up on these people." But in late 1983 and early 1984, as the media began to probe for the first time the relationship between LaRouche and the Reagan administration, Presser followed other Reagan allies in distancing himself from the NCLC.

The LaRouchians suffered a shock when the *Los Angeles Times* revealed in mid-1984 that Presser had been selectively providing information to the FBI since the early 1970s. It took no clairvoyance for them to realize that providing the FBI with information on LaRouche, as well as on minor hoods like John Nardi, Jr., may have been Presser's way of keeping the FBI off his back while he rose to the Teamster presidency. After all, the LaRouchians themselves had been feeding information to the FBI almost as long as Presser had—on Communists, Yippies, and arms merchants—in hopes the FBI would overlook their own improprieties. (In 1987 the Justice Department officially acknowledged Presser's informant role in motions pursuant to a racketeering prosecution of the Teamster chief. Presser's attorney then acknowledged that Presser had had "continuous contact" with the FBI for more than a decade.)

LaRouche aide Edward Spannaus filed a Freedom of Information Act request with the FBI for documents in Presser's informant file "insofar as such documents mention or discuss Lyndon H. LaRouche, Jr. . . . or associates of [his]." When the FBI turned down the request, Spannaus filed suit in federal court in Alexandria, Virginia. After a government motion for summary judgment was denied, *New Solidarity* gleefully announced that it hoped to "lift the veil on Presser's real rise to power in the Teamsters." By this time, *New Solidarity* was no longer calling Presser a heroic Teamster "nation builder," but simply an "accused embezzler."

If the NCLC's alliance with the highest levels of the IBT had turned a cropper, LaRouche simply raised his sights higher—from hoodlums who control unions to those who control nations. After numerous trips to Central America, his intelligence aides latched on to the plight of General Manuel Antonio Noriega. The Panamanian strongman had begun to attract harsh criticism from the U.S. government and media in 1985–86, primarily because of his role in the cocaine traffic. The LaRouchians began to vigorously defend him, just as they had done with the Teamsters.

In early 1986, Senator Jesse Helms (R.-N.C.), a member of the Senate Foreign Relations Committee, raised the issue of Noriega's links to Fidel Castro, involvement in drug trafficking, and responsibility for the murder of Dr. Hugo Spadafora, a former Panamanian Health Minister who had been critical of the regime. Helms stated flatly that Noriega was "head of the biggest drug trafficking operation in the Western Hemisphere."

These charges were not right-wing paranoia. Noriega's drug activities had been confirmed by DEA, CIA, Pentagon, and State Department reports going back to the early 1970s. A 1985 House Foreign Affairs Committee report characterized Panama under Noriega's rule as a "drug and chemical transshipment point and money-laundering center for drug money." In a 1986 *New York Times* article, James LeMoyne compared Noriega's army to the Mafia, because it "skims funds, takes kickbacks, engages in smuggling and has a political structure resembling a racketeering network in which loyal henchmen share in the spoils." An equally good analogy would have been the Teamsters union. Indeed, the parallels between the leadership style of Noriega and the most corrupt Teamster bosses are uncanny. Just as Jimmy Hoffa indulged in the rhetoric of class struggle at union meetings, so Noriega affected a militant populist and anti-imperialist rhetoric to manipulate Panamanian workers. Just as Jackie Presser became an FBI informer in the early 1970s to divert federal authorities from his own misdeeds, so Noriega became a source for the U.S. intelligence community at that time to facilitate his long-range ambitions. Just as Presser had his TRUTH and BLAST—and Tony Pro his team of enforcers—Noriega had his death squads. Just as Rolland McMaster issued denunciations of the evils of drug trafficking for the Michigan Anti-Drug Coalition, so Noriega went to an international anti-drug conference in Vienna, where he described drugs as the "scourge" of mankind. Just as Presser and the Teamsters were willing to deal with the extremist LaRouchians, so Noriega developed ties with M-19, the pro-Castro guerrilla group in Colombia, and with Castro's secret service, the DGI. Just as certain Teamster leaders had Hoffa murdered, so Noriega bumped off his predecessor, General Omar Torrijos Herrera.

In the mid-1980s, NCLC operative Carlos Wesley made several trips to Panama, where a top official of the national construction workers union, was a member of LaRouche's Schiller Institute. After meeting with a pro-Noriega group of businessmen, Wesley announced that they represented "patriotic and nationalist tendencies" and were in substantial agreement with the economic development/anti-IMF program of the Schiller Institute. Soon the LaRouchians had become Noriega's public relations flacks in Washington. As students of Mitch WerBell's classic defense in the 1976 pot-smuggling trial, they knew just how to defend the indefensible. They circulated a white paper on Capitol Hill and other documents that accused Senator Helms of being the "point man" in a State Department conspiracy to overthrow Noriega because of the latter's *opposition* to drugs. Noriega, they said, was being set up by the *real* "drug Mafia," which had learned he was planning a "military War on Drugs." The drug Mafia were in league with narco-terrorists, and thus wanted not only to stop Noriega from cracking down on drugs but also to destabilize Panama so the Soviets could gain control of the Canal. Just why the State Department and Helms should want this was explainable only in terms of LaRouche's theory of secret oligarchical control of the Western world. Not a very convincing scenario to anyone in Washington, but that wasn't the point: The LaRouchians knew that a cover story based on absurd premises, as long as it is internally consistent, can be useful as a smoke screen and a delaying tactic.

The Panamanian embassy in Washington had nothing more convincing to offer the media, especially after Noriega forced figurehead President Nicolas Ardito Barletta to resign at gunpoint for urging an independent investigation of the Spadafora slaying. The embassy referred journalists to the LaRouchians, who said Barletta's resignation was a cause for rejoicing. Was he not a wretched agent of Henry Kissinger and those "who lend their souls to the institutions of usury"? La-

Rouche followers demonstrated outside the Senate hearings on Panama, with signs suggesting that Helms was in the pay of Israel's Mossad. *Executive Intelligence Review* reprinted a speech by Noriega discussing the "transcendental role" of the military in Central America. When the United States suspended aid to Panama in July 1987, the LaRouchians compared the regime's plight to their own problems with federal prosecutors.

Most grotesque was *New Solidarity*'s attitude toward the Spadafora murder. The former Health Minister had been tortured for five hours in a village square, then beheaded and his remains dumped in a U.S. postal bag over the Costa Rican border. According to *New Solidarity,* Spadafora died because he was a left-wing narco-terrorist plotting to launch a Sandinista-style movement in Panama. The charges, made in the context of ridiculing the Spadafora family's grief, were totally untrue. Spadafora was an opponent of communism who had served with Edén Pastora's Contra army in Nicaragua and aided the Miskito Indian resistance. He had been an informant for U.S. intelligence agencies on vital matters of national security. Only days before his murder he had met with DEA officials to supply them with details about Noriega's trafficking.

The relationship between LaRouche and Noriega was touched on in February 9, 1988, testimony before the U.S. Senate Foreign Relations Committee's Subcommittee on Terrorism, Narcotics, and International Operations. José I. Blandón Castillo, Panama's former New York consul general, stated that "Mr. LaRouche works for Mr. Noriega" and that LaRouche's followers had given Noriega intelligence reports on several U.S. senators. "When [the senators] arrived in Panama, we had the information and published it in the papers before they arrived." Blandón added that the LaRouchian propaganda cover story on the death of Spadafora (that he was a left-wing terrorist) was the "official version" of Noriega's G-2 (military intelligence). Blandón also revealed that Mario Parnther, a Panamanian politician close to Noriega, was one of the links to LaRouche. Parnther "came to the States to speak in favor of Lyndon LaRouche . . . he spoke to me of LaRouche's role in connection with Panama, and said that he, Parnther, met with LaRouche in Boston."

Parnther's trip had not been kept a secret by the LaRouchians. *EIR* had reported on it in September 1987, noting that he addressed the Commission to Investigate Human Rights Violations in the United States, an organization set up to protest the federal prosecutions of LaRouche and his followers. Identifying Parnther as a member of the national directorate of Noriega's party, *EIR* had quoted him as praising LaRouche's "unyielding commitment to the truth about Panama" and asserting: "We are fortunate that men emerge such as Lyndon La-Rouche . . ."

In reporting Blandón's testimony, *EIR* implied that LaRouche had advised Noriega, via Parnther, to reject the State Department's plan that he resign in exchange for immunity. *EIR* suggested that this advice had encouraged Noriega's change of mind on the State Department offer—his adoption of the hard line which sent U.S. policy in Central America into a tailspin. Whether or not LaRouche's role was really so crucial, he had apparently indeed suggested that Noriega emulate what he himself was doing in the Boston case: Delay and hang tight until the enemy gets exhausted; in the meantime, create as much ideological obfuscation as possible and threaten to expose everybody in Washington who has ever secretly dealt with you. In early 1988 the Panamanian government produced a 300-page report that backed up the LaRouchian claim that Noriega was Latin America's premier anti-drug warrior. It was a pathetic record of arrests of mules, spraying of pot plantations, and seizure of cocaine from small dealers who hadn't made the proper payoffs. Most of the arrests described were a result either of DEA arm-twisting or else of Noriega enforcing the Medellín cartel's control of the action. But the report showed that Noriega, like his apparent adviser LaRouche, had a certain embarrassment potential: Included was the text of a 1984 letter from DEA chief Francis Mullen, Jr., to Noriega, hailing the dictator's "long-standing" and "very meaningful" support for the DEA and thanking him for "the autographed photograph." Wrote Mullen: "I have had it framed and it is proudly displayed in my office."

In establishing ties with persons like Noriega and Jackie Presser, LaRouche was not just being a crime groupie. He was developing meanwhile his own operation on the grand scale—an effort that brought in over $200 million, much of it via credit-card and loan fraud, while spinning off numerous secondary scams involving federal matching funds, nonprofit foundations, and election campaign committees. Many LaRouchians who participated in these operations developed a predatory frame of mind not just through LaRouche's psychological manipulation but by associating with convicted felons such as Michele Sindona and Rolland McMaster and idolizing the likes of Tony Provenzano. These facts, coupled with the NCLC's eleven-year history of shifting alliances with various underworld figures, suggest that La-Rouche is neither just a political extremist nor simply a white-collar criminal in the Bernie Cornfeld mold. Rather, he is the "boss" (as he puts it) of an organization with striking resemblances to a traditional racketeering enterprise.

In this aspect of his work, LaRouche has revealed the same genius for innovation as in his political organizing. He constructed his businesses on the basis of cultism and ideology rather than ethnic ties and blood oaths. He maximized profits by persuading his followers to devote every waking hour to the organization—and without even having to give them a cut of the action. He operated within the constitutionally protected framework of electoral activity (the first such entrepreneur to do so). He utilized an unincorporated political association that is everywhere and yet nowhere, permeating a bewildering network of corporate shells. Most important, he developed a unique system for warding off prosecutors—not a Maginot line of mob attorneys, but a multilayered defense in depth.

Studying the plight of the Teamsters union, LaRouche observed how intimately prosecutorial initiatives are linked to investigative journalism and the media spotlight. He was able to break that link by aggressive libel suits and pressure on people with media influence, thus diverting the media away from any serious pursuit of him for years. Even though he lost every libel battle, he won the war by making exposés of LaRouche too expensive for the media chains.

But LaRouche took things a step further: When law enforcement agencies *did* begin to investigate him, he immediately counterattacked with civil liberties suits in federal court, charging a conspiracy to undermine his constitutional rights. He kept the FBI tied down for ten years with a suit, still pending in Manhattan, that has cost the government heavily in pretrial litigation costs.

In the early 1980s he also used this technique to keep the Manhattan DA's office, the Illinois state attorney general's office, and Federal Election Commission investigators at bay. When NCLC member Joyce Rubinstein was arrested in 1985 on misdemeanor theft charges in Princeton, New Jersey, the LaRouchians launched a federal suit against the arresting officers and the municipality. (This type of suit makes local police departments think twice about tangling with people who can make more trouble than their arrest seems worth.)

LaRouche and his followers also developed a reputation for making a monumental extra-courtroom nuisance of themselves. Any prosecutor who went after them—or any politician who took a public stand against them that might encourage prosecutors—could expect to be picketed and to become the target of a smear campaign and/or harassing phone calls. In wielding the weapon of the Big Smear, LaRouche had four advantages: the means of gathering intelligence and nasty gossip, the means of distributing smear materials, the freedom from fear of libel suits, and the freedom from having to worry about his own reputation. His publishing entities could crank out leaflets and brochures on a moment's notice, and his followers could pass out hundreds of thousands of copies within days. His publications were meanwhile protected by the NCLC corporate shell game and thus were virtually judgment-proof against libel suits (in fact they were rarely sued—most targeted persons didn't know what else LaRouche might have on them). Likewise, LaRouche didn't have to worry about upholding any moderate image. He could play the mad-dog publisher with impunity, laying out the smears no one else would touch (but occasionally seeing his material picked up by the major media once he had done the spadework). All this served as a powerful incentive—just like his civil liberties suits—for prosecutors to go after easier targets, as well as for politicians and media figures to leave him alone. In New York City in the early 1980s, as we have seen, this tactic protected him as effectively as payoffs and rubouts protect Mafia dons.

Finally, LaRouche used his intelligence community gambit. Although this was far from being a new idea, his attempts to compromise the CIA included new twists.

LaRouche's system was not infallible, and by 1988 he and his followers were embroiled in multiple indictments. Yet for over a decade he had conducted his questionable operations with virtual impunity, thanks to his creative tactics. And what ultimately was this defense-in-depth set up to protect? The full scope of LaRouche's financial activities is only beginning to be known. Veteran LaRouche watchers believe there are still huge gaps in the puzzle of where the money came from to pay for his empire of political, intelligence-gathering, and propaganda fronts in over a dozen countries. As yet, neither law enforcement nor investigative reporters have probed his operations in Colombia, Peru, Panama, and Mexico, his close ties with military officers and members of the landowning elite in Thailand, and his organization's alleged use of offshore bank accounts and couriers to move cash around the world. It is quite probable that the intelligence agencies of more than one country would prefer that these matters never be probed.

# Afterword

# Why LaRouche Was Not Fought

Following the LaRouchian victories in the March 1986 Illinois primaries, some observers argued that the Democratic Party's immune system had broken down. In fact, the problem went far beyond the Democrats. The major media had failed over the years to vigorously unmask
LaRouche. Jewish and black organizations and the left had largely
ignored his dramatic political inroads in the early 1980s, blithely allowing him to operate his international network of hate from midtown
Manhattan with nary a protest. Reagan administration aides, GOP operatives, Teamster leaders, and others on the right had treated him as
just another political ally, to be used as needed.

This see-no-evil attitude contrasted sharply with the opposition that
both liberals and conservatives displayed toward traditional hate
groups such as the Ku Klux Klan and Louis Farrakhan's Nation of
Islam. The double standard was revealed most clearly in the 1984
presidential campaign. When the Klan endorsed President Reagan, it
immediately received a blistering denunciation from him. But when
NBC exposed the administration's ties to LaRouche (while also pointing out LaRouche's ties to the Klan), the White House response was

that it would continue to meet with whomever it pleased. Not a single Jewish or black organization condemned this response, nor did the media take issue with Reagan. Yet the connection between Jesse Jackson and Farrakhan meanwhile became front-page news. Reagan and Bush used the Farrakhan issue to hound Walter Mondale, who was entirely innocent of any links to or sympathy with the Chicago radio preacher. Mondale and the Democratic Party, however, failed to make an issue of the administration's dealings with LaRouche, whose statements against the Jews over the years had been more extreme and much more systematic than Farrakhan's. Furthermore, the Democrats failed to take any steps against LaRouche's massive infiltration of the party primaries that year.

Fundamentally, the political structure's immune system against the ultraright is geared only to oppose overt hate groups led by demagogues who speak their minds frankly. The LaRouchians, like a clever virus, evaded the immune system by mixing right-wing and left-wing ideology and by using code words and a studied kookiness. These tactics made it difficult for the public—and for harried news reporters on deadline—to define LaRouchism. And if one cannot define something, how can one fight it? The NCLC's anti-Semitism did become widely known, but it stirred up little visceral indignation because LaRouche often used Jewish aides to express it. (They would meet with reporters and Reagan administration officials to tell them the NCLC was really only "anti-Zionist," that LaRouche had been misinterpreted, and so on.) Whenever such methods stopped working, LaRouche fell back on his kook act, as if to suggest that even if he were a fascist and a bigot he was a singularly harmless one not worth fighting. This tactic turned out to be his strongest defense. When he came under media attack after the 1986 Illinois primaries, he gave a rambling speech before the National Press Club about assassination plots, and later announced on network television a plan to colonize Mars. The level of opposition to him dropped, enabling his followers to make further grass-roots electoral inroads and to continue raising tens of millions of dollars a year.

LaRouche was also shielded by the middle-class character of his movement. The Klan easily elicits opposition because its members are perceived as ignorant "rednecks." Farrakhan, of course, is widely regarded as a gutter bigot, appealing mostly to low-income blacks. But LaRouche speaks on TV in a cultivated New England accent reminiscent of William F. Buckley's. His followers wear three-piece business suits and often sport degrees from major universities. Several are from prominent families. Thus they often are treated not as hatemongers at all but as misguided idealists or as victims of cult brainwashing. Some media reports have implied that although a Klansman might deserve harsh condemnation, the proper response to a LaRouchian—even one convicted of felonies such as loan fraud—is to offer him psychotherapy and a scholarship to get back into graduate school. (In fact LaRouche's NCLC is no more cultish than Farrakhan's Nation of Islam or the Klan-linked Aryan Nation. Indeed, the LaRouchians, with their higher education levels, would seem to have even less excuse for anti-Semitism.)

The LaRouchian's ability to hide behind middle-class "educated" standards is best illustrated by what happened when their Humanist Academy rented a hall at Columbia University for a public gathering in 1980. If they had worn bed sheets and burned a cross, there would have been an uproar. Instead, they staged Elizabethan dramatist Christopher Marlowe's *The Jew of Malta,* featuring a Jewish villian who strangles a friar, poisons several nuns, betrays his Christian neighbors to the Turks, and meets his end in a cauldron of boiling water. The audience, composed of NCLC members and friends, had been instructed that the play was a weapon in the fight against the international "oligarchy." They hissed and laughed when Barabas the "rich Jew" appeared on the stage. In essence, this was no different from a cross-burning, but a university spokesman defended renting the hall to them. He explained that the LaRouchians, unlike the Klan, fell into a "gray area."

In spite of LaRouche's multileveled smoke screen, his movement would have found fewer allies and more opponents except for the array of positive and negative incentives he offered. This was *intelligent fascism* in action. Alone among American ultraright bigots, LaRouche could offer potential allies something of value: his prowess at intelligence gathering, his sophisticated dirty tricks, and the sometimes formidable efforts of his FEF/*EIR* think tank. Furthermore, those who accepted his help ran almost no risk of being publicly embarrassed: Since LaRouche was not portrayed in the media as especially sinister, those who met with him could always explain it away. The LaRouchians were sensitive to the needs of their allies in this respect. If they had a relationship with a GOP operative, they kept it secret. If they ran a smear campaign against a particular political candidate, they would also throw a few harmless punches against the candidate who was being aided by their smears. For instance, when LaRouche spread rumors about George Bush and the Trilateral Commission during the 1980 New Hampshire primary, he also issued some pro forma criticisms of Reagan.

On the negative side, LaRouche demonstrated that he could make life miserable for powerful people if they crossed him. His smear campaigns against Henry Kissinger and Roy Cohn made this clear. Such prominent figures had always been beyond the reach of the traditional hate groups, but LaRouche carried the battle to their doorsteps. As a result, other powerful people became extremely reluctant to tangle with him. This was not because they were all cowards at heart. Many of them would have denounced him if they had felt an important matter of principle was at stake. But the media's portrayal of LaRouche as a kook and the silence of most Jewish organizations about him sent a message that it simply wasn't worth the effort to oppose him seriously.

But even on the infrequent occasions when vigorous opposition to LaRouche did emerge, there was an astonishing ability on the part of many people to evade the issue of principle. When the Manhattan weekly *Our Town* published a series attacking LaRouche in 1979, NCLC members went around to advertisers and to stores that freely distributed the paper and threatened them with legal action. Four major banks, Consolidated Edison, and the New York Telephone Company gave in immediately and either canceled advertising in *Our Town* or withdrew permission for its circulation on their premises. (Four years later, the telephone company still banned *Our Town*.) Such was the response of the business community; what about the labor movement? In 1980 a top official of the Pennsylvania Federation of Teachers gave several donations to LaRouche's presidential campaign. When Jewish teachers urged the union's board to pass a resolution criticizing the official, the board—reacting to factional problems in the union—instead voted to *commend* him and later censured a union leader who had supported the original resolution.

In neither case were the people who caved in suffering under any great illusions about LaRouche. In the fall of 1979, his followers deluged the streets of New York with leaflets calling for the crushing of the "Zionists." In the PFT situation, the protesting teachers provided abundant documentation of LaRouche's anti-Semitism. As the LaRouchians developed their deceptive tactics to higher levels of sophistication, such incidents multiplied. Each time, the evasion of the issue of principle merely made similar evasions more easy in the future. And for some politically astute people, the smoke screen became something they could hide behind *along with* LaRouche while they conducted their business with him. It provided the basis for them to *pretend* that they didn't know what he was about and *pretend* that they regarded him as a kook.

In fact the LaRouche movement's fascist character and its dangerous (nonkook) side were not really difficult to see. As early as 1976–77, recognition that LaRouche had gone fascist could be found in places as diverse as the newsletter of the Christian Anti-Communist Crusade and the Op-Ed page of *The Washington Post*. In 1980, Lionel Abel suggested in *Dissent* that LaRouche was America's "first serious fascist," while the Anti-Defamation League's Michigan spokesman, Richard Lobenthal, described the NCLC in 1981 as the "closest thing to an American fascist party that we've got." Several writers focused on the neo-Nazi elements in LaRouche's ideology.

If this viewpoint—easily proven by LaRouche's writings, his alliances with ex-Nazis and international neo-fascists, and a simple comparison of his tactics with those of classical fascism—had been adopted and widely publicized by the major media and other opinion makers, La-Rouche would have been stopped dead in his tracks in the early 1980s. There would have been no chats with National Security Council officials, no alliance with top Teamsters, no deals with shadowy GOP operatives, no grass-roots candidates' movement of significant proportions, no passive sufferance by the Democratic Party, and certainly no Illinois primary victories in 1986. All that was needed was for opinion leaders to draw the same clear line they had drawn against the Klan, to name LaRouche for what he really was, to declare his movement beyond the bounds of decency.

The confusion on this point, and the inability to draw a clear line, is best illustrated by the role of the major media and especially the major daily newspapers. The media were certainly not the only lax institution, but their response both reflected and molded that of all other aspects of the political immune system. For instance, from the beginning of LaRouche's rise most major newspapers shied away from analyzing his organization in any but the most superficial terms. They avoided the terms "fascist" and "neo-Nazi," which alone could adequately express his aims and methods. *The New York Times* in its 1979 series on La-Rouche at least kept the *concept,* expressing it through euphemisms and vivid examples, but soon even the euphemisms were dropped. In the early 1980s, some newspapers began to describe LaRouche as a "conservative Democrat" or to adopt other totally misleading labels.

The major media became silent about LaRouche's political actions as well as his ideology. The electoral breakthroughs of his followers were almost totally ignored in the early 1980s. No one in the media sought to find out where the two thousand LaRouche candidates in 1984 had come from. LaRouche's ties to the Teamsters union, exhaustively documented in the left-liberal weeklies and magazines, were ignored by major newspapers that normally jump on *any* scandal involving the Teamsters. Prior to 1986, the Baltimore *Sun* was the only paper to have probed LaRouche's finances, even though court cases involving La-Rouche corporate shells offered an easy score for any investigative reporter.

One reason for the laxness was the fear of libel suits. In the late 1970s, LaRouche and his followers sued the Anti-Defamation League and *Our Town* for libel. At the time, religious and psychological cults were filing numerous libel suits, and many editors assumed LaRouche would be equally aggressive. Although the ADL suit was dismissed and LaRouche quietly dropped the *Our Town* suit (and filed no serious new libel suits until 1984), his followers maintained his litigious reputation by calling up reporters and editors at the drop of a hat to threaten legal action. A Catch-22 resulted: Newspapers toned down their coverage of LaRouche by using "soft" labels and avoiding mention of the nastier aspects of his movement. This soft approach then developed a life of its own. No longer was LaRouche perceived as the dangerous character portrayed by *The New York Times* in 1979. Hence there was no incentive for editors to call his bluff.

LaRouche made what turned out to be one of his shrewdest moves in early 1984. He learned that he would be the subject of an exposé on NBC's *First Camera*. This threatened to undermine his ties with the Reagan administration and the intelligence community. But LaRouche must have known that *First Camera* was not watched by many people. If other media could be prevented from repeating the charges, the damage could possibly be contained. He sued NBC for $150 million prior to the show. The result was that some NBC affiliates didn't air it and many newspapers didn't report on it. Thus most Americans failed to hear that the Reagan administration had been meeting with neo-Nazis who in turn were in bed with racketeers, and that the leader of these neo-Nazis had discussed assassinating Jimmy Carter and other government officials in 1977. Furthermore, the major media failed to follow up *First Camera*'s work, even though it was a presidential election year in which the news value of the story was potentially very great.

One thing the national media did report was the outcome of the *LaRouche* v. *NBC* trial that fall. Finding that NBC had not libeled La-Rouche, the jury awarded it $3 million on a counterclaim (later knocked down to $200,000 by the judge). On the surface, this appeared to be a major defeat for LaRouche, but it was arguably a victory for him on a deeper level. The suit had squelched negative media coverage of him earlier in the year that might have cost him millions of dollars in loans and donations. And in spite of the trial's outcome, the media remained supercautious. For instance, the jury had found that the defendants were not liable for calling LaRouche a "small-time Hitler," but this did not loosen the taboo against hard labels for LaRouche. *The Washington Post* finally followed up the LaRouche-Reagan story (the *only* major paper to do so), but reporter John Mintz was apparently not allowed by his editors to deal forthrightly with LaRouche's political views. The result was that Mintz's excellent series was left with a gaping hole: who, what, when, but no why. This omission was seen in all subsequent major media coverage. LaRouche, it appeared, had established a state of affairs almost strange beyond belief: He was able to run for president of the United States, gain over a million dollars in matching funds, force TV networks to sell him millions of dollars of prime time for his scurrilous campaign ads—and meanwhile deny to the public the opportunity to hear strong criticisms of his policies and program.

After the 1986 Illinois primary, it was more important than ever to give the public accurate information about LaRouche. At first it appeared that blunt, accurate terms might become acceptable. The media did quote Adlai Stevenson III as calling the LaRouchians neo-Nazis. Senator Moynihan likewise used this designation in a Manhattan speech. Many journalists were aware of the truth, but the major media, Jewish organizations, and the Democratic Party decided to stick to soft terms that wouldn't disturb anyone (the *Times* went so far as to censor out the forbidden word in its coverage of Moynihan's speech). Some newspapers continued to call LaRouche a "rightist," but conservatives began to object. *The Wall Street Journal* published an editorial suggesting that LaRouche was really still left-wing (the evidence it cited was conspiracy theories that actually originated on the right). Suddenly the fact that U.S. and West German ultrarightist networks had nurtured LaRouche and provided him with ideas, money, and allies (not to mention weapons training) for the previous ten years became too controversial to dwell on. Newspapers avoided giving offense to the right by adopting the neutral term "political extremist" or by saying LaRouche had a "mixed" philosophy. The *New York Times* called him "eccentric" and a "conspiracy theorist" while announcing that he somehow defied classification in conventional terms. Meanwhile most of the media promoted the kook theory, by reminding the public over and over that LaRouche believes the Queen of England pushes drugs. The *only* serious analysis of LaRouche appeared in smaller unorthodox weeklies such as the Chicago *Reader,* the *Boston Phoenix* and *In These Times.* LaRouche watcher Chip Berlet recalled his frustration at the time: "I talked with dozens of reporters. I'd send them LaRouche's writings. Then I'd lead them step by step through it on the phone, to show them it was classic fascism. I'd cite chapter and verse from Hannah Arendt's *Origins of Totalitarianism*— how LaRouche fit like a glove. They'd say, 'That's nice,' then turn to their word processors and crank out some quip about Queen Elizabeth."

But behind the media's "soft" view of LaRouche there was often the rankest hypocrisy. While newspapers portrayed him as a kook they made editorial judgments based on the assumption that he was indeed potentially dangerous—so dangerous that his activities must be concealed from the public lest the truth help his movement grow. Jerome

Chase of the National Jewish Community Relations Advisory Council, in a 1986 memorandum on LaRouche's Illinois electoral victories, raised questions about this bizarre "quarantine" policy. Inquiries by the NJCRC, he wrote, had uncovered that "the media in Illinois *did* know that [Democratic primary candidates] Fairchild and Hart were LaRouchites, and chose not to headline this information, based on a judgment that to do so would give LaRouche a platform in statewide politics he did not deserve."

This attitude—don't write about an important story because we, the journalists, believe the public can't handle it—would be regarded as downright unethical in every area of journalism *except* the coverage of extremists. Indeed, in other areas it would be called a cover-up. In this case it also involved an almost comical inconsistency: The Chicago and national media had shown no such restraint in the case of Farrakhan, the obscure Chicago preacher whom the Republican Party and the media transformed in 1984 into America's most celebrated anti-Semite.

The "quarantine" policy toward the LaRouchians persisted after the flap over the Illinois primaries. NDPC candidates continued to get high vote percentages in all parts of the country, yet none of the media reported on this in depth. In the fall of 1986, the ADL published a study of the LaRouche grass-roots primary vote nationwide. Many reporters glanced at the figures, noted that the LaRouchians had not won any more major primaries, and declared them to be defeated. It was the double standard once again: If Farrakhan's Nation of Islam or the Ku Klux Klan had run 230 candidates of whom nearly 50 percent received over 10 percent of the vote (the actual statistics in the ADL report) both the ADL and the media would have sounded the alarm from the rooftops. For the media in this case, it was also part of the continuing lack of curiosity about anything beneath the surface relating to LaRouche. *The Washington Journalism Review* did a piece, "Letting LaRouche Off," which commented on the lack of vigorous reporting. It had no effect. When Senate hearings in 1988 unearthed LaRouche's ties to General Noriega, most of the media didn't mention it, much less follow it up, even though anything relating to Noriega was supposedly important news at the time. Again, when the LaRouchians were identified in the summer of 1988 as being behind the false rumors of Michael Dukakis's undergoing psychiatric treatment, no one in the media bothered to look at their antecedent political trickery, and the rumor was thus presented as an isolated incident.

The confusion and see-no-evil attitude toward LaRouche was often far worse in political circles than in the newsrooms. This spell was broken for a while after the Illinois primary victories. Democrats in some states did vigorously oppose LaRouchian candidates, although they were not always successful in preventing them from receiving sizable votes. As we have seen, the two LaRouche AIDS referendums in California gained very large vote totals. But the issue of just how vulnerable to manipulation the voters might become, and just how poorly society's early-warning system had functioned, never had to be confronted seriously. In October 1986, federal and state authorities raided the LaRouche organization's Virginia headquarters and the indictments began. Many observers figured that the downfall of La-Rouche was not far off and that the NCLC would revert to nuisance status. A resurgence of high vote percentages for LaRouche candidates in 1988 was thus largely ignored, and when LaRouche was convicted of loan fraud that December it indeed appeared possible that the end was near for his remarkable political career.

If so, it will be a victory on the cheap. It will not have resulted in *any* sense from a strengthening of the grass-roots resistance to his far-right extremism. On the contrary, it will be a direct result of the *weakness* of that resistance. LaRouche, facing so little opposition and attracting so many closet collaborators in the early and mid-1980s, came to regard himself as invulnerable. For this reason alone, he became reckless in his fund-raising methods, eliciting massive complaints to the authorities from fraud victims. The result was deep legal trouble for his movement and a situation in which his opponents could tell themselves that it was no longer necessary to fight him politically. The problem of strengthening the political immune system was thus postponed until either the LaRouche movement refurbished itself and launched a counterattack or some new ultraright organization emerged to ape LaRouche's brilliant political innovations while avoiding his financial mistakes.

In the meantime, the relief with which the Democratic Party, Jewish organizations, the left, and the media resigned the problem of La-Rouche into the hands of the FBI bore more than a touch of Weimar Republic decadence, all the more so since it was *not* political pressure that led to the indictments but simply LaRouche's out-of-control fund raising. One prosecutor in the LaRouche cases described his annoyance at calls from reporters asking such questions as "Do you think this will destroy LaRouche?" (as if it were the Justice Department's business to wage political battles rather than simply enforce the law).

Those who would project a political role onto law enforcement, hoping it will do what political leaders are unable or unwilling to do, only prove that the moral flabbiness on which demagogues thrive is still with us. Given this fact, the lessons of LaRouche's rise and apparent fall are important. If we study them seriously and act on them, it may turn out that the LaRouche phenomenon was a blessing in disguise—a dry run, under relatively safe conditions, that revealed our hitherto unsuspected weaknesses without our having to pay a heavy price for this knowledge. One thing seems certain: America is too violent and diverse —and too vulnerable to economic crisis—to avoid forever a major internal challenge from some form of totalitarian demagoguery. When that test comes, the story of Lyndon LaRouche may provide the key to an effective and timely response.

# Notes

The following abbreviations are used throughout the notes section:

*EIR: Executive Intelligence Review*
ICLC: International Caucus of Labor Committees
LHL: Lyndon H. LaRouche, Jr.
LM: Lyn Marcus (pen name of LHL prior to 1976)
NCLC: National Caucus of Labor Committees
NDPC: National Democratic Policy Committee
*NS: New Solidarity*
NSIPS: New Solidarity International Press Service
*TC: The Campaigner*
USLP: United States Labor Party

**CHAPTER ONE**

"NASTY DUCKLING": Paul L. Montgomery, "How a Radical-Left Group Moved Toward Savagery," *New York Times,* Jan. 20, 1974.

CHILDHOOD ISOLATION AND BULLYING: LHL, *The Power of Reason: A Kind of an Autobiography* (New York: New Benjamin Franklin Publishing House, 1979), pp. 38–39.

FAMILY SECTARIANISM: LHL, *The Power of Reason,* pp. 35–39; Hezekiah Micajah Jones (Lyndon H. LaRouche, Sr.), *Present Day Quakerism in New England,* privately published pamphlet, 1937; Vin McLellan, "Meet Lyn Marcus: The Marxist Messiah," *Boston Phoenix*, Jan. 29, 1974.

THE "WITCH MOTHER" THEME: LM, "The Politics of Male Impotence," NCLC internal, Aug. 16, 1973; LM, "Mothers' Fears," NCLC internal, Sept. 11, 1973; LM, "The Case of Ludwig Feuerbach," *TC*, Dec. 1973.

RESENTMENT IN HIGH SCHOOL: LHL, *The Power of Reason*, pp. 55–56; LHL, "How the Classics Were Lost," and "Mrs. Babbitt Destroyed the U.S.A.," *TC*, Oct. 1981.

LIFE IN CPS CAMP: LHL, "American Friends of Sodomy Committee," Part II, *NS*, Nov. 10, 1978.

ARMY ENLISTMENT: LM, "The Conceptual History of the Labor Committees," *TC*, Oct. 1974, p. 9; LHL, *The Power of Reason*, pp. 58–59.

MARXIST ACTIVITIES IN INDIA: LM, "The Conceptual History of the Labor Committees," p. 9; *EIR* ed., *LaRouche: Will This Man Become President?*, (New York: New Benjamin Franklin Publishing House, 1983), pp. 44–46.

SANITIZED VERSION OF LEFTIST BACKGROUND: *EIR* ed., *LaRouche: Will This Man Become President?*, p. 46.

MYSTICAL EXPERIENCE: LHL, *The Power of Reason*, pp. 31–34.

"NO REVOLUTIONARY MOVEMENT . . . UNLESS I BROUGHT IT INTO BEING": Paul W. Valentine, "The Newest Left," *Washington Post*, Feb. 17, 1974.

**CHAPTER TWO**

BACKGROUND ON THE SDS YEARS: LM, "The Conceptual History of the Labor Committees," *TC*, Oct. 1974; "The History of the Labor Committee," intermittent series in *Solidarity*, Dec. 18, 1970, through Apr. 12, 1971 (various authors).

PLANS FOR CADRE ORGANIZATION: LM, "How the Workers League Decayed," NCLC internal, June 27, 1970, p. 18.

LEAVING THE TROTSKYIST "SEWER": LM, "The Conceptual History of the Labor Committees," pp. 12–13.

NCLC CLAIMS THAT IT PENETRATED SDS FOR THE GOVERNMENT: *"Anti-Semitism" Libel Against Lyndon Hermyle LaRouche, Jr.*, NDPC pamphlet, Jan. 25, 1983, p. 10.

FBI AND POLICE HARASSMENT: *LaRouche v. Webster*, U.S. District Court, Southern District of New York, 75 Civ. 6010, Plaintiff's Second Amended Complaint, Apr. 2, 1982; Edward Spannaus, "The Documentary History of FBI Operations Against Lyndon LaRouche and the NCLC," *NS* series beginning July 11, 1983.

CYNICAL VIEW OF LEFT-WING FACTIONALISM: LM, "How the Workers League Decayed," pp. 1, 9.

**CHAPTER THREE**

LAROUCHE ON FASCISM: LM, "Growth of Fascist Movements," Part II, *Solidarity*, June 14, 1971.

MOP UP DOCUMENTS: "Deadly Crisis for CPUSA," *NS*, Mar. 12, 1973; "Death of the CPUSA," *NS*, Apr. 9, 1973; "Operation Mop-Up: The Class Struggle Is for Keeps," *NS*, Apr. 16, 1973; "The CP Within Us," NCLC internal, Apr. 22, 1973; "Their Morals and Ours," *NS*, Apr. 23, 1973; "CP Recruiting Pallbearers for Its Own Funeral," *NS*, Apr. 30, 1973; "Mop-Up Has Changed the Way You Think," *NS*, May 21, 1973.

PHILADELPHIA MOP UP: Mark Manoff, "NCLC: The 'Flesh and Bones' Approach," *The Drummer*, May 29, 1973.

FBI INTERVENTION IN MOP UP: *Socialist Workers Party v. Attorney General of the United States*, U.S. District Court, Southern District of New York, 73 Civ. 3160, Final Report of the Special Master (Judge Charles D. Breitel), Feb. 4, 1980. Printed as pamphlet: *What the FBI Spies Did* (New York: Political Rights Defense Fund, 1980).

CHAPTER FOUR

TAKING AWAY BEDROOMS: LM, "The Politics of Male Impotence," NCLC internal, Aug. 16, 1973.

THEORY OF SUDDEN PERSONALITY CHANGE: LM, " 'Trotskyism' As Organized Sexual Impotence," NCLC internal, Aug. 20, 1973.

DEFECTORS' DESCRIPTIONS OF NCLC PSYCHOLOGICAL TECHNIQUES AND SESSIONS: Christine Berl and Henry Weinfeld, open letter to NCLC membership, Apr. 2, 1974; Marian Kester, "Thinking the Unthinkable," NCLC factional document, Aug. 15, 1974.

THE ALLEGED BRAINWASHING OF WHITE: Christopher White, "On the Track of My Assassins," *TC*, Feb.–Mar. 1974; LM, "Uncover CIA-Police Plot to Take Over U.S.—Discover Method to De-program Victims of CIA and Soviet Psycho-Sexual Brainwashing," *NS* special supplement (includes text of LHL's Jan. 3, 1974, speech describing alleged tortures).

WITCHES AND HISSING SOUNDS: Carol White, "Intake Procedure for Suspected Brainwashing Cases," NCLC internal, 1974.

PARANOIA ABOUT CHRISTINE BERL: LM, "Why Christine Berl Could Be Turned into a Zombie," NCLC internal, Apr. 1, 1974.

TECHNIQUES OF BRAINWASHING AS ALLEGEDLY PRACTICED BY CIA AND OTHER NCLC FOES: LM, "The Real CIA—the Rockefellers' Fascist Establishment," *TC*, Apr. 1974; M. Minnicino, "Low Intensity Operations: The Reesian Theory of War," *TC*, Apr. 1974; LM, "Rockefeller's 1984 Plot," *TC*, Feb.–Mar. 1974; LM, "Uncover CIA-Police Plot to Take Over U.S."

CHAPTER FIVE

THEORY OF ETHNIC FASCISM: LM, "Growth of Fascist Movements," Part II, *Solidarity*, June 14, 1971.

"PURE RAGE" SPEECH: LM, "Build a Revolutionary Youth Movement!," *NS*, June 10, 1973 (excerpts).

DRILL-INSTRUCTOR METHODS, RESPONSE OF GANG MEMBERS: Howard Blum, "Marx and the Outlaws: Recruiting in the Ghetto," *Village Voice*, June 6, 1974.

ATTACKS ON BARAKA: Costas Axios (Konstandinos Kalimtgis) and Nikos Syvriotis, *Papa Doc Baraka: Fascism in Newark*, NCLC pamphlet, 1973; "Answer to the CIA: Destroy Baraka!," *NS*, Aug. 17, 1973.

BLACK MEMBERS INTERNALIZE NCLC RACISM: Allen Salisbury and Dennis Speed, "The Fight Against Black Magic," *NS*, June 22, 1974.

CALL FOR ANTI-ZIONIST UNITY: *LaRouche Tells Black Leaders: We'll Destroy the Zionists Politically*, USLP leaflet, Aug. 23, 1979.

CHAPTER SIX

STRATEGY FOR INFILTRATING THE RIGHT: Gregory F. Rose, "The Swarmy Life and Times of the NCLC," *National Review*, Mar. 30, 1979.

LAROUCHE EMBRACES THE *SPOTLIGHT*'S VIEW OF ZIONISM: LHL, "Walter Mondale British Agent," *NS*, Sept. 2, 1977.

"GIDEON'S ARMY": LHL, *What Every Conservative Should Know About Communism* (New York: New Benjamin Franklin House Publishing Company, 1980), p. vi.

EARLY EXAMPLES OF NCLC ANTI-SEMITISM: LM, "The Case of Ludwig Feuerbach," *TC*, Dec. 1973, p. 37; Nancy Spannaus, "Israeli Psychosis: Rockefeller's Solution to the Jewish Question," *TC*, Aug. 1975, p. 59

VIENNESE REFUGEES, CHOLERA CULTURE, "PUS": LHL, *The Case of Walter Lippmann* (New York: Campaigner Publications, 1977), p. 121.

CHRIST KILLERS: LHL, "New Pamphlet to Document Cult Origins of Zionism," *NS*, Dec. 8, 1978.

"KOSHER NOSTRA": Mark Burdman, "Begin Gov't Links to Crime Publicized in France," *War on Drugs*, Nov. 1980.

"PURE EVIL": LHL, "Zionism and the 'Zionist Lobby,' " *NS*, Aug. 22, 1978.

"NATIONAL SECURITY RISK": "Register the Zionist Lobby as Foreign Agents!," *NS*, Sept. 5, 1978.

"ZOMBIE-NATION": LHL, "New Pamphlet to Document the Cult Origins of Zionism."

"NAUSEATING JEWISH HYPOCRISY": "For Peace in the Mideast, Dump the Jewish Lobby!," *NS*, Mar. 17, 1978.

PASSIVITY OF LOWER-LEVEL NCLC MEMBERS: Linda Ray, "Breaking the Silence: An Ex-LaRouche Follower Tells Her Story," *In These Times*, Oct. 29, 1986.

ONLY ONE AND A HALF MILLION KILLED IN HOLOCAUST: LHL, "New Pamphlet to Document Cult Origins of Zionism"; "LaRouche Reaffirms '1.5 Millions' Analysis," NSIPS news release, Jan. 17, 1981.

"MORAL ANAESTHETIZATION" AND THE VOLKSWAGEN JOKE: Alice and Don Roth, "A Method in the Madness," open letter to NCLC members, Feb. 3, 1981.

JEWS ALLEGEDLY PUT HITLER IN POWER: LHL, "Hitler: Runaway British Agent," *NS*, Jan. 10, 1978; LHL, "The Truth About 'German Collective Guilt,' " Part I, *NS*, Oct. 10, 1978.

"SOUND AND INTENSE . . . ENTHUSIASM" OF NAZIS TO CRUSH BRITAIN: LHL, "Hitler: Runaway British Agent."

HITLER'S CRIMES A "SLIGHT MISTAKE" IN COMPARISON TO PLANS OF ZIONISTS: LHL, speech to Michigan Anti-Drug Coalition, May 20, 1979, published in *NS*, June 8, 1979; see editorial correction, June 15, 1979.

WARNING TO JEWISH NCLC MEMBERS: LHL, "New Pamphlet to Document the Cult Origins of Zionism."

**CHAPTER SEVEN**

INSURRECTION FANTASIES: LM, "The Art of Insurrection," *NS*, June 5, 1972.

DOCTRINE OF PARTISAN WARFARE: Uwe Parpart, "Deploying a Revolutionary Army: The Model of Yugoslav Proletarian Brigades," and Warren Hamerman, "The Development of Tito's Revolutionary Army," *NS*, Aug. 31, 1974.

DENUNCIATION OF DEMOCRACY: LHL, "Creating a Republican Labor Party," *NS*, June 22, 1979.

FASCISM BECOMES A MASS MOVEMENT ONLY IF SOCIETY'S "LEADING STRATA" DECIDE TO SPONSOR IT: LM, "The Conceptual History of the Labor Committees," *TC*, Oct. 1974, p. 25.

HOW TO BUILD A COALITION AND FUNCTION AS THE VANGUARD WITHIN IT: LHL, "Creating a Republican Labor Party"; LaRouche, "A Machiavellian Solution for Israel," *TC*, Mar. 1978, esp. pp. 29–31.

THE DEBT CRISIS: LHL, *Operation Juarez*, *EIR* special report, Aug. 2, 1982.

RIDDING THE EARTH OF OLIGARCHS AND CREATING THE "GOLDEN SOULS": LHL, *The Power of Reason* (New York: New Benjamin Franklin Publishing House, 1979), pp. 194–95.

SUPPRESSION OF POLITICAL DISSENT: LHL, "Creating a Republican Labor Party."

REJECTION OF ELECTIONS AND PARLIAMENTS: LHL, "NATO in Caesar's Foolish Footsteps," *NS*, Nov. 1, 1977.

DICTATORSHIP OF MONETARISTS VERSUS DICTATORSHIP OF INDUSTRIAL CAPITALISTS: LHL, *The Case of Walter Lippmann* (New York: Campaigner Publications, 1977), pp. 92, 97, 142.

UNITY OF LABOR AND CAPITAL AGAINST THE MONETARISTS: LHL, *Lippmann*, p. 92; LHL, "Creating a Republican Labor Party."

DICTATORSHIP BY AN ELITE: LHL, *Lippmann*, pp. 91, 144.

ONLY THE ELITE CAN SHAPE LAWS: "The German Constitutional State and Terrorism," *TC*, Feb. 1978, p. 24.

DEFINITION OF FREEDOM: LHL, *Lippmann*, p. 68; also see p. 91.

GOOD AND EVIL THOUGHTS AND STRUGGLE AGAINST EVIL THOUGHTS: LHL, *Lippmann*, pp. 129, 140.

RIGHT TO LIVE AS FREE MAN DEPENDS ON OBEDIENCE TO STATE: LHL, *Lippmann*, p. 69.

THE CRIMINAL MIND: LHL, *Lippmann*, pp. 94–95; "The German Constitutional State and Terrorism," pp. 40–42.

SURGICAL POLICE OPERATIONS: LHL, *U.S. Labor Party Security Services*, brochure, July 15, 1978; "Two Approaches to the Law Enforcement Crisis," *EIR*, Apr. 14, 1981.

THE MULTITIERED ENEMY CONSPIRACY: LHL, "How to Analyze and Uproot International Terrorism," *NS*, Feb. 17, 1978; "Register the Zionist Lobby as Foreign Agents!," *NS*, Sept. 5, 1978.

PURGING THE JEWS: "Register the Zionist Lobby as Foreign Agents!"; "A War-winning Strategy," *NS*, Mar. 21, 1978.

DENIAL OF CITIZENSHIP TO THE MASSES: LHL, "Creating a Republican Labor Party."

CRITIQUE OF HITLER'S VERSION OF TOTAL MOBILIZATION: LHL, *Lippmann*, pp. 8–9.

THE NCLC'S TOTAL MOBILIZATION: LHL, "Free Naval Policy from Geopolitics," *EIR*, Aug. 4, 1981; LHL, "American Rearmament Potential: Why a 'Quick Fix' Won't Work," *EIR*, July 29, 1980; LHL, "What Are Economic Shock Waves?," *EIR*, Dec. 14, 1982; LHL, *Military Policy of the LaRouche Administration*, Citizens for LaRouche campaign pamphlet, 1979; LHL, "Peace-Through-Strength Disorientation," *NS*, Aug. 15, 1978; LHL, "A Return to Federalist-Whig Military Policy," Parts I and II, *NS*, Sept. 8 and Sept. 12, 1978; LHL, "The Political Economy of Military Posture," *NS*, Feb. 11, 1977.

IN-DEPTH WAR-FIGHTING PYRAMID, TRANSFORMATION OF EDUCATIONAL SYSTEM, "SOLDIER-CITIZENS": LHL, *Military Policy of the LaRouche Administration*, pp. 4, 10–13.

WAGE WAR, ESTABLISH GLOBAL HEGEMONY, BRING FORCES OF EVIL UNDER "FIRM-HANDED" RULE: LHL, "The Disorienting Heritage of Clausewitz," *NS*, June 16, 1978.

"PROGRESSIVE LIQUIDATION," VICTORY OVER LAST ENEMY BASTION: LHL, "A Return to Federalist-Whig Military Policy," Part II, *NS*, Sept. 12, 1978.

CRITIQUE OF HITLER'S TWO-FRONT STRATEGY: LHL, "A Return to Federalist-Whig Military Policy," Part II.

BACKHANDED PRAISE OF HITLER ("LONDON'S MOST DEADLY ENEMY") AND CRITICISM OF HIM FOR NOT COMPLETING THE CONQUEST OF BRITAIN: LHL, "Hitler: Runaway British Agent," *NS*, Jan. 10, 1978; LHL, "The Truth About 'German Collective Guilt,' " Part I, *NS*, Oct. 10, 1978; LHL, "London Pushes Toward World War III," *NS*, Mar. 3, 1978.

DENIAL OF THE FULL SOVEREIGNTY OF NATIONS: LHL, *Lippmann*, pp. 170–71.

U.S. SHOULD DECLARE WAR ON BRITAIN: LHL, "Peace-Through-Strength Disorientation"; "A War-winning Strategy."

TOTAL WAR AND "ABC" WARFARE: LHL, "Harold Brown Is Nuts!," *NS*, Jan. 31, 1978; LHL, "London Pushes Toward World War III."

ESTIMATE OF LOSSES: LHL, "London Pushes Toward World War III"; LHL, "Military Policy of the LaRouche Administration."

OCCUPATION POLICY AND CITYBUILDING: LHL, "A Return to Federalist-Whig Military Policy," Part II.

TIMUR AS ROLE MODEL: "Marlowe's Tamburlaine: The Will to Win," *NS*, Jan. 17, 1983.

CHAPTER EIGHT

EARLY LAROUCHIAN SUPPORT FOR STAR WARS WEAPONRY: *Sputnik of the Seventies: The Science Behind the Soviets' Beam Weapon,* USLP pamphlet, 1977.
A. P. ALEKSANDROV: "Soviet Science Chief Rebuts 'Greenies,' " *Fusion,* Feb. 1980.

CHAPTER NINE

LAROUCHE'S RESPONSE TO REAGAN'S STAR WARS SPEECH: "Prominent Democrat Praises Reagan Strategic Policy," *NS,* Apr. 1, 1983.
LAROUCHIANS PUBLISH WINTERBERG ON NUCLEAR WEAPONS: Friedwardt Winterberg, "Some Reminiscences About the Origins of Inertial Confinement," *Fusion,* Nov. 1979. Winterberg, *The Physical Principles of Thermonuclear Explosive Devices* (New York: Fusion Energy Foundation, 1981).
LAROUCHE'S SDI "SPILLOVER" THEORY: LHL, "National Academy of Science Wonders: Is Lyndon LaRouche Also a Scientist?," *NS,* Sept. 22, 1986.
ATTACK ON RICHARD PERLE AS "MOSSAD-LINKED" AGENT: "Japanese Elite Hear Strategic, Economic Dimensions of SDI," *EIR,* May 2, 1986.

CHAPTER TEN

BARDWELL SPEAKS OUT: Steven Bardwell, "Third Rome Hypothesis," ICLC internal, Jan. 13, 1984.
RECURRENT PHOTOGRAPH SUGGESTING A SWASTIKA: *Fusion,* May 1978, p. 40; *NS,* Sept. 3, 1984; *NS,* Feb. 22, 1985; *Fusion,* July–Aug. 1985, p. 25.
LIVING SPACE OF THIRD REICH: *Deutsche-Bergwerks Zeitung,* March 8, 1942, cited in Jean-Michel Angebert, *The Occult and the Third Reich* (New York: Macmillan Publishing Company, 1974), p. 227.
MADOLE'S SWASTIKA MYSTICISM: "NRP Leader Gives Lecture on 'The Occult & Fascism' at New York's Warlock Shop," *The National Renaissance Bulletin,* June–July–Aug. 1977.
LAROUCHE'S GRAND DESIGN, SDI-STYLE: LHL, "Wassily Leontief Acts to Block Effective Implementation of the SDI," *Fusion,* July–Aug. 1985.
ZENKER'S DEFENSE OF NAZI WAR CRIMINALS: Kurt P. Tauber, *Beyond Eagle and Swastika: German Nationalism Since 1945* (Middletown, Conn.: Wesleyan University Press, 1967), Vol. I, pp. 309–10; Vol. II, pp. 1152–53 (nn. VIII, 173–75).
SCHERER'S DEFENSE OF LAROUCHE: "Poison Weapons of Psychological Terror Against Lyndon LaRouche," testimony of Brig. Gen. Paul-Albert Scherer at LaRouchian hearings, Sept. 1987, published in *EIR,* Sept. 25, 1987.
NAZI SCIENTISTS ABSOLVED OF MORAL RESPONSIBILITY FOR ROLE IN WORLD WAR II: LHL, "The Lesson of Nazi Jet Aircraft Development," *EIR,* Aug. 11, 1981.
GLORIFICATION OF PEENEMÜNDE: LHL, "The Lesson of Nazi Jet Aircraft Development"; Marsha Freeman, "The Truth About the German Rocket Scientists: The Men Who Built America's Space Program," *NS,* four-part series, May 20, 1985–June 21, 1985.
LAROUCHE'S FRIENDSHIP WITH EHRICKE: Ken Kelley, "The Interview: The World According to Lyndon LaRouche," San Francisco *Focus,* Nov. 1986, p. 155.
LAROUCHE PUBLICATIONS DEPICT RUDOLPH AS INNOCENT VICTIM: "ADL Spews out Smear Against Eminent German Scientist," *NS,* Apr. 1985.
OPPOSITION TO OSI: "Stop OSI Assault on German-American Scientists!," *NS,* July 1, 1985; "Schiller Meet: Drop OSI, Start Crash SDI Effort," *NS,* June 24, 1985; "Disband the OSI!," *NS,* July 1, 1985.
LIST OF MARTYRS EXPANDS: "Demjanjuk Frame-up Flounders as New Evidence of KGB Fraud Emerges," *EIR,* Feb. 5, 1988; "Brief Case Histories of Some Recent Examples of

KGB Justice Against Some Other American Citizens," fact sheet of the International Human Rights Commission, c/o Schiller Institute, Nov. 1986.

PROCEEDINGS OF KRAFFT EHRICKE CONFERENCE: *Colonize Space! Open the Age of Reason* (New York: New Benjamin Franklin Publishing House, 1985); see esp. LHL, "Krafft Ehricke's Enduring Contribution to the Future Generations of Global and Interplanetary Civilization," pp. 27–54.

CITYBUILDING IN SPACE, COSMIC SPIRALS, INSPIRATION FROM NAZI SCIENTISTS: LHL, "Design of Cities in the Age of Mars Colonization," *EIR*, Sept. 11, 1987.

DEATH-RAY SEMINAR IN MUNICH: LHL, "Nonlinear Radiation: The True Total War," *EIR*, Sept. 18, 1987.

**CHAPTER ELEVEN**

DEBRA FREEMAN'S 1978 CAMPAIGN: *U.S. Labor Party's Freeman Goes to Congress: Ending 200 Years of Zionist Trade in Black Commodities*, TC special report, 1978.

LAROUCHE'S PLANS FOR NEW HAMPSHIRE PRIMARY: "New Hampshire Primary Is a Test for the War on Liberalism," *NS*, Aug. 24, 1979.

EARLY SPLASH IN NEW HAMPSHIRE: " 'Menace' or Best Bet in N.H.?," *Boston Globe*, Nov. 20, 1979.

BIZARRE BEHAVIOR DURING PRIMARY: "LaRouche 'Times' Series 'Lies and Distortion,' " Manchester *Union Leader*, Oct. 12, 1980; "LaRouche Says They're Trying to Murder Him," Manchester *Union Leader*, Feb. 2, 1980.

TARGETING SENIOR CITIZENS IN NEW HAMPSHIRE: "LaRouche's N.H. Campaign Tactics Assailed," *Washington Star*, Feb. 23, 1980.

THEORY OF "CONTAINMENT WALL": LHL, "Keeping a Fixed Identity in a Changing World," NCLC internal, undated, late 1970s.

**CHAPTER TWELVE**

EDWARD KOCH, LAROUCHIANS AND THE DEMOCRATIC PARTY: "Barbaro Criticizes Koch for Refusing to Hold One-on-One Debates," *New York Times*, Aug. 27, 1981; U.S. Senator Daniel Patrick Moynihan, "Lyndon H. LaRouche and the Democratic Party," text of speech delivered at Mount Sinai Jewish Center, New York City, Mar. 23, 1986; Moynihan, "The Links Between LaRouche and New York Corruption," Op-Ed, *New York Times*, Apr. 1, 1986; "For Koch, a Glowing Day," *New York Times*, Sept. 23, 1981.

*NEW YORK TIMES*'S TREATMENT OF KLENETSKY: "Klenetsky Calls Koch a Special-Interest Tool," *New York Times*, Aug. 30, 1981; "Candidates for Mayor on the Issues," *New York Times*, Sept. 20, 1981; "On the Edge in Politics," *New York Times*, Sept. 21, 1981; "Mad Melvin: The Cult Candidate," *Village Voice*, Sept. 2, 1981.

NDPC IN BALTIMORE, 1982–83: "Debra Freeman Unmasked," editorial, Baltimore *Evening Sun*, Dec. 9, 1982, comments on three-part *Evening Sun* series by Mark Arax on Freeman and the NDPC; Phyllis Orrick, "Gearing for Smears: A Look at Local Labor Party Candidates," *City Paper* (Baltimore), May 27, 1983.

NDPC NATIONAL ELECTION ACTIVITY AND INROADS 1982–1983: *What Is the NDPC?*, NDPC pamphlet, 1983; Warren J. Hamerman, "The LaRouche Factor in U.S. Politics: 20%–40% Showing in the Elections," *EIR*, Jan. 4, 1983; Warren J. Hamerman, "Run with the LaRouche Campaign! A Call for Tens of Thousands of Citizen Candidates," *NS*, Oct. 7, 1983.

NEW YORK SCHOOL BOARD RACE, 1983: Stanley E. Michels and Franz S. Leichter, "How New Yorkers Defeated LaRouche," Op-Ed, *New York Times*, Apr. 3, 1986.

SURVEY OF GRASS-ROOTS LAROUCHE SUPPORTERS: John C. Green and James L. Guth, " 'Who Really Controls Us': A Profile of Lyndon LaRouche's Campaign Contributors," unpublished report (Furman University), May 1986.

LAROUCHE TARGETS *THE SPOTLIGHT* READERSHIP AND OTHER RIGHT-WING POPULISTS: LHL, *What Every Conservative Should Know About Communism* (New York: New Benjamin Franklin Publishing House, 1980), pp. v–xiii.

## CHAPTER THIRTEEN

NDPC CAMPAIGNING IN ILLINOIS PRIOR TO PRIMARY: "NDPC Begins 1986 Campaign with Illinois Slate," *NS*, Dec. 23, 1985; "Warrior Angels Campaign for NDPC in Illinois," *NS*, Jan. 31, 1986; "LaRouche Illinois Drive Focused on Rural Areas," *New York Times*, Mar. 31, 1986; "Farm Pitch: LaRouche Cultivates Rural Support," *St. Louis Post Dispatch*, Apr. 7, 1986; "The Last Days of the Illinois Campaign," *NS*, Apr. 14, 1986.

ANALYSIS OF THE LAROUCHE VICTORIES: "Ultraright Victories Scrutinized: Voter Frustration May Explain Results," *Washington Post*, Mar. 26, 1986; "Voters Responded to the Economic Issues," *NS*, Mar. 31, 1986; Tom Johnson, "A Report on 'The LaRouche Factor' in Selected Downstate Counties in the 1986 Illinois Primary Election," unpublished study prepared for American Jewish Committee, Mar. 31, 1986; Rhodes Cook, "LaRouche and His Followers: Angry, Noisy and Persistent," *Congressional Quarterly*, Apr. 5, 1986; "Lyndon LaRouche Tackles the Drug Lobby's Media," *EIR*, Apr. 18, 1986 (text of LHL's Apr. 9, 1986, speech before the National Press Club); Robert B. Albritton, "The LaRouche Victory in Illinois: An Analysis of the 1986 Democratic Primary Election Returns," report commissioned by American Jewish Committee, June 1986.

## CHAPTER FOURTEEN

NATIONWIDE NDPC RESULTS IN 1986: *The 1986 LaRouche Primary Campaign: An Analysis*, ADL report, Oct. 1986.

WHITE SUPREMACISTS HAIL LAROUCHE ILLINOIS VICTORIES: Robert Miles, "USLP Rides Again," *From the Mountain* (newsletter), Mar.–Apr. 1986; "Populists Hail 'Out Group' Victory," *The Spotlight*, Mar. 31, 1986.

OTHER RIGHT-WING GROUPS LEARN FROM LAROUCHE: Leonard Zeskin, "Watch for Far Right to Try a Larger Strategy in '88 Elections," *The Monitor* (organ of Center for Democratic Renewal), Aug. 1987.

## CHAPTER FIFTEEN

DUKAKIS MENTAL HEALTH SMEAR: Rowland Evans and Robert Novak, "Dukakis Depression Rumors Backfire on Bush Campaign," syndicated column, *New York Post*, Aug. 8, 1988; Anthony Lewis, "The Low Road," *New York Times*, Aug. 28, 1988.

COALITION CHALLENGES CARTER'S 1976 VICTORY: "U.S. Labor Party, GOP Join Forces in 4 Vote Challenges," *Washington Post*, Nov. 28, 1976.

SYSTEMATIC ATTEMPTS TO WOO GOP AND CONSERVATIVES IN 1976: Morton Blackwell, *The Right Report*, Nov. 19, 1976.

LAROUCHE'S 1978 POLITICAL PUNDITRY: "LaRouche to Reagan: Build a Strong Whig Force," *NS*, May 19, 1978.

SAYS REAGAN IS BEST CANDIDATE, ATTACKS BUSH: LHL, "The Incompetence of George Bush," front-page editorial, *NS*, Feb. 2, 1979.

PREDICTS CONSERVATIVE GROUND SWELL: *NS*, Sept. 7, 1979.

RECOGNIZES THAT REAGAN IS REPUBLICAN FRONT-RUNNER IN NEW HAMPSHIRE: *NS*, Aug. 24, 1979.

FEARS THAT REAGAN WILL MAKE A "FATAL" PLUNGE INTO THE MAINSTREAM: "LaRouche Begins First National Campaign Tour," *NS*, Aug. 28, 1979.

LAROUCHE'S ATTACKS AGAINST BUSH IN NEW HAMPSHIRE: LHL, *Is Republican George Bush a*

*'Manchurian Candidate'?*, Citizens for LaRouche campaign leaflet, Jan. 12, 1980; George Canning, "The Bones in Bush's Closet," *EIR*, Jan. 22, 1980.

IMPACT OF TRILATERAL/SKULL AND BONES ISSUE: James M. Perry, "Conspiracy Theorists Point Darkly to Bush as a Trilateralist," *Wall Street Journal*, Feb. 26, 1980.

"BORAX" SALESMAN . . . "MINCEMEAT": LHL, open letter to Democratic National Committee, Jan. 4, 1980.

PAUL CORBIN AND "BRIEFINGATE": Jody Powell, *The Other Side of the Story* (New York: William Morrow, 1984).

LAROUCHIANS OPPOSE PROBE: *Briefingate: The KGB-FBI-Manatt Plot to Destroy the U.S. Presidency, NDPC* pamphlet, *1983*.

*EIR* INTERVIEWS WITH HIGH OFFICIALS: "Agriculture Secretary Block Foresees U.S. Farm Export Push," May 12, 1981; "DOD's DeLauer Talks About Technologies," Aug. 25, 1981; "Commerce Undersecretary Olmer on Trade and Foreign Investment," Aug. 11, 1981; "Norman Ture Muses About an Industrial Recovery Under Reagan," Aug. 4, 1981; "Justice Department's D. Lowell Jensen Blasts Drugs and Domestic Terrorism," Apr. 7, 1981; "Weidenbaum: 'We Are All Monetarists and Supply-Siders,'" Apr. 7, 1981; "Senator Hatch Talks About Brilab Approach," Mar. 10, 1981; "Senator Tower on Military Policy," Jan. 27, 1981.

ATTACKS ON HOLTZMAN AND OSI: "The OSI: How Criminals Cloak Their Crimes," *NS*, Aug. 14, 1979; "Justice Dept.'s Bogus Nazi-Hunters," *NS*, July 31, 1979.

ANTI-JERRY BROWN SMEAR CAMPAIGN: Will Wertz, *Tom Hayden's CED: Brownshirts of the 1980s*, Wertz for Senate campaign pamphlet, 1982.

ARTICLES FROM *THE LANDMARK*: "Secret Democratic U.S. Senate Candidates Revealed," Mar. 29, 1984; "Quotes from Hunt's New York City Fundraisers," Mar. 29, 1984; "Jim Hunt Is Sissy, Prissy, Girlish and Effeminate," July 5, 1984; "The Hunt for Senate-Homosexual Connection Is Very Real," Oct. 25, 1984.

ATTACKS ON MONDALE AND PASTOR: *Worse Than Jimmy Carter? The Facts About Mondale, Grenada, and the KGB*, NDPC pamphlet, 1983.

TESTIMONY AT LIBEL TRIAL: *LaRouche* v. *National Broadcasting Company*, U.S. District Court, Eastern District of Virginia, Civ. Docket No. 84-0136-A.

INNIS'S OPINION ON HITLER: Arnold Forster and Benjamin R. Epstein, *The New Anti-Semitism* (New York: McGraw-Hill, 1974), pp. 185–87.

**CHAPTER SIXTEEN**

LAROUCHE'S VIEWS ON PROPAGANDA: LHL, "Woodward's Book on Casey: A Blend of Fact and Fiction," *EIR*, Oct. 16, 1987.

CALLS REAGAN "PUSSYWHIPPED": James Ridgeway, "Secret Agent Man," interview with LHL, *Village Voice*, Oct. 13, 1987.

INDIRECT ALLUSIONS TO THE SO-CALLED JEWISH QUESTION: LHL, *The Pestilence of Usury*, NDPC pamphlet, 1981; "Bring the Usurers to Justice!," *NS*, Jan. 21, 1983; "Does U.S. Mean Uncle Shylock?," *NS*, Aug. 12, 1985; "Milton Friedman Finally Gets His Pound of Flesh," *NS*, May 3, 1985.

CALLS SCHLESINGER "IMP OF EVIL": LHL, "A Query to the President: Is Jimmy Carter Truly a Christian?," *NS*, Oct. 13, 1978.

DRUG-PUSHING ALLEGATION: Konstandinos Kalimtgis et al., *Dope, Inc.: Britain's Opium War Against the U.S.* (New York: New Benjamin Franklin Publishing House, 1978); *Moscow's Secret Weapon: Ariel Sharon and the Israeli Mafia*, *EIR* special report, Mar. 1, 1986, see esp. pp. 12–21.

POLLARD PORTRAYED AS TYPICAL OF JEWS IN U.S. GOVERNMENT: "Pollard Case: Soviet-Israeli Spies Will Be Exposed," *NS*, June 13, 1986.

PURGE OF JEWS FROM U.S. GOVERNMENT DEMANDED: "Pollard Should Be Only the Beginning," *NS*, Mar. 16, 1987.

JEWS AS POLITICAL AGENTS, NOT JUST SPIES: "Register the Zionist Lobby as Foreign Agents!," *NS*, Sept. 5, 1978.

ISRAEL "MAIN INTERMEDIARY" IN STEALING SECRETS FOR SOVIETS: "Pollard Talks: Mossad Agents in U.S. Govt.," *NS*, June 16, 1986.

LAROUCHIANS DENIGRATE THE HOLOCAUST: LHL, "New Pamphlet to Document Cult Origins of Zionism," *NS*, Dec. 8, 1978; Helga Zepp-LaRouche, "The Zionists' Holocaust Today," *NS*, Jan. 26, 1979; Carol White, "Will There Be a Next Generation?," *NS*, Sept. 15, 1978.

SOOBZOKOV DEFENDED: "Who Is Tscherim Soobzokov, and Who Wants Him Dead?," *NS*, Aug. 26, 1985; "Soobzokov Dies; Blood on Hands of FBI, ADL," *NS*, Sept. 13, 1985.

WALDHEIM SUPPORTED: "LaRouche Calls Waldheim Affair 'Gigantic Hoax,'" *EIR*, June 20, 1986.

COMMENTS ON BITBURG: "Victory in Germany," *NS*, May 13, 1985; "The Shocking Truth about Simon Wiesenthal," *EIR*, May 14, 1985.

ATTACK ON KISSINGER: LHL, *Kissinger: The Politics of Faggotry*, NCLC leaflet, Aug. 3, 1982.

SAYS HOMOSEXUALITY WAS "ORGANIZED" BY THE OLIGARCHY: LHL, "The End of the Age of Aquarius?," *EIR*, Jan. 10, 1986.

ALLEGES THAT "SHYLOCKS" ARE BLOCKING ACTION AGAINST AIDS: LHL, "Baker Learns Lesson of Merchants of Venice," *NS*, Oct. 28, 1985.

HITLER ON SYPHILIS: *Mein Kampf*, trans. Ralph Manheim (Boston: Houghton Mifflin, 1943), pp. 246–57.

AIDS THE SPRINGBOARD FOR A NEW NATIONALISM: "New Solidarity Hits 100,000 Subscriptions," *NS*, Aug. 22, 1986.

HANGING AND BURNING SUGGESTED: LHL, "The End of the Age of Aquarius?," pp. 40–41.

GARY BAUER'S VIEWS ON QUARANTINE: "How to Make America Safe for Families," interview, *New York Newsday*, Aug. 19, 1987.

LAROUCHE COMMENTS ON GAY-BASHING: LHL, "Teenage Gangs' Lynchings of Gays Is Foreseen Soon," *NS*, Feb. 9, 1987.

**CHAPTER SEVENTEEN**

LAROUCHIAN POLICY OF NAMING NAMES, SUCH AS KISSINGER: "A War-winning Strategy," *NS*, Mar. 21, 1978.

THE "ZIONIST-BRITISH ORGANISM": "Register the Zionist Lobby as Foreign Agents!," *NS*, Sept. 5, 1978.

REVIEW OF *THE WHITE HOUSE YEARS:* LHL, "Henry Kissinger as a Novelist," *EIR*, Nov. 4, 1980.

KISSINGER'S MASTERS "FAR WORSE THAN HITLER": LHL, *The Pestilence of Usury*, NDPC pamphlet, 1981.

LEADING NEO-NAZI PRAISES LAROUCHE'S ANTI-KISSINGER CAMPAIGN: Robert Miles, *From the Mountain*, May–June 1984, p. 5.

KISSINGER WATCH ANNOUNCED; AIM IS "CONTROLLED AVERSIVE ENVIRONMENT": Mark Burdman, "Dr. K.'s Career Takes a Turn for the Worse," *EIR*, Jan. 4, 1983.

SURVEILLANCE, PRANKS, AND DEMONSTRATIONS: "The Growing Tribulations of Henry Kissinger," *NS*, Nov. 18, 1982; "From Kissinger's Appointment Book," *NS*, Nov. 12, 1982; "Does Henry Kissinger Have AIDS, at 60?," *NS*, June 6, 1983; "Does Dr. Henry Kissinger Still Exist?," *NS*, June 20, 1983; "Henry K. Hops a Catering Truck to Flee

Protest," *New York Post,* Aug. 21, 1982; "Briefly," *EIR,* Nov. 2, 1982; " 'Kissinger— Never Again,' " *NS,* Sept. 26, 1983.

THE ULTIMATE SMEAR: LHL, *Kissinger: The Politics of Faggotry,* NCLC leaflet, Aug. 3, 1982; "LaRouche Challenges Kissinger to Sue Him," *EIR,* Aug. 17, 1982.

KISSINGER INFLUENCE IN WASHINGTON ATTACKED: "Kissinger Behind White House Purge," *NS,* Oct. 21, 1983; *Kissinger's Drive to Take Over the Reagan Administration, EIR* special report, 1983; "Want to Save Lives? Bury Kissinger!," *NS,* June 28, 1985.

DEATH WISH FOR KISSINGER: "Briefly," *EIR,* July 6, 1982; Mark Burdman, "Dr. K.'s Career Takes a Turn for the Worse"; "Is Henry Going off the Deep End?," *NS,* June 10, 1983; "Koestler Takes His Own Advice; Kissinger to Follow?," *NS,* Mar. 14, 1983.

ALLEGED CAR-BOMB SUGGESTION: *NBC Nightly News,* Apr. 7, 1986.

KISSINGER AND ZIONISM: "Kissinger Mafia Pollute the Holy Land," *NS,* Mar. 18, 1983.

LAROUCHIANS BELIEVE KISSINGER IS OUT TO GET THEM: "Kissinger Behind Attacks on LaRouche Organization," *NS,* Aug. 8, 1983; "Kissinger Seeks Revenge," *NS,* July 13, 1984.

**CHAPTER EIGHTEEN**

SCHERER'S VIEW OF LAROUCHE AS SPYMASTER: "Poison Weapons of Psychologial Terror Against Lyndon LaRouche," Brig. Gen. Paul-Albert Scherer, *EIR,* Sept. 25, 1987.

*EIR* ON IRAN-CONTRA AFFAIR: Jeffrey Steinberg, "Billion-Dollar Arms Bust Blows Israel's Khomeini Connection," *EIR,* May 9, 1986; *Moscow's Secret Weapon: Ariel Sharon and the Israeli Mafia, EIR* special report, Mar. 1, 1986.

LAROUCHE'S 1971 PLAN: LHL, "A Comparative Analysis of Intelligence Services," *EIR,* Dec. 4, 1979.

SECRET FRENCH GOVERNMENT MEMO: Milton R. Copulos, *The LaRouche Network,* Heritage Foundation report, July 19, 1984.

RATING OF WORLD SPOOK AGENCIES: LHL, "A Comparative Analysis of Intelligence Services."

"PLODDING PHILISTINES," POETRY VS. SPOOKERY, QUARKS: LHL, "The Day the Bomb Went Off," *TC,* Sept. 1981.

HACK NOVELISTS AS SPOOKS: LM, "Rockefeller's 'Fascism with a Democratic Face,' " *TC,* Nov.–Dec. 1974.

REVIEW OF *THE BOURNE IDENTITY:* "The Robert Ludlum Formula," *NS,* June 18, 1981.

POE AN AGENT: LHL, *Urgent Reforms of the Criminal-Justice System,* NDPC report, Feb. 9, 1981.

SIMILARITIES TO *THE IPCRESS FILE:* LM, "Rockefeller's 1984 Plot," *TC,* Feb. 1974, p. 8.

**CHAPTER NINETEEN**

THEORIES ON GANDHI SLAYING: EIR eds., *Derivative Assassination: Who Killed Indira Gandhi?* (New York: New Benjamin Franklin Publishing House, 1985).

VISIT TO TURKEY: "LaRouche Expresses Solidarity with NATO Ally Turkey," *EIR,* Aug. 14, 1987 (includes text of his Ankara press conference).

LAROUCHE ON MARCOS: Bob Grant Show, WABC-AM Radio, Oct. 8, 1986.

BLAMING MARCOS'S PROBLEMS ON THE ZIONISTS: Paul Goldstein, "President Marcos and General Ver Wage War on Drugs and Terrorism," *EIR,* Jan. 17, 1986.

POLAND: LHL, "Poland: A Trotskyite Insurrection?," *EIR,* Sept. 16, 1980; "Don't Meddle in Poland," *NS,* Jan. 25, 1982; "Poland Targeted by Terror Networks," *EIR,* Aug. 17, 1982.

GUATEMALA: Jeffrey Steinberg et al., *Soviet Unconventional Warfare in Ibero-America: The Case of Guatemala, EIR* special report, Aug. 15, 1985.

SOUTH AFRICA, MID-1980S: "The Fraud of the New Anti-Apartheid Drive," *EIR,* Jan. 8,

1985; "Botha: 'Apartheid Is Outdated, and We Have Outgrown It,' " *EIR*, Feb. 14, 1986; "So. Africa Strikes at ANC Terrorists," *EIR*, May 30, 1986; "South Africa's Great Task: A 'Grand Design' for All of Africa," *EIR*, June 20, 1986.

NCLC ASPIRES TO AN ALLIANCE WITH BROEDERBOND: "The Rembrandt Factor," NCLC internal, Oct. 19, 1977; "Interim Report on Humanist and Pro-Development Tendencies in South Africa," NCLC internal, Jan. 19, 1978.

PROMOTING SOUTH AFRICA'S INTERESTS: *Peace Through Development in Southern Africa*, TC special report, 1978; "Summary of South Africa's Economic Potential for Development," NCLC internal, late 1970s.

PLANS FOR SCIENTIFIC INTELLIGENCE GATHERING: LM, "Functions of the Science Section," ICLC internal, Jan. 4, 1975.

INDIRECT MONITORING BY GOVERNMENT: LHL, "Security: KGB Footprints Around Computron," ICLC internal, Jan. 23, 1981.

GOLDSTEIN WORRIES ABOUT INCIDENT IN SOVIET UNION: "Background Profile on KGB Connection," NCLC security memo, Jan. 19, 1981.

BREZHNEV OBITUARY: "Leonid Brezhnev (1906–82): Nation Builder," *NS*, Nov. 18, 1982.

**CHAPTER TWENTY**

FASCISM REQUIRES HIGH-LEVEL SPONSORS: LM, "The Conceptual History of the Labor Committees," *TC*, Oct. 1974, p. 25.

CRITICIZES CUTBACKS AT LANGLEY: LHL, "In Defense of the Central Intelligence Agency," *NS*, Dec. 1, 1978.

URGES A PARALLEL ORGANIZATION: LHL, "The CIA—Only a Caretaker Force," *EIR*, Oct. 10, 1978.

URGES INCREASED AUTHORITY FOR CIA: LHL, *The Case of Walter Lippmann* (New York: Campaigner Publications, 1977), pp. 178–80.

DEPOSITION OF JEFFREY STEINBERG: June 6, 1984, *LaRouche* v. *NBC*, U.S. District Court, Eastern District of Virginia, Civ. Docket No. 84-0136-A.

BARDWELL ON NCLC'S ALLEGED GOVERNMENT CONNECTIONS: Steve Bardwell, "Third Rome Hypothesis," ICLC internal, Jan. 13, 1984.

**CHAPTER TWENTY-ONE**

FRANKHOUSER'S 1975 TRIAL: *U.S.A.* v. *Roy Frankhouser*, U.S. District Court, Philadelphia, Crim. Docket No. 74-101—see esp. testimony of Edward N. Slamon and his ATF memoranda filed with the court; "Informer's Trial: He Says Uncle Sam Was His Partner in Crime," *Washington Star*, Sept. 15, 1975; "How Klansman Became a U.S. Agent," *Philadelphia Inquirer*, July 13, 1975.

FRANKHOUSER'S DECEPTION OF THE NCLC: *U.S.A.* v. *The LaRouche Campaign et al.*, U.S. District Court, Massachusetts, Crim. Docket No. 86-323-K, Proffer Pursuant to the Classified Information Procedures Act, Aug. 1987; John Mintz, "Sifting the Truth from Informers on LaRouche," *Washington Post*, Oct. 26, 1986.

BARDWELL'S SKEPTICISM: Steve Bardwell, "Third Rome Hypothesis," ICLC internal, Jan. 13, 1984.

FICK'S ALLEGATION ABOUT GOLDSTEIN: *NBC Nightly News*, Apr. 7, 1986.

**CHAPTER TWENTY-TWO**

STALIN AND TROTSKY ARTICLES: LHL, "The Question of Stalinism Today," *TC*, Nov. 1975; LM and K. Ghandi, "The Passion and Second Coming of L. Trotsky," *TC*, Summer 1974.

LAROUCHE ON THE POTENTIAL EXPLOSIVENESS OF HIS CIA CONNECTION: LHL, "Woodward's Book on Casey: A Blend of Fact and Fiction," *EIR*, Oct. 16, 1987.

JUDGE ROBERT KEETON RULES ON CIA DEFENSE AND THE EMERSON PROBLEM: *U.S.A. v. The LaRouche Campaign et al.*, U.S. District Court, Massachusetts, Crim. Docket No. 86-323-K, Memorandum and Order, Apr. 8, 1988.

## CHAPTER TWENTY-THREE

AGENT PROFILES: LM, "Psychological Profile of a Model CIA Agent," NCLC internal, Aug. 19, 1974.

HAMERMAN DEFINES SECURITY'S MISSION: Warren Hamerman, "What Are the Labor Committees and the Labor Parties?," in *How the Labor Party Is Organized to Win*, USLP pamphlet, 1976.

"ANTI-SEMITIC JEWS": Howard Blum and Paul L. Montgomery, "One Man Leads U.S. Labor Party on Its Erratic Path," *New York Times*, Oct. 8, 1979.

CHARLES TATE'S TESTIMONY: *USA v. Roy Frankhouser*, U.S. District Court, Massachusetts, Crim. Docket No. 86-323-K, Nov. 2-4, 1987.

NEW HAMPSHIRE "COVER": "LaRouche Says His Supporters Take Covert Roles in Campaign," *New York Times*, Feb. 16, 1980.

CANON WEST: "Knight of Malta Admits Campaign Against USLP," *NS*, Dec. 12, 1978.

MASQUERADING AS JOURNALISTS: Patricia Lynch, "Is Lyndon LaRouche Using Your Name?," *Columbia Journalism Review*, Mar./Apr. 1985.

NEW HAMPSHIRE "TARGET LIST": "Harassing Telephone Calls Linked to Campaign in New Hampshire," *New York Times*, Mar. 1, 1980.

SMEARS AND OTHER HARASSMENT OF JOURNALISTS: John Mintz, "Critics of LaRouche Group Hassled, Ex-Associates Say," *Washington Post*, Jan. 14, 1985.

DEPOSITION OF JEFFREY STEINBERG: June 6, 1984, *LaRouche v. NBC*, U.S. District Court, Eastern District of Virginia, Civ. Docket No. 84-0136-A.

DEAD CATS: Transcript of NBC *First Camera*, Mar. 4, 1984.

PLANS FOR HARASSING ADL: "Security-Legal Memorandum: NDPC-ADL Counteroperations—Make the ADL Pay Everywhere," NCLC internal, Mar. 7, 1984.

EGAN'S TESTIMONY: Bond hearing of Jeffrey and Michelle Steinberg, Oct. 9, 1986, *USA* v. *Jeffrey Steinberg et al.*, U.S. District Court, Massachusetts, Crim. Docket No. 86-323-K; Violation No. 86-1379-M (Alexandria, Va.).

## CHAPTER TWENTY-FOUR

MEETINGS WITH POLICE IN PACIFIC NORTHWEST: " 'Radical' Group Spies on Left," *Seattle Sun*, Oct. 27, 1976.

SURGICAL ACTION: LHL, *U.S. Labor Party Security Services*, July 15, 1978.

NCLC'S LAW ENFORCEMENT PHILOSOPHY: "Two Approaches to the Law Enforcement Crisis," *EIR*, Apr. 14, 1981.

DEFENDING THE PDID: "The Conspiracy to Destroy Law Enforcement: The Case of the LAPD," *Investigative Leads*, 1980.

NCLC ADMITS IT COOPERATES WITH POLICE: "Plaintiff's Memorandum in Support of Motion to Enjoin Release," *LaRouche v. Webster*, U.S. District Court, Southern District of New York, 75 Civ. 6010, 1978.

CLAMSHELL ALLIANCE: "Two in Labor Party Cited as Police Source," *Concord Monitor*, June 9, 1977; "Strange Bedfellows: Thomson and USLP," *Boston Phoenix*, June 14, 1977.

FBI SAYS REPORTS ARE "FABRICATED": Edward Spannaus, "The Documentary History of FBI Operations Against Lyndon LaRouche and the NCLC," Part III, *NS*, July 18, 1983 (quotes from FBI documents received under FOIA).

FIGHTING THE COUNTERCULTURE: "Cleaning Up the Filth," *NS*, June 25, 1981; LHL, *Special Anti-terrorist Information Report*, NSIPS, May 10, 1979, p. 11.

**CHAPTER TWENTY-FIVE**

WILLIAM BUNDY QUOTED: Howard Blum and Paul L. Montgomery, "U.S. Labor Party: Cult Surrounded by Controversy," *New York Times*, Oct. 7, 1979.

LEVY AND NCLC: Transcript of NCLC interview with Levy, Dec. 1981; "Mordechai Levy: The Profile of Mossad Hit Teams," in *Moscow's Secret Weapon: Ariel Sharon and the Israeli Mafia*, *EIR* special report, Mar. 1, 1986.

**CHAPTER TWENTY-SIX**

DUPONT'S WAR AGAINST ROY: *Now East*, July and Dec. 1980; "Profiles of the Times," Oct. 24, 1982; Nicholas von Hoffman, *Citizen Cohn* (New York: Doubleday, 1988); *People* v. *Dupont*, New York State Supreme Court, New York County, Crim. Docket No. 4995/80.

ROGER STONE'S LETTER: "Judge Releases Cohn Foe," *Village Voice*, Nov. 25, 1981.

NCLC'S REACTION TO MEDIA'S OUTRAGE: "Is N.Y. Times Hanging Roy Cohn Out to Dry?," *NS*, Nov. 5, 1982.

ATTACKS ON MORGENTHAU: *Is the District Attorney the Biggest Crook in Town?*, NCLC leaflet, 1982; "Is Morgenthau a Terrorist Sympathizer or Just His Wife?," *NS*, Dec. 6, 1982; "NCLC Motion Rattles 'Get LaRouche' Prosecutor," *NS*, Dec. 10, 1982.

ATTEMPTS TO INTIMIDATE ABRAMS' OFFICE: "Homosexual Coven Runs N.Y. Attorney General's Office," *NS*, Aug. 4, 1986; "Roy Cohn's Last Vendetta: Alliance with the Dope Lobby," *NS*, Aug. 11, 1986.

**CHAPTER TWENTY-SEVEN**

PURLOINED LETTER: LHL, "A Machiavellian Solution for Israel," *TC*, Mar. 1978, p. 8.

ROLE OF DECEPTION AND CONCEALMENT IN HISTORY AND PHILOSOPHY: LHL, "The Secrets Known Only to the Inner Elites," *TC*, May–June 1978; LHL, "Wall Street's Un-reformed Drunks," *NS*, Mar. 7, 1978; LHL, "What Is a Humanist Academy?," *TC*, Sept.–Oct. 1978; LHL, "A Machiavellian Solution for Israel."

"NOT NECESSARY TO CALL ONESELF A FASCIST TO BE A FASCIST": LHL, "Solving the Machiavellian Problem Today," *NS*, July 7, 1978.

AVOIDING "MORAL SHOCK": "Machiavelli's Notebook: More Crimes Covered Up by Euphemisms," *New York–New Jersey Prosecutor* (NCLC regional newspaper), Sept. 29, 1986.

WORD GAMES: LHL, *The Case of Walter Lippmann* (New York: Campaigner Publications, 1977); TWISTING CUSTOMARY MEANINGS OF WORDS: p. 76; IRONY AND PUNNING: pp. 76–77; "NOMINALIST" PUNS: pp. 54, 69, 85; DISLIKE OF OCCAM: p. 54.

GERMAN RIGHTIST DECEPTIONS: Kurt P. Tauber, *Beyond Eagle and Swastika: German Nationalism Since 1945*, 2 vols. (Middletown, Conn.: Wesleyan University Press, 1967).

**CHAPTER TWENTY-EIGHT**

ALLEGED "KERNEL OF TRUTH" IN THE *PROTOCOLS OF ZION*: LHL, "New Pamphlet to Document Cult Origins of Zionism," *NS*, Dec. 8, 1978.

CONSPIRACY THEORY OF OLIGARCHS VERSUS HUMANISTS: LHL, "The Secrets Known Only to the Inner Elites," *TC*, May–June 1978.

ATLANTIS: LHL, "The New Outline of History," *NS*, Feb. 9, 1979; LHL, "The Truth Concerning Pre-Christian Cultures," *NS*, Mar. 23, 1979; LHL, "Beneath the Waters of Chappaquiddick," Part II, *NS*, Jan. 26, 1979.

OLIGARCHS WROTE OLD TESTAMENT: LHL, "Solving the Machiavellian Problem Today," *NS*, July 7, 1978.

THE EVIL PERSIANS: LHL, "The Secrets Known Only to the Inner Elites," pp. 16–20.

ALLEGED JEWISH POWER IN ANCIENT BABYLON AND PERSIA:  Houston Stewart Chamberlain, *Foundations of the Nineteenth Century*, Vol. I (New York: Howard Fertig [repr.], 1968), pp. 458–63; Oswald Spengler, *The Decline of the West*, Vol. II (New York: Alfred A. Knopf, 1928), p. 209.

EVIL DIONYSIAN CULTS:  LHL, "What Is a Humanist Academy?," *TC*, Sept.–Oct. 1978; LHL, "The Secrets Known Only to the Inner Elites," pp. 20–24.

ISIS AND MODERN ISRAEL:  Mark Burdman, "How Britian's Biggest Racists Created Zionism," *TC*, Dec. 1978, pp. 38–39.

ROSENBERG'S VIEW OF ANCIENT CULTS:  Alfred Rosenberg, *The Myth of the Twentieth Century* (Torrance, Calif.: Noontide Press, 1982); Dionysios: p. 17; Isis: pp. 149, 235.

ROLE OF PIERLIONI FAMILY AND OTHER ROMAN BANKERS IN MEDIEVAL EUROPE:  LHL, "The Secrets Known Only to the Inner Elites," pp. 32–33; LHL, "Two Global Conspiracies," *NS*, Nov. 18, 1977.

THE OLD MAN OF THE MOUNTAIN:  LHL, "How to Analyze and Uproot International Terrorism," *NS*, Feb. 17, 1978.

FREDERICK BARBAROSSA:  "The German Constitutional State and Terrorism," manifesto of the European Labor Party, *TC*, Feb. 1978, pp. 36–37.

BEMOANING OF RACIAL DECLINE:  LHL, "The Looming Extinction of the 'White Race,' " *EIR*, May 21, 1985.

ATLANTIS AND THE ARYAN RACE:  LHL, "The New Outline of History"; Rosenberg, *The Myth of the Twentieth Century*, pp. 4–5; LHL, *The Toynbee Factor in British Grand Strategy*, *EIR* special report, 1982.

LAROUCHE ON STRUGGLE BETWEEN INDUSTRIAL AND LOAN CAPITAL:  LM, *Dialectical Economics* (Lexington, Mass.: D. C. Heath, 1975).

SPENGLER'S STRUGGLE OF THE TWO ELITES:  *The Decline of the West*, Vol. II, p. 506.

**CHAPTER TWENTY-NINE**

NAZI OBSESSION WITH A BRITISH-JEWISH CONSPIRACY:  *Mein Kampf* (Boston: Houghton Mifflin, 1943), p. 637; Himmler quoted in Bradley F. Smith, *Heinrich Himmler: A Nazi in the Making, 1900–1926* (Stanford, Calif.: Hoover Institution Press, 1971), p. 166 Alfred Rosenberg, *The Myth of the Twentieth Century* (Torrance, Calif.: Noontide Press, 1982), p. 414; *World-Battle* quoted in Peter Viereck, *Meta-Politics: The Roots of the Nazi Mind* (New York: Capricorn Books, 1965), p. 307–8; Joseph Goebbels, *The Goebbels Diaries*, ed. and trans. Louis P. Lochner (Garden City, N.Y.: Doubleday, 1948), pp. 285–86 (entry for Dec. 19, 1942).

POPULIST OBSESSION WITH BRITISH-JEWISH PLOT:  Richard Hofstadter, *The Age of Reform* (New York: Vintage, 1955), pp. 70–93.

LAROUCHE'S APPARENT SOURCE FOR HIS THEORIES ABOUT THE "BRITISH":  "Cincinnatus," *War! War! War!*, 3d ed. (Metairie, Louisiana: Sons of Liberty, 1984).

"BRITISH" DEFINED AS BEING IDENTICAL WITH WEALTHY BRITISH JEWS:  LHL, *The Case of Walter Lippmann* (New York: Campaigner Publications, 1977), p. 13; LHL, "Anti-Dirigism Is British Tory Propaganda," *NS*, Feb. 3, 1978.

STAR OF DAVID ILLUSTRATION:  LHL, "Mickey Mouse & Pluto Move to Washington," *NS*, Oct. 17, 1978.

CONSPIRACY OF COSMOPOLITAN FAMILIES:  LHL, "How to Analyze and Uproot International Terrorism," *NS*, Feb. 17, 1978.

KICK THE BRITISH OUT OF WASHINGTON:  LHL, "The Fitness to Command," *NS*, Feb. 14, 1978.

"ZIONIST-BRITISH ORGANISM":  "Register the Zionist Lobby as Foreign Agents!," *NS*, Sept. 5, 1978.

ROTHSCHILDS CONTROL BRITAIN: Christopher R. White, *The Noble Family*, *TC* special report, 1978, p. 14.

**CHAPTER THIRTY**

RACIAL DOCTRINES: LM, *Dialectical Economics* (Lexington, Mass.: D. C. Heath, 1975), pp. 90–91, 457; LHL, "The Secrets Known Only to the Inner Elites," *TC*, May–June 1978, p. 50.

THE HIGHER REALITY THE BRITISH CAN'T COMPREHEND: "The Death of Aldo Moro: The Time for Justice Has Come," Part II, *NS*, May 16, 1978.

PARASITE AND HOST: LHL, "The Secrets Known Only to the Inner Elites," p. 64.

BRITISH A "LOWER ORDER OF MENTALITY": LHL, "The Death of Aldo Moro: The Time for Justice Has Come," Part II.

BRITISH A "PACK OF ANIMALS": LHL, "That Zoo Called 'The House of Lords,' " *NS*, Dec. 29, 1978.

AVOWED ENEMIES OF HUMAN SPECIES: LHL, "How to Analyze and Uproot International Terrorism," *NS*, Feb. 17, 1978.

ALLEGED "SENSUAL APPETITES": LHL, "The Truth Concerning Pre-Christian Cultures," *NS*, Mar. 23, 1979.

BRITISH AN ALIEN SPECIES: Christopher R. White, *The Noble Family*, *TC* special report, 1978, pp. 4, 11.

"POTENTIAL DESTROYER" OF THE OLIGARCHS: LHL, "The Elite That Can't Think Straight," *EIR*, Oct. 17, 1978, p. 56.

DESTROY THE BRITISH SO HUMANITY MIGHT LIVE: White, *The Noble Family*, p. 31.

CHINESE: LM, "What Happened to Integration?," *TC*, Aug. 1975, p. 26.

AMERICAN BLACKS: LHL, *The Case of Walter Lippmann* (New York: Campaigner Publications, 1977), p. 144.

PUERTO RICANS: LM, "What Happened to Integration?," p. 40; Marcus, "The Sexual Impotence of the Puerto Rican Socialist Party," *TC*, Nov. 1973.

ITALIANS AND IRISH: LM, "The Case of Ludwig Feuerbach," *TC*, Dec. 1973, pp. 32–33.

TRIBAL PEOPLES: LHL, "The Truth Concerning Pre-Christian Cultures."

ANNEXATION OF NATIVE AMERICAN AND MEXICAN TERRITORY: LHL, *Lippmann*, p. 30.

RUSSIANS AS SUBHUMANS: LHL, "Ivan Grozny, Timur Timofeev Is a Boyar," *NS*, May 30, 1978.

MOUNT ATHOS: "Bomb the 'Holy Mountain,' " *EIR*, Feb. 21, 1986.

ALLEGED ULTIMATE GOAL OF LAROUCHE'S LIFE: LHL, *The Power of Reason* (New York: New Benjamin Franklin Publishing House, 1979), p. 194.

**CHAPTER THIRTY-ONE**

TYCOON THEORY: LHL, "Shoe Data Processing Comes of Age," undated report.

CRIMINAL CONDITIONING THEORY: LHL, "How to Profile the Terrorist Infrastructure," *EIR*, Sept. 26, 1978.

CONFRONTATIONAL FUND-RAISING TACTICS: Howard Blum and Paul L. Montgomery, "U.S. Labor Party: Cult Surrounded by Controversy," *New York Times*, Oct. 7, 1979.

LAROUCHE ANALYZES LABOR COSTS: LHL, "Economic-Valuation Budgetary Standards," ICLC internal, Jan. 15, 1981.

KALIMTGIS THREATENS TO GO BEFORE A GRAND JURY: Konstandinos Kalimtgis, "Open Letter to Lyndon H. LaRouche, Jr.," Jan. 26, 1981.

COMPUTRON BANKRUPTCY: *In the Matter of Computron*, U.S. Bankruptcy Court, Southern District of New York, Docket No. 81-B-104-77.

LAROUCHE ON PSYCHOLOGICAL BURNOUT: LHL, "Organizational Aspects of Financial Management," NCLC internal, July 25, 1981.

ALLEGED FINANCIAL SCAMS DURING 1980 CAMPAIGN: *Bank Bumiputra Malaysia Berhard* v. *D. Stephen Pepper,* New York State Supreme Court, County of New York, Civ. Docket No. 10750-81; *John J. Parker et al.* v. *Pepper Fine Arts et al.,* New York State Supreme Court, New York County, Civ. Docket No. 12046-84.

**CHAPTER THIRTY-TWO**

REPORT ON FINANCIAL STRUCTURE: *How the Labor Party Is Organized to Win,* NCLC/USLP pamphlet, 1976.

"PROPRIETARY" RELATIONSHIP, SHADOWS, FOOTPRINTS: LHL, *What Are the Labor Committees Today?,* ICLC pamphlet, Dec. 1979.

LERNER'S ALLEGATIONS: Affidavit of Eric Lerner, May 29, 1979, *Gilbertson* v. *Lerner,* New York State Supreme Court, New York County, Civ. Docket No. 09564-79.

NCLC'S FINANCES GO "UNDERGROUND": "Financial Warfare Against the NCLC, Report No. 1," NCLC internal, Sept. 23, 1978.

WERTZ'S POEMS: "The Cathedrals," *NS,* Nov. 25, 1985; "From the Sling of David," *NS,* Dec. 20, 1985; "Sling of David," *NS,* Dec. 27, 1985.

THE "ART" OF CREDIT-CARD FRAUD: Complaint and Jury Demand, July 28, 1986, *First Fidelity Bank* v. *LaRouche et al.,* U.S. District Court, New Jersey, Civ. Docket No. 86-2938.

**CHAPTER THIRTY-THREE**

MARGARET BEYNEN CASE: Declaration of Margaret Beynen, Oct. 9, 1986, U.S. District Court, Northern District of California, Civil Docket No. 86-5820.

RIP-OFFS OF ELDERLY, AN OVERVIEW: CBS's *West 57th,* Oct. 10, 1987.

ELIZABETH ROSE TRANSFORMED INTO HEROINE: "Elizabeth Rose Blasts 'Reign of Terror' Against Elderly in U.S.," *NS,* Nov. 7, 1986; "Elizabeth Rose Inspires Audiences," *NS,* Dec. 19, 1986; "Patriotic 84-Year-Old Begins Tour for Seniors' Rights," *NS,* Nov. 24, 1986.

HELGA ON FINANCIAL "LOGISTICS": Helga Zepp-LaRouche, ICLC daily briefing, Aug. 22, 1986.

**CHAPTER THIRTY-FOUR**

LAROUCHE'S THEORY OF LINKS BETWEEN SPOOKS AND CROOKS: LHL, *The Case of Walter Lippmann* (New York: Campaigner Publications, 1977), pp. 134–35.

CIARDELLI'S DRUG CONNECTION: Mike Royko, "They Hate Drug Pushers, But . . . ," *Chicago Tribune,* Apr. 21, 1986.

NCLC ANALYSIS OF THE DRUG TRAFFIC: Konstandinos Kalimtgis et al., *Dope, Inc.: Britain's Opium War Against the U.S.* (New York: New Benjamin Franklin Publishing House, 1978).

NCLC THEORIES ON MONEY LAUNDERING: David Goldman, "What Does the NSA Know About Dirty Money?," *NS,* Aug. 21, 1979.

THE ROVING DECIMAL POINT: *Bank of Nova Scotia* v. *NCLC,* New York State Supreme Court, New York County, Civ. Docket No. 02829-77; "The Drug Banks Heist $350,000 from LaRouche Organization," *NS,* Nov. 7, 1978.

**CHAPTER THIRTY-FIVE**

LAROUCHIAN DEALINGS WITH TEAMSTERS: "LaRouche Cult Linked to Teamsters," *Our Town,* Dec. 23, 1979, and "Teamsters for LaRouche," *Our Town,* Jan. 27, 1980 Douglas Foster, "Teamster Madness," *Mother Jones,* Jan. 1982.

NCLC ARTICLES GLORIFYING VIOLENCE: "Teamsters Debate PROD," *NS,* Aug. 11, 1978; "Ken Paff—Khomeini's Man in U.S. Labor Movement," *NS,* Feb. 9, 1981.

ANTI-SEMITISM: LHL, "Jack Anderson and the Gang That Killed Hoffa," in *The Gang That Killed Hoffa, TC* special report, 1978.

BACKGROUND ON MCMASTER:   Dan E. Moldea, *The Hoffa Wars* (New York: Paddington Press, 1978).

LAROUCHE PRESIDENTIAL CAMPAIGN AND THE TEAMSTERS:   "The Big Lie Bites Back," *Convoy,* July–Aug. 1979; LHL, "Open Letter to IBT Pres. Fitzsimmons," and TCELP, "Teamster Committee: 'No Time to Be Scared,' " *NS,* Extra, June 22, 1979; "IBT Denies Supporting U.S. Labor Party Candidates," *International Teamster,* July 1979.

NCLC CALLS FOR FIGHT AGAINST AFL-CIO ZIONISTS:   *NS,* Sept. 8 and Sept. 26, 1978.

## CHAPTER THIRTY-SIX

"HAVE A HUNDRED-DOLLAR BILL":   LHL, "Top-Level Dope, Inc. Control of Dalto Conclusively Proven," ICLC internal, Nov. 4, 1981.

MAYER MORGANROTH'S BACKGROUND:   "Florida Lawyer's Role in Teamster Loans Being Investigated by Justice Department," *Wall Street Journal,* Nov. 14, 1977; Dan E. Moldea, *The Hoffa Wars* (New York: Paddington Press, 1978).

## CHAPTER THIRTY-SEVEN

GOOD AND BAD MOBSTERS:   LHL, "The Mafia in U.S. Life," ICLC internal, Nov. 1, 1981.

ANTI-BRILAB LITERATURE:   *The Justice Department Stands Trial,* NDPC pamphlet, 1981; *Brilab-Abscam: Union-Busting in America,* Committee Against Brilab and Abscam pamphlet, 1980.

PROVENZANO FAMILY DEFENDED:   *NS,* Apr. 16, 1981; May 7, 1981; May 21, 1981.

FRANK SHEERAN DEFENDED:   *NS,* Apr. 13, 1981; Apr. 16, 1981; May 18, 1981.

INTERVIEW WITH ORRIN HATCH:   "Senator Hatch Talks About Brilab Approach," *EIR,* Mar. 10, 1981.

CABA IN HOUSTON:   "Committee Against Brilab, Abscam: Controversy Swirling Around Group's Tactics in Fighting 'Conspiracy,' " *Houston Post,* Dec. 7, 1980.

ALLEGED "ARRAY OF MAFIOSO CONNECTIONS":   "FBI Cointelpro Against LaRouche on Trial in Detroit," *NS,* Jan. 24, 1986.

DETROIT SPLIT:   Joe Conason, "Is LaRouche's Cult Collapsing?," *Village Voice,* Nov. 11, 1981.

"DOPE-SOAKED TEETH":   "Max Fisher–United Brands Behind Detroit-Centered Operation," ICLC internal, Nov. 5, 1981.

" 'MAFIA VIOLENCE' AURA":   LHL, "Top-Level Dope, Inc. Control of Dalto Conclusively Proven," ICLC internal, Nov. 4, 1981.

THREATS TO DALTO:   "Dalto May Be Killed by Mafia Soon," ICLC internal, Nov. 1, 1981.

## CHAPTER THIRTY-EIGHT

ANNOYANCE AT IBT LEADERSHIP:   "Teamster Stupidity," *NS,* Jan. 25, 1982.

SUPPORT FOR NORIEGA:   *White Paper on the Panama Crisis: Who's Out to Destabilize the U.S. Ally, and Why, EIR* special report, 1986; "State Department Plots with Nazis to Destroy Panama," *EIR,* Mar. 21, 1986; "U.S. Caught Backing Mob 'Democrats' in Panama," *EIR,* June 27, 1986.

NORIEGA SPEECH:   Manuel Noriega, "The Military's Role in Securing Democracy," *EIR,* Mar. 7, 1986.

ATTITUDE TO SPADAFORA MURDER:   "From the Editor," *EIR,* Mar. 7, 1986.

BLANDON TESTIMONY:   Hearing on Drugs, Law Enforcement and Foreign Policy: Panama, U.S. Senate Committee on Foreign Relations, Subcommittee on Terrorism, Narcotics and International Operations; Feb. 9, 1988.

PARNTHER SPEAKS AT LAROUCHIAN GATHERING: "International Panel Blasts Persecution of LaRouche," *EIR*, Sept. 18, 1987 (photo of Parnther at this event, *EIR*, Sept. 25, 1987, p. 37).

EIR'S RESPONSE TO BLANDÓN TESTIMONY: "José Blandón Paid to Lie," *EIR*, Feb. 19, 1988.

# Acknowledgments

The uncovering of the LaRouche conspiracy in America has been a collective endeavor in which many journalists and editors have made important contributions. Chip Berlet, the dean of LaRouche watchers, has tracked the NCLC since 1975 and has written dozens of articles. Patricia Lynch of NBC-TV first cracked the story of LaRouche's White House connection. Bryan Chitwood was the reporter on the scene in Leesburg, Virginia, who did the most exhaustive work in 1986–88 on their financial dealings. Russ Bellant probed their relations with the Republican Party and their activities in Detroit. Ed Kayatt, publisher and editor of the Manhattan weekly *Our Town*, fought LaRouche for over eight years, in the teeth of lawsuits and harassment which would have caused many publishers to back off.

In addition, this book draws upon the work of John Rees, Greg Rose, Joe Conason, Joel Bellman, Jude Dratt, John Mintz, Chuck Fager, Harvey Kahn, Paul Valentine, Mark Arax, Howard Blum, and Paul Montgomery. Journalists who gave generously of their time on various research points include Bob Windrem, Bruce McColm, Jim Hougan, and Linda Hunt. Dan Moldea's classic investigative work *The Hoffa Wars* was a source of inspiration as well as facts. University of Chicago graduate student Daniel Messinger provided information on LaRouche's election activities. The late Fred Christopher of the New York Conservative Party gave me an initial orientation about LaRouche's conspiracy theories without which I could never have understood them. Former *High Times* news editor Bob LaBrasca warmly encouraged my probe of LaRouche's connections to the Teamsters union.

This book includes materials from interviews and joint investigations conducted with Patricia Lynch, Ronald Radosh, and Kalev Pehme, who have my gratitude. Where John Mintz of *The Washington Post* reinterviewed persons that Radosh and I earlier interviewed for *The New Republic*, I have sometimes quoted from the Mintz interviews with his permission.

I owe a special debt to Kevin Coogan for allowing me to use findings from his unpublished manuscript, "The Mystery of Lyndon LaRouche." Especially, I am indebted to him for digging out the writings of LaRouche's father and for his study of the murky circumstances surrounding Roy Frankhouser's 1975 trial. His manuscript delves into many fascinating areas which my book does not deal with, and I hope it will find a publisher before long.

In the years I tracked LaRouche, I was without the protection of a large news organization. I wish to thank the attorneys who represented me pro bono in lawsuits initiated by the LaRouchians: Steve Bundy and Frank Barron of Cravath, Swaine and Moore in 1980–81; Phil Hirschkop in 1984; and Randolph Scott-McLaughlin, Raphael Lopez, and Morton Stavis of the Center for Constitutional Rights also in 1984. In addition, I am grateful to attorneys Weldon Brewer, Ramsey Clark, Jerry Nadler, and Eli Rosenbaum for their advice at various points.

Financial help in writing this book was provided by the Smith-Richardson Foundation, the Stern Fund, and the League for Industrial Democracy. I especially thank Arch Puddington and Gail Wolfe of the LID for their generous assistance.

For research help, I am deeply indebted to the staff of New York University's Tamiment Institute and to the research and fact-finding divisions of the Anti-Defamation League of B'nai B'rith. Gail Gans at the ADL chased down scores of documents for me over the years, while ADL fact-finding director Irwin Suall offered invaluable advice at many points. For help on LaRouche's early career I thank the staff of the Prometheus Library.

The following individuals provided vital encouragement over the ten years this book was in preparation: John Ranz, Sheldon Ranz, Lenny Lopate, the late Mannie Goldstein, Guy Hawtin, David Hacker, Rita Freedman, A. J. Weberman, Linda Ray, Dave Phillips, Anne-Marie

Vidal, Arnold Sperber, Aron Kay, Bob Roistacher, Stanley Pinsley, Vanessa Weber, John Train, John Hitz, Lyn Wells, Lenny Zeskin, Jack Newfield, Dave Pollock, Marvin Sochet, Frank Touchet, Jack Finn, and my father, Arnold King.

For their special personal support, I wish to thank Denise Beck, Kevin Coogan, Michael Hudson, Katy Morgan, Kalev Pehme, Leslie Smith, and "Simon," as well as my five colleagues to whom this book is dedicated.

Finally, I thank my agents, Peter Miller and Laurie Perkins, and my editor at Doubleday, Patrick Filley.

Michael Hudson and Kalev Pehme did invaluable editorial work on the final manuscript and also provided many insights into LaRouche's financial empire.

# Index

ABOUT THE AUTHOR

Dennis King is regarded as the country's leading expert on Lyndon LaRouche. His work has appeared in *The New Republic* and *Our Town.* Mr. King lives in New York City.